Turbo Libraries

A Programmer's Reference

Related Titles of Interest

Turbo Language Essentials: A Programmer's Reference, Weiskamp, Shammas, and Pronk

Turbo Algorithms: A Programmer's Reference, Weiskamp, Shammas, and Pronk

Power Graphics Using Turbo C, Weiskamp, Heiny, and Shammas

Introducing C to Pascal Programmer's, Shammas

Advanced Turbo C Programmer's Guide, Mosich, Shammas, and Flamig

The Turbo C Survival Guide, Miller and Quilici

C Programming Language: An Applied Perspective, Miller and Quilici

C Wizard's Programming Reference, Schwaderer

Turbo C DOS Utilities, Alonso

Quick C DOS Utilities, Alonso

Turbo C and Quick C Functions: Building Blocks for Efficient Code, Barden

Power Graphics Using Turbo Pascal, Weiskamp, Heiny, and Shammas

Applying Turbo Pascal Library Units, Shammas

Programming with Macintosh Turbo Pascal, Swan

Turbo Pascal DOS Utilities, Alonso

Artificial Intelligence Programming with Turbo Prolog, Weiskamp and Hengl

Mastering HyperTalk, Weiskamp and Shammas

Turbo Libraries
A Programmer's Reference

Keith Weiskamp
Namir Shammas
Ron Pronk

WILEY

John Wiley & Sons, Inc.
New York • Chichester • Brisbane • Toronto • Singapore

Publisher: Stephen Kippur
Editor: Katherine Schowalter
Managing Editor: Ruth Greif
Copy Editor and Proofreader: Brown Editorial Service
Compositor: Loren Heiny

Turbo BASIC, Turbo C, Turbo Pascal, and Turbo Prolog are registered trademarks of Borland International, Inc.

Library of Congress Cataloging-in-Publication Data

Weiskamp, Keith.
    Turbo libraries: a programmers's reference / Keith Weiskamp, Namir
Shammas, Ron Pronk.
        p.   cm.
    ISBN 0-471-61005-4
    1. Programming languages (Electronic computers)   I. Shammas,
Namir Clement, 1954-   . II. Pronk, Ron.   III. Title.
    QA76.7.W45   1989
    005.13'3--dc19   88-35178
                                                                     CIP

Printed in the United States of America
89 90 10 9 8 7 6 5 4 3 2 1

Contents

Preface   **xix**

Section 1 Keyboard and Screen I/O   1

Introduction 2
    Turbo BASIC 2
        Reading from the Keyboard 2
        Character Input 2
        Using the INPUT Statement 3
        Using the INPUT$ Function 3
        Using the INKEY$ Function 4
        String Input 5
        Numeric Input 5
        Writing to the Screen 6
        Formatted Input 7
        Formatted Output 7
        Cursor Control 7
        Specifying the Cursor Location 9
        Querying the Cursor Location 10
    Turbo C 10
        Quick Overview of the I/O System 10
        Reading from the Keyboard 11
        Character Input 11
        ungetc(), ungetch() 12
        Using scanf() to Read a Character 13
        Using bioskey() 14
        String Input 15

Using scanf() to Read Strings   16
Numeric Input   17
getw()   17
Using scanf() to Read Numeric Input   17
Writing to the Screen   18
Character Output   18
Using printf() to Display a Character   20
String Output   20
Using printf() to Display Strings   21
Numeric Output   22
Using printf() to Write Numeric Output   22
Formatted Input with scanf()   23
Reading Numbers   24
Reading Characters and Strings   26
Formatted Output with printf()   27
Numeric Output   28
Outputting Strings   29
Cursor Control   29
Specifying the Cursor Location   30
Getting the Cursor Location   30
Text Windows   31
Defining a Window   32
Accessing a Window   33
Obtaining the Status of a Window   33
Controlling Video   34
Direct Video Output   34
Setting Text Mode   35
Controlling Display Attributes   36
Setting Foreground and Background Colors   36
The textcolor() and textbackground() Functions   36
Using the textattr() Function   38
Setting High, Normal, and Low Video Intensity   38
Turbo Pascal   39
Reading from the Keyboard   39
Character Input   39
Using the Readln Procedure   40
Using the ReadKey Function   40
String Input   41
Numeric Input   41
Writing to the Screen   41
Formatted Input   42
Formatted Output   42
Cursor Control   43

Specifying the Cursor Location   43
Querying the Cursor Location   43
Text Windows   44
Defining a Window   44
Accessing a Window   46
Controlling Video   47
Direct Video Output   47
Test for Snow   48
Setting Text Mode   48
Setting Foreground and Background Colors (Attributes)   49
TextColor and TextBackground Procedures   49
Using the TextAttr Variable   52
Setting High, Normal, and Low Video Intensity   52
Turbo Prolog   53
Reading from the Keyboard   53
Character Input   53
Using the readln to Read a Character   54
Using the inkey Predicate   55
Reading Extended Key Codes   56
String Input   57
Numeric Input   57
Using readln to Read Numeric Input   58
Reading from the Screen   59
Reading Characters   60
Reading Strings   60
Writing to the Screen   62
Character Output   62
Using write and writef to Display a Character   62
String Output   63
Numeric Output   64
Formatted Input   64
Formatted Output   65
Formatting Data with writef   65
Formatting Strings with field_str   65
Cursor Control   66
Specifying the Cursor Location   66
Getting the Cursor Location   67
Defining the Shape of the Cursor   68
Text Windows   68
Creating a Window   69
Controlling Video   70
Direct Video Output   72
Test for Snow   72
Controlling Display Attributes   72

Setting Window Attributes   73
Setting Character and String Attributes   75

Section 2 File I/O Essentials   77

Introduction   78
Turbo BASIC   78
The Organization of Sequential Files   78
The Organization of Random-Access Files   78
The Organization of Binary Files   79
File Management in Turbo BASIC
Creating and Deleting Files   79
Opening Files   79
Closing Files   80
Initializing Files   81
Writing to Files   81
Writing to Sequential Files   81
Writing to Random-Access Files   85
Open the File   85
Map Fields   85
Assign Data Fields   86
Write the Record to the File   86
Close the File   87
Writing to Binary Files   88
Open the File   88
Position the File Pointer   88
Write to the File   88
Close the File   88
Using BSAVE to Write Bytes to a File   89
Reading Files   89
Reading From Sequential Files   89
Reading from the KYBD: 91
Reading from Random-Access Files   92
Open the File   93
Map the Fields   93
Read a Record Directly   93
Copy Data in Field Variables   93
Close Files   94
Reading from Binary Files   95
Open a File   95
Position the File Pointer   95
Read the File   95
Close the File   96

Turbo C   97
  Stream Pointers   98
  File Handles   99
  Streams   99
  Text Streams   99
  Binary Streams   99
  File Buffering   99
  Creating and Deleting Files   100
  Creating Files   100
  Deleting Files   102
  Opening and Closing Files   103
  Opening Files in Stream I/O   104
  Opening Files in Low-Level I/O   106
  Closing Files in Stream I/O   108
  fflush() and fflushall()   108
  Closing Files in Low-Level I/O   109
  Initializing Files   109
  File Status   111
  Writing to Files   112
  Writing in the Stream I/O System   112
  Writing Unformatted Data   112
  Writing Formatted Data   113
  Writing Blocks of Data   117
  Writing Data in Low-Level I/O   119
  Reading Files   121
  Reading with Stream I/O   121
  Reading Unformatted Data   122
  Reading Formatted Data   124
  Reading Blocks of Data   126
  Reading Data in Low-Level I/O   127
  Auxiliary Functions   129
  Detecting the End of a File   129
  Error Handling   130
  Global Error Variables   130
  Stream I/O Error Handling   131
  Low-Level I/O Error Handling   133
Turbo Pascal   133
  The Organization of Text Files   133
  The Organization of Typed Files   133
  The Organization of Untyped Files   134
  File Management in Turbo Pascal   134
  Creating and Deleting Files   134
  Opening Files   134

Closing Files   136
Initializing Files   136
Writing to Files   136
Writing to Text Files   136
Writing to Typed Files   140
Declare a File-Type Variable   140
Assign the Variable   141
Declare an Output Mode   141
Write Data   141
Close the File   142
Writing to Untyped Binary Files   143
Declaring a File-Type Variable   143
Assigning a File-Type Variable to a DOS Filename   143
Declaring an Output Mode   143
Writing Data   143
Closing the File   144
Reading Files   145
Reading From Text Files   145
Reading from Typed Files   147
Declaring a File-Type Variable   147
Assigning a File-Type Variable to a DOS Filename   147
Declare an Output Mode   147
Read Data   148
Close the File   148
Reading from Untyped Binary Files   149
Declare a File-Type Variable   150
Assign a File-Type Variable to a DOS Filename   150
Declare an Output Mode   150
Read Data   150
Close the File   151
Working with File Buffers   152
I/O Redirection in Turbo Pascal   155
Auxiliary Functions and Variables   156
Turbo Prolog   158
I/O Devices   158
Creating Files   158
Deleting Files   160
Opening and Closing Files   161
Initializing Files   163
Writing to Files   164
Writing to ASCII (Text) Files   164
Writing to Output Devices   166
Writing to Text Files Using file_str   169

Writing to Database Files   171
Reading Files   173
Reading from ASCII Files   173
Reading from Text Files Using file_str   175
Reading from Database Files   175
Auxiliary Domains and Predicates   178
Predefined File Domains   178
Detecting the End of a File   179
Reading and Moving the File Pointer   180
Flushing a File Buffer   180
I/O Redirection   182

Section 3 DOS Directory Access and Control   **185**

Introduction   186
     Turbo BASIC   186
          CHDIR   186
          MKDIR   187
          RMDIR   188
          FILES   189
          NAME   189
     Turbo C   190
          getcurdir() and getcwd()   191
          chdir()   192
          mkdir()   193
          rmdir()   194
          rename()   195
          findfirst() and findnext()   197
          searchpath()   199
     Turbo Pascal   200
          GetDir   200
          ChDir   201
          MkDir   202
          RmDir   203
          Rename   204
          FindFirst and FindNext   206
          GetFAttr and GetFTime   208
     Turbo Prolog   211
          disk   211
          system and bios   213
          dir   216
          renamefile   217
          existfile and dir   218

Section 4 The Borland Graphic Interface (BGI)   221

Introduction   222
BGI Quick Overview   222
   Graphic Hardware and Modes Supported   223
   Which Files are Required?   223
   Working with Viewports   225
   Working with Colors   227
      CGA Colors   229
      EGA and VGA Colors   231
   Steps for Using the BGI   231
      Step 1: Initialize the Graphics System   231
      Step 2: Perform Graphics Commands   233
      Step 3: Close Down the Graphics System   233
   Loading Graphics and Font Drivers   235
   Using the Linking Method   235
   Turbo C   235
   Turbo Pascal   236
   Turbo Prolog   237
   What to Do if Something Goes Wrong   238
   Tips for Porting Programs   240
      No BASIC Support   240
      Error Handling   240
      Using Data Structures   240
   The BGI Routines   240
      arc   244
      bar   246
      bar3d   246
      circle   248
      cleardevice   250
      clearviewport   251
      closegraph   252
      detectgraph   252
      drawpoly   254
      ellipse   256
      fillellipse   257
      fillpoly   258
      floodfill   260
      getarccoords   261
      getaspectratio   263
      getbkcolor   265
      getcolor   266
      getdefaultpalette   268
      getdrivername   268

getfillpattern   269
getfillsettings   270
getgraphmode   273
getimage   275
getlinesettings   276
getmaxcolor   277
getmaxmode   277
getmaxx   278
getmaxy   280
getmodename   280
getmoderange   281
getpalette   281
getpixel   284
gettextsettings   284
getviewsettings   286
getx   289
gety   290
graphdefaults   291
grapherrormsg   292
_graphfreemem   292
_graphgetmem   293
graphresult   293
imagesize   295
initgraph   296
installuserdriver   296
installuserfont   297
line   298
linerel   299
lineto   300
moverel   301
moveto   302
outtext   303
outtextxy   304
pieslice   305
putimage   307
putpixel   309
rectangle   310
registerbgidriver   311
registerbgifont   312
restorecrtmode   312
sector   314
setactivepage   315

setallpalette 315
setaspectratio 315
setbkcolor 316
setcolor 316
setfillpattern 317
setfillstyle 317
setgraphmode 318
setlinestyle 318
setpalette 321
setrgbpalette 321
settextjustify 322
settextstyle 323
setusercharsize 324
setviewport 325
setvisualpage 326
setwritemode 326
textheight 327
textwidth 329

Section 5 String Processing 331

Introduction 332
Overview 332
Strings in Turbo BASIC 332
Strings in Turbo C 333
Strings in Turbo Pascal 334
Strings in Turbo Prolog 334
Turbo BASIC 335
ASC 335
BIN$ 335
CHR$ 336
HEX$ 337
INSTR 337
LCASE$ 338
LEFT$ 338
LEN 339
MID$ 339
OCT$ 340
RIGHT$ 341
SPACE$ 341
STR$ 342
STRING$ 342
UCASE$ 343
VAL 343

Turbo C   344
    stpcpy()   344
    strcat()   344
    strchr()   345
    strcmp()   346
    strcmpi()   347
    strcpy()   348
    strcspn()   348
    strdup()   349
    stricmp()   350
    strlen()   351
    strlwr()   352
    strncat()   353
    strncmp()   354
    strncmpi()   355
    strncpy()   356
    strnicmp()   357
    strnset()   358
    strpbrk()   359
    strchr()   360
    strrev()   361
    strset()   362
    strspn()   363
    strstr()   364
    strtod()   365
    strtok()   366
    strtol()   367
    struol()   367
    strupr()   368
Turbo Pascal   369
    Chr   369
    Concat   370
    Copy   370
    Delete   372
    Insert   373
    Length   374
    Ord   375
    Pos   376
    Str   377
    UpCase   377
    Val   378

Turbo Prolog   379
   char_int   379
   format   380
   frontchar   382
   frontstr   385
   fronttoken   386
   isname   389
   str_chr   390
   str_int   391
   str_len   393
   str_real   395
   upper_lower   396

Section 6 Math Routines   399

Introduction   400
Summary of the Math Routines   400
   Turbo BASIC   402
      ABS   402
      ATN   402
      CEIL   402
      COS   403
      DECR   403
      EXP   404
      INCR   404
      INT   405
      LOG   405
      RANDOMIZE   406
      RND   406
      SIN   406
      SQR   407
      TAN   408
   Turbo C   408
      abs()   408
      acos()   409
      asin()   410
      atan()   411
      atan2()   411
      cabs()   412
      ceil()   413
      cos()   413
      cosh()   414
      div()   415
      exp()   416

fabs()   417
floor()   417
fmod()   418
frexp()   419
hypot()   420
labs()   420
ldexp()   421
ldiv()   422
log()   423
log10()   423
max()   424
min()   424
modf()   425
poly()   426
pow()   426
pow10()   427
rand()   428
random()   429
randomize()   430
sin()   430
sinh()   430
sqrt()   431
srand()   432
tan()   433
tanh()   433
Turbo Pascal   434
Abs   434
ArcTan   434
Cos   435
Dec   436
Exp   436
Inc   437
Int   438
Ln   438
Randomize   439
Random   439
Round   440
Sin   441
Sqrt   441
Tan   442
Trunc   442
Turbo Prolog   443
abs   443
arctan   443

cos   444
div   444
exp   445
ln   446
log   446
mod   447
random   447
random   448
round   448
sin   449
sqrt   450
tan   450
trunc   451

Section 7 Command-Line Arguments   453

Introduction   454
 Turbo BASIC   454
  Counting Arguments   456
 Turbo C   457
 Turbo Pascal   459
 Turbo Prolog   460

Index   463

Preface

As you program with one of the Turbo languages, you probably forget—
more often than you'd like to admit —how to use a certain routine. If you
are in the process of translating some code from one language to another,
you'll really find it difficult to keep track of the subtle differences between
the routines in the different languages you are using. What you need is
a resource you can turn to—one that helps you find information quickly;
that provides useful programming examples in the different languages; and
that covers important programming topics, such as the Borland Graphic
Interface, file I/O, keyboard and screen I/O, and string processing. And
that's why we've written this book—to help you get the most out of the
powerful tools that are provided with the Turbo languages.

This book is the second volume of a three-part programmer's reference
series for programmers using Borland's Turbo languages. We designed
each volume to cover a key area of programming with the Turbo languages.
The first book, *Turbo Language Essentials*, presents the fundamentals of
programming with Turbo BASIC, C, Pascal, and Prolog. This book, *Turbo
Libraries*, covers the major functions, procedures, and predicates available
with each of the four languages. The third book, *Turbo Algorithms*, shows
you how to write important algorithms and data structures.

Who Should Read This Book

If you use any of Borland's Turbo languages you'll want to have this book by your side. Programmers who know one of the Turbo languages and want to learn a new language will especially find this book to be a valuable resource. Because similar programming examples are presented in each language, you'll easily be able to compare languages.

If you're like most serious Turbo language programmers, you want a complete reference book that helps you find key information quickly, and not just another user's guide. To fill this need, *Turbo Libraries* presents each language with useful examples and provides you with numerous programming tips and techniques.

What You'll Need

To use this book you'll need one or more of the Turbo language compilers. You'll also need an IBM PC, XT, AT, PS/2, or a compatible computer system. All of the code examples that we present are designed for use with the latest versions of the Turbo language compilers, including the recently released versions: Turbo BASIC, Turbo C 2.0, Turbo Pascal 5.0, and Turbo Prolog 2.0.

A Look Inside

We've designed the book so that you can find information easily and quickly. Instead of the typical alphabetical organization used by most reference books, we've arranged the book by important programming topics. The major library routines of the Turbo languages are presented in 7 sections. Here is a breakdown of the sections in *Turbo Libraries*:

Section 1: *Keyboard and Screen I/O* presents all of the major routines for peforming keyboard and screen I/O operations in each Turbo language. This section also shows you how to perform important tasks such as displaying text windows, setting screen colors, and controlling the keyboard buffer. You'll find this section to be a valuable resource even if you've just started to learn one of the Turbo languages.

Section 2: *File I/O Essentials* includes the descriptions and numerous code examples of the file processing functions, procedures, and predicates. We've also included introductions for each language to explain how the file I/O system works.

Section 3: *DOS Directory Access and Control* shows you how to use the routines provided by each Turbo language for processing DOS directories. Some of the topics covered in this section include how to create, move to, and remove directories; how to read and set the date and time stamps of files and directories; and how to change the attributes of files and directories.

Section 4: *The Borland Graphic Interface (BGI)* covers the routines for performing both low-level and high-level graphics. All of the BGI routines are presented for C, Pascal, and Prolog. The first part of this section explains the basic features and components of the BGI, such as viewports, colors, graphics drivers, and font drivers. In the second part, we show you how to use each routine—over 100 sample programs are provided.

Section 5: *String Processing* introduces the string-processing routines and the techniques for processing strings in each of the languages. To see how to concatenate strings, convert strings to lowercase, or search a string for substrings, this is the place to turn.

Section 6: *Math Routines* covers all of the major math routines available for each of the Turbo languages. We've included numerous sample programs to illustrate how the math routines are used.

Section 7: *Command-Line Arguments* shows you how to process command-line arguments. You'll learn how to use the built-in functions, procedures, and predicates for accessing command-line arguments.

How to Use This Book

This book is packed with material on techniques both for programming with the Turbo languages and for developing PC applications. We'll start with the more basic topics and then progress to more advanced ones. As you use the book, try out as many of the examples as possible. Because each language is so highly interactive, you can quickly learn the subtleties of programming by running the examples and modifying them.

If you take a minute to glance through this book, you'll notice the following set of icons are used to represent the four Turbo languages:

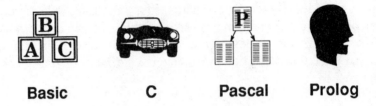

Basic   C   Pascal   Prolog

These icons are included to help you quickly locate the technical discussions on the language that you are working with. In addition, you'll find numerous tips and cautions in the left and right margins. We've used the following icons:

to label the tips and warnings.

Notational Conventions

Because *Turbo Libraries* covers four languages under one cover, we've tried to keep the notational symbols as simple and consistent as possible to avoid any unnecessary confusion. To help you detect any program statements or specials symbols, we've put all of the language keywords, symbols, functions, procedures, variables, constants, and so on in bold type.

Whenever general programming statements are introduced, we use the following format:

```
<function name> ( [<argument 1,> <argument 2,> ... ] )
{

 [<declarations>]

 <statements>

 return (return value);
}
```

The language reserved words and symbols such as return and { } are placed in normal type, and the identifiers that must be supplied by the programmer are placed inside angle brackets and set in italics such as *<function name>*, *<statements>*, and so on. The symbols [ ] are used to indicate optional parts. Bold type is used for language terms, parts of syntax lines, and other code components.

Acknowledgments

We'd like to take this opportunity to thank all those very special people out there whose help was invaluable in getting this book out. We are especially indebted to Dan Shafer who first inspired us to write this book. A big thank you also goes out to Mike Floyd and Jeff Duntemann who provided a wealth of technical feedback. We'd also like to thank the team at Wiley—Teri Zak, Katherine Schowalter, and especially Ruth Greif whose great sense of humor and loving care made the production of this book a snap—well, almost. Nan Borreson of Borland International also was a great help in making sure that we were well stocked with the latest versions of the Turbo compilers.

Rob Mauhar and Lenity Himburg deserve a special note of thanks for sacrificing precious hot-air ballooning time to help with the index. No small amount of thanks goes to Loren Heiny who took time out from chasing robots to oversee the book production and offer his expertise to make sure that this book turned out to be a first-rate product.

Last but not least, we'd like to thank all of you who have taken the time to write to us and share your ideas.

Keyboard and Screen I/0

Introduction

Keyboard and screen I/O (input/output) tasks are important even for the simplest of programs. The Turbo languages provide a variety of tools for reading data typed at the keyboard and writing data to the screen. These I/O routines are called *console I/O functions* because they affect the way your programs obtain and display data at the system console.

In this section we present all of the major keyboard and screen I/O routines for each Turbo language. The topics covered include:

- Character input and output
- String input and output
- Formatted input and output
- Cursor control
- Text windows
- Direct video control

In Section 2, "File I/O Essentials," general discussions are provided to show you how I/O in general is handled in the four Turbo languages. To perform keyboard and screen I/O operations with the Turbo languages, it is not necessary to open or close files when you read data from the keyboard or write data to the screen.

Turbo BASIC

Turbo BASIC supports several categories of console I/O operations. We discuss the categories under two basic sections:

- Reading from the keyboard
- Writing to the screen

Reading from the Keyboard

Turbo BASIC supports keyboard input operations that handle characters, strings, and numbers.

Character Input

Turbo BASIC provides several ways to read characters from the keyboard. Keep in mind that BASIC treats a character as a string that contains a single element. Three general approaches are available for handling character input. You can

- use the general-purpose **INPUT** statement.

- use the **INPUT$** function.
- use the **INKEY$** function.

The **INPUT** statement enables you to type a character, followed by a carriage return.

Using the INPUT Statement

Syntax:

```
INPUT [;] ["<prompt_string>" {;|,}] <variable_list>
```

Parameters:

prompt_string   an optional string displayed as an input query. If the semicolon follows the string, a question mark is added. If a comma is used instead, the question mark is not displayed.

variable_list   a list of numeric or string variables that store the input values you type. The data type of the variables listed must match the data type of your input.

Remarks:

The Backspace key also can erase the typed character. You'll find this programming method useful when you want to give the user some time to verify his or her input. You might also want to include the optional prompt to indicate that only one character is required. This method is identical to typing a string of characters from the keyboard.

Example:

In the following code segment, we've coded an **INPUT** statement along with a prompt message. The program then compares the length of the input string **C$** with the value 1. If the string is longer than one character, it is truncated using the predefined **LEFT$** function. This ensures that **C$** contains no more than one character. Here's the code:

```
INPUT "Enter a character ? ",C$
IF LEN(C$) > 1 THEN C$ = LEFT$(C$,1)
```

This function enables your program to read a specified number of characters from either the keyboard or from a file.

Using the INPUT$ Function

Syntax:

```
INPUT #<file_number> <variable_list>
```

Parameters:

file_number   the number assigned to an opened file.

variable_list   the list of input variables.

Remarks:

To implement **INPUT$** with keyboard character input, use the form **INPUT$(1)**. This causes the function to input a single character from the keyboard immediately, without waiting for the Return key to be pressed. If you want to include a message prompt with this method, use separate **PRINT** statements. Any **PRINT** statements to display a message and/or prompt must be placed before the statement that contains the **INPUT$** function.

Example:

This example prompts the user for a yes/no answer. The input character is assigned to **ANS$** by the **INPUT$(1)** function. Note that we use **DO-LOOP UNTIL** to ensure that the answer is either a Y or an N (with both uppercase and lowercase forms accepted). Here's the code section:

```
DO
   PRINT "Go ahead ? (Y/N) ";
   ANS$ = INPUT$(1)
   PRINT ANS$ : PRINT
LOOP UNTIL INSTR("YyNn",ANS$) > 0
```

**Using the
INKEY$ Function**

This predefined function is a smarter version of the **INPUT$** function.

Syntax:

```
INKEY$
```

Remarks:

In general, **INKEY$** provides flexibility in reading characters from the keyboard. **INKEY$** can read zero, one, or two characters. Pressing [Return] yields a null string (or character), whereas pressing a key whose ASCII code is less than 128 returns a single character. Pressing a special key (keyboard function key or cursor control key) returns two characters. With these options, you should find **INKEY$** to be a useful function for programs that interact with the keyboard.

Example:

Our next example prompts the user for a yes/no answer, with the input character then assigned to **ANS$** by the **INKEY$** function. We use **DO-LOOP UNTIL** to ensure that the answer is either a Y or an N (both lowercase and uppercase forms are accepted). Here's the example:

```
DO
   PRINT "Go ahead ? (Y/N) ";
   ANS$ = INKEY$
   PRINT ANS$ : PRINT
LOOP UNTIL INSTR("YyNn",ANS$) > 0
```

String Input

You can use the **INPUT** statement in your programs to read a keyboarded string of characters that does not contain any commas. With **INPUT**, the user can press the Backspace key to correct erroneously typed characters.

Example:
This example illustrates how you can program a prompt that accepts a single string from the keyboard:

```
INPUT "Enter your name --> ",NM$ : PRINT
PRINT "Greetings ";NM$;". How are you today?"
```

To read a string that contains commas, use **LINE INPUT** instead.

Numeric Input

You can also use the general-purpose **INPUT** statement to read numbers from the keyboard.

Example:
These code lines prompt the user to enter a floating point number and an integer:

```
INPUT "Enter unit price : ",Unit.Price#
INPUT "Enter quantity   : ",Quantity%
PRINT
PRINT "Total due = ";Unit.Price# * Quantity%
```

The general-purpose **INPUT** statement can read multiple variables of different data types from the keyboard. When you implement this approach, the user must delimit each entry with a comma. The following example shows how to input a string, a real number, and an integer:

```
INPUT "Enter a string, a real, and an integer ",A$,B#,C%
```

Writing to the Screen

Turbo BASIC provides the **PRINT** and **WRITE** statements for displaying various types of variables.

Syntax:
```
PRINT [<output_expression_list>] [;]
WRITE [<output_expression_list>]
```

Parameter:
This parameter explanation is for the **PRINT** and **WRITE** formats:

output_expression_list   a list of string and numeric expressions to display.

These statements enable you to form a chain of output composed of constants, variables, and expressions. You delimit these different objects with either a semicolon or a comma. The semicolon instructs the **PRINT** statement to concatenate the output items immediately. By contrast, the comma informs **PRINT** to advance to the next print zone (each print zone is 14 columns wide).

The difference between **WRITE** and **PRINT** is that, with **WRITE**, you delimit data items with commas and enclose strings in double quotation marks. You can also use the **TAB()** and **SPC()** functions to display spaces between different output objects. The **TAB()** function takes one argument, which is the absolute column position of the tab. For example,

```
PRINT TAB(40);5;TAB(60);6
```

places the numbers 5 and 6 in columns 40 and 60, respectively.

You use the **SPC()** function to specify the number of spaces you want to display between output objects. For instance,

```
SPC(40);5;SPC(20);6
```

achieves the same effect as the above **TAB()** example.

Example:
The following set of **PRINT** statements outputs various types of data:

```
PRINT "A" ' character constant
PRINT YOUR.NAME$ ' string variable
```

```
PRINT INDEX% ' integer variable
PRINT "Time is ";TIME$ ' string constant and variable
PRINT "Cost = $ ";Pr# * Qn% ' string constant & expression
T$ = "MAIN MENU"
PRINT SPC(40 - LEN(T$) \ 2);T$ ' centers T$ on a line
PRINT TAB(40 - LEN(T$) \ 2);T$ ' centers T$ on a line
```

Formatted Input

Turbo BASIC does not support a mechanism for implementing formatted input. You have to write custom procedures or functions to provide this capability.

Formatted Output

The **PRINT USING** statement provides some powerful formatted output capabilities. The general syntax for using a **PRINT USING** statement is:

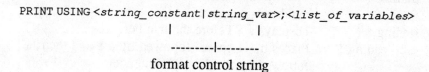

```
PRINT USING <string_constant|string_var>;<list_of_variables>
                        |                |

                    ---------|---------
                    format control string
```

The format control string, which is either a constant or a variable, specifies the combination of text and format settings. These settings are either for strings/characters or for numeric output. Table 1.1 lists the formatting characters that Turbo BASIC supports. Table 1.2 presents a set of examples to show you how the **PRINT USING** statement is used.

Most of the examples included in Tables 1.1 and 1.2 show the output of single data objects. However, you can also use **PRINT USING** to specify multiple data objects. Here's an example:

```
Format1$ = "X(##) = +#.####^^^^  &"
Format2$ = "Mean = #.#### and Sdev = #.#####"
FOR I = 1 TO NData
   PRINT USING Format1$;I, X(I), Units$(I)
NEXT I
PRINT USING Format2$;Mean, Sdev
```

Cursor Control

Turbo BASIC supports several commands for querying and setting the position of the cursor. We discuss these two basic command categories next.

Table 1.1. Turbo BASIC formatting characters

Format Setting	Meaning
\<n spaces>\	Outputs strings using n + 2 spaces. The extra string characters are ignored.
!	Outputs one character of the string
&	Outputs an entire string
#	Outputs an unsigned integer using one space
<n>#	Outputs an unsigned integer using n spaces
<n>#.<m>#	Outputs real with n spaces left to the decimal and m spaces to the right of the decimal
leading +	Includes a sign before the number
trailing −	Includes a sign after the number, if the number is negative
leading $	Displays a $ before the number
<n> leading $	Places n − 1 spaces followed by a $ and then followed by the displayed number
leading *'s	Displays leading *
,	Uses commas to group every three significant figures in the integral portion of a number
trailing ^^^^	Uses scientific notation to display a number
_<char>	Causes the formatting character that immediately follows it to be displayed verbatim

Table 1.2. Examples of the PRINT USING statement

PRINT USING Example	Display
PRINT USING "\\";"ME"	ME
PRINT USING "\\";"MINE"	MI
PRINT USING "\ \";"MINE"	MINE
PRINT USING "!";"MINE"	M
PRINT USING "&";"MINE"	MINE
PRINT USING "#";5	5
PRINT USING "##"; 5	5
PRINT USING "##.##";5	5.00
PRINT USING "+##";5	+5
PRINT USING "+#.###^^^^";5	+5.000E+000

Table 1.2. Examples of the PRINT USING statement (continued)

PRINT USING Example	Display
PRINT USING "$#";5	$5
PRINT USING "$$$#";5	$5
PRINT USING "**#";5	**5
PRINT USING "**#";55	*55
PRINT USING "#–";5	5
PRINT USING "##–";–55	55–
PRINT USING "_##";5	#5
PRINT USING "Num = #";5	Num = 5
PRINT USING "#";55	%55 ¨ needs more spaces

In Turbo BASIC you use **LOCATE** to set the cursor position and also to define its shape.

Specifying the Cursor Location

Syntax:
```
LOCATE <row> [,<column> [,<cursor>,<start>,<stop>]]
```

Parameters:
The following parameters describe **LOCATE**:

row
: specifies the screen row number (1 to 25) where the cursor is to be placed.

column
: specifies the column number (1 to 80) for the cursor position.

cursor
: numeric flag you use to indicate whether the cursor is visible. A 0 value makes the cursor invisible, whereas a 1 makes it visible.

start, stop
: define the cursor size. The top line is zero, whereas the maximum value of the bottom line varies based on the type of display adapter being used. Use the value 7 for a Color Graphics Adapter (CGA) and 13 for a Monochrome Adapter. Thus, the values of **start** and **stop** should be within the appropriate range.

Example:
The following code lines show you can clear the screen and center a heading on the first row:

```
CLS
Heading$ = "M A I N    M E N U"
LOCATE 1, (40 - LEN(Heading$) \ 2) : PRINT Heading$
```

Querying the
Cursor Location

The predefined **CSRLIN** and the **POS** functions return the row and column number for the cursor position. The **CSRLIN** function requires no arguments, but the **POS** function takes one dummy argument (the reason might be historic).

Syntax:
```
CSRLIN
```

Example:
The following procedure moves the cursor to the lower right corner (in this case, down one row and over by one column position to the right):

```
SUB ToLowerRight
   LOCAL XPos, YPos
   XPos = POS(1)
   YPos = CSRLIN
   ' check if cursor is at the border lines
   IF XPos < 80 THEN INCR XPos
   IF YPos < 25 THEN INCR YPos
   LOCATE YPos,XPos
END SUB
```

Turbo C

Turbo C provides an assortment of I/O functions for communicating with the system console. In this section we present the functions and techniques you can use to read and write simple data, to read and write formatted data, and to control the cursor. We also explain other I/O operations that you might find useful, such as controlling the display attributes. First, it can help to review the Turbo C I/O system briefly.

Quick Overview
of the I/O System

Turbo C has a more general, yet more versatile I/O, system than the other Turbo languages. The I/O functions in Turbo C are not built into the language. Rather, they are part of the standard C library. This feature gives

Turbo C its portability. The standard I/O library is divided into three levels:

- Stream I/O
- Console and port I/O
- Low-level I/O

Of the three levels, the *stream I/O* system is the most portable and general. The *console* and *port I/O* system provides functions for reading and writing directly to the system console or other I/O ports. Finally, the *low-level I/O* system provides a set of routines for performing I/O operations at the lowest level possible.

In our presentation of the I/O routines you can use to access the keyboard and screen, we focus on the stream and console and port I/O functions. The Turbo C file system is discussed in much greater detail in Section 10.

Reading from the Keyboard

Turbo C provides numerous stream and console I/O functions you can use to read characters, strings, integers, and other types of data from the keyboard. The input routines can be divided into two categories—*formatted* and *unformatted*. In our presentation in the following sections, we include both categories.

Character Input

Turbo C offers four main functions for reading characters from the keyboard. They are:

- **getc()**
- **getchar()**
- **getch()**
- **getche()**

Both **getc()** and **getchar()** read a character from the standard input stream. These functions wait until a character is available; however, they do not echo the character. The functions **getch()** and **getche()** read a character from the system console. The **getch()** function does not echo the character that's read; however, **getche()** does.

Syntax:

```
#include <stdio.h>
int getc(FILE *stream);
```

```
#include <stdio.h>
int getchar(void);

#include <conio.h>
int getch(void);

#include <conio.h>
int getche(void);
```

Examples:
The first example illustrates how you can read a character using the stream function **getc()**:

```
while ((ch = getc(stdin)) != 'X') {
    if (islower(ch)) arg1 = getval(ch);
    else ...
}
```

In this case, the input character is not displayed. Note also that we must specify the reserved word **stdin** as an argument for **getc()** to indicate that we are reading data from the standard input device.

This second example shows how a character is both read and displayed using the **getche()** function:

```
while ((ch = getche()) != 'X') {
    if (islower(ch)) arg1 = getval(ch);
    else ...
}
```

Here, we don't need to specify the **stdin** for **getche()**, because this function reads from the standard input device by default.

**ungetc(),
ungetch()**

Turbo C also provides two functions that enable you to send a character back to the keyboard.

Syntax:
```
#include <stdio.h>
int ungetc(int c, FILE *stream);

#include <conio.h>
int ungetch(int ch);
```

Parameters:
For **ungetc()**, the **c** and ***stream** parameters are:

c   the character to push back into input stream.
*stream   a pointer to the input stream.

For **ungetch()**, the **ch** parameter is:

ch   the character to push back to the keyboard buffer.

Remarks:
The **ungetc()** function sends back the most recently read character to a specified input stream, whereas **ungetch()** sends the most recently read character back to the keyboard. In using **ungetc()** to send a character back to the keyboard, you must specify the **stdin**, like this:

```
ungetc(ch, stdin);
```

The **ungetch()** function, on the other hand, doesn't require a second argument.

When you use **ungetc()** or **ungetch()**, only one character can be pushed back to the keyboard. After a character is pushed back, another character must be read with one of the **getc()** functions before **ungetc()** or **ungetch()** is called.

Here we describe how **scanf()** is used to read a character.

**Using scanf() to
Read a Character**

Syntax:
```
#include <stdio.h>
int scanf(const char *format-string[,address,...]);
```

Parameters:
*format-string   defines how the function reads in a set of input values.
address   the address of a variable used to hold a numeric or character input.

Remarks:
Although the Turbo C **scanf()** function is a general-purpose routine for reading formatted data, you can also use it to read a character from the

keyboard. The **scanf()** function enables you to type a character followed by a carriage return. The Backspace key can be used to erase the typed character. Hence, this method is helpful when the user may want to pause before typing a character.

Example:
The following code segment illustrates the use of the **scanf()** function.

```
printf("\nEnter a character ");
scanf("%c",&ch);
```

Note that the format string **"%c"** is required to instruct the **scanf()** function that a character is to be input. In addition, the address of the variable where the input character is to be stored must be passed as an argument. In our example, we pass the address of the variable **ch** using the & operator.

We cover the **scanf()** function in much greater detail under the heading "Formatted Input with scanf()."

Using bioskey()   The **bioskey()** function enables you to read a single key from the keyboard by calling **BIOS** directly.

Syntax:
```
int bioskey(int cmd);
```

Parameter:
cmd   specifies the input operation.

Remarks:
This function can read keys that have extended key codes, such as the cursor positioning keys or the function keys. When you use the **bioskey()** function you can specify three modes with the argument **cmd**. The modes are:

- **0** Gets the next key pressed at the keyboard
- **1** Tests to see if a key is available
- **2** Obtains the current Shift key status

Example:
The following example prompts the user for a response. The program calls the **bioskey()** function until the user enters a key. After a key has been entered, **bioskey()** is called again to read the key. The **do-while** loop repeats

until the user presses the Esc key. Here's the example:

```
do {
    printf("\nGo ahead ? (Y/N)");
    while (bioskey(1) == 0);        /* wait for key */
    k = bioskey(0);                 /* read key */
    if (isalnum(k & 0xFF)
        printf("%c", k);
} while (k != ESC);
```

Turbo C provides two main functions that you can use to read unformatted **String Input** strings—**gets()** and **cgets()**.

Syntax:
```
#include <stdio.h>
char *gets(char *s);

#include <conio.h>
char *cgets(char *s);
```

Parameters:
The relevant parameter for **gets()**:

*s   the location where the input string is stored.

With **cgets()**:

*s   the location where the input string is stored.

Remarks:
The **gets()** is a stream I/O function that reads a string from **stdin**. When this function is called, all characters are read until the newline character (\n) is encountered. The **gets()** replaces the newline character with the null character. For example, suppose you type this string at the keyboard:

```
String 1<CR>
```

Turbo C stores this string as:

```
|S|t|r|i|n|g|\0|
```

The **cgets()** function, on the other hand, reads a string from the keyboard and stores both the string and the length of the string. Before **cgets()** is called, you must set the first element of the array variable that will store the returned string to the maximum length of the string to be read. Then, **cgets()** reads the input string until it encounters a return or until it exceeds the string size limit. As an example, if the string size is set to 20 characters and **cgets()** is called as shown here:

```
str[0] = 20;    /* string size */
cgets(str);
```

and the following string is typed in:

```
This is a very very very long string<CR>
```

only the first 20 characters of the string will be read.

Example:
The following example illustrates how you prompt for a single string from the keyboard.

```
printf("\nEnter your name --> ");
gets(name);
printf("\nGreetings, %s. How are you today?", name);
```

Using scanf() to Read Strings

You can also use the Turbo C **scanf()** function to read one or more strings. To read a string, Turbo C requires the format specifier %s.

Examples:
Here's an example that illustrates the use of the **scanf()** function to read a string:

```
printf("\nEnter a string");
scanf("%s",str);
```

The next example shows how you can use **scanf()** to read multiple strings:

```
printf("\nEnter your first, middle, and last names ");
scanf("%s%s%s",first,middle,last);
```

Keep in mind that the **scanf()** function does not accept variable-length strings. You must know how many words (the number of spaces) are in a given string before you attempt to read the string, because white space characters are treated as delimiters.

Turbo C provides only two options for reading numeric data. The first option uses the function **getw()**, and the other uses the **scanf()** function.

Numeric Input

The **getw()** function can only read integers from a stream. To read an integer from the keyboard, use the term **stdio** as the stream pointer.

getw()

Syntax:
```
#include <stdio.h>
int getw(FILE *stream);
```

Parameter:
*stream   a pointer to the input stream.

Example:
The following example shows how you can use **getw()** to read an integer from the keyboard:

```
printf("\nEnter a number from 1 to 10 -->");
n = getw(stdio);
if ((n < 1) || (n > 10))
   printf("\nSorry the number is out of range");
```

If you want to read numeric data other than integers, use the general input function **scanf()**. The **scanf()** function can read numeric data in a variety of formats—including decimal integers, octal integers, hexadecimal integers, and floating-point. Table 1.3 shows a table of the format codes required by Turbo C to read numeric data in the different formats.

Using scanf() to Read Numeric Input

Examples:
The following examples show how you can use the **scanf()** function to read numeric input. The first example reads a decimal integer:

```
printf("\nEnter a number from 1 to 10 -->");
scanf("%d", &n);
if ((n < 1) || (n > 10))
    printf("\nSorry, the number is out of range");
```

Table 1.3. Turbo C format codes for reading numeric data

Format Code	Description
%d	Read a decimal integer
%i	Read a decimal, octal, hex number
%o	Read an octal integer
%u	Read an unsigned integer
%x	Read a hexadecimal integer
%h	Read a short integer
%e	Read a floating-point number
%f	Read a floating-point number

This next example prompts you to enter a floating-point number and an integer:

```
printf("\nEnter unit price : ");
scanf("%f",&unitprice);
printf("Enter quantity : ");
scanf("%d",&quantity);
printf("\nTotal due = %f",unitprice * quantity);
```

You can also use the general-purpose **scanf()** statement to read multiple variables of different data types from the keyboard. Under this approach, the user must include a format code for each entry. The following example shows how to input a string, a real number, and an integer:

```
printf("\nEnter a string, a real, and an integer ");
scanf("%s%f%d",mystr, &myreal, &myint);
```

Writing to the Screen

Turbo C provides numerous stream and console I/O functions that you can use to write characters, strings, integers, and other data to the screen. As is the case for input routines, we can comfortably divide output routines into the two categories, *formatted* and *unformatted*. In our presentation here, we include both categories.

Character Output

Turbo C provides three main functions you can use to display characters on the screen.

Syntax:
```
#include <stdio.h>
int putc(int c, FILE *stream);

#include <conio.h>
int putch(int c);

#include <stdio.h>
int putchar(int c);
```

Parameters:
c   the character to display.
*stream   the designated output stream.

Remarks:
Both **putc**() and **putchar**() send a character to the standard output stream. To use these functions, you must include the header file **stdio.h**. The function **putch**() sends a character to the system console. This function is prototyped in **conio.h**.

Examples:
Our first example below illustrates how you can use the stream functions **getc**() and **putc**() to read and display a character:

```
while ((ch = getc(stdin)) != 'X') {
  if (islower(ch)) putc(ch, stdout);
   else ...
}
```

In this case, the input character read is not displayed. We must specify the reserved word **stdin** as an argument for **getc**() and **stdout** as an argument for **putc**() to indicate that we are reading data from the standard input console and writing data to the standard output device.

This next example shows how a character is displayed using the **putch**() function:

```
if ((ch = getch()) != 'A')
  putch(ch);
```

Here, we don't need to specify the **stdout** for **putch()**, because this function writes to the standard output console by default.

Using printf() to Display a Character

Here we describe how **printf()** is used to display a character.

Syntax:
```
#include <stdio.h>
int printf(const char *format-string[,argument, ...]);
```

Parameters:
*format-string   specifies how the arguments displayed are formatted.
argument   the data element to display.

Remarks:
You can use the Turbo C general-purpose output function **printf()** to display a single character. You use the term **%c** in the format string to indicate that you want a character to be displayed.

Example:
The following code segment illustrates the use of both the **scanf()** and **printf()** functions for reading and displaying a character:

```
printf("\nEnter a character ");
scanf("%c",&ch);
printf("\nYour character is %c", ch);
```

String Output

Turbo C provides two primary functions that you can use to write unformatted strings—**puts()** and **cputs()**. Here are their general formats:

```
#include <stdio.h>
int puts(const char *s);
```

```
#include <conio.h>
int cputs(const char *s);
```

Parameter:
*s   the output string.

Remarks:
The **puts()** is a stream I/O function that sends a string to **stdout**. When this

function is called, Turbo C sends a string terminated with the null character (**\0**) to the standard output device and replaces the null character with the newline (**\n**) character. Therefore, when you display a string with **puts()**, the cursor is advanced to the next line.

The **cputs()** function, on the other hand, sends a string to the system console (display). However, **cputs()** won't include the newline character. For this reason, you should use **cputs()** if you don't want the cursor to advance to the next line following display of the string.

Example:

The following example demonstrates how you can prompt for a single string from the keyboard.

```
puts ("Enter your name --> ") ;
gets (name) ;
cputs ("Greetings, ") ;
cputs (name) ;
cputs (" How are you today?") ;
```

The first output function, **puts()**, displays the specified string and advances the cursor to the next line. We cause the second string to be displayed by calling **cputs()** three times. Because **cputs()** does not append a newline character (**\n**) to the end of each string, the string is displayed on a single line.

You can also use the Turbo C **printf()** function to display one or more strings. To display a string with this approach, use the format specifier %s.

Using printf() to Display Strings

Examples:

This example illustrates how you can use the **printf()** function to write a string:

```
printf ("\nEnter a string ") ;
```

The next example shows how you can write multiple strings with the **printf()** function:

```
printf ("\nYour first name is %s and your last name is %s",
      first, last) ;
```

Numeric Output

You have two options for writing numeric data in Turbo C. With the first option, you use the **putw()** function. With the second option, you use the **printf()** function. The **putw()** function can only be used to send integers to a specified stream.

Syntax:
```
#include <stdio.h>
int putw(int w, FILE *stream);
```

Parameters:
w   the integer to display.
*stream   the selected output stream.

Remarks:
To display an integer on the screen, use the term **stdout** as the stream pointer.

Example:
The following example shows how you can use **putw()** to display an integer on the screen:

```
printf("\nEnter a number from 1 to 10 -->");
n = getw(stdio);
if ((n < 1) || (n > 10))
   putw(n, stdout);
```

Using printf() to Write Numeric Output

If you want to write numeric data other than integers, use the general output function **printf()**. The **printf()** function can write numeric data in a variety of formats—including decimal integers, octal integers, hexadecimal integers, and floating-point. Table 1.4 shows the format codes required to display numeric data in the different formats available.

Example:
The following examples show how you can use the **printf()** function to display numeric data. This first example reads and writes a decimal integer:

```
printf("\nEnter a number from 1 to 10 -->");
scanf("%d", &n);
if ((n < 1) || (n > 10))
   printf("\nSorry, the number is out of range");
else printf("\nYour number is %d", n);
```

Table 1.4. Turbo C format codes for displaying numeric data with printf()

Format Code	Description
%d	Write a decimal integer
%i	Write a decimal, octal, hex number
%o	Write an octal integer
%u	Write an unsigned integer
%x	Write a hexadecimal integer
%h	Write a short integer
%e	Write a floating-point number
%f	Write a floating-point number
%g	Write a floating-point number

This example prompts you to enter a floating-point number and an integer:

```
printf("\nEnter unit price: ");
scanf("%f",&unitprice);
printf("Enter quantity: ");
scanf("%d",&quantity);
printf("\nTotal due = %f",unitprice * quantity);
```

The general-purpose **printf()** statement can display multiple variables of different data types. However, the user must include a format code for each entry. The following example demonstrates how to output a string, a real number, and an integer:

```
printf("\nString is %s Real is %f and integer is %d", str,
        flt, i);
```

Formatted input is performed in Turbo C by using the **scanf()** function. This function uses variable-length arguments.

Formatted Input with scanf()

Syntax:
```
int scanf(char *format-string[,argument-list]);
```

Parameters:
This function uses two parameters; however, the second parameter is optional. The first, **format-string**, is a string constructed according to a set

of formatting rules. This format string tells the **scanf()** function how to read in data from the **stdin**. The second argument, **argument-list**, is actually a list of arguments, and each argument is a pointer to a variable that corresponds with a variable type specified in the format string. When formatted data is read, the data is stored in the arguments included in the argument list. Because this function uses general input pointers, you can perform formatted input operations with any standard Turbo C data type.

The format string determines how data is read. The structure of this string is defined as

```
% [*] [data-width] [F|N] [h|l] type-spec
```

and the function of each component is

%	indicates the beginning of a format string.
*****	indicates that data is to be skipped.
data-width	the number of characters to read.
F|N	flags for overriding the default data pointer size.
h|l	options for converting the data type of the input.
type-spec	the symbol to specify the type of data to read.

Remarks:
Remember that the symbols enclosed in brackets [] are optional parts and can be omitted. In this respect, the simplest format specification string that can be written is of the form

```
%type-spec
```

Because **scanf()** can read three unique classes of formatted data—numbers, characters, and pointers—three types of format specification codes are available. Table 1.5 lists the valid specifications for the type-spec component. The first five values in this table— **%d, %o, %x, %i,** and **%u**—can be specified as uppercase letters such as **%D**. If the uppercase letter is used, the data read is expected to be returned in a long data type. We present the techniques for reading different data types next.

Reading Numbers   To read a number such as an integer, the format string is specified as

```
scanf("%d", &val);
```

Table 1.5. Specifications for the type-spec component

Value	Function
%d	Read a decimal integer
%o	Read an octal number
%x	Read a hexadecimal number
%i	Read a decimal, octal, or hexadecimal number
%u	Read an unsigned integer
%e	Read a floating-point number
%f	Read a floating-point number
Reading Characters and Strings	
%c	Read a character
%s	Read a string
Reading Pointers	
%n	Return the number of characters read
%p	Read a pointer

Note also that we pass the address of the variable used to store the integer input value. The data type of the variable should match the type specified in the format string. Multiple integer values can be read with **scanf()** using calls of the form:

```
scanf("%d%d%d", &val1, &val2, &val3);
```

In this case, if the input consists of the numbers

```
25 32 12
```

scanf() reads these three numbers and stores 25 in the variable **val1**, 32 in the variable **val2**, and 12 in the variable **val3**.

When a format string is specified, other characters besides the predefined format specifiers can be included. Such characters perform pattern matching features. If a character included in the format string is not one of the format specifiers, **scanf()** expects to read that same character in the input string. For example, if a format string is written as "%d$%d" and **scanf()** is called with

```
scanf("%d$%d", &val1, &val2);
```

the function will expect to read numbers in the format

```
21$12
```

When the data is read, however, the character $ is not stored. If this character is missing from the input string, **scanf()** terminates before reading all of the data.

Reading Characters and Strings

The technique of reading formatted characters and strings is similar to that of reading numbers. In this case, either the specifier "%c" or "%s" is used. To read a character, the format is

```
scanf("%c", &c);
```

Note that the **&** operator is required to pass the address of the variable **c** to **scanf()**. When **scanf()** reads strings, it stops reading data when the first whitespace character is encountered. The whitespace characters consist of a blank, tab, and newline characters. Thus, if the following string is typed in

```
"This text is for scanf()"
```

when **scanf()** is called with the arguments

```
scanf("%s", line);
```

where **line** is a pointer to character array, **scanf()** only reads and stores the string **"This."** To read the complete string, **scanf()** must be called multiple times.

To limit the size of the string that **scanf()** reads, the optional width specification can be used. In this case, a call such as

```
scanf("10%s", line);
```

reads the first 10 characters from the string typed and stores the characters in the variable line.

The **scanf()** function can also be used to skip over unwanted data of a specified type. This feature is controlled by the symbol *****. If you include the ***** in a format string, data of the corresponding type will be read but not stored. For example, the **scanf()** call

```
scanf("%*c%c", &c);
```

reads and skips over the first character read; the second character read is stored in **ch**. This feature is useful for clearing the **stdin** of newline characters. For example, if we use **scanf()** to read a string that was terminated by a carriage return, **scanf()** reads the string; however, the carriage return remains in the input buffer. To read the string and remove the carriage return, we can call **scanf()** with

```
scanf("%s%*c",buf);
```

Formatted output is displayed with the general **printf()** function. Like the **scanf()** function, this routine also uses a variable number of arguments.

Formatted Output with printf()

Syntax:
```
int printf(char *format-string[,argument-list]);
```

Parameters:
The **printf()** function also contains two parameters—the format string and the argument list. The format string is similar to the one used by **scanf()**; however, for **printf()**, the format string defines how data is to be written to a stream. The structure of this format string is defined as

```
% [flags] [data-width] [.precision] [F|N] [h|l] type-spec
```

and the function of each component is

%	indicates the beginning of a format string.
flags	specifies options such as justification.
data-width	the number of characters to print.
precision	specifies the number of digits to print.
F|N	flags for overriding the default data pointer size.
h|l	options for converting the data type of the output.
type-spec	specifies the type of data to write

TIP

Remarks:
The symbols enclosed in brackets [] are optional parts and they can be omitted. With **printf()**, the simplest format specification string that can be written is

```
%type-spec
```

The format string can also consist of just a string of data for outputting, such as

```
printf("This is an output string");
```

Numeric Output   The standard **printf()** call for displaying a number is

```
printf("<%number code>", str);
```

where the component **%number code** must be one of the following:

Format Code	Description
%d	Read a decimal integer
%o	Read an octal number
%x	Read a hexadecimal number
%i	Read a decimal, octal, or hexadecimal number
%u	Read an unsigned integer
%e	Read a floating-point number
%f	Read a floating-point number
%g	Read a floating-point number

Examples:
The following examples illustrate how formatted numbers are displayed using the **printf()** function:

```
printf("%d %d %f", 12,20,34.2);
printf("%d %h", ival, hexval);
```

The first call to **printf()** displays two integers and a floating-point number. Note that a space is placed between each number.

The second **printf()** example displays an integer in standard format and an integer in a hexadecimal format.

The standard **printf()** call for displaying a string is

Outputting Strings

```
printf("%s", str);
```

The number of characters to display can also be specified by using the width specifier. For example, the function

```
printf("%7s", str);
```

displays the first seven characters of the string **str**. If **str** contained the string **"one two three four,"** the **printf()** call above would display the string **"one two."**

The width specifier can also be used to pad strings. That is, trailing or leading blanks can be added by specifying a width that is greater than the output string. If **printf()** is called with

```
printf("%25s", str);
```

the function will right justify our string by adding six blanks at the beginning as shown:

```
"        one two three four"
```

To left justify a string, a flag specifier must be used. For this action, here is a sample function call:

```
printf("%-25s", str);
```

which produces the output

```
"one two three four      "
```

Turbo C provides one function for moving the cursor and two functions for obtaining the position of the cursor. These functions—**gotoxy()**, **wherex()**, and **wherey()**—are prototyped in the header file **conio.h**. You must include this file in any program that uses one or more of these functions.

Cursor Control

Specifying the Cursor Location

You use the function **gotoxy()** to set the cursor position.

Syntax:
```
#include <conio.h>
void gotoxy (int row, int column);
```

Parameters:

row   specifies the screen row number (1 to 25) where the cursor is to be placed.

column specifies the column number (1 to 80) for the cursor position.

Example:
The following code example illustrates how to center a message on the screen after first clearing the screen:

```
void center (char *heading)
/* clear screen and center string */
{
    clrscr();
    gotoxy (40 - strlen (heading) / 2, 1);
    cprintf ("%s", heading);
}
```

Getting the Cursor Location

The functions **wherex()** and **wherey()** return the row and column number for the cursor position. Neither of these functions requires an argument, and both return integer-typed results.

Syntax:
```
#include <conio.h>
int wherex (void);
int wherey (void);
```

Example:
The following function moves the cursor to the lower right corner (in this case, down one row and over by one column position to the right):

```
void tolower right (void)
{
    int xpos, ypos;
```

```
    xpos = wherex();
    ypos = wherey();
    /* check whether cursor is at the border lines  */
    if (xpos < 80) xpos++;
    if (ypos < 25) ypos++;
  gotoxy(xpos,ypos);
}
```

The cursor position can also be obtained by calling the **gettextinfo()** function, which is presented next.

$$\mathbf{T}_{\text{IP}}$$

Turbo C provides support for simple text-based windows. Text windows can be created and positioned anywhere on the screen, provided that the screen is currently set to one of the standard text modes. Once a window is defined, all of the output and other I/O routines such as the cursor positioning functions perform their actions relative to the base position (upper left corner) of the window. The first row and column in a text window is also addressed as position (1,1), as shown in Figure 1.1. Keep in mind that when a window is defined, a border is not drawn. Therefore, you cannot actually see the boundaries of a window.

Text Windows

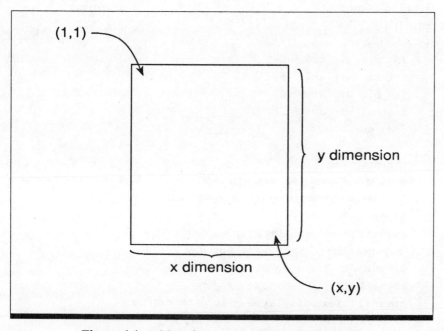

Figure 1.1. Addressing a text window in Turbo C

**Defining a
Window**

The function **window()** is used to define a window.

Syntax:
```
#include <conio.h>
void window(int left, int top, int right, int bottom);
```

Parameters:
left, top   defines the upper left corner of the window.
right, bottom   defines the lower right corner of the window.

Remarks:
In the 80-column text mode, the screen has a default of **window(1,1,80,25)**. Similarly, the default size for the full screen window in 40-column text mode is **window(1,1,25,40)**. If values outside the range of the screen are specified, the window is not created.

Example:
The following example program illustrates how a window is created and text is displayed in the window:

```
#include <conio.h>
main()
{
    int min_win_col = 20;
    int max_win_col = 60;
    int min_win_row = 2;
    int max_win_row = 20;
    char ch;

    clrscr();
    window(min_win_col, min_win_row,
        max_win_col, max_win_row);
    gotoxy(1,5);
    cprintf("Text displayed in window");
    ch = getch();      /* wait for any key */
    textmode(MONO);    /* remove window */
    gotoxy(1,5);
    cprintf("Text displayed in full screen");
    ch = getch();      /* wait for any key */
    clrscr();
}
```

Note that the **textmode()** function sets the default window to the size of the full screen. Because the corner of the first window is located at column 20, row 2, and the function **gotoxy(1,5)** is used to position the cursor in the window, the text string **"Text displayed in window"** is actually written at screen location (20,6).

The text window defined by the **window()** function affects many of the other routines declared in the header file **conio.h**, including the functions shown in Table 1.6.

Accessing a Window

Table 1.6. Description of functions defined with window()

Function	Description
clrscr()	Clear the active window
clreol()	Clear characters from cursor position to end of line
cprintf()	Write formatted data to the active window
cputs()	Write a string to the active window
delline()	Delete a line in text window
getche()	Read a character in active window and echo
gettext()	Copy text from screen to memory
gettextinfo()	Get the textmode video information
gotoxy()	Position the cursor in the window
insline()	Insert a line in text window
movetext()	Copy text from one screen area to another
putch()	Write a character to the active window
puttext()	Copy text from memory to a screen area
wherex()	Get column position of cursor
wherey()	Get row position of cursor

When one of these routines is executed, an input or output operation is performed in relation to the position and size of the current window. Thus a function such as **gotoxy(1,1)** places the cursor at the upper left corner of the screen window and not necessarily the physical screen. Turbo C only defines and uses one window at a time.

Turbo C provides a useful function called **gettextinfo()**, which is useful for obtaining the status of the current window.

Obtaining the Status of a Window

Syntax:
```
#include <conio.h>
void gettextinfo(struct text_info *tinfo);
```

Parameter:

*tinfo   a pointer to the structure that contains the current text related information such as window size, cursor position, and screen attributes.

The data structure **text_info** is defined in the **conio.h** file as:

```
struct text_info {
    unsigned char winleft; /* window coordinates */
    unsigned char wintop;
    unsigned char winright;
    unsigned char winbottom;
    unsigned char attribute; /* screen attributes */
    unsigned char normattr;
    unsigned char currmode;
    unsigned char screenheight;  /* screen size */
    unsigned char screenwidth;
    unsigned char curx;      /* cursor position */
    unsigned char cury;
};
```

Controlling Video

Turbo C provides a set of functions and global variables that control how data is displayed on the screen. With these features you can perform tasks such as writing directly to video memory and displaying text in different foreground and background colors. The functions and variables, along with the techniques for using them, are presented next.

Direct Video Output

Turbo C provides a global variable that controls how output is displayed on the screen. This variable, called **directvideo**, is declared in the header file **conio.h** like this:

```
extern int directvideo;
```

You can set the **directvideo** variable to one of two possible values, as shown in Table 1.7. By default, **directvideo** is set to 0. You can set this variable to the value of 1 to increase the output performance of your program.

Table 1.7. Values for directvideo

Value	Description
0	Use DOS calls to display output (BIOS)
1	Write data directly to video RAM

If you are using video hardware that is not compatible with the IBM standard, setting **directvideo** to 1 might lead to unexpected results.

Example:
Here's a brief program that illustrates the use of the **directvideo** variable:

```
#include <conio.h>
main()
{
    directvideo = 1;
    printf("\nString displayed by writing to video memory");
    directvideo = 0;
    printf("\nString displayed by using a BIOS call");
}
```

Turbo C provides the **textmode()** function for selecting a specific text display mode.

Setting Text Mode

Syntax:
```
#include <conio.h>
void textmode(int mode);
```

Parameter:
mode   used to set the display mode to one of the five modes supported by the PC.

Remarks:
Table 1.8 shows the constants that are defined by the **conio.h** header file to work with the **textmode()** function. The constant **LAST** switches back to the previously selected text mode. This feature is useful if you are switching back and forth between a graphics mode and a text mode.

Table 1.8. Constants defined by conio.h for use with textmode()

Constant	Value	Mode
BW40	0	40 × 25 B/W on a color adapter
C40	1	40 × 25 color on a color adapter
BW80	2	80 × 25 B/W on a color adapter
C80	3	80 × 25 color on a color adapter
MONO	7	80 × 25 B/W on a monochrome adapter
LAST	−1	Last active text mode

Example:
The following code segment illustrates how **textmode()** is used:

```
textmode(C80);
printf("\nDisplay text in color mode");
textmode(MONO);
printf("\nDisplay text in monochrome mode");
textmode(LAST);
printf("\nDisplay text back in color mode");
```

Controlling Display Attributes

Turbo C provides a set of functions you can use to control both the foreground and background colors of text and to control the display intensity.

Setting Text Foreground and Background Colors

Turbo C can set foreground and background colors (attributes) for text that is displayed in text mode. Essentially, two techniques are provided to set the attributes for displayed text. The first technique consists of using the **textcolor()** and **textbackground()** functions to set the background and foreground colors. The second technique involves using the function **textattr()** to set attributes.

The textcolor() and textbackground() Functions

These functions are provided for setting the background and foreground colors of displayed text. They are declared in the header file **conio.h** as:

Syntax:
```
#include <conio.h>
void textbackground(int color);
void textcolor(int color);
```

The function **textcolor()** sets the foreground color, and **textbackground()** sets the background color. For selecting foreground colors, the **conio.h** file provides the constants shown in Table 1.9.

Table 1.9. Constants for selecting foreground colors with textcolor()

Constant	Value
BLACK	0
BLUE	1
GREEN	2
CYAN	3
RED	4
MAGENTA	5
BROWN	6
LIGHTGRAY	7
DARKGRAY	8
LIGHTBLUE	9
LIGHTGREEN	10
LIGHTCYAN	11
LIGHTRED	12
LIGHTMAGENTA	13
YELLOW	14
WHITE	15
BLINK	128

As shown, 16 colors are supported (0–15). In addition, you can make text blink by adding the constant **BLINK** or the value 128 to a color value. For example, the statement

```
textcolor(RED+BLINK);
```

sets the foreground color to red with a blinking attribute.

Background colors are set using any of the first eight colors (0–7). You cannot use the blinking attribute or any of the colors 8–15 when setting the background color.

Example:
The following program demonstrates how background and foreground

colors are set using the text window features of Turbo C. The program first fills the entire screen with yellow dots on a green background. Then a window is defined and located at the middle of the screen. The program issues a **clrscr()**, which only affects the window. Next, red dashes are emitted on a blue background. The **gotoxy()** routine is used to guide the display of these dashes. The program then waits for a key to be pressed, clears the screen, and draws pluses on top of the dashes.

Using the textattr() Function

A function is also provided so you can set both the foreground and background colors at the same time. This function is declared in **conio.h**.

Syntax:
```
void textattr(int attribute);
```

Parameter:
The background, foreground, and blinking attributes are set according to the value specified with the argument **attribute**. This argument is represented with the following bit settings:

Attribute	Bits
foreground	0–3
background	4–6
blinking	7

Example:
The following example shows how the color attributes are set to yellow foreground and red background and the blinking attribute is turned on:

```
textattr(YELLOW + (RED * 16) + BLINK);
```

Setting High, Normal, and Low Video Intensity

Turbo C provides the functions **highvideo()**, **normvideo()**, and **lowvideo()** for controlling the intensity of text output. The **highvideo()** function sets the high intensity bit (bit 3) of the current foreground color setting. Therefore, it performs the following mapping of colors 0–7:

```
0 ------> 8
1 ------> 9
2 ------> 10
3 ------> 11
```

```
4 ------> 12
5 ------> 13
6 ------> 14
7 ------> 15
```

The **lowvideo**() function produces the opposite result, that is, it clears the high intensity bit of the current foreground color setting. Therefore, colors 8–15 are mapped to colors 0–7. Finally, the **normvideo**() function sets the foreground color to the default setting.

Example:
The following code segment illustrates how the video attribute functions are used:

```
cprintf ("Display text in default attributes");
textcolor (RED);
highvideo ();
printf ("\nDisplay text in light red");
textcolor (WHITE);
lowvideo ();
printf ("\nDisplay text in light gray");
normvideo ();
printf ("\nDisplay text in default attributes");
```

Turbo Pascal

Turbo Pascal supports several categories of console I/O operations. We discuss the categories under two basic topics:

- Reading from the keyboard
- Writing to the screen

Turbo Pascal supports keyboard input operations that handle characters, strings, and various numeric types.

Reading from the Keyboard

Turbo Pascal provides two basic ways to read characters from the keyboard. You can:

Character Input

- Use the general-purpose **Readln** procedure
- Use the **ReadKey** function imported from unit **CRT**

Using the
Readln Procedure

The **Readln** procedure enables you to type a character, followed by a carriage return.

Syntax:
```
Procedure Readln([Var F: Text; ] V1 [, V2, ...,Vn]);
```

Parameters:

F   references a text file.
V1, V2 .. Vn   input variables of type **char**, **integer**, **real,** or **string.**

Remarks:
The Backspace key also can be used to erase the typed character. You'll find this programming method useful when you want to give the user some time to think or to verify his or her input.

Example:
The following code segment illustrates how you can use the **Readln** statement to prompt for a character:

```
Write('Enter a character : ');
Readln(Character);
```

Using the
ReadKey Function

This function enables you to read a single character from the keyboard. You can also use the boolean **KeyPressed** function (also imported from unit **CRT**) to detect whether the program user has pressed a key.

Syntax:
```
Function ReadKey: Char;
```

Example:
The following example prompts the user for a yes/no answer. We assign the input character to **Answer** using the **ReadKey** function. Note that we use a **Repeat-Until** loop to ensure that the answer is either a Y or an N (with uppercase and lowercase forms both accepted). Here's the example:

```
Repeat
    Write('Go ahead ? (Y/N) ');
    Answer := ReadKey;
    Writeln(Answer); Writeln;
Until Answer In ['Y','y','N','n'];
```

You can use the **Readln** procedure to read a string of characters from the keyboard. With **Readln**, you can press the Backspace key to correct erroneously typed characters.

Example:
The following example illustrates how you can program a prompt that accepts a single string from the keyboard:

```
Write('Enter your name --> ');
Readln(Name); Writeln;
Writeln('Greetings, ',Name,'. How are you today?');
```

You can also use the general-purpose **Readln** procedure to read numbers from the keyboard.

Example:
These code lines prompt the user to enter a floating-point number and an integer:

```
Writeln('Enter unit price : ');
Readln(UnitPrice);
Writeln('Enter quantity   : ');
Readln(Quantity);
Writeln;
Writeln('Total due = ',UnitPrice * Quantity);
```

The general-purpose **Readln** procedure can read multiple variables of different data types from the keyboard. When you implement this approach, the user must delimit each entry with a space. The following example shows how to input a string, a real number, and an integer:

```
Writeln('Enter a string, a real, and an integer ');
Readln(MyStr, MyReal, MyInt);
```

Turbo Pascal provides the **Write** and **Writeln** procedures for displaying various types of variables. These statements enable you to form a chain of output composed of constants, variables, and expressions.

Syntax:
```
Write(F, V1 [,V2, ..., Vn]);
Writeln([Var F : Text;] V1 [,V2, ..., Vn]);
```

Parameters:

F	references a text file.
V1, V2 .. Vn	input variables of type **char, integer, real,** or **string.**

Example:

The following set of **Writeln** procedures outputs various types of data:

```
Writeln('A'); { character constant }
Writeln(YourName); { string variable }
Writeln(Index); { integer variable }
Writeln('Time is ',Time); { string constant and variable }
Writeln('Cost = $',Pr*Qn); { string constant & expression }
```

Formatted Input

Turbo Pascal does not support a mechanism for implementing formatted input. You have to write custom procedures or functions to provide this capability.

Formatted Output

The **Writeln** and **Write** procedures support rather limited formatted output capabilities. You may specify the width used to display a character, string, or numeric output by placing a colon and the desired width number after the output data object.

For floating-point output, you can specify decimal places by inserting a second colon after the width specifier, followed by the number of decimals.

Example:

This example shows how you can specify decimal places for floating-point output:

```
Writeln(' ':30,'Total = ',Total:4:2,' for ',Num:3,' Items');
```

If the width specifier is a negative number, Turbo Pascal displays the data object flush left (aligned at the left margin). If the decimal-place specifier is negative, the final display format will vary, depending on the width specifier:

• If the width specifier is positive, the number is forced to appear in scientific notation—along with a generous number of digits.

• If the width specifier is negative, the number is left justified and displayed in scientific notation—with only a few significant digits. If you use a negative decimal-place specifier, its magnitude has no effect.

Turbo Pascal supports the following commands that you can use to query and set the position of the cursor. We discuss the two basic command categories next.

Cursor Control

You can use the procedure **GotoXY**, imported from unit **CRT**, to set the position of the cursor.

Specifying the Cursor Location

Syntax:
```
Procedure GotoXY(Row, Column : Byte);
```

Parameters:

Row   specifies the screen row number (1 to 25) where the cursor is to be placed.

Column   specifies the column number (1 to 80) for the cursor position.

Example:
The following code example illustrates how you can clear the screen and then center a heading line:

```
Procedure Center(Heading : String);
{ clear screen and center heading }
Begin
    ClrScr;
    GotoXY((40 - Length(Heading) div 2),1);
    Writeln(Heading);
End;
```

You use the functions **WhereX** and **WhereY**, imported from unit **CRT**, to return the row and column number of the cursor position. Neither function requires an argument, but both functions return **Byte**-typed results.

Querying the Cursor Location

Syntax:
```
Function WhereX : Byte;
Function WhereY : Byte;
```

Example:
The following procedure moves the cursor to the lower right corner (in this

case, down one row and to the right by one column position):

```
Procedure ToLowerRight;

Var XPos, YPos : Byte;

Begin
    XPos = WhereX;
    YPos = WhereY;
    { check if cursor is at the border lines }
    If XPos < 80 Then Inc(XPos);
    If YPos < 25 Then Inc(YPos);
    GotoXY(XPos,YPos)
End;
```

Text Windows

Turbo Pascal provides support for simple text-based windows. Text windows can be created and positioned anywhere on the screen, provided that the screen is currently set to one of the standard text modes. Once a window is defined, all of the output and other I/O routines (such as the cursor positioning functions) perform their actions relative to the base position (upper left corner) of the window. The first row and column in a text window is also addressed as position (1,1). Keep in mind that when a window is defined, a border is not drawn. Therefore, you cannot actually see the boundaries of a window.

Defining a Window

The procedure **Window** is used to define a window. This procedure is exported by library **CRT** and defines the rectangular screen area in text mode.

Syntax:
```
Procedure Window(X1, Y1, X2, Y2 : Byte);
```

Parameters:
X1,Y1   the upper left corner of the window.
X2,Y2   the lower right corner of the window.

In the 80-column text mode, the screen has a default of **Window(1,1,80,25)**. Similarly, the default size for the full screen window in 40-column text mode is **Window(1,1,25,40)**.

Once a window is defined, the boundaries of the window remain in effect until another **Window** procedure is called. If you want to restore the screen to its full range—80 columns by 25 rows in 80-column mode or 40 columns by 25 rows in 40-column mode—you should call **Window** with **Window(1,1,80,25)** or **Window(1,1,25,40)**. You can also reset the size of a window to the size of the full screen by calling the **TextMode** procedure.

TIP

The **Window** procedure only affects the video page zero of a Color Graphics Adapter (CGA, EGA, or VGA).

TIP

Example:
The following sample program illustrates how a window is created and text is displayed in the window:

```
Program Make_Window;

Uses CRT;

Const
    MIN_WIN_COL = 20;
    MAX_WIN_COL = 60;
    MIN_WIN_ROW = 2;
    MAX_WIN_ROW = 20;


Var Ch : Char;

Begin
    ClrScr;
    Window(MIN_WIN_COL, MIN_WIN_ROW,
        MAX_WIN_COL, MAX_WIN_ROW);
    GotoXY(1,5);
    Writeln('Text displayed in window');
    Ch := ReadKey;     { wait for any key }
    TextMode(Mono);    { remove window }
    GotoXY(1,5);
    Writeln('Text displayed in full screen');
    Ch := ReadKey;     { wait for any key }
    ClrScr;
End.
```

Note that the **TextMode** procedure is used to set the default window to the size of the full screen. Because the corner of the first window is located at column 20, row 2, and the function **GotoXY(1,5)** is used to position the cursor in the window, the text string **"Text displayed in window"** is actually written at screen location (20,6).

Accessing a Window

The text window defined by procedure **Window** affects many of the other routines exported by unit **CRT**, including the functions and procedures shown in Table 1.10.

Table 1.10. Routines affected by definitions with Window

Function	Description
GotoXY	Position the cursor in the window
ClrScr	Clear the active window
ClrEol	Clear characters from cursor position to end of line
DelLine	Delete a line
InsLine	Insert a line
Read	Read a character
ReadLn	Read a line of data
Write	Write data
WriteLn	Write a line of data
WhereX	Get column position of cursor
WhereY	Get row position of cursor

When one of these routines is executed, an input or output operation is performed in relation to the position and size of the current window. Thus a function such as **GotoXY(1,1)** places the cursor at the upper left corner of the screen window and not necessarily the physical screen. Turbo Pascal only defines and uses one window at a time.

To access the screen coordinates of the current window, the variables **WindMin** and **WindMax** are provided. Both of these are defined as type **word** and exported by the **CRT** library. When the **Window** procedure is called, **WindMin** is set to the value representing the upper left corner, and **WindMax** is set to the value representing the lower right corner. Each of these variables uses the following representation:

```
7 6 5 4 3 2 1 0
```

Y coordinate	X coordinate

Controlling Video

Turbo Pascal provides a set of routines and variables that control how data is displayed. With these features you can perform tasks such as writing directly to video memory and displaying text in different foreground and background colors. The routines and variables, along with the techniques for using them, are presented in the following sections.

Direct Video Output

The **CRT** unit exports a boolean variable, **DirectVideo**, that plays an important role in causing the **Writeln** and **Write** statements to write directly to the screen memory. When **DirectVideo** is set to **True**, the direct video output enables the **Writeln** and **Write** statements to display data quickly.

By default, this variable is set to **True**. If it is set to **False**, characters are displayed by calling the BIOS output functions. When the BIOS is used to display text, you will notice a substantial decrease in your program's output operations; however, using this technique helps to ensure that your program is compatible with most PC hardware configurations.

Example:
The following code segment illustrates how data is displayed using the BIOS and writing directly to video memory:

```
DirectVideo := False;
Writeln('Text displayed by writing to BIOS');
DirectVideo := True;
Writeln('Text displayed by writing to video memory');
```

Whenever the **TextMode** procedure is called, the **DirectVideo** variable is reset to its default (**True**) value. To ensure that the setting of this variable remains the same throughout the course of a program, save the state of this variable before you call **TextMode** and restore it to its previous value. For example, the following code segment would produce the desired effect:

```
VState := DirectVideo;  { save state }
TextMode(Mono);
DirectVideo := VState;  { restore state }
```

Test for Snow   Occasionally, when characters are written directly to the video memory for CGA adapters, unwanted interference patterns called *snow* appear on the screen. To eliminate this problem, Turbo Pascal provides a variable called **CheckSnow,** which allows you to turn *snow-checking* on or off. This variable, defined as a **Boolean,** is set to **True** by default. When **CheckSnow** is set to **True,** a special test is made to ensure that data is not written to video memory at the wrong time. You can set this variable to **False** to eliminate the *snow-checking* feature.

Setting Text Mode   Turbo Pascal provides the **TextMode** procedure for selecting a specific text display mode. This routine is exported by unit **CRT.** The constants shown in Table 1.11 are defined and exported by **CRT** to work with **TextMode:**

Table 1.11. Constants available for setting TextMode

Constant	Value	Mode
BW40	0	40 × 25 B/W on a color adapter
C40	1	40 × 25 color on a color adapter
BW80	2	80 × 25 B/W on a color adapter
C80	3	80 × 25 color on a color adapter
Mono	7	80 × 25 B/W on a monochrome adapter
Last	−1	Last active text mode

When the **TextMode** procedure is called, the following variables are sent to the indicated values:

Variable	Value
DirectVideo	True
CheckSnow	True

In addition, the active window is set to the full screen size and the current text attribute is set to the normal setting.

TIP   To retain the current window coordinates before **TextMode** is called, you should save these coordinates and use them to call the **Window** procedure after the new text mode is selected.

Example:
The following code segment illustrates how **TextMode** is used:

```
TextMode(C80);
Writeln('Display text in color mode');
TextMode(Mono);
Writeln('Display text in monochrome mode');
TextMode(Last);
Writeln('Display text back in color mode');
```

Turbo Pascal can set foreground and background colors (attributes) for text that is displayed in text mode. Essentially, two techniques are provided that set the attributes for displayed text. The first technique consists of using the **TextColor** and **TextBackground** procedures to set the background and foreground colors, and the second technique involves using the variable **TextAttr** to set attributes.

Setting Foreground and Background Colors (Attributes)

These procedures are exported by unit **CRT** and enable a program to alter the foreground and background color of text displayed in text mode.

TextColor and TextBackground Procedures

Syntax:
```
Procedure TextColor(Color : Byte);
Procedure TextBackground(Color : Byte);
```

The procedure **TextColor** is used to set the foreground color and **TextBackground** is used to set the background color. For selecting foreground colors, the **CRT** unit exports the constants listed in Table 1.12. As shown, 16 colors are supported (0–15). In addition, you can make text blink by adding the constant **Blink** or the value **128** to a color value. For example, the statement:

```
TextColor(Red+Blink);
```

sets the foreground color to red with a blinking attribute.

Background colors are set using any of the first eight colors (0–7). You cannot use the blinking attribute or any of the colors 8–15 when you set the background color.

Example:
The following program demonstrates how background and foreground

Table 1.12. Constants for setting foreground colors

Constant	Value
Black	0
Blue	1
Green	2
Cyan	3
Red	4
Magenta	5
Brown	6
LightGray	7
DarkGray	8
LightBlue	9
LightGreen	10
LightCyan	11
LightRed	12
LightMagenta	13
Yellow	14
White	15
Blink	128

colors are set using the the text window features of Turbo Pascal. The program first fills the entire screen with yellow dots on a green background. Then a window is defined and located at the middle of the screen. The program issues a **ClrScr,** which only affects the window. Next, red dashes are emitted on a blue background. The **GotoXY** routine is used to guide the display of these dashes. The program then waits for a key to be pressed, clears the screen, and draws plus signs on top of the dashes.

```
Program Test_Windows;

Uses CRT;

Const MIN_COL = 1;
    MAX_COL = 80;
    MIN_ROW = 1;
    MAX_ROW = 25;
    MIN_WIN_COL = 20;
    MAX_WIN_COL = 60;
```

```
    MIN_WIN_ROW = 2;
    MAX_WIN_ROW = 20;

Var i, j : Byte;
    Ch : Char;

Begin
    DirectVideo := True;
    ClrScr;
    TextColor(Yellow);
    TextBackground(Green);
    { fill screen with dots }
    For i := MIN_ROW To MAX_ROW Do
        For j := MIN_COL To MAX_COL Do
            Write('.');
    Window(MIN_WIN_COL, MIN_WIN_ROW,
            MAX_WIN_COL, MAX_WIN_ROW);
    ClrScr;

    TextColor(Red);
    TextBackground(Blue);
    { fill window screen with dashes }
    For i := MIN_WIN_ROW To MAX_WIN_ROW Do Begin
        GotoXY(1,i); { place on 1st column of row i }
        For j := MIN_WIN_COL To MAX_WIN_COL Do
            Write('-');
    End;

    Ch := ReadKey; { wait for any key }
    ClrScr;
    { fill window screen with pluses }
    For i := MIN_WIN_ROW To MAX_WIN_ROW Do Begin
        GotoXY(1,i); { place on 1st column of row i }
        For j := MIN_WIN_COL To MAX_WIN_COL Do
            Write('+');
    End;
End.
```

You can modify the program so that the window limits are redefined before the pluses are displayed.

Using the TextAttr Variable

The **CRT** unit also exports a byte-typed variable, **TextAttr**, which you can use in setting the video display attributes for subsequent displayed characters. This variable is also set when the procedures **TextColor** and **TextBackground** are called.

The background, foreground, and blinking attributes are stored in the variable **TextAttr** as:

Attribute	Bits
foreground	0–3
background	4–6
blinking	7

Example:
The following example shows how the color attributes are set to yellow foreground and red background and the blinking attribute is turned on:

```
TextAttr := Yellow + (Red * 16) + Blink;
```

Setting High, Normal, and Low Video Intensity

The **CRT** unit exports the **HighVideo**, **NormVideo**, and **LowVideo** procedures to control the intensity of text output. The **HighVideo** procedure sets the high intensity bit (bit 3) of the value stored in the **TextAttr** variable. Therefore, it performs the following mapping of colors 0–7:

```
0 ------> 8
1 ------> 9
2 ------> 10
3 ------> 11
4 ------> 12
5 ------> 13
6 ------> 14
7 ------> 15
```

The **LowVideo** procedure produces the opposite result, that is, it clears the high intensity bit of the **TextAttr** variable. Therefore, colors 8–15 are mapped to colors 0–7. Finally, the **NormVideo** procedure sets the **TextAttr** variable to the default setting.

Example:
The following code segment illustrates how the video attribute functions are used:

```
Writeln('Display text in default attributes');
TextColor(Red);
HighVideo;
Writeln('Display text in light red');
TextColor(White);
LowVideo;
Writeln('Display text in light gray');
NormVideo;
Writeln('Display text in default attributes');
```

Turbo Prolog

Turbo Prolog supports a window-based I/O system that you can use to read and write unformatted and formatted data. Predicates are provided for reading and writing characters, strings, and numeric data. Many of the predicates that Turbo Prolog provides are *bidirectional*—that is, they can be used both to read and write data. Here we present the predicates and the basic techniques you follow in using these predicates to perform basic console I/O operations.

Turbo Prolog provides a complete set of predicates you can use to read data from the keyboard. The predicates read characters, strings, Turbo Prolog terms, and numeric data—including integers and reals. **Reading from the Keyboard**

Turbo Prolog provides one main predicate for reading a single character from the keyboard. **Character Input**

Syntax:
```
readchar(CharVariable)  (o)
       (char)
```

Parameter:
CharVariable   stores the input character.

Remarks:
Here, **readchar** is the standard predicate that you use to read a single character from the current input device. The input device is, by default, set to the keyboard. The argument you use for **readchar** must be a free variable of the **character domain** type. The **readchar** predicate waits until a

character is typed—if a character is not currently available when the predicate is called. With **readchar**, the character that the user types is echoed on the screen.

Example:
The following code segment shows how you can use **readchar** to read a character:

```
getch(Ch) :-
    write("Enter a character "),
    readchar(Ch).
```

For this code segment to work properly, **Ch** must be a free variable when your program calls **getch**.

Turbo Prolog also provides a predicate that allows you to send a character back to the keyboard buffer. This predicate is defined as:

```
unreadchar(CharVariable)   (i)
        (char)
```

Parameter:
CharVariable   the character to send back to the keyboard buffer.

Remarks:
The **unreadchar** predicate sends the specified character back to the keyboard buffer. This predicate sends back characters until the keyboard buffer is full. If this situation occurs, **unreadchar** will fail.

Example:
In the following call to **readchar**, we illustrate how the character **A** would be pushed back into the keyboard buffer:

```
unreadchar('A')
```

Because the keyboard buffer is represented as a FIFO (first-in, first-out) queue, Turbo Prolog treats the character that is read following the **readchar** as the most recent character pushed back into the keyboard buffer.

Using readln to Read a Character   Turbo Prolog also can use the general **readln** predicate to read a character. This predicate enables you to type a character, followed by a carriage return.

Syntax:
```
readln(StringVar)   (o)
     (string)
```

Parameter:
StringVar   stores the input data.

Remarks:
With **readln**, the user can press the Backspace key to erase the typed character. You'll find this programming method useful when you want to give the user some time to think or to verify his or her input. The **readln** predicate stores the data that it reads as a string. For this reason, you need to use the built-in predicate **str_char** to convert a string into a character representation.

Example:
The following code segment illustrates how you can use the **readln** predicate to read a character:

```
getch(Ch) :-
    write("Enter a character "),
    readln(Str),
    str_char(Str, Ch).
```

In this example, **readln** reads a character and stores it as a string. Turbo Prolog converts the string to a character by calling **str_char**.

Keep in mind that characters and strings are represented differently in Turbo Prolog; therefore, if you use **readln** to read a character, the character is converted into a string.

TIP

The **inkey** predicate enables you to read a single key (character) from the keyboard.

Using the inkey Predicate

Syntax:
```
inkey(CharVar)   (o)
     (char)
```

Parameter:
CharVar   stores the input character.

Remarks:

This predicate differs from **readchar**, because it doesn't wait for the user to press a key. If a key is not available in the standard input, **inkey** fails. The **inkey** predicate actually reads the PC's keyboard buffer. It's useful for tasks such as serial communications.

Example:

The following example illustrates how you can use **inkey** to read a character:

```
getch(Ch) :-
    write("Enter a character "),
    inkey(Ch).
```

TIP

Turbo Prolog also provides a predicate you can use to determine whether a key is currently available in the keyboard buffer. This predicate, called **keypressed**, succeeds if the user has pressed a key but the key has not yet been read by an input predicate. The following example illustrates how you could use **keypressed** to query and wait for the user to enter a key:

```
pause :-
    write("\nEnter a key to continue: "),
    check_key.

check_key :-
    keypressed.
check_key :-
    check_key.
```

Reading Extended Key Codes

You can use the standard **readchar** predicate to read any of the PC's extended keys, such as the cursor positioning keys or the function keys. When the user presses an extended key, **readchar** returns the value 0 to indicate that the key pressed is an extended key. You can call the predicate a second time to get the scan code of the key.

Example:

This example illustrates how you can use **readchar** to read one of the function keys:

```
predicates
  get_f_key(integer)
```

```
clauses
    get_f_key(Key) :-
        readchar(Ch);
        Ch = 0,            /* indicates an extended key */
        readchar(C2),
        char_int(C2, Val),
        Val >= 59,
        Val <= 68,
        Key = Val - 58.
```

The extended codes for the function keys F1 to F10 range from 59 to 68. The **get_f_key** checks whether the extended code that is input is within this range. The **get_f_key** then adjusts the input code to reflect the number of the function key pressed. For example, if you press the F2 function key, the variable **Key** is bound to the value 2.

The **readln** predicate is provided for reading a string of characters from the keyboard. The Backspace key can be used during string entry to correct unwanted characters.   **String Input**

Example:
The following example illustrates how you can use the **readln** predicate to read a string:

```
getstr :-
    write("\nEnter a string "),
    readln(Str).
```

To read multiple strings, call the **readln** function multiple times.

Turbo Prolog supports two methods you can use to read numeric data— **Numeric Input**
including integers and reals. The first method uses the predicates **readint** or **readreal,** whereas the second method uses the general **readln** predicate.

Syntax:
```
readint(IntVar)   (o)
       (integer)

readreal(RealVar)   (o)
        (real)
```

Parameters:

IntVar   stores an integer value.

RealVar   stores a real value.

Remarks:

If you use the **readln** predicate, you must convert the data read by your program into either a **real** or **integer** domain. You use the **str_int** predicate or the **str_real** predicate to perform these conversions. This technique is discussed in more detail next.

    The argument supplied to the program must be the name of a free variable. Both predicates keep reading digits until a carriage return is encountered.

Example:

Our example below shows how you can use **readint** and **readreal** to read numeric data:

```
getnum :-
    write("\nEnter a number from 1 to 10 --> "),
    readint(N),
    N >= 1,
    N <= 10,
    write("\nEnter a real number "),
    readreal(R).
```

Using readln to Read Numeric Input

You can also use the general-purpose **readln** in your Turbo Prolog programs to read integers and reals. However, Turbo Prolog stores any data read with **readln** as a string; therefore, you must convert strings composed of integers or reals to their appropriate numeric domain type. For this conversion, Turbo Prolog provides two predicates, which are defined next.

Syntax:

```
str_int(StringVar, IntVar)   (i,o), (o,i), (i,i)
      (string, integer)

str_real(StringVar, RealVar)   (i,o), (o,i), (i,i)
      (string, real)
```

Parameters:

StringVar   string of decimal or real digits.

IntVal   an integer value.
RealVar   a real value.

Remarks:

The **str_int** predicate converts a string of integer digits into an integer value, whereas **str_real** converts a string representing a real number into a real value.

Examples:

The following examples show how you can use the **readln** predicate to read numeric input. The first example reads a decimal integer:

```
getnum :-
    write("\nEnter a number from 1 to 10 --> "),
    readln(Intstr),
    str_int(Intstr, N),
    N >= 1,
    N <= 10.


getnum :-
    write("\nSorry the number is out of range").
```

Here, if the number entered by the user is not between 1 and 10, the first **getnum** clause fails and the second one is called to display the error message.

This example prompts you to enter a real number and an integer:

```
total :-
    write("\nEnter unit price: "),
    readln(Unitprice),
    str_real(Unitprice, Up),
    write("Enter quantity: "),
    readln(Quantity),
    str_int(Quantity, Q),
    write("\nTotal due = ",Up * Q).
```

In addition to reading data from the keyboard, Turbo Prolog can read characters, strings, and their associated attributes directly from the screen.

Reading from the Screen

Reading Characters

The two Turbo Prolog predicates provided for reading characters and their attributes are **scr_attr** and **scr_char**, respectively. Both of these predicates read data from a specified row and column coordinate.

Syntax:
```
scr_char(Row, Col, CharVariable)   (i,i,i), (i,i,o)
        (integer, integer, char)
```

```
scr_attr(Row, Col, AttrVariable)   (i,i,i), (i,i,o)
        (integer, integer, integer)
```

Parameters:

Row, Col	the row and column position of the character.
CharVariable	the character read or written.
AttrVariable	the attribute code for the character.

You can specify the parameters **CharVariable** and **AttrVariable** as either input or output parameters.

Example:
The following example illustrates how Turbo Prolog reads a character and its attribute from the screen:

```
readscr(X, Y, Ch, Attr) :-
  scr_attr(X, Y, Attr),
  scr_char(X, Y, Ch).
```

If we call **readscr** with

```
readscr(5,10, C, A).
```

the character and its attribute at row 5 column 10 would be read and stored in the variables **C** and **A**.

Reading Strings

Turbo Prolog provides the following three predicates for use in reading a string and its attribute.

Syntax:
```
field_str(Row, Col, Length, StringVar)  (i,i,i,i), (i,i,i,o)
        (integer, integer, integer, string)
```

```
field_attr(Row, Col, Length, AttrVar)  (i,i,i,i), (i,i,i,o)
        (integer, integer, integer, integer)
```

```
window_str(StringVar)  (i), (o)
        (string)
```

Parameters:

Row, Col   the row and column position of the string.
Length   the length of the string (number of characters).
StringVar   stores the string.
AttrVar   the attribute of the string.

Remarks:

Both **field_str** and **field_attr** enable you to specify the location and the length of the string or attribute to be read. You specify the position of the string in relation to the currently active window. The predicate **window_str** reads the entire contents of the active window and binds the input string to the specified string variable.

Examples:

This first example illustrates how you can use **field_str** and **field_attr** to read a string and its attribute:

```
getstr(Str, Attr) :-
  field_str(0,0,80,Str),
  field_attr(0,0,80,Attr).
```

In this case, Turbo Prolog reads the string from the first row in the currently active window. Because the string length is set to 80 characters, we can ensure that the full string will be read.

The next example shows how you can use **window_str** to read the contents of the currently active window:

```
get_w_str(Str) :-
    makewindow(1,7,0,"",0,0,25,80),
    write("This string\nis displayed\non three lines"),
    window_str(Str).
```

In this case, the three-line string written to the window is read and stored in the variable **Str**. The variable will contain the same number of lines as the string displayed in the window.

Writing to the Screen

Turbo Prolog provides a number of predicates for writing data to the screen—including strings and integers. As is true for input routines, we can conveniently divide output routines into two categories: *specialized* output routines and *general* routines that can be used to display formatted data. We include both categories in the following discussions.

Turbo Prolog's screen I/O is based on a dynamic windowing system. The default window is the entire screen, which consists of 25 rows and 80 columns. When an output predicate is called, data is always displayed in the active window.

Character Output

Turbo Prolog displays characters and attributes using the **scr_attr** and the **scr_char** predicates. When these routines are called, a character is displayed or an attribute is set at a specified position in the active window.

Examples:
The following example illustrates how you can display a character and set its attribute at a specified screen location:

```
disp_char(X,Y,Ch,Attr)  :-
   scr_chr(X,Y,Ch),
   scr_attr(X,Y,Attr).
```

If we call **disp_char** with these values

```
disp_char(10,10, ' ', 112).
```

Turbo Prolog displays a reverse-video blank at row 10, column 10, in the active window.

Using write and writef to Display a Character

Here are the general formats for using **write** and **writef** to display a character:

Syntax:
```
write(Arg1, Arg2, Arg3, ..., ArgN)      (i,i,i,...,i)
writef(FormatStr, Arg1, Arg2, Arg3, ..., ArgN)     (i,i,i,...,i)
```

Parameters:
Arg1 ... ArgN   the list of data elements to display.
FormatStr   specifies how the list of arguments is displayed.

Remarks:

The Turbo Prolog general-purpose output functions **write** and **writef** are also useful for displaying a single character. The **write** predicate is a general-purpose output tool that writes values of any domain type. You can also use the **write** predicate to display multiple data items, because it supports a variable number of arguments.

The **writef** predicate is similar to the **write** predicate; however, with **writef** you can specify format information for the data to be written. We cover this predicate in more detail later in the section.

Example:

The following code segment demonstrates the use of the **write** predicate for displaying a character:

```
readc :-
  write("\nEnter a character "),
  readchar(Ch),
  write("\nYour character is ", Ch).
```

In this case, note that we used the **write** predicate to display both a string and a character. Each data item to be displayed must be separated from others by a comma.

String Output

In Turbo Prolog, you use the **write** predicate to display unformatted strings. Because this predicate can take a variable number of arguments, you can display multiple strings with a single call.

In addition to the **write** predicate, Turbo Prolog provides a unique predicate you can use to display a string in a window.

Syntax:

```
window_str(String)   (i), (o)
        (string)
```

The **window_str** predicate controls string output in the current window. If the string displayed is longer than the width of the current window, Turbo Prolog truncates the string.

Examples:

Our first example illustrates the use of the **write** predicate for displaying a string:

```
write("\nEnter a string").
```

Note that we've used the symbols **\n** to display a new line (carriage return-linefeed).

This next example shows how multiple strings can be written with the **write** predicate:

```
write("\nYour first name is ", First, " and your last name is ",
      Last).
```

Numeric Output

You must use the **write** predicate to display unformatted numeric data. This predicate enables you to read both integer and real numbers.

Examples:
The following example shows how you can use **write** to display an integer on the screen:

```
get_num(N) :-
    write("\nEnter a number from 1 to 10 --> ");
    readint(N),
    N <= 10,
    N >= 1,
    write("\nYour number is ", N).
```

The next example prompts you to enter a real value and an integer. Turbo Prolog then calculates a new value and displays the result. Here's the example:

```
total :-
    write("\nEnter unit price : "),
    readreal(Unitprice),
    write("Enter quantity : "),
    readint(Quantity),
    write("\nTotal due = ",Unitprice * Quantity).
```

Formatted Input

Turbo Prolog does not provide any predicates for reading formatted input—other than the **field_attr** and **field_str** predicates. You can, however, use one of the primitive input predicates, such as **readchar** or **scr_char**, to create your own custom formatted input routine.

Turbo Prolog provides the **writef** predicate for use in writing formatted data. In addition, you can format strings using the **field_str** predicate. Both of these predicates are presented in the following two sections. Version 2.0 of Turbo Prolog also provides a predicate called **format** that enables you to format a set of arguments to a string.

The **writef** predicate can justify data in a field, specify a field width, or specify the precision and format for real numbers.

Syntax:
```
writef(<format-string>, <list of parameters>)
```

Parameters:
The **format-string** consists of a set of symbols that define how the output should be displayed. In addition, the **format-string** may also contain standard characters, which are displayed as they are represented. The parameters must be constants or variables belonging to any of the standard domain types.
　　The syntax for indicating a format specification is simply

```
%<code>
```

You include the % symbol to indicate that the symbols that follow are to be used as format specifiers. Table 1.13 lists the formatting characters that Turbo Prolog supports.

Turbo Prolog provides two primary predicates, **field_str** and **field_attr**, that you can use to write unformatted strings and set string attributes, respectively.

Syntax:
```
field_str(Row, Col, Len, Str)
```

Parameters:
The **field_str** predicate displays a string of length **Len** at the specified row and column location. When you display a string with this predicate, you can choose from two techniques available for formatting the string:

1. If the string has more characters than its length specification, the string is truncated.

Table 1.13. Turbo Prolog formatting characters

Format Setting	Meaning
—	Indicates that data are to be left justified
<n>	An integer value that indicates the field width of the output data
.<n>	Specifies the precision of the fractional part of a real number
.<n>	Specifies the maximum number of characters to be displayed in a string
.<n>f	Indicates that a real number is displayed in standard notation (34.67)
.<n>e	Indicates that a real number is displayed in exponential notation (3.467e1)
.<n>g	Indicates that a real number is displayed in the shortest format

2. If the string has fewer characters than its length specification, the string is padded with blank characters.

Cursor Control

Turbo Prolog provides two predicates for controlling the cursor—**cursor** and **cursorform**. These predicates allow you to set the position of the cursor, obtain the position of the cursor, and define the shape (size) of the cursor. You use the predicate **cursor** to both set and read the position of the cursor.

Specifying the Cursor Location

You set the cursor position by calling the **cursor** predicate.

Syntax:
```
cursor(Row, Column)
```

Parameters:

Row   specifies the screen row number (0 to window height) where the cursor is to be placed.

Column specifies the column number (0 to 79) for the cursor position. The full screen consists of 25 rows and 80 columns.

Remarks:

When **cursor** is called, Turbo Prolog positions the cursor in the currently active window. The specified position of the cursor is referenced relative to the upper left corner of the active window. To position the cursor, you must call the **cursor** predicate with integer constants, constant expressions, or integer variables that are currently bound to a value.

In controlling the cursor, Turbo Prolog uses a coordinate system that differs significantly from the system used by the other Turbo languages. In Turbo Prolog, the upper left corner of the screen or active window is referenced as (0,0), whereas in the other languages, this position is referenced as (1,1). If you are converting a program from one of the other Turbo languages to Turbo Prolog, be sure to account for this difference in coordinate systems.

Example:

The following code example illustrates how to center a message on the screen after first clearing the screen:

```
center_str(Str) :-
    clearwindow,
    str_len(Str, Len),
    cursor(1, 40 - Len div 2),
    write(Str).
```

You also use the **cursor** predicate to obtain the position of the cursor. To read the cursor position, you must call **cursor** with arguments that are free variables.

Getting the Cursor Location

Example:

The following predicate **move_cur** moves the cursor to the lower right corner of the screen (in this case, down one row and to the right by one column position):

```
predicates
    move_cur
    test_cur(integer, integer, integer)

clauses
    move_cur :-
```

```
        cursor(Row, Col), /* get position of cursor */
        test_cur(Row, 24, Nrow),
        test_cur(Col, 79, Ncol),
        cursor(Nrow, Ncol).

    test_cur(Old, Val, New) :-
        Old < Val,
        New = Old + 1.
    test_cur(Old, _, Old).
```

Here, we used the predicate **test_cur** to see if the cursor is not currently at the last row and column on the screen.

Defining the Shape of the Cursor

You use the predicate **cursorform** to define the shape of the cursor. In text mode, the cursor is composed of eight scan lines. The **cursorform** predicate enables you to select the number and position of the scan lines to be used in drawing the cursor.

Syntax:
```
cursorform(StartLine, EndLine)
```

Parameters:

StartLine, EndLine   define the starting and ending positions for the cursor. These arguments must be within the range of 1–8.

Examples:
In the following examples, we define three cursor sizes:

```
cursorform(1,8)   /* define full size cursor */
cursorform(1,2)   /* define cursor with two scan lines */
cursorform(7,8)   /* define two line cursor at top */
```

Text Windows

Turbo Prolog provides support for simple text-based windows. Text windows can be created and positioned anywhere on the screen, provided that the screen is currently set to one of the standard text modes. Once a window is defined, all of the output and other I/O routines (such as the cursor positioning functions) perform their actions relative to the base position (upper left corner) of the window. The first row and column in a text window is also addressed as position (1,1).

The window feature in Turbo Prolog is much more powerful than the text based windows supported by the other Turbo languages. In Turbo Prolog windows can be created with different attributes, such as borders and titles. In addition, multiple windows can be displayed at the same time. The complete set of window-related predicates is listed in Table 1.14.

Table 1.14. Turbo Prolog window-related predicates

Predicate	Description
clearwindow	Set a window to its background attribute
colorsetup	Change the color attributes of the active window
existwindow	Determine if the specified window exists
framewindow	Update the frame for the current window
gotowindow	Make the specified window active
makewindow	Create a new window and make it active
removewindow	Remove a specified window
resizewindow	Change the size of a window
scroll	Scroll the text in a window a specified number of times
shiftwindow	Get the active window or move to the specified window
window_attr	Set the attribute of the active window
window_str	Read or write a string to the active window
windowcolors	Set the colors for the active window

Creating a Window

The predicate **makewindow** is used to create a new window. When a window is created with this predicate, the window automatically becomes the active window and all screen I/O predicates direct their actions in this active window. Although Turbo Prolog can display multiple windows, only one window can be active at a time.

Syntax:

Two forms of the **makewindow** predicate are provided. The first uses the following format:

```
makewindow(WNo, Attr, FrAttr, Title,
         Row, Col, Height, Width)
```

and the second **makewindow** predicate uses this format:

```
makewindow(WNo, Attr, FrAttr, Title,
          Row, Col, Height, Width,
          ClearW, TitlePos, BorderCodes)
```

As shown, the second predicate gives you more control over how the window is displayed. In either case, each of these predicates can be called with all bound or free variables. If free variables are supplied, either predicate returns the settings of the current window.

Parameters:
The parameters for each of these predicates are defined in Table 1.15.

Example:
The following sample predicates illustrate how a window is created and text is displayed in the window:

```
clauses
   disp_window1 :-
     makewindow(1,1,7,"Test window1", 2,2,20,60),
     window_str("Display string in window 1").

   disp_window2 :-
     makewindow(1,0,7,"Test window2", 10,22,10,40,
                1, 255, "\218\191\192\217\\179\196"),
     window_str("Display string in window 2").
```

The first clause, **disp_window1**, displays a window with a blue background. The upper right corner of the window is positioned at row 2, column 2, and the window is 20 columns high by 60 columns wide.

The second clause, **disp_window2**, creates a window using the more general version of the **makewindow** predicate. In this case the window is created with a single line border. Note that the numeric ASCII values for the border codes are used.

Controlling Video Turbo Prolog provides a set of predicates that control how data is displayed. With these features you can perform tasks such as writing directly to video memory. These predicates are presented next.

Table 1.15. Arguments for makewindow predicates

Argument	Description
WNo	The window number. Every window is represented by a unique integer value. This number is used to select the window.
Attr	The background screen attribute (color) for the window
FrAttr	The frame (border) attribute. If this argument is 0, the window is created without a border; otherwise, the window border is displayed in the specified color.
Title	The title for the window. If this argument is specified as the empty string "", the window is created without a title.
Row	This argument specifies the row origin (top row) for the window
Col	This argument specifies the column origin (left column) for the window
Height	This argument defines the height of the window in screen rows
Width	This argument defines the width of the window in screen columns
ClearW	This argument is used as a flag to determine if the window region should be cleared when the window is displayed. Two values are supported: 0 window is not cleared. 1 window is cleared.
TitlePos	This argument defines how the title should be positioned. If it is set to the value 255, the title is centered in the window; otherwise, the value specified determines the starting column position for the title.
BorderCodes	This argument is a string that defines how the window border should be displayed. The format of this string is: "<ul><ur><ll><lr><hl><vl>" where the components represent: <ul> the upper left corner. <ur> the upper right corner. <ll> the lower left corner. <lr> the lower right corner. <hl> the horizontal line. <vl> the vertical line.

**Direct Video
Output**

Turbo Prolog does not provide a mechanism for writing directly to video memory. You can, however, use the general purpose **port_byte** predicate to access video memory.

Syntax:
```
port_byte(Portaddress, Data)
```

Test for Snow

In addition, a predicate is provided for testing and setting the *snow* checking for video output. With this **snowcheck** predicate, you can make sure data is displayed on the screen without undesirable snow effects. You declare the **snowcheck** predicate with this format:

```
snowcheck(Status)
```

The argument **Status** can be an input or output parameter of domain type **string**. If the argument is not bound to a value, the predicate returns the current status of the snow checking feature. To turn the snow checking on or off, use these two values:

"on"   turn snow checking on
"off"   turn snow checking off

Example:
In the following clause, you test the snow checking status and set it to **"on"** if it is currently turned off:

```
set_snow_check :--
    snowcheck(Status),
    Status = "off",
    snowcheck("on").
set_snow_check.
```

Note that the example uses two clause definitions. We've done so to make sure that **set_snow_check** succeeds regardless of the current state of the snow checking feature. The first clause gets the current state and sets the snow checking feature to "on" if it is currently off.

**Controlling
Display Attributes**

You control display attributes by setting the attribute of the current display window with **window_attr**, or by using **scr_attr** or **field_attr** to set the display attribute for a character or string. You can use either of these predicates to set both the foreground and background colors of text or the display intensity.

Once you have set a window attribute, all data written to the window are displayed in the set attribute.

Setting Window Attributes

Syntax:
```
window_attr(AttributeCode)
```

Parameter:
AttributeCode takes an integer argument, which corresponds with the desired video attribute. With this predicate, you can set display attributes for both monochrome and color displays. The codes for setting monochrome attributes are listed in Table 1.16.

Table 1.16. Attribute codes for monochrome settings

Attribute Code	Description
0	Black characters on a black background
7	White characters on a black background
12	Black characters on a white background

In addition, if the value 8 is added to any of the codes shown in the table, the white colors displayed will be in high intensity. If the value 128 is added to any of the codes, the data displayed will blink.

Tables 1.17 and 1.18 show the codes that define the foreground and background colors.

Color attributes are actually determined by selecting one background color and one foreground color and adding their attribute codes together. For example, to produce the color attribute red text on a brown background the value would be:

```
4      +    96    = 100
(red)       (brown)
```

A blinking attribute can also be included with color attributes by adding the value 128.

Table 1.17. Codes for defining foreground colors

Attribute Code	Color
0	Black
1	Blue
2	Green
3	Cyan
4	Red
5	Magenta
6	Brown
7	White
8	Gray
9	Light blue
10	Light green
11	Light cyan
12	Light red
13	Light magenta
14	Yellow
15	High intensity white

Table 1.18. Codes for defining background colors

Attribute Code	Color
0	Black
16	Blue
32	Green
48	Cyan
64	Red
80	Magenta
96	Brown
112	White

Example:
The following example illustrates how **window_attr** sets the attribute for a window:

```
clauses
    window_disp :-
        makewindow(1,7,7,"", 0,0,25,80),
        window_attr(33),    /* green with blue background */
        write("Text is in green, background is blue").
```

Character and string attributes are set using the same codes presented for setting window attributes. To set a character or string attribute, the following two predicates are used:

Setting Character and String Attributes

```
scr_attr(Row, Col, Attr)
field_attr(Row, Col, Len, Attr)
```

The predicate **scr_attr** sets the attribute of a character at a specified screen position. The predicate **field_attr**, on the other hand, sets the attribute of a character or string. In this case, the **Len** argument specifies the number of characters to set in the specified attribute.

Example:
The following call to **scr_attr** changes the character displayed at row 5, column 1 to inverse video:

```
scr_attr(5, 1, 12).
```

In the next code segment, the blinking attribute makes the word *see* blink in red in the displayed string:

```
clauses
    blink :-
        write("Can you see the blinking word?"),
        field_attr(1,9,132).
```

File I/O Essentials

Introduction

Each of the Turbo languages provides a rich set of built-in routines and tools for working with files. File I/O tasks are important, because most programs must be able to store and retrieve data. In this section, we present the major file I/O components of each of the Turbo languages. In addition, the techniques for working with different types of files are discussed.

Turbo BASIC

Turbo BASIC supports I/O capabilities for three types of files:

- Sequential
- Random access
- Binary

The Organization of Sequential Files

Sequential files store ASCII text in variable-length records. Each record ends with a pair of carriage-return/linefeed characters. Reading records from sequential files involves scrolling through records in sequence (hence, their name). You cannot go directly to a particular sequential record; you can only read or write the next record in sequence. Turbo BASIC supports two kinds of sequential files:

- Field delimited
- Nondelimited

The difference between the two types lies in the way in which they write each field or data object to a sequential file. Nondelimited files output fields in a manner similar to a screen or printer output that employs **PRINT** and **LPRINT**. With field-delimited sequential files, Turbo BASIC places commas between data objects, or fields, and encloses strings within double quotation marks. Turbo BASIC also enables you to append records to existing data files.

The Organization of Random-Access Files

With Turbo BASIC *random-access* files, you manipulate equal-sized, (fixed-length) records. Consequently, the file I/O system is able to access any record directly, without having to read records in the same sequence in which they are stored. As an analogy, you might consider random-access capabilities to be much like opening a book to the particular page you want to read, without having to flip through preceding pages.

Turbo BASIC supports *binary* file I/O as a way for you to deal with non-ASCII data files. Binary file I/O also enables you to search for a specific byte location in a file. Your programs can go directly to this byte position to start and/or resume input. You use string variables in a binary file to exchange data between your program and your binary data file.

The Organization of Binary Files

All three file types have some common file management steps, including procedures for opening and closing files. File opening procedures access a file, whereas file closing procedures ensure that any data still pending in memory are properly written to a file before the program terminates. Also, by closing a file, you reclaim the buffer area in memory that was allocated when you opened the file.

File Management in Turbo BASIC

   Another feature is common to all Turbo BASIC file types: DOS doesn't require you to specify a maximum file size when you create the file. Consequently, you can expand a file until you reach either your disk storage limitation or the limit allowed with the DOS version you are using.

Turbo BASIC creates a file when you open it for output. If the file does not exist, Turbo BASIC creates a new one automatically. To delete a file, use the **KILL** statement.

Creating and Deleting Files

Syntax:
```
KILL <filename>
```

Parameter:
filename   this argument can be either a string-typed constant, variable, or expression. You can also include a drive name, path name, and even wildcards in the argument.

Example:
Here's an example that enables you to remove ***.BAK** files from any directory you specify:

```
INPUT "Enter directory name ";Path$
' test if you need a \ at the end of the path name
IF RIGHT$(Path$,1) <> "\" THEN Path$ = Path$ + "\"
KILL Path$ + "*.BAK"
```

The first file I/O task your programs will perform involves opening files with the **OPEN** statement. When you open a file, you allocate an I/O buffer in RAM for the file. The contents of the file then become accessible to your

Opening Files

program for processing. Also, you use the **OPEN** statement to indicate the file type, optional record sizes, and the I/O mode that you want.

Turbo BASIC supports these two general formats for the **OPEN** statement.

Syntax:
```
OPEN <filename> [FOR <mode>] AS [#]<file_number> [LEN = <rec_size>]
or
OPEN "<mode character>",[#]<file_number>,<filename>
    [,<record_size>]
```

Parameters:

filename   the *filename* must be unique. You can include an optional file path with the name, but no wildcards. Table 2.1 shows the I/O *mode* and *mode character* options available to you, along with the fileype that each mode supports.

file_number   a buffer or I/O channel number that you can use in file I/O operations.

record_size   specifies the record length of a random access file. The default value is 128 bytes, but you can specify any value between 1 and 32767 bytes.

Table 2.1. The mode and mode character options available in opening a file

Mode	Mode Character	Task	File Type
APPEND	A	Append data	Sequential
BINARY	B	Data I/O	Binary
INPUT	I	Read data	Sequential
OUTPUT	O	Write data	Sequential
RANDOM	R	Data I/O	Random access

Closing Files

You use the **CLOSE** statement to close files, which is the final file I/O task your program will perform.

Syntax:
```
CLOSE [#<file1> [,#<file2>[,...]]]
```

If you use **CLOSE** with no specifiers, Turbo BASIC closes all files that are currently open. Hence, this is a quick and efficient way to ensure that all of your files are closed. However, you'll certainly want to close files selectively for some programming applications. To perform selective file closing, you list the buffer numbers associated with the particular files you wish to close.

By closing a file, you ensure that any related data still pending in memory are properly written to the file. In addition, closing a file reclaims the buffer area in memory allocated when you opened the file.

Initializing Files

Turbo BASIC doesn't support any statements explicitly intended for performing file initialization.

Writing to Files

Because Turbo BASIC supports three types of files, we'll discuss outputs for each method separately.

Writing to Sequential Files

When you open a *sequential file*, Turbo BASIC requires you to specify the desired I/O mode: **INPUT**, **OUTPUT**, or **APPEND**. Thus, you can select either the **OUTPUT** or the **APPEND** mode for data output. The **OUTPUT** mode rewrites and truncates the contents of any existing data file. By contrast, the **APPEND** mode extends the opened file by placing any new data after the last current record. Consequently, you select the output mode that is meaningful to your application.

When you write data to a sequential file, you also can choose whether you want to send data in a field-delimited fashion. Usually, you output field-delimited records for applications that write data in special formats—often to supply data to other commercial products. By contrast, Turbo BASIC outputs nondelimited records to a file in a format that parallels the one used to output to a line printer or screen.

You use the **PRINT #** and **PRINT # USING** statements to output records to nondelimited sequential files. Here are the general formats for these statements.

Syntax:
```
PRINT #<file number>, [USING <format>;]<expression list>[;]
```

The **PRINT #** and **PRINT # USING** work just like **PRINT** and **PRINT USING**, which send output to a screen, and like **LPRINT** and **LPRINT USING**, which send data to a line printer.

Examples:
In this example, we demonstrate how you can store a small numeric

database in a sequential file. Sequential files are suitable for relatively small-scale applications—where you can read the entire database into memory. Here's the example:

```
DEFINT A-Z
DEFDBL X
DIM X(10,100) ' matrix of data
DATA "Sample Data"
DATA 2,3
DATA 1,2,3,4,5,6,7,8,9
RESTORE
READ Title$,NVar, NData
FOR I = 1 TO NData
   FOR J = 1 TO NVar
      READ X(I,J)
   NEXT J
NEXT I
' create and open sequential file
OPEN "O",1,"Sample.dat"
PRINT #1,"DATA1"  ' emit file ID name
PRINT #1,Title$  ' write title
PRINT #1,Date$    ' write date and time
PRINT #1,Time$
PRINT #1,NVar     ' write number of variables
PRINT #1,NData     ' write number of data
' nested loops to write data matrix
FOR I = 1 TO NData
   FOR J = 1 TO NVar
      PRINT #1, X(I,J)
   NEXT J
NEXT I
CLOSE #1
END
```

Turbo BASIC also supports a number of file-like devices. Table 2.2 lists and provides the filenames for devices that you can open just like output files.

Outputting to the **SCRN:** device is identical to the approach used with the **PRINT** and **PRINT USING** statements. Similarly, outputting to a line printer functions like **LPRINT** and **LPRINT USING**.

Table 2.2. Turbo BASIC device/filenames

Output Device	Filename
Screen	SCRN:
Line printers 1, 2, and 3	LPT1:, LPT2:, and LPT3:
Communication ports 1 and 2	COM1: and COM2:

Our program below reads a data file and looks for certain user-specified words. A text line that matches any of the sought words is simultaneously displayed on the screen, printed, and stored in an output text file. The program places a caret symbol below each matching line to point to the corresponding location of the user-supplied search words.

```
OPTION BASE 1
DEFINT A-Z
CLS
INPUT "Enter filename ";F$ : PRINT
OPEN "I",4,F$ ' open input data file
DO
    INPUT "Enter number of search words ";N : PRINT
LOOP UNTIL N > 0
DIM DYNAMIC WORD$(N) ' custom dimension array of words
FOR I = 1 TO N
  PRINT "Enter word #";I;
   INPUT " ? ",WORD$(I) : PRINT
NEXT I
DIM DEV$(3)
DEV$(1) = "SCRN:"
DEV$(2) = "LPT1:"
INPUT "Enter output filename ";DEV$(3) : PRINT
' Open all three output devices
FOR I = 1 TO 3
  OPEN "O",I,DEV$(I)
NEXT I
Count = 0
DO WHILE NOT EOF(4)
   LINE INPUT #4,L$
   INCR Count
```

```
    FOR I = 1 TO N
        Index = INSTR(L$,WORD$(I))
        IF (Index > 0) THEN
            FOR J = 1 TO 3
                PRINT #J, USING "###: &";Count,L$
                PRINT #J, SPC(Index+4);"^"
            NEXT J
        END IF
    NEXT I
LOOP
PRINT #2, CHR$(140) 'formfeed
' close all file buffers
CLOSE #1, #2, #3, #4 ' or simply CLOSE
END
```

You use the **WRITE #** statement to write field-delimited records to
sequential files. This statement enables you to send output delimited by
commas and strings enclosed in double quotation marks.

In this example, we've modified the program in the previous example
so that we can use the **WRITE #** statement. By doing so, we can send
multiple variables with a single **WRITE #** statement. We can then read
these variables back to the file easily, without having to write special
parsing routines (as would be the case if we use **PRINT #**). Here's the
example:

```
DEFINT A-Z
DEFDBL X
DIM X(10,100) ' matrix of data
DATA "Sample Data"
DATA 2,3
DATA 1,2,3,4,5,6,7,8,9

RESTORE
READ Title$,NVar, NData
FOR I = 1 TO NData
    FOR J = 1 TO NVar
        READ X(I,J)
    NEXT J
NEXT I
' create and open sequential file
```

```
OPEN "O",1,"Sample.dat"
' write four strings on one line
WRITE #1,"DATA1",Title$,Date$,Time$
' write two numeric variables on the same line
WRITE #1,NVar,NData
' nested loops to write data matrix
FOR I = 1 TO NData
   FOR J = 1 TO NVar
      WRITE #1, X(I,J)
   NEXT J
NEXT I
CLOSE #1
END
```

Writing to Random-Access Files

When you send output to *random-access files*, you'll have to prepare a bit more than you do to write to sequential files. The extra preparation will pay off, though, because your programs will be able to read any existing record directly from a random-access file. Follow these five general steps in writing to a random-access file:

1. Open the file using **OPEN**.
2. Establish a map using **FIELD** for the fields that make up each random-access record.
3. Assign data to the declared fields using **LSET** or **RSET**.
4. Write the record to the file using **PUT**.
5. Close the file using **CLOSE**.

Open the File

To open the file, you specify the random-access mode and the length of each record with the **OPEN** statement. Here are the two general formats you can use for **OPEN**.

Syntax:
```
OPEN "R",<file number>,<filename>,LEN = <record_length>
```
or
```
OPEN <filename> FOR RANDOM AS <file number> LEN = <rec_len>
```

Map Fields

You use **FIELD** to establish a map for the fields that make up each random-access record. The **FIELD** declaration specifies both the size and name of related field variables. Use this general format for **FIELD**.

Syntax:
```
FIELD <file number>, <width1> AS <str1>[,<width2> AS <str2>...]
```

**Assign Data
Fields**

Use either **LSET** (left-justified string assignment) or **RSET** (right-justified string assignment) to assign data fields to a record. Because all of the fields are string-typed, you must convert all numeric data into coded and packed fixed-size strings.

Syntax:
```
LSET <field-var> |
RSET <field-var> =  <string-var> |
  MKI$(<integer-var>)          |
  MKL$(<long integer-var>)  |
  MKS$(<single real-var>)    |
  MKD$(<double real-var>)    |
  MKMS$(<single real-var>)   |
  MKMD$(<double real-var>)   |
```

Table 2.3 shows the predefined functions you can use to convert numeric variables into packed strings.

Table 2.3. Functions for converting numeric variables into packed strings

Functions	Converts from	Format Comment
MKI$	Integer	
MKL$	Long integer	
MKS$	Single prec-real	
MKD$	Double prec-real	
MKMS$	Single prec-real	Special Microsoft format
MKMD$	Double prec-real	Special Microsoft format

**Write the Record
to the File**

After the field assignments of a record have been completed, you can write the record using the **PUT** statement.

Syntax:
```
PUT #<file_number>[,<record_number>]
```

If you omit the *record_number,* the **PUT** statement simply writes to the next record in sequence. So, you use the *record_number* to specify a record

position that you want to write to directly. The operating system expands
the file size if you specify a record number that exceeds the current number
of records in the file.

At the end of random access file I/O, close the file using the **CLOSE**   **Close the File**
statement. It is used in the same manner described earlier for sequential
files.

Example:

To illustrate the use of random-access files, we've written a program that
prompts for the average temperatures for days of an entire week, as well
as for a week number. The numeric data are packed and stored in one
random access record. This is the program:

```
OPTION BASE 1
DEFDBL A-Z
DEFINT I-O
DIM Week.Data(7)
CLS
INPUT "Enter week number ";Week.Num% : PRINT
FOR I = 1 TO 7
   PRINT "Enter temperature for day ";I;
   INPUT " ? ",Week.Data(I) : PRINT
NEXT I


' open random access file
OPEN "R",1,"TempStat.DAT",56
' map fields of the record
FIELD #1,  8 AS D1$,  8 AS D2$,  8 AS D3$,  8 AS D4$,_
        8 AS D5$,  8 AS D6$,  8 AS D7$
LSET D1$ = MKD$(Week.Data(1))
LSET D2$ = MKD$(Week.Data(2))
LSET D3$ = MKD$(Week.Data(3))
LSET D4$ = MKD$(Week.Data(4))
LSET D5$ = MKD$(Week.Data(5))
LSET D6$ = MKD$(Week.Data(6))
LSET D7$ = MKD$(Week.Data(7))
PUT #1,Week.Num% ' write the record
CLOSE #1
END
```

Writing to Binary Files

Binary file I/O shares some of the features of random-access file I/O. One such feature is the ability to read from and write to the same file after you've opened the file. Four general I/O steps are involved (although the second step is optional).

1. Open the file using **OPEN**.
2. Position the file pointer using **SEEK**.
3. Write to the file using **PUT$**.
4. Close the file using **CLOSE**.

Open the File

You use the **OPEN** statement to open a binary file. You may use either of these two general formats.

Syntax:
```
OPEN "B",<file number>,<filename>
```
or
```
OPEN <filename> FOR BINARY AS <file number>
```

Position the File Pointer

Turbo BASIC provides the option to position the file pointer using the **SEEK** statement.

Syntax:
```
SEEK <file number>,<byte location in file>
```

Write to the File

You use **PUT$** to write data to a binary file.

Syntax:
```
PUT$ <file number>,<binary data stored in a string>
```

Remarks:
Whenever you use the **PUT$** function, Turbo BASIC automatically advances the byte location in the file so that you can successfully use subsequent **PUT$** statements.

Close the File

When binary file I/O has terminated, close the file using the **CLOSE** statement. Use **CLOSE** in the same manner that we've described earlier for sequential files.

Example:
Our next program simply copies the contents of one binary file to a new

one. The copy process occurs byte-by-byte. This is the program:

```
CLS
INPUT "Enter source file ";S$ : PRINT
INPUT "Enter destination file ";D$ : PRINT
OPEN "B",1,S$
OPEN "B",2,D$
SEEK 2,1
WHILE NOT EOF(1)
   GET$ 1,1,C$
   PUT$ 2,C$
WEND
BEEP : PRINT "DONE"
CLOSE
END
```

Turbo BASIC also supports **BSAVE** for writing (or actually copying) bytes from memory to a DOS file.

Using BSAVE to Write Bytes to a File

Syntax:
```
BSAVE <filename>,<offset address>,<number of bytes copied>
```

As this format suggests, you need to preset the segment address using the **DEF SEG** statement. One of the more popular uses for **BSAVE** involves saving screen outputs to files.

Example:
This example shows a portion of code used to save a color screen image to the file **SCREEN.000**:

```
CLS
<statements that place data on the screen to be saved>
DEF SEG = &HB800 ' assume color monitor
BSAVE "SCREEN.000",0, 4000
```

Because Turbo BASIC supports three types of files, we discuss the procedures for reading from each type of file separately.

Reading Files

When you open a sequential file, specify the **INPUT** mode your program uses to read data. Also, before your program can read data from a sequential

Reading from Sequential Files

file, you have to denote whether the data have been stored in a field-delimited fashion.

When you read multiple variables from a single record in a field-delimited sequential file, Turbo BASIC automatically places the data into the input variables. However, with nondelimited records, the operation imposes more responsibility on you to parse the record you want to read. This fact makes it more attractive and convenient to read records with single data items.

You may input data from a sequential file using the **INPUT #** and **LINE INPUT #** statements, or by implementing the **INPUT$** function.

Syntax:

```
INPUT #<file number>,<list of variables>
LINE INPUT #<file number>,<one string variable>
<string-var> = INPUT$(<number of chars to read>,<file number>)
```

Remarks:

INPUT # is suitable for reading a list of variables, especially from field-delimited records. The **LINE INPUT #** is suitable for reading text files, particularly because it doesn't read commas as delimiters for variables. You'll probably use the string-typed **INPUT$** function only for more specialized applications. This function enables you to specify the number of characters that you want to read from the file.

Turbo BASIC also provides the predefined logical function **EOF(*<file number>*)**, which detects the end of a sequential file. Using this function, you don't have to keep track of the number of records that have been processed.

Example:

This example demonstrates how you can read a small numeric database from a sequential file. Sequential files are suitable for small-scale applications where you can read the entire database into memory.

```
DEFINT A-Z
DEFDBL X
' open sequential file
OPEN "I",1,"Sample.dat"
INPUT #1,File.ID$
IF File.ID$ <> "DATA1" THEN
    CLOSE
```

```
    PRINT "Sorry, bad data file"
    END
END IF
INPUT #1,Title$    ' read title
INPUT #1,Creation.Date$ 'read date and time for file
' creation
INPUT #1,Creation.Time$
INPUT #1,NVar      ' read number of variables
INPUT #1,NData     ' read number of data
' create dynamic matrix
DIM DYNAMIC X(NData,NVar)
' nested loops to read data matrix
FOR I = 1 TO NData
   FOR J = 1 TO NVar
       INPUT #1, X(I,J)
       PRINT X(I,J)
   NEXT J
NEXT I
CLOSE #1
END
```

Turbo BASIC also supports one file-like device for reading data: **KYBD:**. **Reading from** The filename for the input device that you can open in the same way you **the KYBD:** would open input files is **KEYBOARD**.

Example:

In a previous example, we used the **WRITE #** statement to write to a small numeric database. With the program below, we can read the data back to the database:

```
DEFINT A-Z
DEFDBL X

' open sequential file
OPEN "I",1,"Sample.dat"
' read four strings on one line
INPUT #1,File.ID$
IF File.ID$ <> "DATA1" THEN
    CLOSE
    PRINT "Sorry, bad data file"
    END
```

```
END IF
INPUT #1,Title$,Creation.Date$,Creation.Time$
' read two numeric variables on the same line
INPUT #1,NVar,NData
DIM DYNAMIC X(NData,NVar) ' create dynamic matrix of
' data
' nested loops to read data matrix
FOR I = 1 TO NData
   FOR J = 1 TO NVar
      INPUT #1, X(I,J)
   NEXT J
NEXT I
CLOSE #1
END
```

TIP

Keep in mind that Turbo BASIC provides you with the predefined end-of-file function, **EOF**, for use with sequential files. The general syntax for the function is:

```
EOF(<file number>)
```

Usually, you'll use the **EOF** function in a **WHILE** loop. The idea is to detect the final record so that your program doesn't erroneously attempt to read past the end of the file. Follow the general formats below in using the **EOF** function for this purpose:

```
WHILE NOT EOF(<file number>)
   <sequence of statements>
WEND
```

or

```
DO WHILE NOT EOF(<file number>)
   <sequence of statements>
LOOP
```

Reading from Random-Access Files

With random-access files, you'll need to prepare a bit more than you do for sequential files. However, there's a payoff for your effort: Your application programs will be able to read any existing record directly, without having to follow the sequential order of the file.

Follow these four general steps in reading from a random-access file:

1. Open the file using **OPEN**.
2. Establish a map for the fields in each random-access record using **FIELD**.
3. Read a desired record using **GET**.
4. Copy data for any field variables into normal variables.
5. Close the file using **CLOSE**.

To open a random-access file, you use the **OPEN** statement and specify the random access mode and the length of each record. Here are the two general formats available.

Open the File

Syntax:
```
OPEN "R",<file number>,<filename>,LEN = <rec len>
or
OPEN <filename> FOR RANDOM AS <file number> LEN = <rec len>
```

You use the **FIELD** declaration to establish a map for the fields in each random-access record. **FIELD** specifies the size and name of related field variables.

Map the Fields

Syntax:
```
FIELD <file number>, <width1> AS <str1>[,<width2> AS <str2>...]
```

Use the **GET** statement to read a record directly.

Read a Record Directly

Syntax:
```
GET #<file number>[,<record number>]
```

If you omit the **record number**, the **GET** statement simply reads the next record. In other words, you use the **record number** to specify the record location that you want to read directly.

You must copy data for any field variables into normal variables. The values of fields that contain character-typed data need only be assigned to the program's string variables. By contrast, for fields that hold packed, coded numbers, you should unpack their data using the **CVI, CVL, CVS, CVD, CVMS,** and **CVMD** string unpacking functions. Table 2.4 shows you which numeric type corresponds with each function.

Copy Data in Field Variables

Table 2.4. Numeric types for converting field variables

Functions	Converts to	Format Comment
CVI	Integer	
CVL	Long integer	
CVS	Single prec-real	
CVD	Double prec-real	
CVMS	Single prec-real	Special Microsoft format
CVMD	Double prec-real	Special Microsoft format

Close Files

Following the end of random access file I/O, close the file using the **CLOSE** statement. Use this statement in the same manner described earlier for sequential files.

Example:

In the program below, we read the average temperatures for all days of a given week. These temperature values were stored in a random-access file by running the program shown earlier.

```
OPTION BASE 1
DEFDBL A-Z
DEFINT I-O
DIM Week.Data(7)
CLS
INPUT "Enter week number ";Week.Num% : PRINT
' open random access file
OPEN "R",1,"TempStat.DAT",56
' map fields of the record
FIELD #1, 8 AS D1$, 8 AS D2$, 8 AS D3$, 8 AS D4$,_
          8 AS D5$, 8 AS D6$, 8 AS D7$
GET #1,Week.Num% ' read data record
' copy fields into normal numeric arrays
Week.Data(1) = CVD(D1$)
Week.Data(2) = CVD(D2$)
Week.Data(3) = CVD(D3$)
Week.Data(4) = CVD(D4$)
Week.Data(5) = CVD(D5$)
Week.Data(6) = CVD(D6$)
```

```
Week.Data(7) = CVD(D7$)
' display data read
FOR I = 1 TO 7
PRINT Week.Data(I)
NEXT I
CLOSE #1
END
```

Turbo BASIC also supports the predefined function **LOC**, which you can use to return the number of a previously read random-access record.

Syntax:
```
LOC(<file number>)
```

Binary file I/O shares some of the features available with random-access file I/O. One such feature is the ability to read from and write data to the same file after it has been opened. In reading from a binary file, follow these four general steps (note that the second step is optional):

Reading from Binary Files

1. Open the file using **OPEN**.
2. Position the file pointer using **SEEK**.
3. Read from the file using **GET$**.
4. Close the file using **CLOSE**.

You use the **OPEN** statement to open a binary file.

Open a File

Syntax:
```
OPEN "B",<file number>,<filename>
```
or
```
OPEN <filename> FOR BINARY AS <file number>
```

You may, as an option, position the file pointer using the **SEEK** statement.

Position the File Pointer

Syntax:
```
SEEK <file number>,<byte location in file>
```

Use the **GET$** statement to read from a binary file.

Read the File

Syntax:
```
GET$ <file number>,<number of bytes to read>,<string-var>
```

Close the File   When binary file I/O has terminated, close the file using the **CLOSE** statement. Use **CLOSE** in the same manner that we've described for sequential files.

Example:
The following program simply copies the contents of one file to a new one. The copy process moves one byte at a time. This is the program:

```
CLS
INPUT "Enter source file ";S$ : PRINT
INPUT "Enter destination file ";D$ : PRINT
OPEN "B",1,S$
OPEN "B",2,D$
SEEK 2,0
WHILE NOT EOF(1)
    GET$ 1,1,C$
    PRINT C$;
    PUT$ 2,C$
WEND
BEEP : PRINT "DONE"
CLOSE
END
```

Turbo BASIC also supports the predefined function **LOC** to return the sought position of a binary file.

Syntax:
```
LOC(<file number>)
```

You can use still another predefined function, **LOF**, on binary files. **LOF** returns the length of a file.

Syntax:
```
LOF(<file number>)
```

Turbo BASIC also supports **BLOAD** for reading (or actually copying) bytes from a DOS file into memory.

Syntax:
```
BLOAD <filename>[,<offset address>]
```

As this general syntax suggests, you need to preset the segment address using the **DEF SEG** statement. One popular application for **BLOAD** involves loading help screens from files.

Example:

This example demonstrates how you can load screens into memory from files. In this case, the help screens are stored as **SCREEN.0** to **SCREEN.10**. To move from one screen to another, the user presses any key:

```
CLS
NUM.HELP.SCREENS = 10
DEF SEG = &HB800 ' assume color monitor
FOR I = 1 TO NUM.HELP.SCREENS
  BLOAD "SCREEN." + MID$(STR$(I),2)
  A$ = INPUT$(1)
NEXT I
END
```

Turbo C

Turbo C provides a full set of functions that you can use to perform a wide range of I/O tasks—from reading and writing data files to accessing directories. Essentially, the I/O functions are divided into two distinct categories:

- The stream I/O system
- The low-level I/O system

The stream I/O system, often called *standard I/O,* is the most portable and general. The functions in this category provide the highest level tools for performing file I/O operations. All data are treated as a stream of characters. Also, many of the details involved in file manipulation operations—such as data conversion, buffering, and formatting—are automatically taken care of by Turbo C. To use the functions from the stream I/O system, you must include the header file **stdio.h** in your programs.

The low-level I/O system is closer in function to the operating system. To access files with this system, you must perform many of the low-level tasks—such as buffering, formatting, and data conversion—that are normally handled by the stream I/O system.

The low-level routines, however, are very powerful because you use them to take more control over the way in which files are accessed. In addition, the low-level routines are more efficient and thus can improve the performance of your programs. The header file **io.h** must be included in all programs that use functions from the low-level I/O category.

In both I/O systems, all data are treated as a stream or sequence of elements. This stream approach provides you with a consistent interface for performing both file I/O operations and I/O operations with other devices, such as the console or the printer.

To use the Turbo C file system, there are some important terms and concepts with which you should be familiar. These are presented in the following discussions.

Stream Pointers

In the stream I/O system, data are written to and read from a file using a stream pointer. The pointer keeps track of the location in the file where data are being read or written. Turbo C provides a special structure of type **FILE**, which contains the necessary information to perform operations on a file. When a stream is opened, a pointer to the **FILE** structure is returned. This pointer is later used to access the file.

When a Turbo C program is executed, the five predefined stream pointers shown in Table 2.5 are opened.

Table 2.5. Stream pointers opened with execution of a Turbo C program

Pointer	Description
stdin	Access the standard input
stdout	Access the standard output
stderr	Access the standard error device
stdaux	Access the auxiliary I/O
stdprn	Access the printer

You can use these pointers with any of the stream I/O functions that require a stream pointer of type **FILE**. The pointers **stdin**, **stdout**, and **stderr** refer to the system console (the keyboard and the screen). The **stdaux** pointer references one of the PC's serial communication ports. Finally, the **stdprn** pointer is used to send data to the printer.

A *file handle* is a positive integer value used to reference a file opened in the low-level I/O system. Each file opened in a program is given a unique file handle. This file handle is used by the low-level I/O functions to perform read, write, and other operations involved in file access.

File Handles

Turbo C provides three predefined file handles. We've listed these handles and their values here:

Handle	Value
stdin	0
stdout	1
stderr	2

Note that these handles have the same names as the first three predefined stream pointers.

Turbo C provides two types of streams: *text* and *binary*. Therefore, data can be stored in text files or binary files. These files differ in the way in which data are stored.

Streams

In a text stream, the end-of-line characters, carriage return, and linefeed are translated into the newline character (\n). When a text file is written to disk, however, the newline character is replaced with the carriage return and linefeed characters.

Text Streams

In the binary stream, the end-of-line conversion doesn't occur. The binary stream also uses a technique for representing numbers that is different from the one used with text streams. In a text stream, all numbers are represented as individual characters. For example, you would represent the number 213 as 2, 1, 3. In the binary stream, this same number would be represented as a single integer value in the binary stream. Therefore, it takes less storage space to represent a number in the binary stream than in the text system.

Binary Streams

Files opened in the stream I/O system are buffered. This means that, when data are read from or written to a stream, they are first collected in an intermediate storage area, or *buffer*. When data are read from a stream, the data are actually read from the buffer until the buffer becomes empty. At that point, the buffer is filled with more data. When data are written to a stream, the reverse procedure is used. Both of these techniques drastically

File Buffering

increase the performance of file I/O operations over nonbuffered operations.

Turbo C uses a 512-byte buffer by default. However, you can change the size of this buffer to increase its efficiency, or you can eliminate file buffering altogether. Files opened in the low-level I/O system are not buffered.

Creating and Deleting Files

Turbo C provides separate options for creating and deleting files. The separation exists because Turbo C supports both the stream and low-level I/O systems. We'll divide these two topics into separate discussions.

Creating Files

In Turbo C, you can create new files at the time they are opened for output. If a file specified for output doesn't exist, Turbo C creates a new one automatically. In addition, you can create a file in the low-level I/O system using any of the functions shown in Table 2.6.

Table 2.6. Turbo C file creation functions

Function	Description
creat()	Creates a new file or rewrites an existing file
_creat()	Same as creat()
creatnew()	Creates a new file only
creattemp()	Creates a unique filename

All of these functions are declared in the header file **io.h** in this manner:

```
int creat (char *filename, int permission_code);
int _creat (char *filename, int attribute);
int creatnew (char *filename, int attribute);
int creattemp (char *filename, int attribute);
```

The first argument in each function specifies the filename, whereas the second argument contains either the permission code or the attribute code (depending on which function you want to call). You can use the permission codes and symbols defined in the header file **stat.h**. Table 2.7 provides the value, symbol, and a description for each permission code.

The attribute codes and symbols are defined in the header file **dos.h**, as shown in Table 2.8.

Table 2.7. Permission codes

Value	Symbol	Description
0x0080	S_IWRITE	Permission to write
0x0100	S_IREAD	Permission to read
0x0180	S_IREAD I S_IWRITE	Read and write

Table 2.8. Turbo C file attribute codes

Value	Symbol	Description
0	Not available	Read and write access
1	FA_RDONLY	Read-only
2	FA_HIDDEN	Hidden file
4	FA_SYSTEM	System file

The function **creat**() writes over the specified file if the file already exists and if the permission code is set to the write permission. When you use the **_creat**(), **creatnew**(), or **creattemp**() functions, the specified file is opened in the mode indicated by the attribute code. The **creatnew**() function won't open the specified file if it already exists. The **creattemp**() function creates a file by giving it a unique name. When you call **creattemp**(), Turbo C uses the argument **filename** to specify the name of the destination directory path for the new file.

Each of the low-level file creation functions returns a file handle if the file that you have specified can be created and opened. If an error occurs in the file creation process, the value –1 is returned.

Files created with one of the **creat**() functions are created in the default translation mode, which is specified by the global variable **_fmode**. To create a file in a selected mode, you should first assign this variable to the desired mode before calling one of the **creat**() functions. Remember that Turbo C only supports two file modes: *text* and *binary*.

TIP

Examples:
This first example shows how you can use the **creat**() function to create and open a file for reading and writing:

```
fh = creat("\\turboc\\new.c", S_IREAD | S_IWRITE);
```

Note that the filename includes the path specification. In addition, the **creat()** function returns an integer value, called the file handle, which is saved in the variable **fh**. When you create or open a file, it is important to save the file handle so that the file can be accessed with other I/O functions.

The next example shows how you can use _**creat()** to create a file:

```
fh = _creat("story.doc", FA_HIDDEN);
```

In this case, we create **story.doc** as a hidden file. After this file has been created, it is automatically opened for both reading and writing.

These next two examples illustrate how you might use **creatnew()** and **creattemp()**:

```
if ( (fh = creatnew("list.c", FA_RDONLY) ) == -1)
  printf("\nThe file cannot be created--it already exists");
strcpy(fstr, "\\turboc\\");
fh = creattemp(fstr, FA_SYSTEM);
printf("\nThe file created is %s", fstr);
```

The **creatnew()** function will not attempt to create a file if the file that you specify already exists. Therefore, note in our example that we check the return value of the function.

The **creattemp()** function, on the other hand, creates its own filename. Therefore, we only provide the name of the path where we want to store the file. In this case, a file is created as a system file and stored in the directory **\turboc**. Note also that after **creattemp()** has been called, the argument **fstr** contains the name of the created file.

Deleting Files

The standard technique for deleting a file in Turbo C involves using the **unlink()** function. You can use this function to delete any type of file, except for read-only files. The **unlink()** function is prototyped in **dos.h.**

Syntax:
```
int unlink(char *filename);
```

Parameter:
filename   specifies the full path name for the file.

Remarks:
If the file is deleted, the function returns the value 0. If the file is not found or it is a read-only file, **unlink**() returns –1 to indicate that an error has occurred. Turbo C also provides a macro, called **remove**, which performs the same task as **unlink**(). This macro is provided for compatibility reasons.

If you need to delete a read-only file, you can first change the file's mode using the **chmod**() function.

TIP

Example:
Our next example illustrates how the file tlink.c (stored in the directory **\system\csc**) is deleted:

```
if (unlink("\\system\\csc\\tlink.c") == -1)
    printf("\nFile cannot be deleted");
```

Turbo C provides an assortment of functions that support I/O operations for opening and closing files. We've listed the functions available to you in Table 2.9.

Opening and Closing Files

Table 2.9. Turbo C functions for opening and closing files

Function	I/O Category	Description
fopen()	Stream	Open a file stream
freopen()	Stream	Reassign a file pointer
creat()	Low-level	Create and open a file
_creat()	Low-level	Create and open a file
creatnew()	Low-level	Create and open a file
creattemp()	Low-level	Create and open a file with a unique name
open()	Low-level	Open a file
_open()	Low-level	Open a file
sopen()	Low-level	Open a file
fclose()	Stream	Close a file
fcloseall()	Stream	Close all files
fflush()	Stream	Flush a stream buffer
fflushall()	Stream	Flush all stream buffers
close()	Low-level	Close a file
_close()	Low-level	Close all files

As Table 2.9 shows, you can open and close files using either stream I/O functions or low-level I/O functions. Because Turbo C provides numerous options for opening and closing files, we'll present each task separately.

Opening Files in Stream I/O

You access files in the stream I/O system using stream pointers. When a file is opened or created, Turbo C returns a stream pointer, which in turn is used to perform read and write operations on the file. The main function you use to open a file in stream I/O is **fopen()**.

Syntax:
```
FILE *fopen(char *filename, char *type);
```

Parameters:

filename   the name of the file to open.

type   a string that specifies the attribute and mode for the file. The attribute defines the type of operations that you can perform on the file. Turbo C supports six attributes, which we describe in Table 2.10.

Table 2.10. Turbo C file attributes

Mode	Description
r	Open a file for reading
r+	Open a file for reading and writing
w	Open a file for writing
w+	Open a file for reading and writing
a	Open a file for appending
a+	Open a file for reading and appending

Remarks:
A file will be created automatically if the file you want to open does not exist and if you have specified one of the modes **w**, **w+**, **a**, or **a+**.

When you specify the argument type, you may also include a character that indicates the mode of the file. The two modes available to you are described in Table 2.11. You can combine the mode symbols with the attribute symbols to define the complete access specification for opening a file. As an example, the string

```
"r+b"
```

Table 2.11. File modes

Mode	Description
t	Open a file in text mode
b	Open a file in binary mode

indicates that we want to open a file for read and write access in binary mode. If you do not specify binary or text mode, Turbo C opens the file opened in the global mode, which is determined by the global variable **_fmode**. This variable by default is set to **O_TEXT**.

You can use the global variable **_fmode** to indicate the mode in which you want all files to be opened. Turbo C provides two symbolic constants for setting this global variable. You define these constants in the header file **fcntl.h**, with this format:

```
#define O_TEXT     0x4000
#define O_BINARY   0x8000
```

As an example, if you want to make sure all files in a program are opened in binary mode, include the following statement at the start of your program:

```
_fmode = O_BINARY;
```

Example:
The first part of our example illustrates how you might open a read-only file in stream I/O:

```
fp = fopen("file1.doc", "r");
```

With the next call to **fopen()**, we open the file as a read and write binary file:

```
fp = fopen("file1.doc", "r+b");
```

In both cases, the variable **fp** stores the stream pointer for use in accessing the file.

TIP

Opening Files in Low-Level I/O

With the low-level I/O system, you access files by using file handles. When a file is opened or created, Turbo C returns a file handle that, in turn, performs read and write operations on the file. A file handle is simply an integer value. Each file opened in a program is given a unique file handle.

The two main functions for opening a file in low-level I/O are **open()** and **_open()**.

Syntax:

```
int open(const char *filename, int access[,int permission]);
int _open(const char *filename, int access);
```

Parameters:

filename   specifies the name of the file (including the full path name if desired).

access   defines how the file is to be used. Note also that the **open()** function contains an optional argument called **permission**. You use this argument by calling **open()** to specify the permission code for files.

Remarks:

Both of these functions are used to open a file that already exists. If you want to create a new file, use one of the **creat()** family of functions (presented in the section on creating files).

We've listed the major access codes that Turbo C provides in Table 2.12.

Table 2.12. Turbo C access codes

Value	Symbol	Description
1	O_RDONLY	Opens file for reading only
2	O_WRONLY	Opens file for writing only
4	O_RDWR	Opens file for reading and writing
0800h	O_APPEND	Opens file for appending
0100h	O_CREAT	Creates the file if it does not exist
0200h	O_TRUNC	Opens the file and truncates its length to 0
8000h	O_BINARY	Opens the file in binary mode
4000h	O_TEXT	Opens the file in text mode

Any of the first three access codes can be combined with the other access codes to open files in different modes. For example, you can open a read-only file in binary mode by **OR**ing the following codes:

```
O_RDONLY | O_BINARY
```

The permission codes supported are shown in Table 2.13.

Table 2.13. File permission codes

Value	Symbol	Description
0x0080	S_IWRITE	Permission to write
0x0100	S_READ	Permission to read
0x0180	S_IREAD	S_IWRITE	Read and write

Note, however, that these permission codes are only used when a file is opened with the **open()** function and when the access code for the file is specified as **O_CREAT**. This technique enables you to create and open a new file using the **open()** function.

If a file is successfully opened by **open()** or **_open()**, Turbo C returns a non-negative file handle. If the file cannot be opened, –1 is returned to indicate that an error has occurred.

Examples:
In this first example, we use the function **open()** to illustrate how a file is opened in the low-level I/O system:

```
fh = open("list.c", O_RDWR);
```

Here, the file **list.c** is opened for reading and writing.

In the next example, we show how **open()** can be used to create a file that does not already exist:

```
fh = open("list.c", O_CREAT, S_IWRITE);
```

Note that we've used the permission argument to specify the attribute for creating the file.

Our third and final example illustrates how you can use **open()** to open a file in binary mode:

```
if ( (fh = open("io.h", O_RDONLY | O_BINARY) ) == -1)
  printf("\nThe file cannot be opened");
```

Closing Files in Stream I/O

Turbo C provides two functions that you can use to close files in stream I/O.

Syntax:
```
int fclose(FILE *stream);
int fcloseall(void);
```

Parameter:
*stream   pointer to the opened I/O stream.

Remarks:
The function **fclose()** closes only the specified file. However, you can use the function **fcloseall()** to close all open files in a program. Closing files ensures that any related data still pending in memory are properly written to the file. In addition, closing a file reclaims the buffer area in memory allocated when the file was opened. Use the **fclose()** function to close a single file specified by the file pointer. Use **fcloseall()** to close all open files in a program.

fflush() and fflushall()

Turbo C also provides two functions that you can use to flush stream buffers.

Syntax:
```
int fflush(FILE *stream);
int flushall(void);
```

Parameter:
*stream   pointer to the I/O stream to flush.

Remarks:
For an input buffer, the **flush()** operation clears the buffer. If, on the other hand, the buffer is an output buffer, the **flush()** operation writes the contents of the buffer to its respective file.

Examples:

In this first example, we use **fclose()** to close a specified file:

```
if (fclose("file1.doc") != 0)
   printf("\nThe file cannot be closed");
```

The function **fcloseall()** is useful for closing all open files in a program. As illustrated in the next example, **fcloseall()** returns the number of files closed:

```
n = fcloseall();
printf("The number of files closed is %d", n);
```

The Turbo C functions for closing files in low-level I/O are **close()** and **_close()**. Both functions are declared in the header file **io.h**.

Closing Files in Low-Level I/O

Syntax:

```
int close(int handle);
int _close(int handle);
```

Parameter:

handle   the file handle associated with the opened file.

Remarks:

These two functions are very similar; however, **close()** writes a Ctrl-Z character at the end of a file when it is closed. Both functions return a value of 0 if the specified file is closed. If the file cannot be closed, a value of −1 is returned.

Example:

This example illustrates how you can close a file with the **close()** function:

```
if (close(fh) != 0)
   printf("\nThe file cannot be closed");
```

Turbo C provides three functions that perform different types of file initialization tasks in the stream I/O system. These three functions are declared in the following manner.

Initializing Files

Syntax:
```
FILE *fdopen(int handle, const char *type);
```

Parameters:
handle   the handle associated with the file.
*type   string that specifies the file mode type.

Syntax:
```
FILE *freopen(const char *filename, const char *type, FILE *stream);
```

Parameters:
*filename   the DOS filename.
*type   string that specifies the file mode type.
*stream   the file stream pointer.

Syntax:
```
int rewind(FILE *stream);
```

Parameter:
*stream   the file stream pointer.

Remarks:
The function **fdopen()** associates a stream with an opened file handle. The stream pointer can then be used to access the file. The function **freopen()** is used to substitute a new file with a currently opened stream. When this substitution is made, the stream replaced is automatically closed.

The last function, **rewind()**, repositions a stream pointer to the beginning of a file. This is a useful function if you are working with a file and you need to start at the beginning of the file to read or write data. If **rewind()** succeeds, it returns the value 0; otherwise, it returns a nonzero value.

Example:
The first example illustrates how the **fdopen()** function exchanges a file handle with a stream pointer:

```
fh = creat ("new.doc", S_IWRITE);
fp = fdopen (fh, "w");
```

In this case, the file **new.doc** is created with the **creat()** function, and the file handle is used to obtain a stream pointer (**fp**) that can be used to access the file. Note that because the file is created with the **S_IWRITE** permission, its file handle must be converted to a stream pointer that is also opened in the write-only mode.

The next example shows how **freopen**() exchanges a file pointer with a specified file:

```
fp1 = fopen("file1.doc", "r+");
fp2 = freopen("file2.doc", "r+", fp1);
```

Here the file **file1.doc** is opened with **fopen**() and then the second file **file2.doc** is substituted for the file pointer created by opening the first file.

This code illustrates how the **rewind**() function moves a file pointer to the beginning of a file:

```
fp = fopen("text.1", "r+");
fprintf(fp, "Write this text to the file\n");
rewind(fp);
```

File Status

Turbo C provides a variety of functions you can use to determine the status of files. Functions are provided in both the stream and low-level I/O system. Table 2.14 lists and describes all of these functions for both categories.

Table 2.14. Turbo C functions for determining file status

Function	Category	Description
fileno()	Stream	Gets file handle for a stream
fgetspos()	Stream	Gets position of file pointer
ftell()	Stream	Locates position of stream pointer
fstat()	Low-level	Gets data about an open file
access()	Low-level	Determines access code of file
filelength()	Low-level	Gets the size of a file
getsftime()	Low-level	Gets file's date and time
isatty()	Low-level	Determines device type of file handle
lseek()	Low-level	Reads position of file pointer
tell()	Low-level	Reads position of file pointer
_chmod()	Low-level	Gets the access mode of a file

Writing to Files

Because Turbo C supports two types of I/O systems, we discuss outputs for each method separately. In general, the manner in which you open a file determines which category of output functions you can use.

Writing in the Stream I/O System

The stream I/O system provides flexibility by enabling you to write data in different formats—such as characters, formatted and unformatted strings, and blocks. We've put together Table 2.15 to describe the complete set of stream functions available to you for writing data to files.

Table 2.15. The set of Turbo C stream I/O output functions

Function	Type	Description
fprintf()	Formatted	Writes formatted data to a stream
fputc()	Unformatted	Writes a character to a stream
fputchar()	Unformatted	Writes a character to a stream
fputs()	Unformatted	Writes a string to a stream
fwrites()	Both	Writes a block to a stream
vfprintf()	Formatted	Writes formatted data to a stream

The techniques you follow in writing to binary and text files are identical. Therefore, we only describe the different methods for writing formatted, unformatted, and block data.

Writing Unformatted Data

You can write unformatted data to files as characters and strings. For these tasks, Turbo C provides the functions **fputc()**, **fputchar()**, and **fputs()**, which are essentially the same as the standard output functions **putc()**, **putchar()**, and **puts()**. Each function writes data to a specified stream.

Syntax:
```
int fputc(int ch, FILE *stream);
int fputchar(int ch, FILE *stream);
int fputs(const char *string, FILE *stream);
```

Parameters:

ch   the character to write to the file.
*string the string to write to the file.
*stream the file stream pointer.

Remarks:

The functions **fputc()** and **fputchar()** send a character to a stream, whereas **fputs()** sends a string to a stream. When **fputs()** writes a null terminated string, it doesn't append the newline (\n) character. The return value for **fputc()** and **fputchar()** is the character written. The return value for **fputs()** is the final character written. If an error occurs when your program is writing data to a file, each of these functions returns the **EOF** (end-of-file) constant.

Example:

This first example illustrates the use of the **fputc()** function for writing characters to a file. This program copies the contents of a file and writes a new file.

```
main()
{
    FILE *fp1, *fp2;            /* file pointers */
    char buffer[2000];         /* buffer to store input file */
    int ch, i, j;

    if (!(fp1 = fopen("file1.doc","r"))) {/* open input file */
      printf("File cannot be opened: file1.doc\n");
       exit(1);
    }
    if (!(fp2 = fopen("file2.c","w"))) { /* open output file */
      printf("File cannot be opened: file2.c\n");
       exit(1);
    }
    i = 0;
    while ( (ch = fgetc(fp1)) != EOF ) /* read file */
       buffer[i++] = ch;
    j = 0;
    while ( --i >= 0 )              /* write to file */
       fputc(buffer[j++], fp2);
    fclose(fp1);            /* close input file */
    fclose(fp2);            /* close output file */
}
```

Writing Formatted Data

You write formatted data to files using the **fprintf()** and **vfprintf()** functions.

Syntax:

```
int fprintf(FILE *stream, const char *format[,argument,...]);
int vfprintf(FILE *stream, const char *format, va_list param);
```

Remarks:

The file output versions of **fprintf()** and **vfprintf()** work just like their counterparts for writing to the screen—**printf()** and **vprintf()**. The **fprintf()** and **vfprintf()** functions support a wide variety of formatted output capabilities. You can use these functions to output all of the standard Turbo C data types—such as integers, characters, floating-point, and so on.

Parameters:

Both functions require you to use a formatted string in this general syntax:

```
% [flags] [width spec] [.precision] [size] type
```

Note that all of the specifiers are optional, except for the type **term**. The type specifies the data type of the object that you want to write. You can specify the display width for a character, a string, or numeric output by including a numeric value for the width specifier. The following statement shows how this is done:

```
fprintf(fp," %30s", str);
```

In this case, we want the argument **str** displayed in a field of 30 characters. The string is padded if it is smaller than the width specification, and the string is truncated if it is larger that the width specification. If the width specifier is a negative number, Turbo C displays the data object justified to the right.

To format floating-point output, you specify decimal places by using a period, followed by the number of decimals than you want. As an example, the following statement displays a floating-point value with five decimal places:

```
fprintf(fp, "%.5f", num);
```

Examples:

In this example, we've used the **printf()** function to store a small numeric database in a text file.

```
#include <stdio.h>
#include <string.h>
main()       /* store data base */
{
    const int max_data = 100;
    const int max_var = 10;
    float x[max_data][max_var];
    char title[64];
    int i, j, nvar, ndata;
    FILE *fp;

    strcpy(title, "Sample Data");
    nvar = 2; ndata = 3;
    x[0][0] = 1.0; x[1][0] = 2.0; x[2][0] = 3.0;
    x[0][1] = 4.0; x[1][1] = 5.0; x[2][1] = 6.0;
       /* create and open text file */
    if ( (fp = fopen("Sample.Dat","w")) == NULL) {
      printf("\nSorry, file cannot be opened");
      exit(1);
    }
    fprintf(fp,"DATA1");          /* emit file ID name */
    fprintf(fp,"\n%s",title);     /* write title */
    fprintf(fp,"\n%d",nvar);      /* write number of vars */
    fprintf(fp,"\n%d",ndata);     /* write number of data */
       /* nested loops to write data matrix */
    for (i = 0; i < ndata; i++)
      for (j = 0; j < nvar; j++)
        printf(fp,"%f", x[i][j]);
    fclose(fp);   /* close file */
}
```

In addition to writing data to a file, you can use any of the predefined stream pointers to write data to other devices—such as the screen or a printer.

The following program reads a data file and looks for certain user-specified words. A text line that matches any of the words we are seeking is simultaneously displayed on the screen and stored in an output text file. Each matching line has a carat symbol below it, pointing to the matching location of the user-supplied search words:

```c
#include <stdio.h>
#include <string.h>
main()      /* search for strings */
{
    int const max_words = 100;
    char words[100][40];
    char line[80], *index;
    char filename[64], outname[64];
    FILE *fp1, *fp2;
    int n, i, count, pos;

    printf("Enter filename ");
    scanf("%s",filename);
    if ( (fp1 = fopen(filename,"r")) == NULL) {
        printf("\nSorry, file cannot be opened");
        exit(1);
    }
    do {
        printf("\nEnter number of search words : ");
        scanf("%d",&n);
    } while ( (n < 1) || (n > max_words) );
    for (i = 1; i <= n; i++) {
        do {
            printf("\nEnter word # %d ", i);
            scanf("%s", line);
        } while (strlen(line) > 40);
        strcpy(words[i-1],line);
    }
    printf("\nEnter output filename ");
    fgets(line,80,fp1);
    if ( (fp2 = fopen(outname,"w")) == NULL) {
        printf("\nSorry, file cannot be opened");
        exit(1);
    }
    count = 0;
    while ( !feof(fp1) ) {
        fscanf(fp1, "%s", line);
        count++;
        for (i = 0; i < n; i++)  {
            if ( (index = strstr(line, words[i]) ) != NULL ) {
```

```
            pos = (strlen(line) - strlen(index)) +
                  strlen(words[i]);
            fprintf(fp2, "%d  %s", count, line);
            fprintf(fp2, "%*s\n, pos, "-*^");
            fprintf(stdout, "%d  %s", count, line);
            fprintf(stdout, "%*s\n", pos, "-*^");
        }
      }
   }
   fcloseall();   /* close all file buffers */
}
```

You can also output data in blocks, which provides a quick way to write data stored in arrays or C structures.

Writing Blocks of Data

Syntax:
```
int fwrite(void *buffer, int size, int nitems, FILE *stream);
```

Parameters:

*buffer   references a buffer of data to be written to a specified output stream.

size   contains the number of bytes in each data object written.

nitems   contains the number of data objects that are to be written.

*stream   the file stream pointer.

The function returns the total number of bytes written, which is computed as:

```
size * nitems
```

Examples:

In the program below, we use the block write function, **fwrite()**, to copy the contents of one file to another. Here's the program:

```
#include <stdio.h>
#include <io.h>
#include <alloc.h>

main()
{
```

```
FILE *fp1, *fp2;      /* file pointers */
char *buffer;       /* buffer to store input file */
int fh;
char sfile[64], dfile[64];
long fsz;

    /* open input file */
printf("\nEnter source file ");
scanf("%s", sfile);
if ((fp1 = fopen(sfile,"r")) == NULL) {
    printf("File cannot be opened: %s\n", sfile);
    exit(1);
}
    /* open output file */
printf("\nEnter destination file ");
scanf("%s", dfile);
if ((fp2 = fopen("file2.c","w")) == NULL) {
    printf("File cannot be opened: %s\n", dfile);
    exit(1);
}
fh = fileno(fp1);          /* get file handle */
fsz = filelength(fh);      /* get file size */
buffer = malloc(fsz);      /* allocate buffer */
fread(buffer, 1, fsz, fp1);
fwrite(buffer, 1, fsz, fp2);
fclose(fp1);               /* close input file */
fclose(fp2);               /* close output file */
}
```

In this example, note that we used the functions **fileno()** and **filelength()** to determine the size of the input file. The function **fileno()** obtains the file handle for a specified stream, while **filelength()** returns the length of a file.

Using block I/O operations, we can read and write the file with only two function calls. This is the fastest way to perform I/O operations with the stream functions.

The next program illustrates how you can write data to a file from a C structure. This program prompts you for the average temperature for each day of a given week, in addition to the week number. The numeric data for each week are stored in a single random-access record:

```
#include <stdio.h>

main()
{
    typedef struct {
        float temp[7];
    } weekarray;

    weekarray week_data;
    FILE *fp1;              /* file pointer */
    int i, week_num;

    printf("\nEnter week number : ");
    scanf("%d", &week_num);

    for ( i = 0; i < 7; i++)    {
        printf("\nEnter temperature for day %d : ", i+1);
        scanf("%d", &week_data.temp[i]);
    }
    if ((fp1 = fopen("E:\\tempstat.dat","r+")) == NULL)   {
        printf("File cannot be opened");
        exit(1);
    }
        /* get position of record */
    fseek(fp1,sizeof(week_data) * week_num, 0);
    fwrite(&week_data, sizeof(week_data), 1, fp1);
    fclose(fp1);
}
```

In this example, note that we've used the function **fseek()** to locate a position in the output file. In this way, the block I/O routines enable us to perform random-access operations.

Turbo C provides two functions for writing data to files in the low-level I/O system. These functions, called **write()** and **_write()**, are declared in the **io.h** file.

Writing Data in Low-Level I/O

Syntax:
```
int write(int handle, void *buffer, int byte_count);
int _write(int handle, void *buffer, int byte_count);
```

Parameters:

handle   specifies the file handle.

buffer   contains the data to be written to the file.

byte_count contains the number of bytes of data to be written to the
                file.

Remarks:

Both **write()** and **_write()** perform a similar task to that of the stream block
write function **fwrite()**. In this case, a specified buffer of data is written
to a file. If the byte count is less than the size of the data buffer, only part
of the data in the buffer is written to the file. For example, if the **write()**
function is called with the arguments:

```
write(fh1, charray, 20);
```

where the variable **charray** is defined as:

```
char charray[40];
```

only the first 20 elements of the array are written to the file.

Both functions return the number of bytes written. The function **write()**
treats linefeed characters differently from the function **_write()**. When
write() is used with text files, linefeed characters are translated into the
carriage return-linefeed combination.

Example:

The following example uses the low-level file operations to list the contents
of one or more files to the screen or the printer. The program obtains
arguments from the command line and enables you to direct the output to
the printer by calling the program with the following command:

```
list prn <file1> <file2> ...
```

where the components **file1, file2,** and so on specify the files to list. Here
is the program:

```
#include <io.h>
#include <fcntl.h>
#include <string.h>
#define BUFLEN 128
```

```
main(int argc, char *argv[])
{

    int fh1, fh2;            /* file handles */
    int i, n_bytes;
    char fbuffer[BUFLEN];    /* input buffer */

    if ( argc < 2 ) {        /* check arguments */
        printf("\nInvalid number of arguments");
        printf("\nTry: flist filename filename ... ");
        exit(1);
    }
    i = 1; /* initialize argument counter */
    if (strcmp(argv[1],"prn") == 0 ) {
        fh2 = 4;             /* list files to printer */
        i++; /* skip over argument */
    }
    else fh2 = 1;            /* list files to screen */
    while (i < argc) {       /* open input file */
        if ( (fh1 = open(argv[i], O_RDONLY | O_TEXT)) < 0)
            printf("\nFile cannot be opened: %s\n", argv[i]);
        else {
            while ( !eof(fh1) ) {    /* read input file */
                n_bytes = read(fh1, fbuffer, BUFLEN); /* read */
                write(fh2, fbuffer, n_bytes);  /* write bytes */
            }
            close(fh1);      /* close input file */
        }
        i++;                 /* increment argument count */
    }
}
```

As is true for output functions, Turbo C provides two classes of input routines for accessing both the stream and low-level I/O systems.

Reading Files

The manner in which you open a file also determines which category of input functions you can use. In the following discussions, we cover the functions and techniques for reading data with each system.

The stream I/O system provides a great deal of flexibility in reading data, enabling you to read such different formats as characters, formatted and

Reading with Stream I/O

unformatted strings, and blocks. Table 2.16 shows the complete set of stream functions you can use to read data.

Table 2.16. Turbo C stream functions for reading data

Function	Type	Description
fgetc()	Unformatted	Read a character from a stream
fgetchar()	Unformatted	Read a character from a stream
fgets()	Unformatted	Read a string from a stream
fread()	Both	Read a block from a stream
fscanf()	Formatted	Read formatted data from a stream
vfscanf()	Formatted	Read formatted data from a stream

Reading Unformatted Data

You can read unformatted data from files as characters and strings. For these tasks, Turbo C provides the functions **fgetc()**, **fgetchar()**, and **fgets()**, which are essentially the same as the standard input functions **getc()**, **getchar()**, and **gets()**. Each of these functions reads data from a specified stream.

Syntax:
```
int fgetc(FILE *stream);
int fgetchar(void);
char *fgets(char *string, int str_len,FILE *stream);
```

Remarks:
The function **fputc()** gets a character from a specified stream, whereas **fputchar()** gets a character from the predefined stream **stdin**. You use the **fgets()** function to get a string from a stream. When **fgets()** reads a string, it keeps reading characters until it either encounters the newline (\n) character or reads **str_len – 1** characters. When **fgets()** reads the newline character, it appends the character to the end of the returned string.

The return value for **fgetc()** and **fgetchar()** is the character that the function reads. The return value for **fgets()** is a pointer to the string that the function reads. If an error occurs as your program reads data from a file, each of these functions returns the **EOF** constant.

TIP

When you use one of the unformatted-input routines to read data from a file, it is a good idea to check the input value to determine whether the end of the file has been reached. As an example, consider that we include this **while** statement in a program:

```
while ( (ch = fgetc(fp)) != EOF )
    buffer[i++] = ch;
```

This statement would keep reading data from a file until the end of the file was reached.

Example:

This example illustrates how you can use the **gets()** function to read from a file. Our program produces a screen listing of the contents of a specified set of input files. The syntax for running the program is:

```
<program name> <file1> <file2> <file3> ...
```

Here's the program:

```
#include <stdio.h>

#define LINELEN 80

main(int argc, char *argv[])
{
    FILE *fp1;                  /* file pointer */
    int lcount, i;
    char line[LINELEN + 1];     /* read input strings */

    if ( argc < 2 ) {           /* check arguments */
        printf("\nInvalid number of arguments");
        printf("\nTry: flist filename filename ... ");
        exit(1);
    }


    for (i = 1; i < argc; i++) {
        if ((fp1 = fopen(argv[i],"r")) == NULL) {
            printf("\nFile cannot be opened: %s\n", argv[i]);
        }
        else {
            lcount = 1;                 /* set line counter */
            printf("\nListing file: %s\n", argv[i]);
            while ( !feof(fp1) )  {  /* read input file */
                fgets(line, 80, fp1); /* read a line */
                printf("%s",line);    /* write line to screen */
```

```
        lcount++;    /* increment line counter */
    }
    printf("\n %d line(s) read in file %s\n",--lcount,
        argv[i]);
    fclose(fp1);              /* close input file */
    }
  }
}
```

Reading
Formatted Data

You use the **fscanf()** and **vfscanf()** functions to read formatted data from files.

Syntax:
```
int fscanf(FILE *stream, const char *format [,argument,...]);
int vfscanf(FILE *stream, const char *format, va_list param);
```

The file input versions of **fscanf()** and **vfscanf()** work just like their counterparts for reading from the keyboard, **scanf()** and **vscanf()**. The **fscanf()** and **vfscanf()** functions support a wide variety of formatted input capabilities. You can use both functions to read all of the standard Turbo C data types, including integers, characters, floating-point, and so on.

Parameters:
Both of these functions require a formatted string in the following general syntax:

```
% [*] [width spec] [size] [address type] type
```

Note that all of the specifiers are optional, except for the **type** term. You must use the **type** specifier to denote the data type of the object that you want to read. Notice that you can specify the width in which you want to display a character, a string, or numeric output. You do this by including a numeric value for the width specifier. Here's an example:

```
fprintf(fp," %30s", str);
```

In this case, we've specified that we want the argument **str** to be displayed in a 30-character field. The string is padded if it is smaller than the width specification and truncated if it is larger than the width specification. If the width specifier is a negative number, the data object is displayed justified to the right.

To format floating-point output, you can specify the number of decimal places you want to include by using a period followed by the number of decimals. Here's a sample statement that displays a floating-point value with five decimal places:

```
fprintf(fp, "%.5f", num);
```

Example:
In the following example, we use the **fscanf()** function to retrieve a small numeric database from a text file:

```
#include <stdio.h>
#include <string.h>
main()        /* read database file */
{
    const int max_data = 100;
    const int max_var = 10;
    float x[100][10];
    char title[64];
    char fileid[80];
    int i, j, nvar, ndata;
    FILE *fp;

       /* open text file for reading */
    if ((fp = fopen("sample.dat","r")) == NULL) {
      printf("\nSorry, file cannot be opened");
      exit(1);
    }
    fscanf(fp,"%s", fileid);
    if (strcmp(fileid, "Sample Data") != 0) {
      printf("\nBad data file");
      fclose(1);
      exit(1);
    }
    fscanf(fp,"%s", title);  /* read title */
    fscanf(fp,"%d",&nvar);    /* read number of variables */
    fscanf(fp,"%d",&ndata);   /* read number of items */
```

```
        /* nested loops to read data  */
    for (i = 0; i < ndata; i++)
       for (j = 0; j < nvar; j++)
           fscanf(fp,"%f", x[i][j]);
    fclose(fp);   /* close file */
}
```

Reading Blocks of Data

You can also read blocks, a technique that provides you with a quick way to read and store data in arrays and C structures.

Syntax:

```
int fread(void *buffer, int size, int nitems, FILE *stream);
```

Parameters:

buffer   references the buffer in which you want to store input data.
size   contains the number of bytes in each data object that is read.
nitems   contains the number of data objects that you want to read.

Remarks:

The function returns the total number of bytes read, which is computed as:

```
size * nitems
```

Example:

The following program illustrates how you can read and store data from a file into a C structure. This program reads the average temperature for each day of a week, given the week number. Our program stores the numeric data for each week in one random access record. Here's the program:

```
#include <stdio.h>
main()
{
    typedef struct {
       float temp[7];
    } weekarray;
    weekarray week_data;
    FILE *fp1;          /* file pointer */
    int i, week_num;

    printf("\nEnter week number : ");
```

```
scanf("%d", &week_num);
if ((fp1 = fopen("E:\\tempstat.dat","r")) == NULL) {
    printf("File cannot be opened");
    exit(1);
}
    /* get position of record */
fseek(fp1, sizeof(week_data) * week_num, 0);
fread(&week_data, sizeof(week_data), 1, fp1);
for ( i = 0; i < 7; i++)
    printf("\n%d", week_data.temp[i]);
fclose(fp1);
}
```

Note that we've used the function **fseek()** to locate a position (record) in the input file. By doing so, we can use the block I/O routines to perform random access operations.

Like the low-level write routines, two functions are also provided for reading data form files in the low-level I/O system. These functions, called **read()** and **_read()**, are declared in **io.h**.

Reading Data in Low-Level I/O

Syntax:
```
int read(int handle, void *buffer, int byte_count);
int _read(int handle, void *buffer, int byte_count);
```

Parameters:
Both **read()** and **_read()** perform a similar task to that of the stream block read function **fread()**. In this case, a specified buffer of data is read from a file. The first argument, **handle**, specifies the file handle, and the second argument, **buffer**, contains the data to be read from the file. The last argument contains the number of bytes of data to be read. If the byte count is less than the size of the data buffer, only part of the data buffer is filled with data from the file. For example, if the **read()** function is called with the arguments

```
write(fh1, charray, 20);
```

where the variable **charray** is defined as

```
char charray[40];
```

only the first 20 elements of the array will contain data read from the file.

Remarks:

Both functions return the number of bytes read. The function **read()** treats linefeed characters different than does the function **_read()**. When **read()** is used with text files, carriage returns are removed and the function detects the end-of-file marker when a Ctrl-Z character is encountered. Because the **_read()** function does not perform any translation, it performs a direct call to MS-DOS and is therefore more efficient.

Example:

In the program below, we use the low-level **read()** and **write()** functions to copy the contents of one file to another. Here's the program:

```
#include <stdio.h>
#include <io.h>
#include <alloc.h>
#include <fcntl.h>

main()
{
    int fh1, fh2;       /* file handles */
    char *buffer;       /* buffer to store input file */
    char sfile[64], dfile[64];
    long fsz;

        /* open input file */
    printf("\nEnter source file ");
    scanf("%s", sfile);
    if ( (fh1 = open(sfile, O_RDONLY | O_TEXT)) < 0) {
        printf("\nFile cannot be opened: %s\n", sfile);
        exit(1);
    }
        /* open output file */
    printf("\nEnter destination file ");
    scanf("%s", dfile);
    if ( (fh2 = open(dfile, O_RDONLY | O_TEXT)) < 0) {
        printf("\nFile cannot be opened: %s\n", dfile);
        exit(1);
    }
```

```
fsz = filelength(fh1);          /* get file size */
buffer = malloc(fsz);           /* allocate buffer */
read(fh1, buffer, fsz);
write(fh2, buffer, fsz);

close(fh1);       /* close input file */
close(fh2);       /* close output file */
}
```

In this example, note that the **filelength**() function is called to determine the size of the input file. The size of the file is used as an argument for read and write.

Turbo C also provides special functions and variables you can use to test for end-of-file conditions and to handle error conditions.

Auxiliary Functions

Turbo C provides two boolean end-of-file functions, **feof**() and **eof**(), that enable your program to detect the end of a file before it attempts to read data. You use the **feof**() function to check for the end-of-file marker in files that are accessed in the stream I/O system. Use the **eof**() function in the low-level I/O system. The **feof**() function is declared in **stdio.h**.

Detecting the End of a File

Syntax:
```
int feof(FILE * stream);
```

Remarks:
This function returns a nonzero value if the end-of-file marker is detected. This condition indicates that the file pointer is currently at the end of the file.
    In turn, **eof**() is declared in **io.h** in this manner:

```
int eof(int *handle);
```

The function **eof**() returns the value 1 if the end-of-file marker is detected. If a value of –1 is returned, this condition indicates that some type of error has occurred.

Examples:
The first example illustrates how **feof**() is used in a loop to read a line of data from an input file:

```
while ( !feof(fp1) ) {
    fgets(line, 80, fp1);
    savedata(line);
}
```

The condition statement in the loop always checks to see if the end of file has been reached before the body of the loop is allowed to execute.

TIP

Keep in mind that the constant **EOF** can also be used to detect the end of file when I/O operations are performed. For example, the following statement shows how data can be read from an input file:

```
while ( (ch = fgetc(fp)) != EOF)
    buf[i++] = ch;
```

This second example illustrates how the low-level **eof()** function is used in a loop to read a line of data from an input file:

```
while ( !eof(fh1) ) {
    read(fh1,line, 80);
    savedata(line);
}
```

Note the similarity between this function and the stream routine **feof()**.

Error Handling

To ensure that I/O operations are performed correctly, Turbo C provides some routines and global variables for I/O error checking. The techniques for using the error-checking features are dependent on the I/O system (stream or low-level) in use. Here we present the error-handling features and techniques for using them in separate sections.

Global Error Variables

Turbo C provides three global variables for representing and accessing error messages. These variables are **sys_errlist**, **errno**, and **sys_nerr**. The system error messages are stored as a table of strings that is referenced by the variable **sys_errlist**. When a stream or low-level error occurs, the variable **errno** contains the number of the error in the table that references the appropriate error message. The third variable, **sys_nerr**, stores the number of the error messages in the table.

The error messages stored in the table can be accessed at any time. If you suspect that an I/O error has occurred in a program, you can test the value of **errno**; if it is nonzero, you can display the corresponding error message. The technique for doing this is illustrated by the following code segment:

```
if (errno != 0)
  printf("\nError message is %s", sys_errlist[errno]);
```

Keep in mind that the error messages stored in the system error table are used for other errors besides I/O errors. The error messages that are used for I/O errors are listed in Table 2.17.

TIP

Table 2.17. Turbo C I/O error messages

Error Number	Message
2	No such file or directory
3	Path not found
4	Too many open files
5	Permission denied
6	Bad file number
12	Invalid access code
15	No such device
18	No more files

Many types of errors can occur when you perform stream I/O operations. To detect and control such errors, Turbo C provides three functions, which are declared in **stdio.h**.

Stream I/O Error Handling

Syntax:
```
int ferror(FILE *stream);
void clearerr(FILE *stream);
void perror(char *string);
```

Remarks:
The function **ferror**() is actually implemented as a Turbo C macro that tests the specified stream to see if a read or write error has occurred. If an error is detected, **ferror**() returns a nonzero value.

The second function, **clearerr**(), clears the error detection status of a stream. Once an error occurs, the error status of a stream remains set until it is cleared or until the stream either is initialized with the **rewind**() function or is closed.

The last function, **perror()**, sends an error message to the **stderr** device. The error message is displayed in the following format:

```
user_error_msg : system_error_msg
```

where the first component, **user_error_msg,** is the string that is specified as the argument to **perror()**. The second error component is the system error message that results from an illegal read or write operation. The system error message references one of the error messages stored in the global error message table.

Example:
The following example keeps reading a line of text from the keyboard and writes the line to a file. After each write operation, the error status of the stream is checked with the **ferror()** function. If an error occurs, it is displayed with **perror()**. The program terminates when the user types a period.

```c
#include <stdio.h>
#include <string.h>
main()
{
    FILE *fp;
    char line[81];

    if ((fp = fopen("test.c", "w")) == NULL) {
      printf("File cannot be opened");
      exit(1);
    }
    do  {
      printf("\nInput a line of data");
      gets(line);
     fprintf(fp,"%s\n",line);
      if (ferror(fp)) {
        perror("Error writing to file");
        clearerr(fp);
        exit(1);
      }
    } while (strcmp(line, ".") != 0);
}
```

Errors are accessed in the low-level I/O system using the global variables presented in the previous discussion. The low-level I/O functions set the global variable **errno** to a nonzero value whenever an error occurs.

**Low-Level I/O
Error Handling**

Example:
The following code segment illustrates how the global variables **errno** and **sys_errlist** display errors detected during low-level I/O operations:

```
if ( (fh1 = open("test.c", O_RDONLY)) == -1) {
  printf("File error is: %s", sys_errlist[errno]);
  exit(1);
}

if (read(fh1, buffer, 80) == -1)
  printf("File error is: %s", sys_errlist[errno]);
```

Note that the low-level functions **open()** and **read()** return a value of –1 if an error occurs. This condition indicates that the global variable **errno** is set to the corresponding error number.

Turbo Pascal

Turbo Pascal supports I/O operations for these three types of files:

- Text
- Typed
- Untyped

Text files store ASCII text in variable-length records, with each record ending in a pair of carriage return-linefeed characters. Reading records from text files involves scrolling through the records in sequence. You cannot go directly to a particular sequential record; you can only read or write the next record in sequence. Turbo Pascal also enables you to append more text to the contents of an existing text file.

**The Organization
of Text Files**

With Turbo Prolog typed files, you manipulate equal-sized (fixed-length) records. Consequently, the file I/O system is able to access any record directly, without having to read records in the same sequence in which they are stored. As an analogy, you might consider this random-access capability

**The Organization
of Typed Files**

to be much like opening a book to the particular page you want to read, without having to flip through preceding pages.

The Organization of Untyped Files

Turbo Pascal supports untyped file I/O as a way for you to tackle files of binary data that don't correspond to any Pascal record structure. I/O operations on untyped file read and write bytes in blocks.

File Management in Turbo Pascal

All three file types have some common file management steps, including procedures for opening and closing files. File opening procedures enable you to access a file, whereas file-closing procedures ensure that any data still pending in memory are properly written to a file before the program terminates. Also, by closing a file, you reclaim the buffer area in memory that was allocated when you opened the file.

Another feature is common to all Turbo Pascal file types: DOS doesn't require you to specify a maximum file size when you create the file. Consequently, you can expand a file until you reach either your disk storage limitation or the limit allowed with the DOS version you are using.

Creating and Deleting Files

Turbo Pascal creates a file when you open it for output. If the file does not exist, Turbo Pascal creates a new one automatically. To delete a file, you use the following procedure.

Syntax:
```
Procedure Erase(Var Filename);
```

Parameter:

Filename   specifies the name of the file to be deleted. The argument can be of any valid file type.

Example:
Here's an example that removes a single file from any directory that we specify:

```
Write('Enter filename : ');
Readln(PurgedFile); Writeln;
Assign(FileVar, PurgedFile);
Erase(FileVar);
```

Opening Files

The first file I/O task your programs will perform involves opening files with the **Assign** intrinsic, which connects a DOS filename or device with a file-type variable. When you open a file, you allocate an I/O buffer in RAM for the file. The contents of the file then become accessible to your program for processing.

You need to perform two basic steps when you open a file with a Turbo Pascal program: first, you use **Assign** to connect a DOS filename or device with a file-typed variable. This variable then becomes the handle that Turbo Pascal uses to perform I/O and other file operations, such as **Rename** and **Erase**.

Syntax:
```
Procedure Assign(Var FileVar; Filename : String);
```

Parameters:

FileVar   specifies a file of any valid file type.

Filename   a DOS filename that can include the full path name.

Remarks:

The **Assign** intrinsic has an interesting feature: The file variable continues to represent the associated **Filename** even after you have closed the file and until you assign the file variable to a new filename. This means you can use **Assign** once to open a file for output, close it, reopen it for input, and then close it again. Even though you've closed a file and reopened it for a different I/O operation, you need not repeat the same **Assign** statement.

After you have assigned a filename to a file variable, you can perform the file operations shown in Table 2.18, which includes operations for opening a file for input or output.

Table 2.18. Intrinsics for opening a file in Turbo Pascal

I/O Intrinsic	Purpose
Append(FileVar)	Append to an existing file
Reset(FileVar)	Open a file for input
Rewrite(FileVar)	Open/Create a file for output
Flush(FileVar)	Flush contents of file buffer
Erase(FileVar)	Erase file
Rename(FileVar)	Rename a file
SetTextBuf(<FileVar>, <Buffer>[,<Size>])	Set buffer size for text file I/O

Closing Files

You use the **Close** statement to close individual files, which is the final I/O task your program will perform.

Syntax:
```
Procedure Close(Var FileVar);
```

Parameter:
FileVar   specifies a file of any valid file type.

Remarks:
By closing a file, you ensure that any related data still pending in memory are properly written to the file. In addition, closing a file reclaims the buffer area in memory allocated when you opened the file.

Initializing Files

Turbo Pascal doesn't support any statements explicitly intended for performing file initialization.

Writing to Files

Because Turbo Pascal supports three types of files, we discuss outputs for each method separately. The **Assign** intrinsic determines the type of file to be used for output by examining the supplied type of the file variable.

Writing to Text Files

When the file-typed variable is of type **Text**, **Assign** prepares for text file I/O. Keep in mind that, although **Text** is an abbreviation for the type declaration **File Of Char**, you can't use **Text** and **File Of Char** interchangeably.

Your program using **Rewrite** or **Append** informs the system that text output is about to take place. So, you can use **Rewrite** to overwrite and truncate the contents of any existing data file. By contrast, **Append** extends the opened file by placing any new incoming data after the final record. Consequently, you select the output mode that is meaningful to your application.

You use **Writeln** and **Write** to write to Turbo Pascal text files.

Syntax:
```
Writeln(<file var>, <expression list>);
Write(<file var>, <expression list>);
```

Remarks:
The file output versions of **Writeln** and **Write** work in the same manner as the standard versions. (As a matter of fact, Pascal automatically inserts

the standard output device handles when you use the "standard" **Writeln** and **Write**. Consequently, by using this programming trick, you can redirect output from the standard output device to a text file, a printer, or another device.)

The **Writeln** and **Write** procedures support relatively limited formatted output capabilities. You may specify the width used to display a character, a string, or numeric output by placing a colon and the desired width number after the output data object. For floating-point output, you can specify the decimal places by placing a second colon, followed by the number of decimal places you want. This procedure is an example:

```
Writeln(FileVar,' ':30,'Total = ',Total:4:2,' for ',
      Num:3,' items');
```

If the width specifier is a negative number, the data object is displayed justified to the left. If the decimal-place specifier is negative, the final display format will vary based on these width-specifier criteria:

1. If the width specifier is positive, the number is forced to appear in scientific notation, with a generous number of digits.

2. If the width specifier is negative, the number is justified to the left and displayed in scientific notation with relatively few significant digits. When you use a negative decimal-place specifier, its magnitude has no effect.

Example:
In this example, we demonstrate how you can store a small numeric database in a text file. Text files are suitable for relatively small-scale applications for which you can read the entire database into memory. Here's the example:

```
Procedure Store_Data_Base;

Const MAX_DATA = 100;
    MAX_Var = 10;

Var X : Array [1..MAX_DATA,1..MAX_Var] OF Real;
    Title : String[64];
    I, J, NVar, NData : Integer;
    FileVar : Text;
```

```
Begin
    Title := 'Sample Data';
    NVar := 2;
    NData := 3;
    X[1,1] := 1.0; X[2,1] := 2.0; X[3,1] := 3.0;
    X[1,2] := 4.0; X[2,2] := 5.0; X[3,2] := 6.0;
    {create and open text file}
    Assign(FileVar,'Sample.Dat');
    Rewrite(FileVar);
    Writeln(FileVar,'DATA1');   {emit file ID name}
    Writeln(FileVar,Title);     {write title}
    Writeln(FileVar,NVar);      {write number of variables}
    Writeln(FileVar,NData);     {write number of data}
    {nested loops to write data matrix}
    For I = 1 To NData Do
       For J = 1 To NVar Do
         Writeln(FileVar,X[I,J]);
    Close(FileVar);             {close file}
End.
```

Turbo Pascal also supports a number of file-like devices. Table 2.19 lists and provides the filenames for devices that you can open just like output files.

Table 2.19. Turbo Pascal device/filenames for opening files

Output Device	Filename
Screen	CON
Line Printers 1, 2, and 3	LPT1, LPT2, and LPT3
Communication Ports 1 and 2	COM1 and COM2
NUL device (ignores output)	NUL

Outputting to the **CON** device is identical to the approach used with the standard **Writeln** and **Write** procedures.

Example:
Our program below reads a data file and looks for certain user-specified words. A text line that matches any of the words being searched for is

simultaneously displayed on the screen, printed, and stored in an output text file. We place a caret symbol below each matching line to point to the corresponding location of the user-supplied search words:

```
Program_Demo_Echo;

Uses CRT;
Const MAX_WORDS = 100;

Type TextLine = String[80];
    WordStr = String[40];

Var Words : Array [1..MAX_WORDS] Of WordStr;
    Line : TextLine;
    Filename : String[64];
    SrcTextFileVar : Text;
    N, I, J, Count, Index : Integer;
    DevName : Array [1..3] Of String[64];
    Dev : Array [1..3] Of Text;

Begin
    Write('Enter filename ');
    Readln(Filename); Writeln;
    Assign(SrcTextFileVar, Filename);
    Reset(SrcTextFileVar);
    Repeat
        Write('Enter number of search words : ');
        Readln(N); Writeln
    Until N In [1..MAX_WORDS];
    For I := 1 To N Do Begin
        Repeat
            Write('Enter word # ',I,' ? ');
            Readln(Line); Writeln
        Until Length(Line) <= SizeOf(WordStr);
        Words[I] := Line;
    End;
    DevName[1] := 'CON';
    DevName[2] := 'LPT1';
    Write('Enter output filename ? ');
    Readln(DevName[3]); Writeln;
```

```
      For I := 1 To 3 Do Begin    {open all three output devices}
        Assign(Dev[I],DevName[I]);
        Rewrite(Dev[I])
      End;
      Count := 0
      While Not Eof(SrcTextFileVar) Do Begin
        Readln(SrcTextFileVar,Line);
        Inc(Count);
         For I := 1 To N Do Begin
           Index := POS(Words[I],Line);
           If (Index > 0) Then
               For J := 1 To 3 Do Begin
                 Writeln(Dev[J],Count:3,' ',Line);
                  Writeln(Dev[J],'^':(Index + 4))
                End; {for}
         End; {for}
      End; {while}
      Close(SrcTextFileVar);          {close all file buffers}
      For I := 1 To 3 Do
         Close(Dev[I]);
   End.
```

Writing to Typed Files

When you send output to typed files, you must declare the file-type variables (that handle the output) as

```
File Of <type>
```

Essentially, typed file I/O is a random-access approach. In other words, your application programs can directly read from and write to any existing record. Follow these five general steps in writing to a typed file:

1. Declare a file-type variable.
2. Assign the variable.
3. Declare an output mode.
4. Write data.
5. Close the file.

Declare a File-Type Variable

You declare a file-type variable using

```
File Of <type>
```

The *type* may be a simple or complex data type. Turbo Pascal stores the information in typed files in binary form.

Assign the file-typed variable by including a DOS filename.

Assign the Variable

Syntax:
```
Assign(<file var>:<file-var type>,<filename>:String);
```

Use **Rewrite** or **Append** to declare the data output mode that you want to employ.

Declare an Output Mode

Syntax:
```
Procedure Rewrite(Var FileVar);
Procedure Append(Var FileVar);
```

Parameter:
FileVar   specifies a file of any valid file type.

You write data to a typed file by using the **Write** (but not **Writeln**) procedure.

Write Data

Syntax:
```
Write(<file variable>:<file-variable type>,<list of variables>);
```

You randomly access records by including the **Seek** intrinsic, which requires the following arguments:

```
Seek(<file variable>:<file-variable type>,<record num>:Longint);
```

Also, you need to establish the relationship between the data type of the file variable and the variables with this format:

```
<file-variable type> = File Of <type for written variables>;
```

In addition, Turbo Pascal provides you with the **Truncate** option in case you want to truncate a file at the current file-pointer location. Follow this general syntax for the **Truncate** intrinsic:

```
Truncate(<file variable>:<file-variable type>);
```

Typically, to position the pointer at a desired location, you call **Seek** before you use **Truncate**.

Close the File

At the end of random access file I/O, close the file using the **Close** statement. You use **Close** in the same manner that we described earlier for text files.

TIP

Turbo Pascal also supports the predefined functions **FileSize** and **FilePos** to return the size of the file and the current file pointer location. Each function takes one argument, a file-typed variable, and returns a long integer-typed result.

Example:

To illustrate the use of type files, we've written a program that prompts for the average temperatures for days of an entire week, as well as for a week number. The program stores the numeric data for each week in one random-access record. Here's the program:

```
Program Save_Data_In_Typed_File;

Uses CRT;

Type WeekArray = Record
     Temp : Array [1..7] Of Real;
     End;

     DataFileType = File Of WeekArray;

Var Week_Data : WeekArray;
    DataFile : DataFileType;
    Week_Num : 1..52;
    I : Integer;

Begin
    ClrScr;
    Write('Enter week number : ');
    Readln(Week_Num); Writeln;
    For I := 1 To 7 Do Begin
      Write('Enter temperature for day ',I,' : ');
      Readln(Week_Data.Temp[I]); Writeln;
    End;
```

```
{open random access file}
Assign(DataFile,'E:\TempStat.DAT');
Rewrite(DataFile);
Seek(DataFile,Week_Num-1); {write the record}
Write(DataFile,Week_Data);
Close(DataFile);
End.
```

Untyped file I/O shares some of the features of typed file I/O. One such feature is the ability to read and write data to the same file after you've opened the file. Use these five basic steps as a guideline:

Writing to Untyped Binary Files

1. Declare a file-type variable.
2. Assign the file-type variable to a DOS name.
3. Declare an output mode.
4. Write data.
5. Close the file.

You declare a file-type variable for an untyped file simply by including the keyword **File**, without specifying a data type. Turbo Pascal stores untyped files in binary format.

Declaring a File-Type Variable

You use the **Assign** statement to associate a file-type variable with a DOS file name. Here's the format:

Assigning the File-Type Variable to a DOS Filename

```
Assign(<file var>:<file-var type>,<filename>:String);
```

You declare a data output mode by employing **Rewrite** or **Append**. Use these general formats:

Declaring an Output Mode

```
Rewrite(<file variable>:<file-variable type>);
Append(<file variable>:<file-variable type>);
```

You use the **BlockWrite** statement to write data to an untyped file. **BlockWrite** provides a quick way to perform binary input and can take these two general formats:

Writing Data

```
BlockWrite(<file variable> : File;
    <untyped buffer variable>;
    <requested number of bytes written> : Word);
```

or
```
BlockWrite(<file variable> : File;
    <untyped buffer variable>;
    <requested number of bytes written> : Word;
    <actual number of bytes written> : Word);
```

Notice that with **BlockWrite** you can include an optional argument that returns the actual number of bytes written. This value will be equal to or less than the number of output bytes you requested.

You can also include the **Seek** intrinsic to access a record directly. **Seek** requires the following arguments:

```
Seek(<file variable>: File, <byte number>:Longint);
```

As an option, you can include the **Truncate** intrinsic if you want to truncate the file at the current file-pointer location. Use this general syntax for **Truncate**:

```
Truncate(<file variable> : File);
```

Typically, to position the pointer at a desired location, you call **Seek** before you use **Truncate**.

Closing the File   At the end of random access file I/O, close the file using the **Close** statement. You use **Close** in the same manner that we've described earlier for text files.

TIP   Turbo Pascal also supports the predefined functions **FileSize** and **FilePos** to return the size of the file and the current file pointer location. Each function takes one argument, a file-type variable, and returns a long integer-type result.

Example:
The program below simply copies the contents of one file to a new one. The copy process moves 1024 bytes at a time. This is the program:

```
Program Test_Untyped_File_IO;

Uses CRT;

Const BUFFER_SIZE = 1024;
```

```
Var InFile, OutFile : File;
    Buffer : Array [1..BUFFER_SIZE] Of Char;
    Source, Destination : String[64];
    Err1, Err2 : Byte;
    Actual_Write, Actual_Read : Word;

Begin
    ClrScr;
    Write('Enter source file ');
    Readln(Source); Writeln;
    Write('Enter destination file ');
    Readln(Destination); Writeln;
    Assign(InFile,Source);
    Assign(OutFile,Destination);
    {$I-} Reset(InFile,1); {$I-}
    Err1 := IOResult;
    {$I-} Rewrite(OutFile,1); {$I-}
    Err2 := IOResult;
    If (Err1 + Err2) = 0 Then Begin
       Repeat
         BlockRead(InFile, Buffer, BUFFER_SIZE, Actual_Read);
         BlockWrite(OutFile, Buffer, Actual_Read, Actual_Write)
       Until (Actual_Read = 0) Or
             (Actual_Read <> Actual_Write);
       Writeln(^G,'Done')
    End; {If}
    If Err1 = 0 Then Close(InFile);
    If Err2 = 0 Then Close(OutFile);
End.
```

Reading Files

Because Turbo Pascal supports three types of files, we discuss the procedures for reading from each type of file separately.

Reading from Text Files

When the file-type variable is of type **Text**, you use **Assign** to prepare for text file I/O. Keep in mind that, although **Text** is an abbreviation for the type declaration **File Of Char**, you can't use **Text** and **File Of Char** interchangeably.

Also, use **Reset** in your program to inform the system that you are entering text.

You use **Readln** or **Read** to read data from text files.

Syntax:
```
Readln(<file var>, <expression list>);
Read(<file var>, <expression list>);
```

Remarks:
The file input versions of **Readln** and **Read** operate in the same manner as the standard versions. (In fact, Pascal automatically inserts the standard input device handles in the "regular" **Readln** and **Read**. Consequently, this programming trick enables you to redirect the input from a file to another input device.)

Example:
Our example below demonstrates how to retrieve a small numeric database stored in a text file. A text file is suitable for relatively small applications, where you can read the entire file or database into memory.

```
Procedure Recall_Database;

Const MAX_DATA = 100;
    MAX_Var = 10;

Var X : Array [1..MAX_DATA,1..MAX_Var] Of Real;
    Title : String[64];
    FileID : String[80];
    I, J, NVar, NData : Integer;
    FileVar : Text;

Begin
    Assign(FileVar, 'Sample.Dat');        {open text file}
    Reset(FileVar);
    Readln(FileVar,FileID); {read file ID name}
    If FileID <> 'DATA1' Then Begin
      Writeln('Bad data file');
      Close(FileVar);
       Halt
    End;
    Readln(FileVar,Title);    {read title}
    Readln(FileVar,NVar);     {read number of variables}
    Readln(FileVar,NData);    {read number of data}
    {nested loops to write data matrix}
    For I = 1 To NData Do
```

```
      For J = 1 To NVar Do Begin
      Readln(FileVar,X[I,J]); Writeln(X[I,J]);
      End;
   Close(FileVar); {close file}
End.
```

Turbo Pascal also supports one file-like device for reading data: **CON**. The filename for the input device that you can open in the same way you would open an input file is **Keyboard**. Reading from the **CON** device works just like ordinary **Readln** and **Read** procedures.

To input data from typed files, you must declare the file-type variables that Turbo Pascal will use to handle data input. Declare each variable this way:

Reading from Typed Files

```
File Of <type>
```

Essentially, I/O for a typed file follows a random-access approach. In other words, your application programs can directly read from and write to any existing record; it isn't necessary to follow the sequential ordering of records. Five general steps are involved in reading from a typed file:

1. Declare a file-type variable.
2. Assign a file-type variable to a DOS name.
3. Declare an output mode.
4. Read data.
5. Close the file.

As we've stated above, you declare a file-type variable using **File Of** <*type*>. The <*type*> may be a simple or complex data type. Turbo Pascal stores typed files in binary format.

Declaring a File-Type Variable

You use the **Assign** statement to associate your file-type variable with a DOS filename. Here's the format:

Assign the File-Type Variable to a DOS Name

```
Assign(<file var>:<file-var type>,<filename>:String);
```

Use **Reset** to declare the output mode you want.

Declare an Output Mode

Syntax:
```
Procedure Reset (Var FileVar);
```

Parameter:
FileVar   specifies a file of any valid file type.

Read Data

With a typed file, you read data by using the **Read** (not **Readln**) procedure.

Syntax:
```
Read(<file variable>:<file-variable type>,<list of variables>);
```

Remarks:
You also have to use this **File Of** format to specify the relationship between the data type of the file variable and the type for written variables:

```
<file-variable type> = File Of <type for written variables>;
```

If you want to access records randomly, include the **Seek** intrinsic, which requires these arguments:

```
Seek(<file variable>:<file-variable type>,<record num>:Longint);
```

As an option, you can use the **Truncate** intrinsic to truncate a typed file at the current file-pointer location.

Syntax:
```
Procedure Truncate(Var FileVar);
```

Parameter:
FileVar   specifies a file of any valid file type.

Remarks:
To position the file pointer at a particular location, you typically call **Seek** prior to using **Truncate**.

Close the File

At the end of random-access file I/O, close the file using the **Close** statement. Use **Close** in the same manner described earlier for text files.

TIP

Turbo Pascal also supports the predefined functions **FileSize** and **FilePos**, which return the size of the file and the current file pointer location. Each function takes one argument, a file-type variable, and returns a long integer-type result.

Example:

This program reads a typed file to retrieve the average temperatures for the days of a particular week, given the week number. We used the program described earlier to store the random-access data in a typed file. Here's the program:

```
Program Recall_Data_From_Typed_File;

Uses CRT;
Type WeekArray = Record
    Temp : Array [1..7] Of Real;
    End;
    DataFileType = File Of WeekArray;

Var Week_Data : WeekArray;
    DataFile : DataFileType;
    Week_Num : 1..52;
    I : Integer;

Begin
    ClrScr;
    Write('Enter week number : ');
    Readln(Week_Num); Writeln;
    {open random access file}
    Assign(DataFile,'E:\TempStat.DAT');
    Reset(DataFile);
    Seek(DataFile,Week_Num-1); {Write the record}
    Read(DataFile,Week_Data);
    For I := 1 To 7 Do Begin
      Writeln(Week_Data.Temp[I]); Writeln;
    End;
    Close(DataFile);
End.
```

Reading from Untyped Binary Files

Untyped file I/O shares some of the features available with typed file I/O. One such feature is the ability to read from and write data to the same file after you have opened it. Follow these five general steps:

1. Declare a file-type variable.
2. Assign the file-type variable to a DOS name.

3. Declare an output mode.
4. Read data.
5. Close the file.

Declare a File-Type Variable

For an untyped binary file, you declare a file-type variable simply by including the keyword **File**, without specifying a data type. Turbo Pascal stores untyped files in binary form.

Assign the File-Type Variable to a DOS name

Use this general **Assign** format to associate a file-type variable for an untyped file with a DOS filename:

```
Assign (<file var>:<file-var type>,<filename>:String);
```

Declare an Output Mode

You use **Reset** to declare the mode in which you want to output data stored in an untyped file.

Syntax:
```
Reset (<file variable>:<file-variable type>);
```

Read Data

You use the **BlockRead** statement to read data from an untyped file. **BlockRead** provides you with a quick, efficient way to read binary files and is available in these two general formats:

```
BlockRead (<file variable> : File;
    <untyped buffer variable>;
    <requested number of bytes written> : Word);
```

or

```
BlockRead (<file variable> : File;
    <untyped buffer variable>;
    <requested number of bytes written> : Word;
    <actual number of bytes written> : Word);
```

Notice in the second format that you can, as an option, include an argument to return the actual number of bytes that are output. This value will be equal to or less than the number of output bytes that you have requested.

Include the **Seek** intrinsic if you want direct access to records. **Seek** requires the arguments shown in this general format:

```
Seek (<file variable>: File, <byte number>:Longint);
```

As an option, you can use the **Truncate** intrinsic to truncate an untyped file at the current file-pointer location. Here's the format for **Truncate**:

```
Truncate (<file variable> : File);
```

To position the file pointer at a particular location, it is typical to call **Seek** prior to using **Truncate**.

At the end of random-access file I/O, close the file using the **Close** statement. Use **Close** in the same manner that we've described earlier for text files.

Close the File

Turbo Pascal also supports the predefined functions **FileSize** and **FilePos**, which return the size of the file and the current file pointer location. Each function takes one argument, a file-type variable, and returns a long integer-type result.

TIP

Example:
This simple program copies the contents of one untyped file to a new one. The copy process moves 1024 bytes at a time. Here's the program:

```
Program Test_Untyped_File_IO;

Uses CRT;

Const BUFFER_SIZE = 1024;

Var InFile, OutFile : File;
    Buffer : Array [1..BUFFER_SIZE] Of Char;
    Source, Destination : String[64];
    Err1, Err2 : Byte;
    Actual_Write, Actual_Read : Word;

Begin
    ClrScr;
    Write('Enter source file ');
    Readln(Source); Writeln;
    Write('Enter destination file ');
    Readln(Destination); Writeln;
    Assign(InFile,Source);
```

```
            Assign(OutFile,Destination);
            {$I-} Reset(InFile); {$I-}
            Err1 := IOResult;
            {$I-} Rewrite(OutFile); {$I-}
            Err2 := IOResult;
            If (Err1 + Err2) = 0 Then Begin
               Repeat
                  BlockRead(InFile, Buffer, BUFFER_SIZE, Actual_Read);
                  BlockWrite(OutFile, Buffer, Actual_Read, Actual_Write)
               Until (Actual_Read = 0) Or (Actual_Read <> Actual_Write);
               Writeln(^G, 'Done')
            End; {If}
            If Err1 = 0 Then Close(InFile);
            If Err2 = 0 Then Close(OutFile);
          End.
```

Working with File Buffers

Turbo Pascal provides a procedure called **SetTextBuf** that enables you to adjust the buffer size for text file I/O. The declaration of **SetTextBuf** is:

```
Procedure SetTextBuf(Var FileVar : Text;
                     Var Buffer [; Size : Word ]);
```

The default buffer size is 128 bytes. With **SetTextBuf** this number can be increased, which can help to improve the performance of programs that work with large files.

Example:
The following example is a practical utility that converts WordStar files, up to but not including version 5, into standard ASCII files. The general syntax for using the program (assuming it is compiled as **WS2ASCII.EXE**) is:

```
WS2ASCII infile outfile Y|N
```

The input and output files must be different; otherwise, the utility prompts you for a different filename. The Y/N option enables you to decide whether to convert WordStar paragraphs into single long lines. The program uses the **InBuff** and **OutBuff** character arrays as 16K buffers.

```
PROGRAM WordStar_to_ASCII;
{$B-}
Uses CRT;
Const BUFFER_SIZE = 16384; {16 Kbyte buffer}

Type String64 = String[64];

   Var Ch : Char;
   OK, First, Eliminate_Soft_CR : Boolean;
   Source, Target : String64;
   InBuff, OutBuff : Array [1..BUFFER_SIZE] Of Char;
   InFile, OutFile : Text;

Procedure UpCaseStr(Var Strng : String64);

Var i, n : Byte;

Begin
   n := Length(Strng);
   For i := 1 To n Do
   Strng[i] := UpCase(Strng[i]);
End;

Begin
   ClrScr;
   If ParamCount < 3 Then Begin
     Writeln('Proper usage: ws2ascii <infile> <outfile> <Y|N>');
     Writeln;
     Exit;
   End;
   Source := ParamStr(3);
   Eliminate_Soft_CR := Source[1] In ['Y','y'];
   First := TRUE;
   Repeat
     If First Then Begin
        Source := ParamStr(1);
        First := FALSE
     End
     Else Begin
        Write('Enter Source Filename -> ');
```

```
                    Readln(Source); Writeln;
               End;
               Assign(InFile, Source);
               SetTextBuf(InFile, InBuff);
               {$I-} Reset(InFile); {$I+}
               OK := IOResult = 0;
               If Not OK Then Begin
                    Writeln('Error: Cannot open ',Source);
                    Writeln;
               End;
          Until OK;
          First := TRUE;
          Repeat
               If First Then Begin
                    Target := ParamStr(2);
                    First := FALSE
               End
               Else Begin
                    Write('Enter Target Filename -> ');
                    Readln(Target); Writeln;
               End;
               Assign(OutFile, Target);
               SetTextBuf(OutFile, OutBuff);
               {$I-} Rewrite(OutFile); {$I+}
               OK := (IOResult = 0);
               If Not OK Then Begin
                    Writeln('Error: Cannot open ',Target);
                    Writeln;
               End;
               UpCaseStr(Source);
               UpCaseStr(Target);
               OK := OK And (Source <> Target);
               If Not OK Then Begin
                    Write('Sorry! Source and target filenames ');
                    Writeln('must be different');
                    Writeln;
               End;
          Until OK;
          While Not Eof(InFile) Do Begin
               If Eliminate_Soft_CR And (ORD(Ch) = $8d) Then
```

```
            Read(InFile,Ch) {Get rid of LF too}
       Else Begin
            Ch := CHAR(ORD(Ch) AND $7F); {Get rid of high bit}
            If Ch = ^O Then Ch := ' ';    {Hard space convert}
            If (Ch >= ' ') Or (Ch = ^I)   Or
               (Ch = ^J)   Or (Ch = ^M) Then
            Write(OutFile,Ch);
       End;
   End;
   Write(OutFile,^Z);
   Close(InFile);
   Close(OutFile);
End.
```

Using the **CRT** unit, I/O redirection is accomplished by reassigning the standard input and output files to the standard DOS devices. Normally, these files are automatically assigned to **CRT**. The following **Assign** procedures are used in preparing the input and output files for redirection:

I/O Redirection in Turbo Pascal

```
Assign(Input,''); Reset(Input);
Assign(Output,''); Rewrite(Output);
```

That's all there is to it! The Pascal program employing the above procedures is ready for I/O redirection. The **SetTextBuf** intrinsic may be used to increase the I/O buffer sizes.

Example:
The following example is a practical utility that converts WordStar files, up to but not including version 5, into standard ASCII files. The general syntax for using the program (assuming it is compiled as WS2ASCII.EXE) is:

```
WS2ASCII <infile> outfile
```

The input and output files must be different. The program uses the **SetTextBuf** intrinsic with the **InBuff** and **OutBuff** character arrays as 16K buffers.

```
Program WordStar_to_ASCII_Using_IO_Redirection;
Uses CRT;
```

```
Var Ch : Char;
    Input, Output : Text;
    InBuff, OutBuff : Array [1..16384] Of Char;

Begin
    ClrScr;
    Assign(Input,'');
    Reset(Input);
    SetTextBuf(Input, InBuff);
    Assign(Output,'');
    Rewrite(Output);
    SetTextBuf(Output, OutBuff);
    While NOT Eof(Input) Do Begin
      Read(Input, Ch);
      If ORD(Ch) = $8d Then
          Read(Input,Ch) {Get rid of LF too}
      Else Begin
          Ch := Char(Ord(Ch) And $7F); {Get rid of high bit}
          If Ch = ^O Then Ch := ' ';    {Hard space convert}
          If (Ch >= ' ') Or (Ch = ^I)    Or
             (Ch = ^J)   Or (Ch = ^M) Then
          Write(Output,Ch);
        End;
      End;
    Close(Input);
    Close(Output);
End.
```

Auxiliary Functions and Variables

Turbo Pascal supports the boolean end-of-file function call **Eof**.

Syntax:
```
Function Eof(FileVar) : Boolean;
```

Parameter:
FileVar   specifies a file of any valid file type.

This protects your program from reading past the end of a file. In other words, **Eof** enables your program to detect the end of a file before it reads data. Normally, you accomplish this using the **Eof** function within a **While-Do** loop, in this manner:

```
While Not Eof(<file-var>) Do Begin
   <i/o and other statements>
End;
```

Turbo Pascal also supports **IOResult,** a predefined integer-typed variable that you can use to return a file I/O error status after any file I/O operation. Table 2.20 lists and describes the values for possible I/O errors that can be detected by your Turbo Pascal programs.

Table 2.20. I/O error descriptions

Value Returned	Error by IOResult
0	No error
2	File not found
3	Path not found
4	Too many files are open
5	File access is denied
6	Invalid file handle
12	Invalid file access code
15	Invalid drive number
16	Unable to remove current subdirectory
17	Unable to rename across drives
100	Error in disk read
101	Error in disk write
102	File has not been assigned
103	File has not been opened
104	File has not been opened for input
105	File has not been opened for output
107	Invalid numeric format for Read and Readln

The use of **IOResult** implements the **{$I-}** compiler directive, which prevents the runtime error handler from halting the program when an I/O error occurs. We highly recommend that you reactivate this same error detection mechanism by including **{$I+}** at the end of the protected critical I/O statement. In other words, your critical I/O statements should have this general syntax:

```
{$I-} <critical file I/O statement>; {$I+}
```

Turbo Prolog

The file I/O system in Turbo Prolog is similar to the one you would use with Turbo Pascal. Essentially, Turbo Prolog supports three types of files:

- Text
- Binary
- Consultable or database files

Text files store lines of ASCII data within variable-length records. Each record ends with the carriage return-linefeed combination.

Turbo Prolog provides a complete set of predicates for creating, reading, writing, and modifying text files. In addition, Turbo Prolog provides a few high-level predicates that read the contents of a file into a string variable.

Turbo Prolog provides a predicate that opens a binary file in either *binary mode,* which does not perform any translations on the file, or in *text mode,* which removes all carriage returns when your program reads a file. In turn, when data are written, the text mode replaces each linefeed character with the carriage return-linefeed combination.

Consultable or *database* files are created in Turbo Prolog by saving the asserted database facts in a program. Once these database files have been created, they can be read by using the built-in **consult** predicate. These files are easy to use because you don't have to use the normal steps for accessing files—such as opening a file, assigning a file to an I/O device, and closing a file.

I/O Devices

The file I/O system in Turbo Prolog is based on the underlying principle of I/O devices. At any given time, you can have two I/O devices opened in a program—one for reading and one for writing data. An I/O device can be a text file or a device—such as a printer or screen. When a program executes, the keyboard is assigned as the default input device and the screen is assigned as the default output device.

Your programs read to or write from files by assigning a filename to either the read or write I/O device. Once a file has been assigned to an I/O device, your program can access the file by using any of the standard I/O predicates shown in Table 2.21.

Creating Files

A file is created in Turbo Prolog when your program opens the file with the **openwrite** predicate. If the file does not exist, Turbo Prolog creates a new one automatically.

Table 2.21. Turbo Prolog predicates for accessing data

I/O Predicate	Description
readchar	Reads a character
readint	Reads an integer
readln	Reads a string (line of text)
readreal	Reads a real number
readterm	Reads a Turbo Prolog term
write	Writes data
writef	Writes formatted data

Syntax:
```
openwrite(SymbolicName, FileName) (i,i)
      (file, string)
```

Parameters:

SymbolicName   the name used to reference the file after it has been created.

FileName   a string that specifies the DOS filename.

Example:
Here is an example of a call to this predicate:

```
openwrite(outfile, "New.dat")
```

This example creates and opens a file named **New.dat**, and associates the filename with the term **outfile**. You need to declare this output file in the domains section of your program by using the standard file domain. Here's the approach to use:

```
domains
    file = outfile
```

If the file that you specify in the **openwrite** predicate currently exists, Turbo Prolog will delete the file. So, take care when you use the **openwrite** predicate. If you don't want to overwrite an existing file, you can use the **existfile** predicate before calling **openwrite** to make sure that the file doesn't already exist. The general form of this predicate is shown next.

Syntax:
```
existfile(FileName)   (i)
        (string)
```

Parameter:

FileName   specifies the name of a file in the current directory. If the file
is found, **existfile** succeeds; otherwise it fails.

Deleting Files   To delete a file, you use the predicate **deletefile**. Use the following general
format.

Syntax:
```
deletefile(FileName)   (i)
          (string)
```

Parameter:

FileName   a string that specifies the DOS filename for the file you want
to delete.

Example:

This example illustrates how you can create a new file with the **openwrite**
predicate:

```
domains
    file = newfile

predicates
    create_file

clauses
    create_file :-
        write("\nEnter new file to create: "),
        readln(Fname),
        not(existfile(Fname)),
        openwrite(newfile, Fname).

    create_file :-
        write("\nThe file already exists").
```

Note that the **existfile** predicate is used to determine if the file already exists.

If the file doesn't exist, it is opened. If it is found, on the other hand, the first clause, **create_file**, fails; the second clause is called to display an error message.

Example:
This next example shows how you can use the **deletefile** predicate to delete a file:

```
erase_file :-
    write("\nEnter filename to delete: "),
    readln(Fname),
    deletefile(Fname).
```

Opening and Closing Files

In Turbo Prolog, you must open a file before it can be accessed. When a file is opened, you need to associate the actual filename with a symbolic name. The **readdevice** and **writedevice** predicates use this symbolic name in directing input and output. In addition, other predicates, such as **eof** and **filepos**, use the symbolic name to access an opened file.

We've developed Table 2.22 to describe the Turbo Prolog predicates you can use to open files.

Table 2.22. Predicates for opening files in Turbo Prolog

Predicate	Description
openappend	Opens a file for reading and writing
openmodify	Opens a file for reading and writing
openread	Opens a file for reading only
openwrite	Opens a file for writing

The predicates **openread** and **openappend** issue an error message if the file that you specify to be opened doesn't already exist. If the error is not handled properly, your program will terminate. The predicates **openmodify** and **openwrite**, on the other hand, create the file if it does not exist.

Each predicate takes two arguments, as we've illustrated with the following general format for **openappend**.

Syntax:
```
openappend(SymbolicName, FileName)  (i,i)
        (file, string)
```

Parameters:

SymbolicName   symbolic name used to access the file once it is opened.
FileName   a valid DOS filename.

Remarks:

Turbo Prolog opens the DOS file specified by the argument **FileName** and associates it with the **SymbolicName**. You must declare the symbolic file as a **file** domain type. For example, these two statements illustrate the steps you need to follow in opening a file:

```
domains
    file = testfile
```

```
goal
    openappend(testfile, "test.pro").
```

Here, we've opened the file **test.pro** and assigned it to the symbolic name **testfile**.

Once you have opened a file with one of the **open** predicates, you must assign the file to an input or output device by using **readdevice** or **writedevice**. This is necessary to perform any read or write operations on the file. Next we show the general formats for **readdevice** and **writedevice**.

Syntax:

```
readdevice(SymbolicName)   (i), (o)
        (symbol)
```

```
writedevice(SymbolicName)    (i), (o)
        (symbol)
```

Parameter:

SymbolicName   the symbolic filename used to access a file.

Closing a file, the final I/O task your program will perform, requires the **closefile** predicate. The general format of this predicate is shown next.

Syntax:

```
closefile(SymbolicName)   (i)
        (file)
```

Parameter:
SymbolicName   the symbolic filename used to access a file.

Remarks:
The argument **SymbolicName** is the symbolic name that your program associates with a DOS filename when the file is opened. By closing a file, you ensure that any related data still pending in memory are properly written to the file. In addition, when a file is closed in Turbo Prolog, the system reclaims the buffer area in memory that was allocated when your program opened the file.

If a file that you open for a writing operation is not closed before your program terminates, the data written to the file will be lost.

Example:
In this example, we open a file for reading and assign it to the input device:

```
domains
    file = infile
predicates
    open_file

clauses
    open_file :-
        write("Enter the filename for reading: "),
        readln(Fname),
        openread(infile, Fname),
        readdevice(infile).
```

Turbo Prolog provides one predicate that enables you to initialize binary files. You do this by specifying the mode in which you want to access the files.   **Initializing Files**

Syntax:
```
filemode(SymbolicName, Mode)   (i,i), (i,o)
        (file, integer)
```

Parameters:
SymbolicName   the symbolic name used to access a file.
Mode   the file mode.

Two file modes are provided, which we describe in Table 2.23.

Table 2.23. File modes for initializing binary files

Mode	Description
0	Text mode
1	Binary mode

If you select the text mode, all carriage returns are ignored when your program reads data from the file. However, when data are written to a binary file in text mode, each linefeed character is replaced with the carriage return-linefeed combination. Files opened in binary mode are not translated.

You call the **filemode** predicate immediately after a file is opened. As an example, the following two statements illustrate the steps you need to follow to set the mode of a binary file:

```
openread(bfile, "test.exe"),
filemode(bfile, 1).
```

In this case, we are opening the binary file **test.exe** in the binary mode.

Writing to Files

We can conveniently divide the techniques for writing to Turbo Prolog files into two sections: writing to ASCII files and writing to consultable or database files.

Writing to ASCII (Text) Files

Most of the files you will use in your Turbo Prolog programs will be standard ASCII or text files. To write to such a file, you must first open the file with the **openwrite**, **openappend**, or **openmodify** predicate. Next, you have to assign the file's symbolic name to the write device by using the **writedevice** predicate.

Examples:
In this brief example, the **init_file** clause opens a file called **test.doc** for writing and then assigns the file to the standard write (output) device:

```
init_file :-
    openwrite(outfile, "test.doc"),
    writedevice(outfile).
```

When you open a file, the file pointer is set to a predetermined location in the file. All write operations then begin at this position. If you open a file with the **openwrite** predicate, the file pointer is positioned at the beginning of the file. If you use the **openappend** predicate to open an output file, the file pointer is positioned at the end of the file.

If you want to control where the file pointer is placed, you can use the **openmodify** predicate to open the file and then use the **filepos** predicate to set the file pointer.

Here's a simple clause that illustrates how you can open a file and then set the pointer to a position that you specify:

```
set_pointer :-
    openmodify(outfile, "test.doc"),
    writedevice(outfile),
    filepos(outfile, 50.0, 0).
```

After a file has been opened and initialized for the current write device, you can write to it by using either the **write** or **writef** predicate. Data are written to the file in the same manner that they would be written to the standard output device (the screen).

In this example, we show how you can store a small numeric database in a standard text file:

```
domains
    file = outfile
    rlist = real*

predicates
    write_file(integer, rlist)

clauses
    write_file(Ndata, Data) :-
      openwrite(outfile, "Sample.Dat"),
      writedevice(outfile),
      write("Data1"), nl,
      write("Sample Data"), nl,
      write(Ndata), nl,
      write(Data),
      closefile(outfile).
```

We call the **write_file** predicate with two arguments: the number of data items to write to the file and a list of real numbers. As an example, the goal

```
write_file(6,  [1.0,2.0,3.0,4.0,5.0,6.9]).
```

writes the list of six real numbers to the file.

Note that we write all data to the file using the **write** predicate. You can even use this predicate to write lists, which we illustrate with the statement:

```
write(Data)
```

Writing to Output Devices

Turbo Prolog also supports a number of file-like devices. Table 2.24 provides the output devices and device names that you can access in the same way you would access output files.

Table 2.24. Output device names

Output Device	Device Name
The screen	Screen
The line printer	Printer
The communication port 1	Com1

Example:

Our program example below reads a text file and looks for certain user-specified words. A text line that matches any of the user-specified words is simultaneously displayed on the screen and sent to the printer. To write the matching lines, we've specified the screen and printer as output devices:

```
domains
    file = infile

database
    wlist(string)

predicates
    search_file()
```

```
    get_no_words(integer)
    get_words(integer)
    for(integer, integer, integer)
    find_pos(string, string)
    repeat
    strsfind(string, string, integer)
    matchs(string, string, integer, integer)

goal
    makewindow(1,7,0,"",0,0,24,80),
    search_file.

clauses
    search_file :-
        write("Enter filename "),
        readln(Fname), nl,
        openread(infile, Fname),
        get_no_words(No),
        get_words(No),
        readdevice(infile),
        repeat,
        readln(Line),
        wlist(Word),
        find_pos(Line, Word),
        eof(infile).
    search_file :-
        closefile(infile).

    find_pos(Line, Word) :-
        strsfind(Line, Word, Pos),
        write("\nMatch in line: ", Line),
        write("\nWord matched : ", Word),
        write("\nPosition of match :", Pos), nl,
        writedevice(printer),
        write("\nMatch in line: ", Line),
        write("\nWord matched : ", Word),
        write("\nPosition of match :", Pos), nl,
        writedevice(screen).
    find_pos(_, _).
```

```
get_no_words(N) :-
   write("Enter number of search words: "),
   readint(Val),
   Val <= 100,
   Val > 0,
   N = Val.
get_no_words(N) :-
   get_no_words(N).

get_words(N) :-
   for (0, N, X),
   write("\nEnter word:  "),
   readln(Word),
  assert(wlist(Word)),
   fail.
get_words(_).

strsfind(Srcstr, Substr, Pos):-
   str_len(Srcstr, Size),  /* get length of string  */
   str_len(Substr, Ssize), /* get length of substring */
   matchs(Srcstr, Substr, Ssize, Sub1), !,
   Pos = Size - (Ssize + Sub1) + 1.

matchs(Str1, _, _, _):-   /* fail on null string */
   Str1 = "", fail.
matchs(Str1, Str2, Size, Sub1):-
   frontstr(Size, Str1, First, Rest),
   First = Str2,              /* substring matches  */
   str_len(Rest, Sub1).
matchs(Str1, Str2, Size, Sub1):-
   frontchar(Str1, _, Rest),
   matchs(Rest, Str2, Size, Sub1).

for(I, _, I).
for(I, Limit, Inc) :-
   New = I + 1,
   New < Limit,
   for(New, Limit, Inc).
```

```
repeat.
repeat :- repeat.
```

You can also use the **file_str** predicate to write a string of text to a file. This technique is the easiest way to create a text file.

Syntax:
```
file_str(FileName, String)   (i,o), (i,i)
     (string, string)
```

Parameters:
FileName   specifies the name of a DOS file.
String   a string constant or a string variable that is bound to a string.

Examples:
In the following example, the goal

```
file_str("New.dat", "line 1\nline 2\nline 3").
```

creates a file called **New.dat** and stores the specified string as:

```
line 1
line 2
line 3
```

Although you'll find this predicate useful for creating files and saving data stored in a string, you should keep in mind that **file_str** overwrites a file if the file already exists. You can, however, check to see if a file exists by using the **existfile** predicate before you attempt to write to the file. Our second example shows how you would do this.

The following example shows how the **file_str** predicate is used to write a string to a text file. This program uses the built-in **edit** predicate so you can first create a string and then specify the filename where the string is to be stored:

```
goal
    makewindow(1,7,7,"Create Data", 0,0,25,80),
    edit("", Outstr),
    write("Enter filename to store data: "),
    readln(Fname),
```

```
    file_str(Fname, Outstr),
    dir("","*.*", TempFile),
    file_str(TempFile, Str),
    display(Str).
```

We can easily modify the program above using the **existfile** predicate, which checks to see if the file exists before we overwrite it. If the file exists, the user is given two options: append data to the new file or overwrite the data. Here's the modified program:

```
predicates
    write_file(string, string)

goal
    makewindow(1,7,7,"Create Data", 0,0,25,80),
    edit("", Outstr),
    write("Enter filename to store data: "),
    readln(Fname),
    write_file(Fname, Outstr).

clauses
    write_file(F, Str) :-
      existfile(F),
      write("\nThe file ", F, " already exists."),
      write("\nSelect an option."),
      write("\n (a)ppend data"),
      write("\n (o)verwrite data"),
      readchar(Ans),
      Ans = 'a',
      file_str(F, InStr),
      concat(Instr, Str, Outstr),
      file_str(F, Outstr),
      dir("","*.*", TempFile),
      file_str(TempFile, Str),
      display(Str).
    write_file(Fname, OutStr) :-
      file_str(Fname, Outstr),
      dir("","*.*", TempFile),
      file_str(TempFile, Str),
      display(Str).
```

The first **write_file** clause tests to see if the file exists. If the file is found, the clause then asks the user to select the manner in which the file should be written. If the user chooses to append the data, the clause continues; otherwise, the clause fails, and the second clause is called to overwrite the data in the file.

In Turbo Prolog, you can also easily write the facts asserted in a database to a file. This enables you to store data in record-like structures that can be later read into a program using the **consult** predicate. Database files are easy to create because you can store data in them without opening the files or assigning them to the standard write device.

Writing to Database Files

To create a database file, you call the **save** predicate.

Syntax:
```
save(FileName)    (i)
    (string)
```

Parameter:
FileName   specifies the DOS filename, not the symbolic filename.

When your program executes the **save** predicate, all of the facts currently asserted in the database are written to the named file.

Example:
In this program, we show how you can assert a set of facts to a database, then save them to a text file using the **save** predicate.

```
domains
    file = outfile
    database
    person(string, string, integer, integer)

predicates
    write_file
    get_no_rec(integer)
    for(integer, integer, integer)

clauses
    write_file :-
      get_no_rec(N),
```

```
        for (0, N, X),
        writedevice(screen),
        write("\nEnter last name: "),
        readln(Last),
        write("\nEnter first name: "),
        readln(First),
        write("\nEnter age: "),
        readint(Age),
        write("\nEnter code: "),
        readint(Code),
        assert(person(Last,First,Age,Code)),
        fail.

write_file :-
        write("Enter filename: "),
        readln(Fname), nl,
        save(Fname).

get_no_rec(N) :-
        write("Enter number of records to write: "),
        readint(Val),
        Val <= 100,
        Val > 0,
        N = Val.

for(I, _, I).
for(I, Limit, Inc) :-
        New = I + 1,
        New < Limit,
        for(New, Limit, Inc).
```

With this program we can specify the number of data records we want to create. Note that we've used the following general format to represent each record:

```
person(<last name>, <first name>, <age>, <code>)
```

Therefore, when we write the facts to a file with the **save** predicate, the file will be stored in the following form:

```
person("Parks", "Bill", 42, 1001).
person("Bhajan", "Yogi", 82, 1002).
person("Mecham", "Ev", 58, 1003).
person("VanOmen", "Debbie", 28, 1004).
```

Turbo Prolog provides an alternative here. Instead of using the **consult** predicate to read the facts in a file created with the **save** predicate, you can use the **readterm** predicate to read each fact.

TIP

We can conveniently divide the techniques for reading Turbo Prolog files into two sections: reading from ASCII files and reading from consultable or database files.

Reading Files

To read from an ASCII or standard text file, you must first open the file with either the **openread** or **openmodify** predicate. Then, you have to assign the file's symbolic name to the read device by using the **readdevice** predicate.

Reading from ASCII Files

Example:
In this example, we use the **init_file** clause to open a file called **test.doc** for reading and then assign the file to the standard read (input) device:

```
clauses
    init_file :-
      openread(infile, "test.doc"),
      readdevice(infile).
```

When you open a file with **openread**, the file pointer is set to the beginning of the file. All read operations then begin at that position. If a file is opened with the **openmodify** predicate, you can then specify the position of the file pointer by calling the **filepos** predicate.

Examples:
This simple clause illustrates how a file is opened for reading and the file pointer is set to the end of the file:

```
clauses
    set_pointer :-
      openmodify(infile, "test.doc"),
```

```
      readdevice(infile),
       filepos(infile, 0, 1).
```

Once a file has been opened and initialized for the current read device, you can read data from the file using any of the following predicates:

- **readchar**
- **readint**
- **readln**
- **readreal**
- **readterm**

Data are read from the file in the same manner as they would be read from the standard input device (the keyboard).

The next example illustrates how you can retrieve a small numeric database from a standard text file.

```
domains
    file = infile
    rlist = real*

predicates
    read_file(integer, rlist)

clauses
    read_file(Ndata, Data) :-
      openread(infile, "Sample.Dat"),
      readdevice(infile),
      readln(FileID),
       FileID = "Data1",
      readln(Title),
      readint(Ndata),
      readterm(rlist,Data),
      closefile(infile),!.

    read_file(_, _) :-
      write("\nBad data file"),
      closefile(infile).
```

The **read_file** predicate obtains two data objects from the input file: The first is the number of values read, and the second is a list of real numbers.

You can use the **file_str** predicate—presented earlier as a method for writing a string to a file—to read a file and store the contents of the file in a string variable. This is a powerful and convenient file-reading technique, because you don't have to worry about opening the file or assigning it to the standard read device.

Reading from Text Files Using file_str

Syntax:
```
file_str(FileName, StringVariable)  (i,o), (i,i)
      (string, string)
```

Parameters:

FileName   a DOS file name.

StringVariable used to read or write data from or to a file. The data is represented as a string.

The **file_str** predicate can only read files up to 64K in size. To read a file that is larger, you must use the **openread** predicate and one of the read predicates.

Example:

Here's an example that shows how you use the **file_str** predicate to copy the contents of one text file to another:

```
goal
    makewindow(1,7,7,"Copy files", 0,0,25,80),
    write("Enter source filename: "),
    readln(Fname1), nl,
    write("Enter destination filename: "),
    readln(Fname2), nl,
    file_str(Fname1, Instr),  /* read source file */
    file_str(Fname2, Instr). /* write to file */
```

In Turbo Prolog, you can also easily read the facts saved in a database file and add them to the database of the current program. This enables you to read data that have been stored in record-like structures by the **save** predicate. With database files, your program can read them without having to open them or assign them to the standard read device.

Reading from Database Files

To read the facts in a database file, you call this predicate:

```
consult(FileName)    (i)
      (string)
```

Parameter:
FileName   a DOS filename that references a database file.

Remarks:
The argument **FileName** specifies the DOS filename, not the symbolic
filename. When this predicate executes, all of the facts currently stored in
the file are read and asserted to the database of the current program.

Examples:
Assume that we have a database file, called **dbase.1**, which contains these
facts:

```
part(car, motor).
part(bike, clutch).
part(hot_air_balloon, envelope).
part(plane, wing).
```

Now, if we declare a database section in our program as

```
database
    part(symbol, symbol)
```

we can then call the **consult** predicate, which will read the file **dbase.1** and
assert the four facts stored in the file to the database. We would call the
consult predicate like this:

```
consult("dbase.1").
```

The database file cannot contain extra characters that are not part of the
specified facts. This restriction includes extra spaces and lines. In most
respects, the database file should be treated like program code. To ensure
that a database file will be read correctly, you should use the **save** predicate
to create each database file.

The next example illustrates how you can read a database file with the
consult predicate. The database file contains facts in this format:

```
person(<last name>, <first name>, <age>, <code>)
```

After the facts are read and asserted in the database with the **consult** clause,
we can list them at the display. Here's the example:

```
domains
    file = infile
    database
    person(string, string, integer, integer)

predicates
    read_file
    get_no_rec(integer)
    for(integer, integer, integer)

clauses
    read_file :-
      write("Enter filename: "),
      readln(Fname), nl,
      consult(Fname),
      get_no_rec(N),
       for (0, N, X),
      writedevice(screen),
      retract(person(Last,First,Age,Code)),
       write("\nThe last name is: ", Last),
       write("\nThe first name is: ", First),
       write("\nThe age is: ",Age),
       write("\nThe code is: ", Code),
       fail.
    read_file.

    get_no_rec(N) :-
      write("Enter number of records to display: "),
      readint(Val),
      Val <= 100,
      Val > 0,
      N = Val.

    for(I, _, I).
    for(I, Limit, Inc) :-
```

```
New = I + 1,
New < Limit,
for(New, Limit, Inc).
```

Auxiliary Domains and Predicates

Turbo Prolog provides predefined domains for accessing I/O devices. Other predicates also are available for performing such tasks as testing for the end of a file and controlling the file pointer. We'll describe these auxiliary domains and predicates next.

Predefined File Domains

Turbo Prolog provides four predefined symbolic file domains that you can use to direct input and output to other devices, such as the keyboard and the printer.

Table 2.25 describes the complete set of domains available to you for this purpose.

Table 2.25. Predefined file domains

Domain	Device Type	Description
com1	input/output	Reads and writes to serial COM port
keyboard	input	Reads from the keyboard
printer	output	Writes to the printer
screen	output	Writes to the screen

Use these domains as arguments for either the **readdevice** or **writedevice** predicate.

Example:
The following example shows how you can use the predefined printer I/O device to send a file to the printer:

```
goal
    write("\nEnter filename: "),
    readln(Fname),
    file_str(Fname, Fstr),
    writedevice(printer),
    write(Fstr).
```

In this case, we use the **writedevice** predicate to assign the printer to the standard write (output) device. After this assignment has been made, all data written with one of the Turbo Prolog write predicates are sent to the printer.

Turbo Prolog provides the **eof** predicate, which tests the current position of a file pointer to determine whether the end of the file has been reached. If the file pointer is at the end of the file when **eof** is called, the predicate succeeds; otherwise, it fails.

Detecting the End of a File

Syntax:
```
eof(SymbolicName)    (i)
   (file)
```

Parameter:

SymbolicName   must be the symbolic name that you associate with the DOS name of an opened file.

Examples:
Typically, you use the **eof** predicate with a **repeat-fail** loop in order to read a file. Here's an example:

```
repeat,
    readdevice(infile),
    readln(Line),
    do_something(Line),
    eof(infile).
```

If we define the **repeat** predicate as

```
repeat.
repeat :- repeat.
```

the loop continues (due to the backtracking feature) until the **eof** predicate succeeds.
   Another way to use the **eof** predicate to read a file involves testing the file with the built-in **not** predicate. Here's an example:

```
clauses
    read_file :-
      readdevice(infile),
      not(eof(infile)),
```

```
    readln(Line),
   do_something(Line),
    read_file.
 read_file.
```

In this code, the first **read_file** clause calls itself recursively until the **eof** predicate succeeds (the end of the file is reached). This causes the second **read_file** clause to be called, which terminates the recursive loop.

TIP

The **eof** predicate looks for a null terminator, whereas DOS ends files with a ^Z (control Z). This can cause problems if you're using files not created by Turbo Prolog.

Reading and Moving the File Pointer

By using the **filepos** predicate to read and move a file pointer, you can gain complete control over the locations at which data are read from and written to your files. You call this predicate after you have opened a file.

Syntax:
```
filepos(SymbolicName, Position, Mode)  (i,i,i), (i,o,i)
        (file, real, integer)
```

Parameters:

SymbolicName   specifies the symbolic name of the opened file.
Position   specifies the offset position for the file pointer.
Mode   specifies the mode for positioning the file pointer.

Remarks:
The second argument, **Position**, specifies whether to read or set the position of the file pointer. If you supply the **Position** argument with a real constant or a variable bound to a real value, the file pointer is set. If the argument is a free variable, the position of the file pointer is returned.

The argument **Mode** provides the flexibility to read and set the pointer at different locations. You can supply this argument with any of the three values shown in Table 2.26.

Flushing a File Buffer

Turbo Prolog provides a built-in predicate that you use to flush the contents of an internal file buffer. When data is written to a file, it is first sent to an internal buffer, which is maintained by the Turbo Prolog system. Whenever the buffer becomes full, its contents are written to the corre-

Table 2.26. File mode arguments

Mode	Description
0	Read/set file pointer relative to top of file
1	Read/set file pointer relative to current position
2	Read/set file pointer relative to the end of file

sponding file or I/O device, such as a serial port. The **flush** predicate overrides the normal system for flushing an internal buffer.

Syntax:
```
flush(SymbolicName)   (i)
    (file)
```

Parameter:
SymbolicName   the symbolic name of an opened file.

Example:
The following example illustrates how **flush** is used to clear an internal buffer:

```
clauses
    write_data :-
        write("\nEnter name of output file "),
        readln(Fname),
        openwrite(outfile, Fname),
        window_str("\nEnter a line of text:\n"),
        readln(Text),
        writedevice(outfile),
        write(Text),
        flush(outfile),
        closefile(outfile).
```

Because data is first written to an internal buffer, the statement **write(Text)** does not guarantee that the data are actually written to the output file. When the **flush** predicate is called, however, the contents of the buffer are written to the file even if the buffer is not full.

I/O Redirection

The predefined file domains **stdin, stdout,** and **stderr** can be used to redirect input and output in standalone Turbo Prolog programs. For I/O redirection, the following two symbols are used:

< input redirection
> output redirection

When you use input redirection, all data read with one of the standard input routines, such as **readln**, are automatically read from the specified input device or file. With output redirection, on the other hand, all data are written to the named output device or file.

Using the I/O redirection feature is a two-step process. First, you must use one of the three predefined file domains with the **readdevice** or **writedevice** predicate to establish a redirection link. For example, the statement

```
readdevice(stdin)
```

sets the **stdin** device (keyboard) as the current input device for redirection. The statement

```
writedevice(stdout)
```

sets the **stdout** device (screen) as the current output device for redirection.

Once the redirection link is made using one of these domains, you can redirect input or output when a program is executed from the command line. The syntax for performing this task is:

```
program_name <input >output
```

where the terms input and output refer to the names of I/O devices or files.

TIP

You can redirect output to the printer using the predefined Turbo Prolog name for the printer (**prn**). For example, the command

```
list >prn
```

would execute the program called **list** and send its output to the active printer.

Example:

The following short program illustrates how the I/O redirection feature is used to copy the contents of one file to another:

```
predicates
    repeat

goal
    readdevice(stdin),
    writedevice(stdout),
    repeat,
    readln(Line),
    write(Line),
    eof(stdin).

clauses
    repeat.
    repeat :- repeat.
```

If this program is compiled and linked as a standalone program, you can call it using the redirection symbols to read from and write to files. For example, the command

```
cpy <finput.doc >foutput.doc
```

would copy the contents of the file **finput.doc** to the file **foutput.doc** (assuming the name of the compiled program is **cpy.exe**).

DOS Directory Access and Control

3

Introduction

In the previous section, we presented the tools and techniques you can use to construct and access files in each of the Turbo languages. In this section, we turn our attention to the functions, procedures, and predicates that the Turbo languages provide for accessing DOS directories.

The file system supported by DOS is a tree-structured directory system. As a result, you need to use special routines to access files in this system. Here's a brief sampling of some of the basic applications for which you'll need specialized file-handling routines:

- To create, move to, and remove directories
- To read and set the date and time stamps of files and directories
- To change the attributes of files and directories

Turbo BASIC

Turbo BASIC provides a set of versatile built-in routines for creating and accessing DOS directories. However, with Turbo BASIC, you can't implement predefined routines to search for directory files, or to set and/ or query file attributes.

Turbo BASIC supports a set of intrinsic DOS commands that empower you to manipulate directories. They are **CHDIR**, **MKDIR**, **RMDIR**, **FILES**, and **NAME**.

CHDIR

This command changes the current directory.

Syntax:
CHDIR pathname

Parameter:
pathname   a string that specifies a DOS directory path name.

Example:
The following brief program enables you to list the directory entries for as many as 10 subdirectories:

```
DIM Path$ (10)
CLS
```

```
DO
    INPUT "Enter number of subdirectories ";N
LOOP UNTIL (N > 0) AND (N < 11)
FOR I = 1 TO N
    PRINT "Enter path for subdirectory # ";I;
    INPUT " ? ";Path$(I)
NEXT I
ON ERROR GOTO Bad.Dir
FOR I = 1 TO N
    CLS
    CHDIR Path$(I)
    SHELL("DIR /P")
    PRINT "press any key to continue";
    A$ = INPUT$(1)
    Jump:
NEXT I
END

Bad.Dir:
    PRINT "Cannot access ";Path$(I)
    RESUME Jump
```

The above program also illustrates how you can handle bad directory names. The label **Bad.Dir** contains code to inform you that the currently requested path is invalid.

This command creates a new DOS subdirectory.   **MKDIR**

Syntax:
MKDIR pathname

Parameter:
pathname   a string that specifies a DOS directory path name.

Example:
The following brief program enables you to create subdirectories:

```
CLS
DO
    INPUT "Enter number of subdirectories ";N
```

```
LOOP UNTIL (N > 0)
ON ERROR GOTO Bad.Dir
FOR I = 1 TO N
    PRINT "Enter path for subdirectory # ";I;
    INPUT " ? ",Path$
    MKDIR Path$
NEXT I
END

Bad.Dir:
    PRINT "Cannot create ";Path$
    RESUME NEXT
```

The program above also shows how you can handle bad directory names. The label **Bad.Dir** contains code that informs you that an invalid name has been supplied to **MKDIR**.

RMDIR

This command removes DOS subdirectories.

Syntax:
```
RMDIR pathname
```

Parameter:
pathname   a string that specifies a DOS directory path name.

Example:
This brief program enables you to remove terminal subdirectories (in other words, those without nested subdirectories):

```
CLS
DO
    INPUT "Enter number of subdirectories ";N
LOOP UNTIL (N > 0)
ON ERROR GOTO Bad.Dir
FOR I = 1 TO N
    PRINT "Enter path for subdirectory # ";I;
    INPUT " ? ",Path$
    CHDIR Path$
    SHELL("DEL *.*")
    CHDIR "\" ' go to the root directory
```

```
    RMDIR Path$
    Jump:
NEXT I
END

Bad.Dir:
    PRINT "Cannot delete ";Path$
    RESUME Jump
```

The above program also demonstrates how you can handle bad directory names. The label **Bad.Dir** contains code to inform you that an invalid directory name has been supplied to **CHDIR**.

This command displays the contents of a DOS directory.   **FILES**

Syntax:
```
FILES [<filename or wildcard>]
```

Parameter:
filename   a valid DOS filename or the wildcard symbols * or ?.

Remarks:
If you don't provide an argument, **FILES** displays all of the files in the current directory. The string-typed argument enables you to select the files you want displayed.

Example:
These code lines illustrate how you can use **FILES** to display all of the .COM and .EXE files in a directory:

```
FILES "*.COM"
FILES "*.EXE"
```

The above instructions are similar to:

```
SHELL("DIR *.COM /W")
SHELL("DIR *.EXE /W")
```

This command renames a file. This statement has an interesting feature: **NAME**
NAME can move files from one directory to another on the same disk. The trick is to alter the filename simply by changing its path name.

Syntax:
```
NAME <old filename> AS <new filename>
```

Parameters:

old filename   the DOS filename of the file to be renamed.

new filename   the DOS filename for the new file.

Example:

In our example below, we exploit the file-moving feature of **NAME**. The program prompts for a filename (**press [Enter] to exit**), and the source and destination directories.

```
' Assign initial default directories
S$ = "\"
D$ = "\TBASIC\"
DO
    INPUT "Enter filename press [Enter] to exit ";F$
    IF F$ = "" THEN EXIT LOOP
    PRINT
    INPUT "Source directory ?";A$ : PRINT
    IF A$ <> "" THEN S$ = A$
    IF RIGHT$(S$,1) <> "\" THEN S$ = S$ + "\"
    INPUT "Destination directory ?";A$ : PRINT
    IF A$ <> "" THEN D$ = A$
    IF RIGHT$(D$,1) <> "\" THEN D$ = D$ + "\"
    NAME S$ + F$   AS   D$ + F$
LOOP
END
```

In the above example, Turbo BASIC examines the final character in each directory name you supply. If this last character is not a backslash (\), the program will append one.

Turbo C

Turbo C provides you with a set of useful functions to create and access DOS directories, and to search for files. To use these routines, you must include the header file **dir.h** at the beginning of your program.

These two functions obtain the name of the current directory.

getcurdir() and getcwd()

Syntax:
```
int getcurdir(int drive, char *dir_name);
```

Parameters:

drive   specifies a disk drive.

*dir_name   a string variable that holds the name of the directory.

Syntax:
```
int getcwd(char *path_name, int strlength);
```

Parameters:

*path_name   a string variable that holds the name of the directory.

strlength   the number of characters to be used to store the directory name.

Remarks:

The function **getcurdir()** determines the name of the current directory on a specified drive. The first argument, **drive**, contains a code to indicate which drive should be accessed. These codes are listed in Table 3.1.

Table 3.1. Drive codes for use with getcurdir()

Code	Drive
0	Default drive
1	A
2	B
3	C
4	D

The second argument, **dir_name**, stores the name of the current directory. This returned name does not include the drive specification and it does not begin with a backslash (\).

If you want to obtain the full path name of the current working directory, use **getcwd()**. This function gets the active directory name on the current

TIP

drive. Here, the second argument, **strlength**, specifies the size of the path name that is to be returned.

Example:
The following program displays the name of the current directory:

```
#include <dir.h>
#include <stdio.h>
main()
{
    char pathname[80];
    int drive_no = 0;

    getcurdir(drive_no, pathname);
    printf("You are in the directory: %s", pathname);
}
```

chdir()

This function changes the current directory.

Syntax:
```
int chdir(const char *new_pathname);
```

Parameter:
*new_pathname   the name of the new directory to move to.

Remarks:
The **chdir()** function tries to select the directory specified by **new_pathname** as the working directory. The path name you specify can also include the drive on which the directory can be found.

If **chdir()** succeeds in selecting the specified directory as the new working directory, a value of 0 is returned. Otherwise, **chdir()** returns a value of –1.

Example:
The following brief program enables you to list the directory entries for as many as 10 subdirectories:

```
#include <dir.h>
#include <conio.h>
#include <process.h>
```

```
main()
{
    char path[10][64];
    int i, n;

    clrscr();
    /* get number of subdirectories */
    do {
        printf("\nEnter number of subdirectories : ");
        scanf("%d", &n);
    } while ( (n < 1) || (n > 10) );
    for (i = 0; i < n; i++) {   /* get names */
        printf("\nEnter path for subdirectory # %d ",i + 1);
        scanf("%s",path[i]);
    }
    for (i = 0; i < n; i++) {
        clrscr();
        if (chdir(path[i]) == 0) {
            system("DIR /P");
            printf("\npress any key to continue");
            getch();
        }
    }
}
```

This function creates a new DOS subdirectory. **mkdir()**

Syntax:
```
int mkdir(const char *new_pathname);
```

Parameter:
*new_pathname   the name of the new directory to create.

Remarks:
The **mkdir()** function tries to create the directory specified by **new_pathname**. The path name you specify can also include the drive on which you want the directory to reside.

   If **mkdir()** succeeds in creating the specified directory, a value of 0 is returned. Otherwise, **mkdir()** returns a value of –1 to indicate that an error has occurred.

Example:

Here's a brief program that illustrates how you can use Turbo C to create subdirectories:

```c
#include <dir.h>
#include <conio.h>
#include <process.h>
main()
{
    char path[64];
    int i, n;

    clrscr();
    do {         /* get number of subdirectories */
        printf("\nEnter number of subdirectories : ");
        scanf("%d", &n);
    } while ( n < 0 );
    for (i = 1; i <= n; i++) {   /* get names */
        printf("\nEnter path for subdirectory # %d ",i);
        scanf("%s",path);
        if (mkdir(path) != 0)
         printf("\nError: Cannot create %s",path);
    }
}
```

rmdir()

This function removes DOS subdirectories.

Syntax:

```c
int rmdir(const char *path_name);
```

Parameter:

*new_pathname   the name of the new directory to remove.

Remarks:

The **rmdir()** function tries to remove the directory specified by **new_pathname**. The path name you specify can also include the drive on which the directory resides.

   If **rmdir()** succeeds in deleting the specified directory, a value of 0 is returned. Otherwise, **rmdir()** returns a value of –1 to indicate that an error has occurred. Note that to remove a directory, DOS requires the directory itself to be empty.

Example:

The following brief program enables you to remove terminal subdirectories
(in other words, those without directories):

```
#include <dir.h>
#include <conio.h>
#include <process.h>
main()
{
    char path[64];
    int i, n;

    clrscr();
  /* get number of subdirectories */
    do {
      printf("\nEnter number of subdirectories : ");
      scanf("%d", &n);
    } while ( n < 0 );
    for (i = 1; i <= n; i++) {   /* get names */
      printf("\nEnter path for subdirectory # %d ",i);
     scanf("%s",path);
      if (chdir(path) == 0)  {
        system("DEL *.*");
        chdir("\\");
        rmdir(path);
      }
      else printf("\nError: Cannot delete directory %s",path);
    }
}
```

This function renames a file and can move a file from one directory to **rename()**
another. The trick in moving a file is to include a different path name within
the new filename.

Syntax:

```
rename(const char *old_pathname, const char *new_pathname);
```

Parameters:

*old_pathname   the path name of the directory to be renamed.

*new_pathname   the path name of the new directory.

Remarks:

The **rename()** function tries to rename the file specified by **old_pathname** to **new_pathname**. The path name you specify can also include the drive on which you want the file to reside.

  If **rename()** succeeds in renaming the specified file, a value of 0 is returned. Otherwise, **rename()** returns a value of −1 to indicate that an error has occurred.

Example:

The file-moving feature of **rename()** is illustrated in this example. The program prompts for a filename (**press [Enter] to exit**), and the source and destination directories.

```c
#include <dir.h>
#include <conio.h>
#include <process.h>
#include <string.h>

main()
{
    char filename[64], dummy[64], source[64], dest[64];

    clrscr();
    do {
        printf("\nEnter filename [press [Enter] to exit ] ");
        gets(filename);
        if (strcmp(filename, "") == 0) exit(1);
        printf("\nSource directory ? ");
        gets(dummy);
        if (strcmp(dummy, "") != 0)
        strcpy(source, dummy);
        if ( source[strlen(source) - 1] != '\\')
        strcat(source, "\\");
        printf("\nDestination directory ? ");
        gets(dest);
        if ( dest[strlen(dest) - 1] != '\\')
        strcat(dest, "\\");
        strcat(source, filename);
        strcat(dest, filename);
        if (rename(source, dest) != 0)
```

```
        printf("\nError: File cannot be moved %s",source);
    } while ( 1 );
}
```

These two functions search for files or directories in a specified directory.

Syntax:

```
int findfirst(const char *pathname, struct ffblk *fdata, int attr);
int findnext(struct ffblk *fdata);
```

Parameters:

*pathname   the name of the path and the file to search for.

*fdata   the data structure where the information for the found file is stored.

attr   the attribute(s) for the file to search for.

Remarks:

You use **findfirst()** to locate the first occurrence of a file or directory. The arguments **pathname** and **attr** are used to specify the search criteria. Use **findnext()** to locate other files that match the search criteria indicated by the **findfirst()** function.

In **findfirst()**, **pathname** is the search string that you construct by using the following format:

```
[<drive>] [<directory path>] <file or directory name>
```

Note that the **drive** and **directory path** components are optional. If you omit these components, the default directory and drive are used to search for the file. You can construct the **file** or **directory name** component by using the DOS wildcard characters ***** and **?**.

The second search criterion that **findfirst()** requires is the file attribute, represented by the argument **attr()**. We've provided the available attribute codes for this argument in Table 3.2. You can use either the value or the symbol to specify an attribute. The symbols are defined in the header file **dos.h**. Note also that you can combine the values to create multiple attributes. For example, the code to search for a hidden directory is:

```
16 + 2 = 18
```

When a file is located with either **findfirst()** or **findnext()**, Turbo C returns information about the file—such as the file's name, attribute, and

Table 3.2. File attribute codes for findfirst()

Attribute	Value	Symbol
Read only	1	FA_RDONLY
Hidden file	2	FA_HIDDEN
System file	4	FA_SYSTEM
Volume label	8	FA_LABEL
Directory	16	FA_DIREC
Archive	32	FA_ARCH

size—in a special predefined structure. This structure, called **ffblk**, is defined in the header file **dir.h** as:

```
struct ffblk  {
    char ff_reserved[21];
    char ff_attrib;
    char ff_ftime;
    char ff_fdate;
    char ff_fsize;
    char ff_name[13];
};
```

When Turbo C calls **findfirst()** or **findnext()**, it passes a pointer—the argument **fdata**—to this structure. The components of the structure are filled in when either function returns.

If **findfirst()** or **findnext()** succeeds in locating the specified file, a value of 0 is returned. Otherwise, the function returns a value of –1 to indicate that an error has occurred.

Example:
In the following code segment, we use **findfirst()** and **findnext()** to illustrate how you can list all of the directories contained in the root directory:

```
if (findfirst("\\*.*", &fdata, FA_DIREC) == 0) {
    printf("\nDirectory: %s", fdata.ff_name);
    while (findnext(&fdata) == 0)
    printf("\nDirectory: %s", fdata.ff_name);
}
```

Note that we call **findfirst()** to set the search criteria and to locate the first directory. After **findfirst()** has been called, we can find the remaining directories by using **findnext()**, because the search criteria have already been set. If we need to change the search criteria, we would have to call **findfirst()** again.

This function searches the predefined MS-DOS path for a specified file-   **searchpath()**
name.

Syntax:
```
char *searchpath(const char *filename);
```

Parameter:
*filename   the name of the file to search for.

Remarks:
The search begins with the current directory. If the file is not found, Turbo C then uses the **PATH** environment variable. Each directory specified in this environment variable is searched. The search terminates when either the file is located or all of the directories have been searched.

The **searchpath()** function returns a pointer to the name of the full path where the file is located. If **searchpath()** cannot find the file, it returns the **NULL** pointer.

Example:
```
#include <stdio.h>
#include <dir.h>

main()
{
    char fname[12];
    char *path;

    printf("\nEnter filename to search for: ");
    scanf("%s", fname);
    if ( (path = searchpath(fname)) != NULL)
      printf("\nThe file is in the directory: %s", path);
    else {
      path = getenv("PATH");
      printf("\nThe file cannot be found in the current \
```

```
                          directory or the DOS path %s", path);
        }
    }
```

In this example, note that the function **getenv()** is called to obtain the name of the DOS **PATH** variable. This allows the user to see what directories have been searched in case the file cannot be found.

TIP

If you want to have greater control over which directories are searched when **searchpath()** is called, you can use the **putenv()** function to set the DOS **PATH** variable before calling **searchpath()**. For example, if you want to search for the file **test1.c** in the directories

```
\turboc
\turboc\src\version1
```

you can use the functions:

```
putenv("PATH=C:\\turboc;C:\\turboc\\src\\version1");
path = searchpath("test1.c");
```

Turbo Pascal

Turbo Pascal provides a set of useful functions to create and access DOS directories, and to search for files. To use these routines, your application program must use the standard DOS library unit. Turbo Pascal supports a set of intrinsics that you can use to manipulate DOS directories. They are **GetDir**, **ChDir**, **MkDir**, **RmDir**, and **Rename**.

GetDir

This procedure gets the current directory of a specified drive.

Syntax:
```
Procedure GetDir(Drive_Num : Byte; Var Dir_Name : String);
```

Parameters:

Drive_Num the disk drive number.
Dir_Name the name of the directory returned.

Use Table 3.3 to determine the appropriate numeric code that you use to specify drives.

Table 3.3. Drive specification codes

Code	Drive
0	Default drive
1	A
2	B
3	C
4	D

Example:
This simple program displays the name of the current directory:

```
Procedure Where_Am_I;
Var Drive_Num : Byte;
   Here : String[64];
Begin
   Drive_Num := 0; { current drive }
   GetDir(Drive_Num, Here);
   Writeln('You are in directory ',Here);
End.
```

This procedure changes the current directory.   **ChDir**

Syntax:
```
Procedure ChDir(NewPathName : String);
```

Parameter:
NewPathName   the name of the DOS directory path.

Example:
The following brief program illustrates how you can list the directory
entries for as many as 10 subdirectories:

```
Program Test_ChDir;
Uses CRT, DOS;
{$M 8912, 8912, 655350}


Const MAX_DIR = 10;
```

```
Type DirRange = 1..MAX_DIR;
Var Path : Array [DirRange] Of String[64];
    I, N : Integer;
    Ch : Char;


Begin
   ClrScr;
   Repeat
     Write('Enter number of subdirectories : ');
     Readln(N)
   Until N In [1..MAX_DIR];
   For I := 1 To N Do Begin
     Write('Enter path for subdirectory # ',I,' : ');
     Readln(Path[I])
   End;
   For I := 1 To N Do Begin
     ClrScr;
     {$I-} ChDir(Path[I]); {$I+}
     If IOResult = 0 Then Begin
       Exec('C:\COMMAND.COM','/C DIR /P');
        If DosError <> 0 Then
        Writeln('Dos Error = ',DosError);
        Write('press any key to continue');
         Ch := ReadKey;
     End;
   End;
End.
```

The **FOR** loop in the example above performs two major tasks. First, it changes the current directory using **ChDir(Path[I])**. Second, if the directory most recently changed is valid, the loop executes a copy of the DOS command line processor, which in turn executes a DOS **dir/p** command.

MkDir   This procedure creates a new DOS subdirectory.

Syntax:
```
Procedure MkDir(NewPathName : String);
```

Parameter:
NewPathName   the name of the DOS directory path.

Example:

The following brief program demonstrates how you can create subdirectories:

```
Program Test_MkDir;
Uses CRT;
Var I, N : Integer;
    Path : String[64];
Begin
    ClrScr;
    Repeat
        Write('Enter number of subdirectories : ');
        Readln(N)
    Until (N > 0);
    For I := 1 To N Do Begin
        Write('Enter path for subdirectory # ',I,' : ');
        Readln(Path);
        {$I-} MkDir(Path); {$I+}
        If IOResult <> 0 Then
        Writeln('Error: Cannot create ',Path);
    End;
End.
```

This procedure removes DOS subdirectories.   **RmDir**

Syntax:
```
Procedure RmDir(PathName : String);
```

Parameter:

PathName   the name of the DOS directory path.

Example:

The following brief program illustrates a method for removing terminal subdirectories (in other words, those without nested subdirectories):

```
Program Test_RmDir;
Uses CRT, DOS;
{$M 8912, 8912, 200000}
Var I, N : Integer;
    Path : String[64];
```

```
Begin
    ClrScr;
    Repeat
        Write ('Enter number of subdirectories : ');
        Readln (N)
    Until (N > 0);
    For I := 1 To N Do Begin
        Write ('Enter path for subdirectory # ',I,' : ');
        Readln (Path);
        {$I-} ChDir (Path); {$I+}
        If IOResult = 0 Then Begin
            Exec ('C:\COMMAND.COM','/C DEL *.*');
            If DosError = 0 Then Begin
                ChDir ('\'); { go to the root directory }
                RmDir (Path)
            End
            Else
                Writeln ('Dos Error = ',DosError);
        End;
    End;
End.
```

The **For** loop in the example above performs two major tasks: First, it changes the current directory using **ChDir(Path[I])**. Second, if the directory most recently changed is valid, the loop executes a copy of the DOS command line processor, which in turn executes a DOS **dir *.*** command.

If the latter task proceeds without any error, the program moves to the root directory (because this directory always exists). Once the root directory has been entered, the program removes the most recently deleted directory.

Rename

This procedure renames an unopened file. You need to use the **Assign** procedure along with **Rename**. The **Assign** procedure has an interesting feature that enables you to move files from one directory to another on the same disk. The trick is to include a different path name within the new filename.

Syntax:

```
Assign (<file variable>:<file-var type>,<old filename> : String);
Rename (<file variable>:<file-var type>,<new filename> : String);
```

Example:

In this example, we exploit the file-moving feature of **Rename**. The program prompts for a filename (**press [Enter] to exit**), and for the source and destination directories.

```
Program Test_Rename;
Uses CRT;
Var Error : Integer;
    Source, Destination, Filename, Dummy : String[64];
    FileVar : File;
    Stop : Boolean;

Begin
    ClrScr;
    Stop := FALSE;
    Source := '\';
    Destination := '\';
    Repeat
      Write('Enter filename [press [Enter] to exit ] ');
     Readln(Filename);
      If Filename = '' Then Exit;
      Writeln;
      Write('Enter source directory : ');
     Readln(Dummy); Writeln;
      If Dummy <> '' Then Source := Dummy;
      If Source[Length(Source)] <> '\' Then
         Source := Source + '\';
      Write('Enter destination directory : ');
      Readln(Dummy); Writeln;
      If Dummy <> '' Then Destination := Dummy;
      If Destination[Length(Destination)] <> '\' Then
         Destination := Destination + '\';
      Assign(FileVar, Source + Filename);
      {$I-} Rename(FileVar, Destination + Filename); {$I+}
      Error := IOResult;
      If Error <> 0 Then
        Writeln('Error number ',Error,' has occurred');
    Until Stop;
End.
```

The **REPEAT** loop in the above program simulates an open loop. So, you don't need to reenter the source and destination directories each time—if they are the same as the directories in the previous loop iteration. The program checks to determine whether the final character in each directory name is a backslash (\). If not, a backslash is appended.

FindFirst and FindNext

These procedures search for files or directories. They are exported from the Turbo Pascal DOS library unit.

Syntax:
```
Procedure FindFirst (DOS_Path : String; Attr : Byte;
                     Var Find : SearchRec);
Procedure FindNext (Var Find : SearchRec);
```

Parameters:

DOS_Path   the name of the DOS directory path.
Attr   the file attribute(s).
Find   the record that stores the information about the found file.

Remarks:
The **DOS_Path** is composed of an optional directory path and either an unambiguous filename or a wildcard file mask (such as ***.***). The **Attr** parameter specifies the attribute of the files and/or directories that you are seeking. The DOS library exports the file attribute shown in Table 3.4.

Table 3.4. DOS file attributes

Constant	Value
ReadOnly	$01
Hidden	$02
SysFile	$04
VolumeID	$08
Directory	$10
Archive	$20
AnyFile	$3F

You can add the above attribute values as a way to logically **AND** them. For example, if you want to search for directory entries that are **ReadOnly** and **Directory** names, you add **$01** and **$10**, which results in the **Attr** argument **$11**.

The **SearchRec** data type is a record structure exported by the DOS library. You define it this way:

```
SearchRec = Record
    Fill : Array [1..21] Of Byte; { unused }
    Attr : Byte;
    Time : LongInt;
    Size : LongInt;
    Name : String[12];
End;
```

The **Find** parameter in both **FindFirst** and **FindNext** returns the directory entry that matches the search criteria. If **Find** does not identify a matching entry, the exported integer-typed variable, **DosError**, is set to a nonzero value.

Example:

The following program prompts you for an optional directory path and search file mask. The program displays all matching directory entries:

```
Program Find_Files;
Uses CRT, DOS;
Var DOS_Path, Mask : String[80];
    Find : SearchRec; { from unit DOS }
Begin
    ClrScr;   Write('Enter DOS path -> ');
    Readln(DOS_Path); Writeln;
    Repeat
      Write('Enter file mask -> ');
      Readln(Mask); Writeln;
    Until Mask <> '';
    DOS_Path := DOS_Path + '\' + Mask;
    { look for first matching entry }
    FindFirst(DOS_Path, AnyFile, Find);
    While DosError = 0 Do Begin
      Writeln(Find.Name);
      FindNext(Find); { Find next directory entry }
    End;
End.
```

In the program above, the search begins by using **FindFirst**, which attempts to locate the first matching directory entry. If the search is successful, the value of **DosError** is set equal to zero. This enables the **WHILE** loop to execute and search for all other matching entries.

GetFAttr and GetFTime

These procedures query the attribute and time/date stamp of a file that has been assigned, but not opened. The Turbo Pascal standard DOS library unit exports these procedures.

Syntax:
```
Procedure GetFAttr(Var FileVar; Var Attr : Byte);
Procedure GetFTime(Var FileVar; Var Time : LongInt);
```

Parameters:

FileVar a file variable of any valid file type.
Attr the returned file attribute code.
Time the returned time stamp for the file.

The **Attr** parameter of **GetFAttr** matches any of the file attribute constants exported by DOS. Table 3.5 presents the constants available to you.

Table 3.5. The attribute constants

Constant	Value
ReadOnly	$01
Hidden	$02
SysFile	$04
VolumeID	$08
Directory	$10
Archive	$20
AnyFile	$3F

You unpack the **Time** parameter in the **GetFTime** procedure by using the **UnPackTime** procedure (also exported by the DOS library unit).

Syntax:
```
Procedure UnPackTime(Time : LongInt;
                Var File_Date_Time : DateTime);
```

Parameters:

Time	the packed time data.
File_Date_Time	the unpacked file and date data.

The **DateTime** is a record type, declared in the DOS library in this manner:

```
DateTime = Record
    Year,
    Month,
    Day,
    Hour,
    Min,
    Sec   : Word
End;
```

Examples

This function example returns a string message that defines the attribute of the file parameter:

```
Function Say_Attr(Var Filename : Any_String) : Any_String;
{ The program that uses this function must USE unit DOS }
Var FileVar : File; { untyped file }
    Attr : Byte;
Begin
    Assign(FileVar, Filename);
    GetFAttr(FileVar, Attr);
    If DosError <> 0 Then Begin
      Say_Attr := 'File does not exist');
      Exit;
    End;
    Case Attr Of
      $01 : Say_Attr := 'ReadOnly';
      $02 : Say_Attr := 'Hidden';
      $04 : Say_Attr := 'SysFile';
      $08 : Say_Attr := 'VolumeID';
      $10 : Say_Attr := 'Director';
      $20 : Say_Attr := 'Archive';
      $3F : Say_Attr := 'AnyFile';
    End;
End;
```

Our next example below is a procedure that returns the strings containing the image of the time and date stamps:

```
Procedure Get_Stamps(Filename : String; Var Time_Stamp,
                     Date_Stamp : String;
{ Time_Stamp is in the format hh:mm:ss
  Date_Stamp is in the format Month/Day/Year
  The program using this function must USE unit DOS }

Var Time : LongInt;
    Stamp : DateTime; { from unit DOS }
    Strng : String[10];
    FileVar : File; { use untyped file }
Begin
    Assign(FileVar, FileName);
    GetFTime(FileVar, Time);
    If DosError <> 0 Then Begin
      Time_Stamp := '00:00:00';
      Date_Stamp := '01/01/80';
       Exit;
    End;
    UnPack(Time, Stamp);
    Str(Stamp.Moth:2,Strng);
    Date_Stamp := Strng;
    Str(Stamp.Day:2,Strng);
    Date_Stamp := Date_Stamp + '/' + Strng;
    Str(Stamp.Year:4,Strng);
    Date_Stamp := Date_Stamp + '/' + Strng;
    Str(Stamp.Hour:2,Strng);
    Time_Stamp := Strng;
    Str(Stamp.Minute:2,Strng);
    Time_Stamp := Time_Stamp + ':' + Strng;
    Str(Stamp.Second:2,Strng);
    Time_Stamp := Time_Stamp + ':' + Strng;
End;
```

You create the time and date string images using the built-in Turbo Pascal **Str** routine. If the filename you supply is invalid, the time and date stamp are returned as **00:00:00** and **01/01/80**, respectively.

Turbo Prolog

Turbo Prolog provides most of the routines available in the other Turbo languages for creating and accessing directories. You can easily simulate the routines that Turbo Prolog doesn't provide by using the built-in system predicate.

This predicate gets the current directory.   **disk**

Syntax:
```
disk(PathName)     (i), (o)
    (string)
```

Parameter:

PathName   stores or returns the default drive and path name.

Remarks:

When **disk** is called, it binds the string argument to the current drive and directory. The full path that **disk** returns is formatted as:

<drive name>:<path name>

The predicate **disk** is also used to change the current directory. To change to a new directory, the argument that you pass to **disk** must be bound to the name of the destination directory. For example, to move to the directory **\prolog** on the C drive, you would call **disk** with:

```
disk("C:\\prolog").
```

You can also use the built-in **bios** predicate to change the current directory. The following predicate, called **chdir**, illustrates how this is done:

```
predicates
    chdir(string)
clauses
    chdir(Dir) :-
      Ax = $3B00,
     ptr_dword(Dir, Ds, Dx),
     bios($21, reg(Ax,0,0,Dx,0,0,Ds,0),_).
```

In this case, we call the **bios** predicate with the value $21, which indicates that we want to call interrupt 21h.

Examples:
The example we've provided below displays the name of the current directory:

```
predicates
    getdir
clauses
    getdir :-
        disk(Curdir),
        write("\nYou are in the directory ", Curdir).
```

The following example demonstrates how you can list the directory entries for as many as 10 subdirectories:

```
database
    dlist(string)
predicates
    chdir(string)
    getdir(integer)
    putdir(integer)
    list
    for(integer, integer, integer)
clauses
    list :-
      write("\nEnter number of subdirectories :"),
      readint(N),
       N > 0,
       N <= 10,
      getdir(N),
      putdir(N).
    getdir(N) :-
       for (0, N, X),
      write("\nEnter path for subdirectory "),
      readln(Path),
     assert(dlist(Path)),
       fail.
    getdir(_).
    putdir(N) :-
```

```
   for (0, N, X),
  retract(dlist(Path)),
   write("\nThe path is ", Path),
  chdir(Path),
  system("Dir"),
   fail.
 putdir(_).
 for(I, _, I).
 for(I, Limit, Inc) :-
   New = I + 1,
   New < Limit,
   for(New, Limit, Inc).
 chdir(Dir) :-
   Ax = $3B00,
   ptr_dword(Dir, Ds, Dx),
  bios($21, reg(Ax,0,0,Dx,0,0,Ds,0),_).
```

The program prompts you to enter the names of a set of subdirectories. The subdirectory names then are stored by using **asserts**. Next, the program moves to each specified directory and displays the contents of the directory by using the built-in predicate system.

Turbo Prolog does not provide you with a built-in predicate for creating **system and bios** a directory; however, you can easily write one using the **system** predicate or the **bios** predicate.

You use the **system** predicate to execute a DOS command.

Syntax:
```
system("Mkdir <directory name>").
```

As an example, you can create the directory **\prolog\source** by specifying the goal:

```
system("Mkdir \\prolog\\source").
```

You use the **bios** predicate to execute a DOS interrupt function. The code for this predicate is:

```
predicates
   mkdir(string)
clauses
```

```
mkdir(Dir) :-
    Ax = $3900,
    ptr_dword(Dir, Ds, Dx),
    bios($21, reg(Ax,0,0,Dx,0,0,Ds,0),_).
```

Turbo Prolog also does not provide a built-in predicate for removing a directory. You can, however, easily write one by using the **system** predicate or the **bios** predicate. The format for this statement is:

```
system("Rmdir <directory name> ").
```

This predicate removes the directory specified by *directory name*. As an example, you can create the directory **source** in the directory **\prolog** by writing:

```
system("Rmdir \\prolog\\source").
```

The second technique involves the use of the **bios** predicate, which allows you to execute a DOS interrupt function. The code for this predicate is:

```
predicates
    rmdir(string)
clauses
    rmdir(Dir) :-
        Ax = $3A00,
        ptr_dword(Dir, Ds, Dx),
        bios($21, reg(Ax,0,0,Dx,0,0,Ds,0),_).
```

Examples:
In the following example, we use the predicate **make** to demonstrate how you can make subdirectories:

```
predicates
    mkdir(string)
    make
    getdir(integer)
    for(integer, integer, integer)
clauses
    make :-
        write("\nEnter number of subdirectories :"),
```

```
   readint(N),
    N > 0,
    getdir(N).
  getdir(N) :-
    for (0, N, X),
   write("\nEnter path for subdirectory "),
   readln(Path),
   mkdir(Path),
    fail.
  getdir(_).
  for(I, _, I).
  for(I, Limit, Inc) :-
    New = I + 1,
    New < Limit,
    for(New, Limit, Inc).
  mkdir(Dir) :-
    Ax = $3900,
   ptr_dword(Dir, Ds, Dx),
   bios($21, reg(Ax,0,0,Dx,0,0,Ds,0),_).
```

The following example shows how you can remove terminal subdirectories from the root directory:

```
predicates
    rmdir(string)
    chdir(string)
    remove
    getdir(integer)
    for(integer, integer, integer)
clauses
    remove :-
     write("\nEnter number of subdirectories :"),
     readint(N),
     getdir(N).
    getdir(N) :-
      for (0, N, X),
     write("\nEnter path for subdirectory "),
     readln(Path),
     chdir(Path),
     system("Del *.*"),
     chdir("\\"),
```

```
        rmdir(Path),
        fail.
    getdir(_).
    for(I, _, I).
    for(I, Limit, Inc) :-
        New = I + 1,
        New < Limit,
        for(New, Limit, Inc).
    rmdir(Dir) :-
        Ax = $3A00,
        ptr_dword(Dir, Ds, Dx),
        bios($21, reg(Ax,0,0,Dx,0,0,Ds,0),_).
    chdir(Dir) :-
        Ax = $3A00,
        ptr_dword(Dir, Ds, Dx),
        bios($21, reg(Ax,0,0,Dx,0,0,Ds,0),_).
```

To remove a subdirectory, you first must remove all files that are currently stored in the subdirectory. Therefore, note that our program uses the **chdir** predicate to move into the directory to be deleted, then removes all of the files with the predicate **system("Del *.*")**. Once the files have been removed, we can move to the root directory and delete the specified subdirectory.

dir   This predicate reads and displays the files stored in a directory.

Syntax:
```
dir(<full_path>, <file_spec>, <filename>)    (i,i,o)
   (string, string, string)
```

Parameters:
full_path   the directory path to be searched.
file_spec   the search criteria. You can provide an actual filename or use the wildcard characters * and ? to generalize the search.
filename   the name of the file selected.

Remarks:
When the **dir** predicate is called, all of the filenames in the specified directory that meet the search specification are displayed in a window. You can then select a file by using the cursor positioning keys and the Return

key. The file selected is returned as the third argument. For example, the goal

```
dir("\\prolog", "*.pro", Fname).
```

would display all of the **.pro** files in the **\prolog** directory. Also, the filename that the user selects would be bound to the variable **Fname**. If you do not want to select a file, you can terminate the **dir** predicate by pressing the Esc key. In this case, the predicate would fail.

Example:
The following example illustrates how **dir** is used to list all of the files in a specified directory. If a file is selected, Turbo Prolog displays the contents of the file in a window:

```
predicates
    getfile
clauses
    getfile :-
        write("\nEnter the directory: "),
        readln(Dirname),
        dir(Dirname, "*.*", Fname),
        file_str(Fname, Str),
        display(Str).
```

In this example, we've used the built-in predicate **file_str** to convert the file into a string. This string is then used to display the file.

Turbo Prolog provides a predicate, **renamefile**, that allows you to rename a file in the current directory. This predicate, however, can't be used to move a file from one directory to another.

renamefile

Syntax:
```
renamefile(OldFile, NewFile)    (i,i)
         (string, string)
```

Parameters:
OldFile   the current name of the file to be renamed.
NewFile   the new name for the file. The old and new filenames don't include the path, because we can only rename a file in the current directory.

Example:

The following example illustrates how you can use the **dir** predicate to select a file and then rename the selected file by using **renamefile**:

```
predicates
    rename
clauses
    rename :-
        write("\nEnter the directory: "),
        readln(Dirname),
        dir(Dirname, "*.*", Fname),
        write("\nEnter new name for file"),
        readln(Nname),
        renamefile(Fname, Nname).
```

existfile and dir

These predicates offer two options for searching for a file. The first option involves using the predicate **existfile** to determine if a specified file is in the current directory. The **dir** predicate provides you with capabilities to denote both the directory and the file specification for a search.

Syntax:
```
existfile(FileName)    (i)
        (string)
```

Parameter:

FileName   the name of a valid DOS filename or a variable that is bound to a filename.

Remarks:

Because the **existfile** predicate only searches the current drive and directory, you should not specify a file path. If the specified filename is found in the current directory, **existfile** succeeds. Otherwise, it fails.

Under the second technique, you can use the **dir** predicate to perform more general file searches.

TIP

Turbo Prolog does not provide any file searching predicates that enable you to specify file attributes. You can use the **bios** predicate to write one of your own, however.

Example:

This example shows how you could use the **existfile** predicate to test to determine whether a specified file exists in the current directory.

```
predicates
    check_file
clauses
    check_file :-
        write("\nEnter the filename: "),
        readln(Str),
        existfile(Str),
        write("\nThe file ", Str, " exists").
    check_file :-
        write("\nThe file does not exist").
```

The Borland Graphic Interface (BGI)

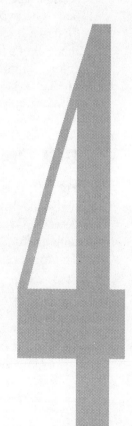

Introduction

In this section, we present the BGI (Borland Graphic Interface), which consists of the set of routines for performing both low-level and high-level graphics. All of the BGI routines are presented for Turbo C, Pascal, and Prolog. (Turbo BASIC does not support the BGI.) This section also presents the important techniques for using the BGI system to help you write graphics programs in the Turbo languages. When you refer to this section, keep in mind that the BGI is provided with all of the Turbo languages except Turbo BASIC. Our presentation is divided into two parts. First, we'll look at the basic features and components of the BGI and the fundamental programming techniques, such as working with viewports and colors, initializing the BGI, and tips for porting graphics programs from one Turbo language to another. The second part includes a short summary with examples for each of the BGI routines.

BGI Quick Overview

The BGI is a unique graphics package because it enables you to perform high- and low-level graphics using a variety of PC graphics hardware devices. Over 70 graphics routines are provided for performing tasks ranging from detecting graphics adapters to drawing and filling polygons. The routines can be divided into the following categories:

- Initialization
- Graphics query
- Graphics error handling
- Color control
- Drawing and filling
- Screen and viewport control
- Text display

The initialization routines are used to set up and shut down the graphics system and load hardware and font driver files. The graphics query routines are used to obtain information about the state of the graphics system. With these routines you can perform tasks such as determining the current drawing line style and color, obtaining the name of the installed graphics driver, and reading the color of a given pixel. The graphics error-handling routines obtain error codes and error messages for illegal operations.

A set of color processing routines are also provided for controlling both the colors of displayed pixels and the colors stored in color palettes. The drawing and filling routines provide all of the major tools needed to draw lines, arcs, circles, rectangles, polygons, pie slices, and so on. The screen and viewport control routines provide greater control over how graphics are displayed on the screen. The last category, the text display routines, offers the necessary tools for displaying different font styles and sizes in graphics mode. With these routines you can create presentation-quality graphics.

Graphic Hardware and Modes Supported

The BGI supports the three IBM standard graphic adapters—CGA, EGA, VGA—and other industry standard graphics adapters, including the Multi Color Graphics Array (MCGA), the Hercules Graphics Adapter, the AT&T 400-line Graphics Adapter, the 3270 PC Graphics Adapter, and the IBM 8514 Graphics Adapter. The complete set of adapters and modes supported is shown in Table 4.1. Note that this table contains the C, Pascal, and Prolog labels for referencing these modes. The graphics hardware drivers supported by the BGI are shown in Table 4.2. You use the names of the adapters and modes listed in these tables when you perform initialization tasks with routines such as **initgraph** and **setgraphmode**. The drivers and modes listed in Tables 4.1 and 4.2 are used in the **initgraph**, **detectgraph**, **getdrivername**, **getmodename**, **getmoderange**, **setgraphmode**, **getgraphmode**, and **getmaxmode** routines. To reference a driver or mode, you can use the symbolic name or its associated integer value.

Keep in mind that each graphic adapter supported has a set of selectable modes. The mode defines the resolution and the number of colors available.

Which Files Are Required?

To use the BGI, special files must be available in the same directory as where you are using one of the Turbo compilers. If the files are not in the current working directory, you must specify the path where the files are stored when you use one of the initialization routines, such as **initgraph**. These files are divided into three categories which are listed in Tables 4.3, 4.4, and 4.5. The BGI include files contain the definitions for all of the data structures; constants; and function, procedure, or predicate definition for each of the graphics routines. The character font files contain the defitions

Table 4.1. Adapters and modes supported by the BGI

Adapter (Driver)	Mode	Size	No. Colors	No. Pages	C	Pascal	Prolog
CGA	0	320 × 200	4	1	CGAC0	CGAC1	cgaC0
	1	320 × 200	4	1	CGAC1	CGAC2	cgaC1
	2	320 × 200	4	1	CGAC2	——	cgaC2
	3	320 × 200	4	1	CGAC3	——	cgaC3
	4	640 × 200	2	1	CGAHI	CGAHI	cgaHI
EGA	0	640 × 200	16	4	EGALO	EGALo	egaLo
	1	640 × 350	16	2	EGAHI	EGAHi	egaHi
EGA64	0	640 × 200	16	1	EGA64LO	EGA64Lo	ega64LO
	1	640 × 350	4	1	EGA64HI	EGA64Hi	ega64HI
EGAMONO	0	640 × 350	2	1	EGAMONOHI	EGAMonoHi	egaMONOHI
VGA	0	640 × 200	16	2	VGALO	VGALo	vgaLO
	1	640 × 350	16	2	VGAMED	VGAMed	vgaMED
	2	640 × 480	16	1	VGAHI	VGAHi	vgaHI
	3	640 × 480	2	1	——	VGAHi2	——
MCGA	0	320 × 200	4	1	MCGAC0	MCGAC1	mcgaC0
	1	320 × 200	4	1	MCGAC1	MCGAC2	mcgaC1
	2	320 × 200	4	1	MCGAC2	——	mcgaC2
	3	320 × 200	4	1	MCGAC3	——	mcgaC3
	4	640 × 200	2	1	MCGAMED	MCGAMed	mcgaMED
	5	640 × 480	2	1	MCGAHI	MCGAHi	mcgaHI
HERC	0	720 × 348	2	2	HERCMONOHI	HercMonoHi	hercMONOHI
ATT400	0	320 × 200	4	1	ATT400C0	ATT400C1	att400C0
	1	320 × 200	4	1	ATT400C1	ATT400C2	att400C1
	2	320 × 200	4	1	ATT400C2	——	att400C2
	3	320 × 200	4	1	ATT400C3	——	att400C3
	4	640 × 200	2	1	ATT400MED	ATT400Med	att400MED
	5	640 × 400	2	1	ATT400HI	ATT400Hi	att400HI
PC3270	0	720 × 350	2	1	PC3270HI	PC3270Hi	pc3270HI
IBM8514	0	640 × 480	256	1	IBM8514LO	IBM8514LO	ibm8514LO
	1	1024 × 768	256	1	IBM8514HI	IBM8514HI	ibm8514HI

for each of the font styles supported by the BGI. If you are using one of the built-in fonts, you must make sure the appropriate ***.chr** file is in the current directory. Otherwise, you must specify the full path name where

Table 4.2. BGI graphics drivers

| Value | Label Names | | |
	C	Pascal	Prolog
0	DETECT	Detect	detect
1	CGA	CGA	cga
2	MCGA	MCGA	mcga
3	EGA	EGA	ega
4	EGA64	EGA64	ega64
5	EGAMONO	EGAMono	egamono
6	IBM8514	IBM8514	ibm8514
7	HERCMONO	HercMono	hercmono
8	ATT400	ATT400	att400
9	VGA	VGA	vga
10	PC3270	PC3270	pc3270

the file is stored when the graphics system is initialized. The graphics driver files contain the information required to control one of the supported graphics adapters. The file that corresponds with the adapter you are using must be in the current directory; otherwise, its full path name must be specified when the driver is loaded.

Table 4.3. The BGI include files

Filename	Description
graphics.lib	The main graphics library (Turbo C)
graphics.h	The graphics header file that must be included in all programs that use graphics (Turbo C)
graph.tpu	Graphics definitions (Turbo Pascal)
grapdecl.pro	Turbo Prolog include file (Turbo Prolog)

Working with Viewports

The BGI system allows you to display graphics in selected areas of a screen, which are called *viewports*. After a viewport is defined, all of the graphics output is sent to the defined region. Figure 4.1 presents an example of how

Table 4.4. Character font files

Filename	Description
goth.chr	The font driver for the gothic character set
litt.chr	The font driver for the small character set
sans.chr	The font driver for the san serif character set
trip.chr	The font driver for the triplex character set

Table 4.5. Graphics driver files

Filename	Description
att.bgi	The driver for the AT&T graphics adapter
cga.bgi	The driver for the CGA graphics adapter
egavga.bgi	The drivers for EGA and VGA graphics adapters
herc.bgi	The driver for the Hercules graphics adapter
ibm8514.bgi	The driver for the IBM 8514 graphics adapter
pc3270.bgi	The driver for the PC3270 graphics adapter

a viewport works. Here the screen's border is drawn with a solid line and the viewport is drawn with the dashed line. The coordinates of the full screen are (0, 0, 639, 199) and the coordinates of the viewport are (250, 50, 400, 150). When graphics are displayed, the upper left corner of the viewport is treated as the origin (0,0). This means that if a line is drawn with coordinates, such as

```
line(0,0,50,50);
```

the line will be drawn starting from the upper left corner of the viewport instead of the upper left corner of the screen.

By default, the viewport is initialized to the boundary of the full screen when the BGI is initialized. To define a different viewport, you must use the **setviewport** routine.

TIP

One of the main advantages of using viewports is that you can easily both clip and move graphic objects and thus easily create animation effects. *Clipping* means that the parts of a graphic object, such as a rectangle, are

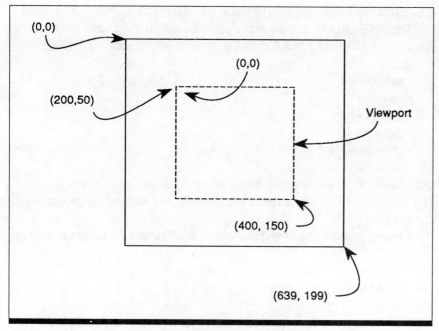

Figure 4.1. Accessing a viewport

not drawn if they extend beyond the region of a defined viewport. All of the graphics drawing and query routines are designed to work with viewports. There are, however, a few routines that are very useful for accessing and initializing viewports. These routines are:

- **clearviewport**
- **getviewsettings**
- **getx**
- **gety**
- **setviewport**

Working with Colors

To use the color drawing and filling capabilities of the BGI, it is necessary for you to understand how colors are displayed on your PC's screen. The screen is divided into discrete units called *pixels*. Each pixel is an addressable memory location; pixels are arranged like a two-dimensional array with rows and columns. Because these pixels can be displayed in different colors, we are able to draw and fill graphic objects in colors.

The BGI provides five main routines for setting and reading the foreground and background drawing colors, which are:

- **setbkcolor**
- **setcolor**
- **getbkcolor**
- **getcolor**
- **getmaxcolor**

Only one foreground and one background color can be selected at a time. The available colors are stored in what is called a *color palette*, which we'll discuss next.

When a graphic object is drawn, such as a line or a rectangle as shown:

```
line(100,100, 200, 200);
rectangle(40,40, 80, 110);
```

the current selected drawing color serves as an index to the color palette. (You can think of the color palette as a table.) The palette actually stores the value required to display a pixel in the selected color. To see how this system works, study Figure 4.2. As indicated by this illustration, only the

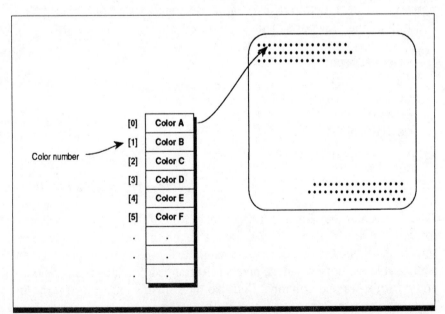

Figure 4.2. Indexing colors

colors stored in the current palette can be displayed. The BGI provides special routines for accessing the color palette. These routines are:

- **setpalette**
- **setallpalette**
- **getpalette**
- **getdefaultpalette**
- **getpalettesize**
- **setrgbcolor**

The number of colors that can be displayed at the same time is determined by the size of the current color palette. Each graphics adapter supports a different size color palette; however, the first entry in the palette table always functions as the background color. As an example, the color palette for the CGA adapter contains four colors, and the palette for the EGA adapter contains sixteen colors. We'll present the colors for the CGA, EGA, and VGA adapters in the following two discussions.

CGA Colors

The CGA adapter supports two modes: low resolution and high resolution. In the low resolution mode, four different colors can be displayed at the same time. The colors that are available are listed in Table 4.6 (modes 0 to 3). In the high resolution mode, only two colors can be displayed, and the background color must always be black. The foreground color can be set to any of the colors listed in Table 4.7.

In the low resolution mode, the foreground colors are predefined. For example, if you choose mode 1 as shown in Table 4.6, the foreground colors

Table 4.6. Available CGA colors

Mode	Background Color (0)	Foreground Colors (1,2,3)
0	User Selectable	light green, light red, yellow
1	User Selectable	light cyan, light magenta, white
2	User Selectable	green, red, brown
3	User Selectable	cyan, magenta, light gray
4	Black	User Selectable (1)

are light cyan, light magenta, and white. You can, however, choose your own background color by using any of the colors in Table 4.7. A background color is selected by using the **setbkcolor** routine. For example, the command

```
setbkcolor(MAGENTA);
```

would set the background color to magenta.

Table 4.7. Available background colors (CGA)

| Color # | Symbolic Name | | |
	C	Pascal	Prolog
0	BLACK	Black	black
1	BLUE	Blue	blue
2	GREEN	Green	green
3	CYAN	Cyan	cyan
4	RED	Red	red
5	MAGENTA	Magenta	magenta
6	BROWN	Brown	brown
7	LIGHTGRAY	LightGray	lightgray
8	DARKGRAY	DarkGray	darkgray
9	LIGHTBLUE	LightBlue	lightblue
10	LIGHTGREEN	LightGreen	lightgreen
11	LIGHTCYAN	LightCyan	lightcyan
12	LIGHTRED	LightRed	lightred
13	LIGHTMAGENTA	LightMagenta	lightmagenta
14	YELLOW	Yellow	yellow
15	WHITE	White	white

TIP

The different foreground colors (modes 0 to 3) in the low resolution mode can be selected by using the **setgraphmode** routine. If you are using the CGA in high resolution mode, you set the foreground color using the **setbkcolor** routine. This might seem like the opposite of what you are suppose to do; however, in the high resolution mode, the foreground color is treated as the background color. If you are in the high resolution mode and you use the **setcolor** routine to change the foreground color, it will not have any effect.

The EGA and VGA adapters are much more versatile than the CGA. Both of these adapters provide a color palette that is completely definable by the user. The color palette contains 16 entries; however, there are 64 colors available to choose from. The default color set consists of the colors listed in Table 4.7.

EGA and VGA Colors

Because its color palettes can be altered, the BGI provides a set of routines for accessing color palettes. These routines are:

- **getmaxcolor**
- **getpalette**
- **getpalettesize**
- **getdefaultpalette**
- **setpalette**
- **setallpalette**

The **getmaxcolor** routine determines the maximum color value stored in a palette, and **getpalette** returns the set of codes for the colors stored in the palette. The other two palette query routines, **getpalettesize** and **getdefaultpalette**, return the size of the current palette and the settings for the default palette, respectively. The **setpalette** and **setallpalette** routines place new colors in the palette.

The BGI provides a set of constants for selecting some of the EGA colors. These constants, along with their associated values, are listed in Table 4.8.

Steps for Using the BGI

To use the BGI routines, there are a few steps that you must follow. We'll present these steps in the order in which they must be followed.

Before any of the BGI graphics drawing routines can be used, you must initialize the graphics system by calling the **initgraph** routine. This routine loads the appropriate graphics driver file and sets the mode of the graphics adapter that is installed in your computer.

Step 1: Initialize the Graphics System

The **initgraph** routine can be called in one of two ways: manual mode and autodetection mode. In the manual mode you are required to specify the name and modes (integer codes) of the graphics driver you wish to load. As an example, the following statements illustrate how an EGA driver is initialized in each of the three Turbo languages:

Table 4.8. Available background colors (EGA)

Color #	C	Symbolic Name Pascal	Prolog
0	EGA_BLACK	EGABlack	ega_BLACK
1	EGA_BLUE	EGABlue	ega_BLUE
2	EGA_GREEN	EGAGreen	ega_GREEN
3	EGA_CYAN	EGACyan	ega_CYAN
4	EGA_RED	EGARed	ega_RED
5	EGA_MAGENTA	EGAMagenta	ega_MAGENTA
7	EGA_BROWN	EGABrown	ega_BROWN
20	EGA_LIGHTGRAY	EGALightGray	ega_LIGHTGRAY
56	EGA_DARKGRAY	EGADarkGray	ega_DARKGRAY
57	EGA_LIGHTBLUE	EGALightBlue	ega_LIGHTBLUE
58	EGA_LIGHTGREEN	EGALightGreen	ega_LIGHTGREEN
59	EGA_LIGHTCYAN	EGALightCyan	ega_LIGHTCYAN
60	EGA_LIGHTRED	EGALightRed	ega_LIGHTRED
61	EGA_LIGHTMAGENTA	EGALightMagenta	ega_LIGHTMAGENTA
62	EGA_YELLOW	EGAYellow	ega_YELLOW
63	EGA_WHITE	EGAWhite	ega_WHITE

```
/* Turbo C */
graphdriver = EGA;
graphmode = EGAHI;
initgraph(&graphdriver, graphmode, "");
```

```
{Turbo Pascal}
GraphDriver = EGA;
GraphMode = EGAHi;
InitGraph(GraphDriver, GraphMode, '');
```

```
/* Turbo Prolog */
initgraph(ega, egaHI, GraphDriver, GraphMode, "")
```

With the autodetection mode you can initialize the appropriate driver for the currently installed graphics adapter without specifying its name. In this mode, the **initgraph** routine calls the **detectgraph** routine to determine which graphics adapter is installed. An example of how the autodetection feature is used is presented later.

Before you initialize the graphics system, you can call the **detectgraph** routine to determine which graphics adapter is currently installed. This routine returns the integer code for your system's graphics adapter and its highest resolution mode.

TIP

Once the graphics system is initialized, you can call any of the drawing, filling, system query, and initialization routines. You can even switch back and forth between a graphics drawing mode and the standard text mode without having to initialize the graphics system each time.

Step 2:
Perform Graphics
Commands

After a graphics driver is installed, the BGI enables you to change graphics modes for the installed driver by calling the **setgraphmode** routine. This routine is often used with **restorecrtmode** for switching back and forth between graphics and text modes.

TIP

After you are done using the BGI routines, you should always call **closegraph** to shut down the graphics system. This routine removes the graphics driver from memory and returns the screen to its default video mode (text).

Step 3: Close
Down the
Graphics System

Examples:

Here is an example program presented in each Turbo language that illustrates the three basic steps required to initialize the graphics system and display graphics.

```
/* Turbo C */
/* graphics.h is required to use graphics */
#include <graphics.h>
main()
{
    /* DETECT is defined in graphics.h */
    int graphdriver = DETECT;
    int graphmode;

    /* Step 1 */
    /* initialize the graphics system */
    initgraph(&graphdriver, &graphmode, "");

    /* Step 2 */
    rectangle( 0, 0, 639, 199 );
```

```
        /* draw circle with radius of 100 units */
        circle(320,100,100);
        getch();
        /* Step 3 */
        closegraph();
}
```

```
Program Init_Demo;         {Turbo Pascal}
Uses Graph;
Var
     GraphDriver, GraphMode : Integer;
Begin
       {Step 1}
     GraphDriver := Detect;
     initgraph(GraphDriver, GraphMode, "");
       {Step 2}
     Rectangle( 0, 0, 639, 199 );
         {draw circle with radius of 100 units}
     Circle(320,100,100);
     Readln;
       {Step 3}
     CloseGraph;
End.
```

```
include "GRAPDECL.PRO"         /* Turbo Prolog */
predicates
     init_demo
clauses
     init_demo :-
       /* Step 1 */
       /* initialize the graphics system */
         initgraph(detect, 0, GraphDriver, GraphMode, ""),
       /* Step 2 */
         rectangle( 0, 0, 639, 199 ),
       /* draw circle with radius of 100 units */
         circle(320,100,100),
         readchar(_),
       /* Step 3 */
         closegraph.
```

Loading Graphics and Font Drivers

A graphics driver is typically loaded at run-time using the **initgraph** routine, as we discussed previously. The font driver files are also loaded at run-time whenever a particular font style is selected. When the graphics or font driver is loaded, memory is allocated for the driver, and the appropriate **.bgi** or **.chr** file is loaded from disk. Of course, this process can slow down the execution of a graphics program. In addition, if you write a program that uses the BGI features and you run this program on other computer systems, you must ensure that the appropriate driver files are available on the new system. To get around this problem, you can link the graphics device drivers and font drivers into your executable program. We'll discuss these techniques next.

Using the Linking Method

The method for linking driver files is different for each of the three languages; thus, we'll treat each separately.

Turbo C

In Turbo C you can link one or more driver files using the **bgiobj** utility. The technique consists of converting the **.bgi** and **.chr** files you wish to use into **.obj** files. Converting a driver or font file into an object file is a simple process. You simply call the **bgiobj** utility with the following general syntax:

```
bgiobj <driver filename>
```

Once the object files are created, you can add them to the main graphics library **graphics.lib** with the following statement:

```
tlib graphics +<object filename> [+ <object filename> ...]
```

If you don't want to add the driver object files to the graphics library, you must add them to the list of files in your linker project file so that they are included when your program is linked.

The last step involves registering the drivers in your graphics program. For this task, two routines are provided:

- **registerbgidriver** — registers a graphics hardware driver
- **registerbgifont** — registers a font driver

The following programs illustrate how the drivers are registered in a graphics program with these routines:

```
#include <graphics.h>   /* Turbo C */
main()
{
    /* DETECT is defined in graphics.h */
    int graphdriver = DETECT;
    int graphmode;

    /* must register driver first */
    if (registerbgidriver(EGAVGA_driver) < 0) exit(1);
    if (registerbgifont(small_font) < 0) exit(1);
    initgraph(&graphdriver, &graphmode, "");
    rectangle( 0, 0, 639, 199 );
    outtextxy(100,100, "Text displayed in small font");
    getch();
    closegraph();
}
```

Turbo Pascal

The procedure for linking a graphics driver file in Turbo Pascal is similar to the one used in Turbo C. Here a driver or font file must be converted into a **.obj** file using the **BINOBJ** utility. The syntax for this conversion tool is:

```
BINOBJ <source filename> <object filename> <public name>
```

where the source file is one of the **.bgi** or **.chr** files. The public name is the user-defined name for the procedure that is linked in as the driver routine. As an example, the following statements illustrate how both a graphics driver and a font file are converted:

```
BINOBJ egavga.bgi egavga EGAVGADriver
BINOBJ litt.chr litt SmallFont;
```

The next step involves creating a unit that links the drivers into a single
module. The following interface unit should be compiled:

```
Unit Drivers;
Interface
Procedure EGAVGADriver;
Procedure SmallFont;
Implementation
Procedure EGAVGADriver; External;
{$L EGAVGA.OBJ}
Procedure SmallFont; External;
{$L LITT.OBJ}
End;
```

The last step consists of writing a program that uses the **RegisterBGIFont**
and **RegisterBGIDriver** routines to register the drivers. The following
program performs this step:

```
Program Driver_Demo;         {Turbo Pascal}
Uses Graph, Drivers;
Var GraphDriver, GraphMode : Integer;
Begin
    If RegisterBGIDriver(@EGAVGADriver) < 0 Then Exit;
    If RegisterBGIFont(@SmallFont) < 0 Then Exit;
    GraphDriver := Detect;
    Initgraph(GraphDriver, GraphMode, "");
    Rectangle( 0, 0, 639, 199 );
    OuttextXY(100,100, "Text displayed in small font");
    Readln;
    CloseGraph;
End.
```

Turbo Prolog

Turbo Prolog uses a different system for linking graphics hardware and font
drivers than C and Pascal. To link in a driver you must use one of the

bgidriver and/or **bgifont** directives in your program to inform the compiler that a linked-in driver is to be used. The following program illustrates how these directives are used:

```
bgidriver "_EGAVGA_driver_far"
bgifont "_small_font_far"
include "GRAPDECL.PRO"

predicates
    driver_demo
clauses
    driver_demo:-
        initgraph(detect, 0, GraphDriver, GraphMode, ""),
        rectangle( 0, 0, 639, 199 ),
        outtextxy(100,100, "Text displayed in small font"),
        readchar(_);
        closegraph().
```

To compile this example and create a standalone program, you must also link in the graphics library **BGI.LIB**. This is done by specifying the graphics library with the *Options/Link* menu item in the Turbo Prolog integrated environment. In Turbo Prolog, it is not necessary to register the drivers as is done in C and Pascal.

What to Do if Something Goes Wrong

If you suspect a problem after loading a graphics driver or performing one of the BGI drawing or initialization routines, you can call **graphresult** (Turbo C and Pascal). This routine returns an integer error code for the last graphics routine called. The error codes supported are listed in Table 4.9.

Table 4.9. Graphics error codes

Code	Language	Description
0	C and Pascal	No error
−1	C and Pascal	Graphics not installed
−2	C and Pascal	Graphics hardware not detected
−3	C and Pascal	Device driver file not found
−4	C and Pascal	Invalid device driver file

Table 4.9. Graphics error codes (continued)

Code	Language	Description
–5	C and Pascal	Not enough memory to load driver
–6	C and Pascal	Out of memory in scan fill
–7	C and Pascal	Out of memory in flood fill
–8	C and Pascal	Font file not found
–9	C and Pascal	Not enough memory to load font
–10	C and Pascal	Invalid graphics mode for driver
–11	C only	Graphics error
–12	C only	Graphics I/O error
–13	C only	Invalid font file
–14	C only	Invalid font number
–15	C only	Invalid device number
–18	C only	Invalid version number

Turbo Prolog treats graphics errors differently than Turbo C and Pascal. If an error is detected in Turbo Prolog, the program stops executing and an error message is displayed. The error messages are listed in Table 4.10.

Table 4.10. Turbo Prolog error messages

Code	Message
6000	BGI graphics not installed
6001	Graphics hardware not detected
6002	Device driver file not found
6003	Invalid device driver file
6004	Not enough memory to load driver
6005	Out of memory in scan fill
6006	Out of memory in flood fill
6007	Font file not found
6008	Not enough memory to load font
6009	Invalid graphics mode for selected driver
6010	Graphics error
6011	Graphics I/O error
6012	Invalid font file
6013	Invalid font number
6014	Invalid device number

Tips for Porting Programs

If you are using the BGI routines in one of the Turbo languages and you wish to rewrite your program in one of the other languages, here are some important tips to keep in mind.

No BASIC Support

Remember that Turbo BASIC does not provide any of the BGI routines. Graphics commands are provided for performing limited drawing tasks, such as drawing lines and circles; however, they are not compatible with the BGI routines.

Error Handling

Each of the languages is different in the way that graphics errors are handled. Turbo C and Pascal are very similar; however, there are some slight differences in the error codes that are supported. Turbo Prolog uses a different error-handling technique than C and Pascal. Turbo Prolog does not provide the **graphresult** or **grapherrormsg** routines that are found in C and Pascal. Whenever a graphics error is encountered in a Prolog program, the program stops executing and the error message is displayed. Programs written in C and Pascal continue to execute when a graphics error is produced unless the error is a fatal error.

Using Data Structures

All of the Turbo languages provide special predefined data structures to support the BGI routines. The structures provided with Turbo C and Pascal are very similar; however, the names used for the components of some of the structures are not always compatible between the two languages. Make sure that you check the names of all data structure components when switching programs between C and Pascal.

In Turbo Prolog, the data structures used are represented as lists; therefore, some conversion is required if you are switching between C or Pascal and Prolog.

The BGI Routines

The BGI provides over 70 graphics routines for tasks ranging from initializing graphics hardware to drawing and filling basic shapes. The complete set of routines that are provided with Turbo C, Pascal, and Prolog are listed in Table 4.11.

Table 4.11. BGI routines for the three languages

Routine	Description
Arc	Draws a circular arc
Bar	Draws a rectangular bar
Bar3D	Draws a 3-D bar
Circle	Draws a circle
ClearDevice	Clears the graphics screen
ClearViewPort	Clears the active viewport
CloseGraph	Shuts down the graphics
DetectGraph	Checks hardware for graphics driver and mode
DrawPoly	Draws a polygon
Ellipse	Draws an ellipse
FillEllipse	Draws and fills an ellipse
FillPoly	Draws and fills a polygon
FloodFill	Flood-fills a bounded region
GetArcCoords	Gets the coordinates to the recent arc command
GetAspectRatio	Determines the current aspect ratio
GetBkColor	Gets the current background color
GetColor	Gets the current drawing color
GetDefaultPalette	Obtains the current color palette in use
GetDriverName	Obtains name of current graphics driver
GetFillPattern	Copies a fill pattern into memory
GetFillSettings	Gets the current fill pattern and color
GetGraphMode	Obtains the current graphics mode
GetImage	Copies a screen bit image into memory
GetLineSettings	Gets line setting information
GetMaxColor	Obtains the highest color in the current color palette
GetMaxMode	Obtains maximum mode name for a given driver
GetMaxX	Obtains maximum horizontal coordinate
GetMaxY	Obtains maximum vertical coordinate
GetModeName	Obtains name of a graphics mode
GetModeRange	Obtains the range of modes supported by the active graphics adapter
GetPalette	Obtains information about the colorpalette
GetPaletteSize	Gets the size of the color palette
GetPixel	Gets the color of a pixel

Table 4.11. BGI routines for the three languages (continued)

Routine	Description
GetTextSettings	Obtains information about current text settings
GetViewSettings	Gets information about the current viewport
GetX	Gets the current horizontal coordinate
GetY	Gets the current vertical coordinate
GraphDefaults	Resets all graphics to default settings
GraphErrorMsg	Returns an error message string
_GraphFreeMem	Deallocates user-modifiable graphics memory
_GraphGetMem	Allocates user-modifiable graphics memory
GraphResult	Obtains an error code for last invalid graphics call
ImageSize	Obtains number of bytes needed to store a bit image
InitGraph	Initializes the graphics system
InstallUserDriver	Installs a user graphics driver
InstallUserFont	Installs a user font style
Line	Draws a line
LineRel	Draws a line using relative coordinates
LineTo	Draws a line from current position to a new position
MoveRel	Moves the current position a relative distance
MoveTo	Moves the current position to a new position
OutText	Displays a text string at current position
OutTextXY	Displays a text string at specified position
PieSlice	Draws and fills a pie slice
PutImage	Copies a bit image onto the screen
PutPixel	Displays a pixel
Rectangle	Draws a rectangle
RegisterBgiDriver	Registers a linked-in graphics driver
RegisterBgiFont	Registers a linked-in stroked font
RestoreCRTMode	Restores the screen to its original mode
Sector	Draws and fills an elliptical pie slice
SetActivePage	Sets active page for graphics display
SetAllPalette	Changes all palette colors
SetAspectRatio	Changes the default aspect ratio
SetBkColor	Sets the background color
SetColor	Sets the active drawing color
SetFillPattern	Selects a user-defined fill pattern
SetFillStyle	Selects a fill pattern and color
SetGraphBufSize	Sets the size of the internal graphics buffer

Table 4.11. BGI routines for the three languages (continued)

Routine	Description
SetGraphMode	Sets the system to graphics mode
SetLineStyle	Sets the current line width and style
SetPalette	Changes a palette color
SetRGBColor	Changes one color in the palette for RGB-type displays
SetRGBPalette	Changes a palette for an RGB type monitor
SetTextJustify	Sets the text justification style
SetTextStyle	Sets the current text style
SetUserCharSize	Sets the user-defined character size
SetViewPort	Sets the current viewport
SetVisualPage	Sets the visual graphics page number
SetWriteMode	Sets the writing mode for line drawing
TextHeight	Obtains the height of a text string
TextWidth	Obtains the width of a text string

Next, we'll provide a quick reference for the complete set of BGI routines. To use any of these routines in Turbo C, include the statement

```
#include <graphics.h>
```

at the beginning of your program. In C, the file **graphics.h** contains the data structure definitions and the function prototypes for all of the BGI routines.

In Turbo Pascal, you must include the following unit:

```
Uses Graph;
```

If you want to see the names of all the constants and type declarations for Turbo Pascal, you should examine the file **GRAPH.TPU**.

Finally, in Turbo Prolog, you must include the following file at the start of your program:

```
include "GRAPDECL.PRO"
```

This file contains all of the definitions for Prolog and should be stored in the same directory you are compiling your program in.

arc

Draws a circular arc at a specified starting point (center) with a fixed radius. The arc is drawn from a start angle to a stop angle.

Syntax:

```
void far arc(int x, int y, int stangle, int endangle, int radius);
Procedure Arc(X, Y : Integer; StAngle, EndAngle, Radius: Word);
arc(X, Y, StAngle, EndAngle, Radius)      (i,i,i,i,i)
    (integer, integer, integer, integer, integer)
```

Parameters:

x, y   the center of the arc specified in absolute coordinates.
stangle   the starting angle specified in degrees.
endangle   the ending angle specified in degrees.
radius   the radius specified in pixels.

Examples:

The following examples illustrate how a set of different sized arcs can be drawn with the **arc** routine.

```
#include <graphics.h>            /* Turbo C */
#define MAX_ARCS    5            /* draw five arcs */

main()
{
    int graphdriver = DETECT, graphmode;   /* autodetection */
    int i, first[MAX_ARCS], last[MAX_ARCS], radius[MAX_ARCS];

    initgraph(&graphdriver, &graphmode, ""); /* initialize */
    first[0] = 0;
    last[0] = radius[0] = 10;
    for (i = 1; i < MAX_ARCS; i++) {
      first[i] = first[i-1] + 25;
      last[i] = last[i-1] + 35;
      radius[i] = 10 * (i+1);
    }
    for (i = 0; i < MAX_ARCS; i++)
       arc(100, 100, first[i], last[i], radius[i]);
    getch();
    closegraph();
}
```

```
Program Draw_Arcs;    {Turbo Pascal}
Uses Graph;
Const
    MAX_ARCS = 5;
Var
    GraphDriver, GraphMode, I : Integer;
    First, Last, Radius : Array [1..MAX_ARCS] Of Word;
Begin
    GraphDriver := Detect;
    InitGraph(GraphDriver, GraphMode, '');
    First[1] := 0;
    Last[1] := 10;
    Radius[1] := 10;
    For I := 2 To MAX_ARCS Do Begin
        First[I] := First[I-1] + 25;
        Last[I] := Last[I-1] + 35;
        Radius[I] := 10 * I;
    End;
    For I := 1 To MAX_ARCS Do
        Arc(100,100, First[I],Last[I],Radius[I]);
    Readln;
    CloseGraph;
End.

include "GRAPDECL.PRO"       /* Turbo Prolog */
predicates
    draw_arcs
    for(integer, integer, integer)
clauses
    for (Init, _, Init).
    for (I, Limit, Next) :-        /* simulated for loop */
        I2 = I + 1,
        I2 < Limit,
        for (I2, Limit, Next).
    draw_arcs :-
        initgraph(detect, 0, GraphDriver, GraphMode, ""),
        for (0, 5, I),
        A = I * 25, B = 10 + I * 35, C = 10 + I * 10,
        arc(100,100, A, B, C),
        fail.
```

```
draw_arcs :-
    readchar(_),
    closegraph.
```

Reference:
circle, ellipse, getarccoords, getaspectratio, pieslice, sector, setaspectratio

Remarks:
This routine uses the aspect ratio of the active graphics driver and mode to ensure that the arc drawn is as round and as smooth as possible. You can read and set the aspect ratio by calling **getaspectratio** or **setaspectratio**. To draw an arc as a full circle, make sure the start and stop angles cover a span of 360 degrees.

bar

Draws a filled-in rectangular bar with the current drawing color and fill pattern.

Syntax:
```
void far bar(int left, int top, int right, int bottom);
Procedure Bar(Left, Top, Right, Bottom : Integer);
bar(Left, Top, Right, Bottom)        (i,i,i,i)
    (integer, integer, integer, integer)
```

Parameters:
left, top   the upper left corner of the bar.
right, bottom the lower right corner.

Examples:
See **bar3d**.

Reference:
bar3d, line, rectangle, setcolor, setfillpattern, setfillstyle

Remarks:
The **bar** routine does not draw an outline for a bar. If you need an outline, use the **rectangle** or **bar3d** routine.

bar3d

Draws a filled-in 3-D rectangular bar with the current drawing color and fill pattern.

Syntax:

```
void far bar3d(int left, int top, int right, int bottom,
               int depth, int topflag);
Procedure bar3d(Left, Top, Right, Bottom : Integer;
               Depth : Word, TopFlag : Boolean);
bar3d(Left, Top, Right, Bottom, Depth, TopFlag)    (i,i,i,i,i,i)
      (integer, integer, integer, integer, integer, integer)
```

Parameters:

left, top	the upper left corner of the bar.
right, bottom	the lower right corner.
depth	the 3-D depth of the bar specified in pixels.
topflag	indicates if a 3-D top is used for the bar. A nonzero value specifies that a top is drawn.

Examples:

The following examples illustrate how both 2-D and 3-D bars are drawn
with the **bar** and **bar3d** routines.

```
#include <graphics.h>         /* Turbo C */
main()
{
    int graphdriver = DETECT, graphmode;   /* autodetection */

    initgraph(&graphdriver, &graphmode, "");
    setfillstyle(SOLID_FILL, RED);
    bar(100, 100, 140, 160);             /* draw 2-D bar */
    setfillstyle(LINE_FILL, CYAN);
    bar3d(160, 100, 190, 160, 6, 1); /* 3-D bar with top */
    bar3d(50, 100, 80, 160, 5, 0);   /* 3-D bar without top */
    getch();
    closegraph();
}


Program Draw_Bars;    {Turbo Pascal}
Uses Graph;
Var
    GraphDriver, GraphMode : Integer;
Begin
    GraphDriver := Detect;
```

```
        InitGraph(GraphDriver, GraphMode, '');
        SetFillStyle(SolidFill, Red);
        Bar(100, 100, 140, 160);               {draw 2-D bar}
        SetFillStyle(LineFill, Cyan);
        Bar3d(160, 100, 190, 160, 6, True);    {3-D bar with top}
        Bar3d(50, 100, 80, 160, 5, False);     {3-D bar without top}
        Readln;
        CloseGraph;
    End.


    include "GRAPDECL.PRO"      /* Turbo Prolog */
    predicates
        draw_bars
    clauses
        draw_bars :-
            initgraph(detect, 0, GraphDriver, GraphMode, ""),
            setfillstyle(solid_FILL, red),
            bar(100, 100, 140, 160),           /* draw 2-D bar */
            setfillstyle(line_FILL, cyan),
            bar3d(160, 100, 190, 160, 6, 1),   /* 3-D bar with top */
            bar3d(50, 100, 80, 160, 5, 0),     /* 3-D bar without top */
            readchar(_),
            closegraph.
```

Reference:
bar, line, rectangle, setcolor, setfillstyle

circle

Draws a circle with a fixed radius at a specified starting point (center). The circle is drawn in the current drawing color.

Syntax:
```
void far circle(int x, int y, int radius);
Procedure Circle(X, Y : Integer; Radius: Word);
circle(X, Y, Radius)       (i,i,i)
        (integer, integer, integer)
```

Parameters:
x, y   the center of the circle specified in absolute coordinates.
radius the radius specified in pixels.

Examples:

Each example draws a circle with a radius of 50 pixels.

```
#include <graphics.h>            /* Turbo C */
main()
{
    int graphdriver = DETECT, graphmode;   /* autodetection */

    initgraph(&graphdriver, &graphmode, "");
    circle(100, 100, 50);
    getch();
    closegraph();
}


Program Draw_Circle;    {Turbo Pascal}
Uses Graph;
Var
    GraphDriver, GraphMode : Integer;
Begin
    GraphDriver := Detect;
    InitGraph(GraphDriver, GraphMode, '');
    Circle(100,100, 50);
    Readln;
    CloseGraph;
End.


include "GRAPDECL.PRO"      /* Turbo Prolog */
predicates
    draw_circle
clauses
    draw_circle :-
        initgraph(detect, 0, GraphDriver, GraphMode, ""),
        circle(100,100, 50),
        readchar(_),
        closegraph.
```

Reference:

arc, ellipse, getaspectratio, getarccoords, pieslice, sector, setaspectratio, setlinestyle

Remarks:
Circles, arcs, ellipses, and pie slices can only be drawn with the default line style (solid line). The thickness of the line can, however, be set before drawing one of these objects using the **setlinestyle** routine.

cleardevice

Clears the entire graphics screen and moves the current position (CP) to 0,0 in the active viewport.

Syntax:
```
void far cleardevice(void);
Procedure ClearDevice;
cleardevice
```

Examples:
The following examples illustrate techniques for clearing both a viewport and the full screen.

```
#include <graphics.h>          /* Turbo C */
#include <conio.h>
main()
{
    int graphdriver = DETECT, graphmode;   /* autodetection */

    initgraph(&graphdriver, &graphmode, "");
    line(0, 0, 200, 200);     /* use full screen */
    setviewport(100, 100, 200, 200, 1);
    line(0, 0, 100, 100);
    getch();
    clearviewport();   /* clear viewport only */
    getch();
    cleardevice();     /* clear complete screen */
    closegraph();
}

Program Clear_Screen;   {Turbo Pascal}
Uses Graph;
Var
    GraphDriver, GraphMode : Integer;
Begin
    GraphDriver := Detect;
    InitGraph(GraphDriver, GraphMode, '');
```

```
    Line(0, 0, 200, 200);          {use full screen}
    SetViewPort(100, 100, 200, 200, True);
    Line(0, 0, 100, 100);
    Readln;
    ClearViewPort;   {clear viewport only}
    Readln;
    ClearDevice;     {clear complete screen}
    CloseGraph;
End.
```

```
include "GRAPDECL.PRO"      /* Turbo Prolog */
predicates
    clear_screen
clauses
    clear_screen :-
        initgraph(detect, 0, GraphDriver, GraphMode, ""),
        line(0, 0, 200, 200),    /* use full screen */
        setviewport(100, 100, 200, 200, 1),
        line(0, 0, 100, 100),
        readchar(_),
        clearviewport,    /* clear viewport only */
        readchar(_),
        cleardevice,        /* clear complete screen */
        closegraph.
```

Reference:
clearviewport, closegraph, initgraph, setviewport

Remarks:
The **cleardevice** routine should be used whenever you need to clear the
full screen, even if the viewport is set to a size smaller than the full screen.
If you only need to clear the current viewport, you should use the **clearviewport** routine.

Clears the active viewport and moves the current position (CP) to 0,0 in   **clearviewport**
the active viewport.

Syntax:
```
void far clearviewport(void);
Procedure ClearViewPort;
clearviewport
```

Examples:
See **cleardevice.**

Reference:
cleardevice, closegraph, getviewsettings, initgraph, setviewport

Remarks:
Only the active viewport is cleared. If the viewport is smaller than the full screen, then the area outside the viewport is not altered.

closegraph   Shuts down the BGI graphics system and deallocates the memory allocated for graphics drivers, fonts, and buffers.

Syntax:
```
void far closegraph(void);
Procedure CloseGraph;
closegraph
```

Examples:
See **cleardevice.**

Reference:
cleardevice, clearviewport, initgraph, setgraphbufsize

Remarks:
The screen is restored to the mode it was in before the BGI was initialized. You should always call this routine whenever your program no longer needs the BGI routines so that memory will be freed up.

detectgraph   Checks hardware to determine which graphics driver and mode to use. This routine always selects the mode that will give the highest resolution possible for the installed adapter.

Syntax:
```
void far detectgraph(int far *graphdriver, int far *graphmode);
Procedure DetectGraph(Var GraphDriver, GraphMode : Integer);
detectgraph(Graphdriver, Graphmode)      (o,o)
          (integer, integer)
```

Parameters:

graphdriver   returns an integer code to indicate which graphics driver
                     is installed.

graphmode   returns an integer code to indicate the graphics mode that
                     is used.

Examples:

The following examples illustrate how the **detectgraph** routine determines
whether a graphics driver is installed.

```
#include <graphics.h>          /* Turbo C */
main()
{
    int graphdriver, graphmode;

    detectgraph(&graphdriver, &graphmode);
    if (graphdriver == -2)   {
      printf("\nNo driver installed--quitting");
      exit(1);
    }
    initgraph(&graphdriver, &graphmode, "");
    /* ... perform drawing commands */
    closegraph();
}


Program Graph_Check;          {Turbo Pascal}
Uses Graph;
Var
    GraphDriver, GraphMode : Integer;

Begin
    DetectGraph(GraphDriver, GraphMode);
    If (GraphDriver = -2)   Then Begin
       Writeln('No driver installed--quitting');
       Exit;
    End;
    InitGraph(GraphDriver, GraphMode, '');
    { ... perform drawing commands}
    CloseGraph;
End.
```

```
include "GRAPDECL.PRO"      /* Turbo Prolog */
predicates
    graph_check(integer, integer)
clauses
    graph_check(GraphDriver, GraphMode) :-
        detectgraph(GraphDriver, GraphMode),
        GraphDriver = -2, !,
        fail.
    graph_check(GraphDriver, GraphMode) :-
        initgraph(GraphDriver, GraphMode, NewGD, NewGM, ""),
        /* ... perform drawing commands */
        closegraph.
```

Reference:
getgraphmode, getmodename, getmoderange, initgraph

Remarks:
The codes for the graphics drivers and graphics modes are presented with the **initgraph** routine. If for some reason **detectgraph** does not detect a graphics adapter, the **graphdriver** parameter is set to –2.

drawpoly   Draws a polygon using the current drawing color and line style.

Syntax:
```
void far drawpoly(int numpoints, int far *polypoints);
Procedure DrawPoly(NumPoints : Word; Var PolyPoints);
drawpoly(PolyPoints)      (i)
        (bgi_ilist)
```

Parameters:
numpoints the number of points used to draw the polygon.

polypoints a list of the points for the polygon. Each point is represented by an X and Y coordinate pair. In Turbo C these points are represented as a pointer to an array. In Turbo Pascal they are represented as an untyped parameter, and in Turbo Prolog they are represented as a list of domain type **bgi_ilist** which is the same as a list of integers (**integer***).

Examples:
The following examples illustrate how a set of coordinate pairs are joined by using the **drawpoly** routine.

```
#include <graphics.h>    /* Turbo C */
main()
{
    int graphdriver = DETECT, graphmode;  /* autodetection */
    int data[] = {45,80,  60,60,  75,35,  15,65,  45,80};

    initgraph(&graphdriver, &graphmode, "");
    drawpoly(5, data);
    getch();
    closegraph();
}


Program Draw_Polygon;   {Turbo Pascal}
Uses Graph;
Const   MAX_POINTS = 5;
    Data : Array [1..MAX_POINTS] Of PointType =
                    (( X :  45; Y :  80),
                     ( X :  60; Y :  60),
                     ( X :  75; Y :  35),
                     ( X :  15; Y :  65),
                     ( X :  45; Y :  80) );
Var
    GraphDriver, GraphMode : Integer;
Begin
    GraphDriver := Detect;
    InitGraph(GraphDriver, GraphMode, '');
    DrawPoly(MAX_POINTS, Data);
    Readln;
    CloseGraph;
End.


include "GRAPDECL.PRO"     /* Turbo Prolog */
predicates
    draw_it
clauses
    draw_it :-
        initgraph(detect, 0, GraphDriver, GraphMode, ""),
        drawpoly([45,80,  60,60,  75,35,  15,65,  45,80]),
        readchar(_),
        closegraph.
```

Reference:
fillpoly, getlinesettings, line, rectangle, setlinestyle

Remarks:
The first and last points must be the same for the polygon to be drawn as
a closed figure.

ellipse Draws an elliptical arc at a specified starting point (center) with fixed
horizontal and vertical radii. The ellipse is drawn from the start angle
(**stangle**) to the end angle (**endangle**).

Syntax:
```
void far ellipse(int x, int y, int stangle, int endangle,
                 int xradius, int yradius);
Procedure Ellipse(X, Y : Integer;  StAngle, EndAngle,
                 XRadius, YRadius : Word);
ellipse(X,Y,StAngle,EndAngle,XRadius,YRadius)    (i,i,i,i,i,i)
        (integer, integer, integer, integer, integer, integer)
```

Parameters:

x, y   the center of the arc specified in absolute coordinates.
stangle, endangle   the starting and ending angles specified in degrees.
xradius, yradius   the horizontal and vertical radii in pixels.

Examples:
The following examples draw an ellipse that spans a 90-degree angle and
a complete ellipse that is filled in with a line pattern.

```
#include <graphics.h>          /* Turbo C */
main()
{
    int graphdriver = DETECT, graphmode;   /* autodetection */

    initgraph(&graphdriver, &graphmode, "");
    ellipse(100, 100, 30, 120, 50, 75);
    setfillstyle(LINE_FILL, 1);
    fillellipse(200, 200, 40, 20);
    getch();
    closegraph();
}
```

```
Program Draw_Ellipse;    {Turbo Pascal}
Uses Graph;
Var
    GraphDriver, GraphMode : Integer;
Begin
    GraphDriver := Detect;
    InitGraph(GraphDriver, GraphMode, '');
    Ellipse(100, 100, 30, 120, 50, 75);
    SetFillStyle(LineFill, 1);
    FillEllipse(200, 200, 40, 20);
    Readln;
    CloseGraph;
End.
```

```
include "GRAPDECL.PRO"      /* Turbo Prolog */
predicates
    draw_ellipse
clauses
    draw_ellipse :-
        initgraph(detect, 0, GraphDriver, GraphMode, ""),
        ellipse(100, 100, 30, 120, 50, 75),
        setfillstyle(line_FILL, 1),
        fillellipse(200, 200, 40, 20),
        readchar(_),
        closegraph.
```

Reference:
arc, circle, fillellipse, getaspectratio, getarccoords, pieslice, sector, setaspectratio

Remarks:
You can draw a complete ellipse (the ends join) by setting the starting angle to 0 and the ending angle to 360. The ellipse is drawn in a counterclockwise direction, where 0 degrees is at 3 o'clock and 90 degrees is at 12 o'clock.

Draws and fills an ellipse in the current fill pattern and color.   **fillellipse**

Syntax:
```
void far fillellipse(int x, int y, int xradius, int yradius);
Procedure FillEllipse(X, Y : Integer;
                      XRadius, YRadius : Word);
```

```
fillellipse(X, Y, XRadius, YRadius)    (i,i,i,i)
            (integer, integer, integer, integer)
```

Parameters:

x, y   the center of the ellipse specified in absolute coor-
                         dinates.

xradius, yradius   the horizontal and vertical radius in pixels.

Examples:
See **ellipse**.

Reference:
arc, circle, ellipse, getaspectratio, getarccoords, pieslice, sector, setaspectratio, setfillpattern, setfillstyle

Remarks:
These routines will draw a full ellipse. If you wish to draw a partial ellipse, use the **ellipse** routine.

fillpoly   Draws and fills a polygon using the current line and fill styles and drawing
                         and filling colors.

Syntax:
```
void far fillpoly(int numpoints, int far *polypoints);
Procedure FillPoly(NumPoints : Word; Var PolyPoints);
fillpoly(PolyPoints)    (i)
        (bgi_ilist)
```

Parameters:

numpoints   the number of points used to draw and fill the polygon (C
                 and Pascal only).

polypoints   a list of the points for the polygon. Each point is represented
                 by an X and Y coordinate pair. In Turbo C these points are
                 represented as a pointer to an array; in Turbo Pascal they
                 are represented as an untyped parameter; and in Turbo
                 Prolog they are represented as a simple list of domain type
                 bgi_ilist, which is the same as a list of integers (**integer***).

Examples:
The following examples illustrate how a polygon is drawn and filled:

```c
#include <graphics.h>    /* Turbo C */
main()
{
    int graphdriver = DETECT, graphmode;   /* autodetection */
    int data[] = {45,80, 160,160, 75,35, 45,80};

    initgraph(&graphdriver, &graphmode, "");
    fillpoly(4, data);
    getch();
    closegraph();
}
```

```pascal
Program Draw_Polygon;   {Turbo Pascal}
Uses Graph;
Const
    MAX_POINTS = 4;
    Data : Array [1..MAX_POINTS] Of PointType =
                    (( X : 45; Y : 80),
                     ( X : 160; Y : 160),
                     ( X : 75; Y : 35),
                     ( X : 45; Y : 80) );
Var
    GraphDriver, GraphMode : Integer;
Begin
    GraphDriver := Detect;
    InitGraph(GraphDriver, GraphMode, '');
    FillPoly(MAX_POINTS, Data);
    ReadLn;
    CloseGraph;
End.
```

```prolog
include "GRAPDECL.PRO"   /* Turbo Prolog */
predicates
    draw_it
clauses
    draw_it :-
        initgraph(detect, 0, GraphDriver, GraphMode, ""),
        fillpoly([45,80, 160,160, 75,35, 45,80]),
        readchar(_),
        closegraph.
```

Reference:
drawpoly, floodfill, line, setfillstyle

Remarks:
If you want to draw a polygon without filling it, use **drawpoly**.

floodfill   Flood-fills a bounded region with the current color and fill pattern.

Syntax:
```
void far floodfill(int x, int y, int border);
Procedure FloodFill(X, Y, Border : Word);
floodfill(X, Y, Border)      (i,i,i)
          (integer, integer, integer)
```

Parameters:

x, y   the location of a region to fill. If this position is inside an en-
              closed area, then the region is filled. If the position is outside
              an enclosed area, then everything is filled except the enclosed
              region.

border   the color code of the border.

Examples:
The following examples illustrate how a bounded region can be filled with
a specified color and pattern style.

```
void fill_it(int x1, int y1, int x2, int y2, int color, int pattern)
{
    int regcolor, xloc, yloc;
    struct fillsettingstype currentfill;

    xloc = (x1 + x2) / 2;               /* get x midpoint */
    yloc = (y1 + y2) / 2;               /* get y midpoint */
    getfillsettings(&currentfill);
    /* set up new fill and color */
    setfillstyle(pattern, color);
    regcolor = getpixel(x1, y1);
    floodfill(xloc, yloc, regcolor);
    setfillstyle(currentfill.pattern, currentfill.color);
}
```

```
Procedure Fill_It (X1, Y1, X2, Y2 : Integer; Color, Pattern : Word);
Var
    RegColor, XLoc, YLoc : Integer;
    CurrentFill : FillSettingsType;
Begin
    XLoc = (X1 + X2) / 2;       {get x midpoint}
    YLoc = (Y1 + Y2) / 2;        {get y midpoint}
    GetFillSettings (CurrentFill);
    SetFillStyle(Pattern, Color);    {set up new fill and color}
    RegColor = GetPixel(X1, Y1);
    FloodFill(XLoc, YLoc, RegColor);
    SetFillStyle(CurrentFill.Pattern, CurrentFill.Color);
End;


include "GRAPDECL.PRO"   /* Turbo Prolog */
predicates
    fill_it(integer, integer, integer, integer, integer, integer)
clauses
    fill_it(X1, Y1, X2, Y2, Color, Pattern) :-
        XLoc = (X1 + X2) / 2,       /* get x midpoint */
        YLoc = (Y1 + Y2) / 2,          /* get y midpoint */
        getfillsettings(FPattern, FColor),
        /* set up new fill & color */
        setfillstyle(Pattern, Color),
        getpixel(X1, Y1, RegColor),
        floodfill(XLoc, YLoc, RegColor),
        /* restore color, pattern */
        setfillstyle(FPattern, FColor).
```

Reference:
drawpoly, fillpoly, getfillsettings, setfillstyle

Remarks:
If the specified point for the flood fill is outside a bounded region, everything but the bounded region is filled.

Gets the coordinates to the most recent arc drawing command. The **getarccoords** coordinates returned are the arc center point and the starting and ending end point coordinates.

Syntax:

```
void far getarccoords(struct arccoordstype far *arccoords);
Procedure GetArcCoords(Var ArcCoords : ArcCoordsType);
getarccoords(X, Y, Xstart, Ystart, Xend, Yend)    (o,o,o,o,o,o)
              (integer, integer, integer, integer, integer, integer)
```

Parameters:

arccoords   Turbo C and Turbo Pascal use a predefined data type called **arccoordstype** to store the coordinates for a given arc. These data types are defined as:

```
struct arccoordstype {          /* Turbo C */
    int x, y;                    /* center point */
    int xstart, ystart, xend, yend; /* end points */
};


Type    {Turbo Pascal}
    ArcCoordsType = Record
        X, Y : Integer;
        Xstart, Ystart, Xend, Yend : Word;
    End;
```

In Turbo Prolog, the parameters are:

X, Y   the arc center point.
Xstart, Ystart   the starting position.
Xend, Yend   the ending position.

Examples:

The following examples illustrate how **getarccoords** is used to read the coordinates of a drawn arc.

```
#include <graphics.h>          /* Turbo C */
main()
{
    int graphdriver = DETECT, graphmode;   /* autodetection */
    struct arccoordstype recentarc;

    initgraph(&graphdriver, &graphmode, "");
    arc(100, 100, 30, 90, 50);
    getarccoords(&recentarc);
    if (recentarc.xend > getmaxx()) exit(1); /* check for error */
```

```
    /* ... drawing commands */
    closegraph();
}


Program Check_Arc;   {Turbo Pascal}
Uses Graph;
Var
    GraphDriver, GraphMode : Integer;
    RecentArc : ArcCoordsType;
Begin
    GraphDriver := Detect;
    InitGraph(GraphDriver, GraphMode, '');
    Arc(100, 100, 30, 90, 50);
    GetArcCoords(RecentArc);
    If RecentArc.Xend > GetMaxX  Then Exit; { check for error }
    { ... drawing commands}
    CloseGraph;
End.


include "GRAPDECL.PRO"     /* Turbo Prolog */
predicates
    check_arc
clauses
    check_arc :-
        initgraph(detect, 0, GraphDriver, GraphMode, ""),
        arc(100, 100, 30, 90, 50),
        getarccoords(_,_,_,_, Xend, _),
        getMaxX(MaxX),
        Xend <= MaxX, /* check for error */
        /* ... drawing commands */
        closegraph().
check_arc :- exit.
```

Reference:
arc

Determine the current aspect ratio of the active graphics driver and mode.   **getaspectratio**

Syntax:
```
void far getaspectratio(int far *xasp, int far *yasp);
Procedure GetAspectRatio(Var Xasp, Yasp : Word);
```

```
getaspectratio(Xasp, Yasp)      (o,o)
                  (integer, integer)
```

Parameters:

xasp, yasp   variables used to return the X and Y aspect ratio.

Examples:

The following examples illustrate how the **getaspectratio** and **setaspectratio** routines are used to control the aspect ratio.

```c
#include <graphics.h>          /* Turbo C */
main()
{
    int graphdriver = DETECT, graphmode;   /* autodetection */
    int xratio, yratio;

    initgraph(&graphdriver, &graphmode, "");
    getaspectratio(&xratio, &yratio);
    if (xratio != yratio) setaspectratio(xratio, xratio);
    circle(100, 100, 50);
    getch();
    closegraph();
}
```

```pascal
Program Draw_Circle;   {Turbo Pascal}
Uses Graph;
Var
    GraphDriver, GraphMode : Integer;
    XRatio, YRatio : Word;
Begin
    GraphDriver := Detect;
    InitGraph(GraphDriver, GraphMode, '');
    GetAspectRatio(XRatio, YRatio);
    If XRatio <> YRatio Then  SetAspectRatio(XRatio, XRatio);
    Circle(100,100, 50);
    Readln;
    CloseGraph;
End.
```

```
include "GRAPDECL.PRO"      /* Turbo Prolog */
predicates
```

```
    draw_circle
    check_ratio(integer, integer)

clauses
    draw_circle :-
        initgraph(detect, 0, GraphDriver, GraphMode, ""),
        getaspectratio(XRatio, YRatio),
        check_ratio(XRatio, YRatio),
        circle(100,100, 50),
        readchar(_),
        closegraph.

    check_ratio(X, X).
    check_ratio(X, Y) :- setaspectratio(X, Y).
```

Reference:
arc, circle, ellipse, fillellipse, pieslice, sector, setaspectratio

Returns the current background color. The background color is returned   **getbkcolor**
as an integer code that can range from 0 to 15.

Syntax:
```
int far getbkcolor(void);
Function GetBkColor : Word;
getbkcolor(BkColor)     (o)
            (integer)
```

Parameter:
bkcolor   (Turbo Prolog only) returns the color code for the current
background color.

Examples:
See **getcolor**.

Reference:
getcolor, getmaxcolor, getpalette, setbkcolor, setcolor

Remarks:
In Turbo C and Pascal the background color is returned as the function
return value. The table of background color codes is presented in the
discussion entitled Working with Colors.

getcolor

Returns the current drawing color. The drawing color is returned as an integer code, which can range from 0 to 15.

Syntax:

```
int far getcolor(void);
Function GetColor: Word;
getcolor(Color)     (o)
        (integer)
```

Parameter:

color   (Turbo Prolog only) returns the color code for the current drawing color.

Examples:

The following example illustrates how drawing and background colors are accessed.

```
#include <graphics.h>          /* Turbo C */
main()
{
    int graphdriver = DETECT, graphmode;   /* autodetection */
    int oldbkcolor, olddrwcolor;

    initgraph(&graphdriver, &graphmode, "");
    oldbkcolor = getbkcolor();
    olddrwcolor = getcolor();
    if (oldbkcolor == BLUE)
        setbkcolor(GREEN);     /* change background color*/
    if (olddrwcolor == RED)
        setcolor(CYAN);        /* change drawing color */
    /* ... drawing commands */
    setbkcolor(BLUE);
    setcolor(RED);
    closegraph();
}


Program Set_Colors;   {Turbo Pascal}
Uses Graph;
Var
    GraphDriver, GraphMode : Integer;
```

```
    OldBkColor, OldDrwColor : Integer;
Begin
    GraphDriver := Detect;
    InitGraph(GraphDriver, GraphMode, '');
    OldBkColor := GetBkColor;
    OldDrwColor := GetColor;
    If OldBkColor = Blue Then
        SetBkColor(Green);      {change background color}
    If OldDrwColor = Red Then
        SetColor(Cyan);         {change drawing color}
    { ... drawing commands}
    SetBkColor(Blue);
    SetColor(Red);
    CloseGraph;
End.
```

```
include "GRAPDECL.PRO"       /* Turbo Prolog */
predicates
    set_colors
    check_draw(integer)
    check_back(integer)
clauses
    set_colors :-
        initgraph(detect, 0, GraphDriver, GraphMode, ""),
        getbkcolor(Oldbkcolor),
        getcolor(Olddrwcolor),
        check_back(Oldbkcolor),
        check_draw(Olddrwcolor),
        /* ... drawing commands */
        setbkcolor(blue),
        setcolor(red),
        closegraph.
    check_back(Oldbkcolor) :-
        Oldbkcolor = blue,
        setbkcolor(green),    /* change background color */
    check_back(_).
    check_draw(Olddrwcolor) :-
        Olddrwcolor = red,
        setcolor(cyan),       /* change drawing color */
    check_draw(_).
```

Reference:
getbkcolor, getmaxcolor, getpalette, setbkcolor, setcolor

Remarks:
In Turbo C and Pascal the background color is returned as the function return value. The table of foreground color codes is presented in the discussion entitled Working with Colors.

getdefaultpalette   Returns the color codes contained in the default color palette.

Syntax:
```
struct palettetype *far getdefaultpalette(void);
Procedure GetDefaultPalette(Var DefPalette : PaletteType);
getdefaultpalette(DefPalette)     (o)
                 (bgi_ilist)
```

Parameter:
DefPalette   the set of colors in the default palette. In Turbo Prolog the colors are returned in a list and in Turbo Pascal the colors are stored in a predefined data structure.

Examples:
See **getpalette**.

Reference:
getmaxcolor, getpalette, getpalettesize, setallpalette, setpalette

Remarks:
The default palette size for CGA is 4 colors in low resolution mode and 2 colors in high resolution mode. Both the EGA and VGA have 16 colors in their default palettes. In Turbo C and Pascal, the palette information is returned in a predefined data structure, which is presented in the discussion on the **getpalette** routine.

getdrivername   Returns the name of the currently installed graphics driver.

Syntax:
```
char *far getdrivername(void);
Function GetDriverName : String;
getdrivername(DriverName)     (o)
        (string)
```

Parameter:

DriverName   (Turbo Prolog) the name of the currently installed driver.

Examples:

See **getgraphmode**.

Reference:

getgraphmode, getmodename, initgraph

Remarks:

The names of the drivers for each of the languages are presented in Table 4.1.

    This routine is helpful for determining the name of the driver that is installed whenever the autodetection feature of **initgraph** is used.

Obtain the bit setting for the user-defined fill pattern. The 64-pixel fill pattern is represented as a sequence of 8 bytes, where each byte corresponds to 8 pixels in fill pattern.

getfillpattern

Syntax:

```
void far getfillpattern(char far *upattern);
Procedure GetFillPattern(Var FillPattern : FillPatternType);
getfillpattern(PatternList)      (o)
            (bgi_ilist)
```

Parameters:

upattern   the user-defined fill pattern (Turbo C). This parameter is a pointer to an 8-byte sequence (bit pattern).

FillPattern   the user-defined fill pattern (Turbo Pascal). This parameter uses the following predefined data:

```
Type
    FillPatternType = Array[1..8] Of Byte;
```

PatternList   the user-defined fill pattern (Turbo Prolog). This parameter is a list of 8 bytes.

Examples:

See **getfillsettings**.

Reference:
getfillsettings, setfillpattern, setfillstyle

Remarks:
This routine also does not return the active fill color. If you need to determine the fill color, use **getfillsettings**.

getfillsettings   Gets the current fill pattern and color.

Syntax:
```
void far getfillsettings(struct fillsettingstype far *fillinfo);
Procedure GetFillSettings(Var FillInfo : FillSettingsType);
getfillsettings(FillPattern, FillColor)      (o,o)
                (integer, integer)
```

Parameters:
In Turbo C and Pascal:
fillinfo   data structure that contains the fill pattern and the fill color. This data structure is defined as:

```
struct fillsettingstype    {        /* Turbo C */
    int pattern;
    int color;
};


Type FillSettingsType = Record      { Turbo Pascal }
    Pattern : Word;
    Color : Word;
End;
```

In Turbo Prolog the parameters are:
FillPattern   an integer code (0–12) that indicates the current fill pattern.
FillColor   an integer code that specifies the current fill color.

The set of fill patterns available for each of the languages are listed in Table 4.12.

Examples:
The following examples illustrate how the fill routines—**getfillpattern, getfillstyle, setfillpattern,** and **setfillstyle**—are be used to control the fill patterns.

Table 4.12. Fill patterns

Value	C Name	Pascal Name	Prolog Name
0	EMPTY_FILL	EmptyFill	empty_FILL
1	SOLID_FILL	SolidFill	solid_FILL
2	LINE_FILL	LineFill	line_FILL
3	LTSLASH_FILL	LtSlashFill	ltslash_FILL
4	SLASH_FILL	SlashFill	slash_FILL
5	BKSLASH_FILL	BkSlashFill	bkslash_FILL
6	LTBKSLASH_FILL	LtBkSlashFill	ltbkslash_FILL
7	HATCH_FILL	HatchFill	hatch_FILL
8	XHATCH_FILL	XHatchFill	xhatch_FILL
9	INTERLEAVE_FILL	InterleaveFill	interleave_FILL
10	WIDE_DOT_FILL	WideDotFill	widedot_FILL
11	CLOSE_DOT_FILL	CloseDotFill	closedot_FILL
12	USER_FILL	UserFill	user_FILL

```c
#include <graphics.h>    /* Turbo C */
main()
{
    int graphdriver = DETECT, graphmode;  /* autodetection */
    struct fillsettingstype filldata;
    char newpattern[] = { 0xBD, 0xA1, 0x43, 0x78,
                          0xA1, 0xBD, 0x47, 0xA1 };
    char oldpattern[8];
    initgraph(&graphdriver, &graphmode, "");
    getfillsettings(&filldata);
    if (filldata.pattern != USER_FILL) { /* use default pattern */
       rectangle(30,30,150,100);
       setfillstyle(LINE_FILL, RED);
       floodfill(100, 75, getcolor());
        /* restore */
       setfillstyle(filldata.pattern, filldata.color);
    }
    else {      /* use a user-defined pattern */
      getfillpattern(oldpattern);
      setfillpattern(newpattern, MAGENTA);
      circle(50,50, 100);
```

```
        floodfill(50,50, getcolor());
          /* restore pattern */
        setfillpattern(oldpattern, filldata.color);
    }
    getch();
    closegraph();
}


Program Get_Set_Fill;   {Turbo Pascal}
Uses Graph;
Const
    NewPattern : FillPatternType =   ( $BD, $A1, $43, $78,
                                       $A1, $BD, $47, $A1 );
Var
    GraphDriver, GraphMode : Integer;
    FillData : FillSettingsType;
Begin
    GraphDriver := Detect;
    InitGraph(GraphDriver, GraphMode, '');
    GetFillSettings(FillData);
    If FillData.Pattern <> UserFill Then Begin
        Rectangle(30,30,150,100);
        SetFillStyle(LineFill, Red);
        FloodFill(100, 75, GetColor);
        SetFillStyle(FillData.Pattern, FillData.Color);
    End
    Else Begin      {use a user-defined pattern}
        SetFillPattern(NewPattern, Magenta);
        Circle(50,50, 100);
        FloodFill(50,50, GetColor);
    End;
    ReadLn;
    CloseGraph;
End.


include "GRAPDECL.PRO"      /* Turbo Prolog */
predicates
    get_set_fill
    fill_it(integer, integer)
clauses
```

```
get_set_fill :-
    initgraph(detect, 0, GraphDriver, GraphMode, ""),
    getfillsettings(FillPat, FillClr), !,
    fill_it(FillPat, FillClr),
    readchar(_),
    closegraph.
fill_it(user_FILL, FillClr) :-
    NewPattern = [$BD, $A1, $43, $78, $A1, $BD, $47, $A1 ],
    getfillpattern(OldPattern),
    setfillpattern(NewPattern, magenta),
    circle(50,50, 100),
    getcolor(Color),
    floodfill(50,50, Color),
    setfillpattern(OldPattern, FillClr). /* restore pattern */
fill_it(FillPat, FillClr ) :-
    rectangle(30,30,150,100),
    setfillstyle(line_FILL, red),    /* new fill style */
    getcolor(Color),
    floodfill(100, 75, Color),
    setfillstyle(FillPat, FillClr). /* restore */
```

Reference:
getfillpattern, setfillpattern, setfillstyle

Remarks:
Remember that once a new fill pattern and color are set, these attributes are used for the fills created by the **bar, bar3d, fillpoly, floodfill, pieslice,** and **sector** routines.

Obtains the current graphics mode for the installed graphics driver.   **getgraphmode**

Syntax:
```
int far getgraphmode(void);
Function GetGraphMode : Integer;
getgraphmode(GraphMode)        (o)
         (integer)
```

Parameter:
graphmode   (Turbo Prolog only) a returned integer code for the current mode.

Examples:

The following examples illustrate how **getgraphmode**—along with the other graphics query routines, **getdrivername, getmodename,** and **getmoderange**—are used.

```c
#include <graphics.h>     /* Turbo C */
#include <conio.h>
main()
{
    int graphdriver = DETECT, graphmode;   /* autodetection */
    int grmode, lomode, himode;
    char *grname, *drname;

    initgraph(&graphdriver, &graphmode, "");
    drname = getdrivername();
    grmode = getgraphmode();
    grname = getmodename(grmode);
    getmoderange(graphdriver, &lomode, &himode);
    restorecrtmode();
    printf("The driver name is %s\n", drname);
    printf("The mode name is %s, the range is %d to %d",
           grname, lomode, himode);
}
```

```pascal
Program Get_Mode;   {Turbo Pascal}
Uses Graph;
Var
    GraphDriver, GraphMode, LoMode, HiMode : Integer;
    GrMode : Word;
    GrName, DrName : String;

Begin
    GraphDriver := Detect;
    InitGraph(GraphDriver, GraphMode, '');
    DrName := GetDriverName;
    GrMode := GetGraphMode;
    GrName := GetModeName(GrMode);
    GetModeRange(GraphDriver, LoMode, HiMode);
    RestoreCrtMode;
    Writeln('The driver name is ', DrName);
```

```
    Writeln('The mode name is ', GrName, ' the range is ',
            LoMode,' to ', HiMode);
End.


include "GRAPDECL.PRO"   /* Turbo Prolog */
predicates
    get_modes
clauses
    get_modes :-
        initgraph(detect, 0, GraphDriver, GraphMode, ""),
        getdrivername(DrName),
        getgraphmode(GrMode),
        getmodename(GrMode, GrName),
        getmoderange(GraphDriver, Lomode, Himode),
        restorecrtmode,
        write("The driver name is ", DrName), nl,
        write("The mode name is ", GrName," the range is ",
            Lomode," to ", Himode),
        closegraph.
```

Reference:
getmodename, getmoderange, initgraph, setgraphmode

Remarks:
The integer codes that correspond with the graphics modes for the different adapters are presented in Table 4.1.

Copies a rectangular screen bit image into memory. The image can be **getimage** restored later by calling **putimage**.

Syntax:
```
void far getimage(int left, int top, int right, int bottom,
                  void far *bitmap);
Procedure GetImage(Left, Top, Right, Bottom : Word; Var BitMap);
getimage(Left, Top, Right, Bottom, BitMap)    (i,i,i,i,o)
        (integer, integer, integer, integer, string)
```

Parameters:
left, top   the upper left corner of the screen rectangle.
right, bottom   the lower right corner of the screen rectangle.

bitmap references the location in memory where the bit image is stored (Turbo C and Pascal). In Turbo Prolog this parameter serves as an integer index to reference the stored bit image.

Examples:
See **putimage**.

Reference:
imagesize, putimage

Remarks:
The bitmap parameter in Turbo Prolog can be used like any other variable; however, it cannot be asserted or retracted in a database.

getlinesettings Gets the line setting information including the current line style, pattern, and thickness.

Syntax:
```
void far getlinesettings(struct linesettingstype far *lineinfo);
Procedure GetLineSettings(Var LineInfo : LineSettingsType);
getlinesettings(LineStyle, Upattern, Thickness)     (o,o,o)
                (integer, integer, integer)
```

Parameters:
lineinfo Turbo C and Turbo Pascal use a predefined data type called **linesettingstype** to store the line settings data. These data types are defined as:

```
struct linesettingstype  {      /* Turbo C */
    int linestyle;
    unsigned upattern;
    int thickness;
};

Type      {Turbo Pascal}
    LineSettingsType = Record
        LineStyle : Word;
        Pattern   : Word;
        Thickness : Word;
    End;
```

In Turbo Prolog, the parameters used are:

LineStyle   an integer code for the current line style (0–4).
Upattern   the line style pattern for user-defined patterns.
Thickness   an integer code for the line thickness (1,3).

Examples:
See **setlinestyle**.

Reference:
setlinestyle

Obtains the maximum color value in the active color palette.   **getmaxcolor**

Syntax:
```
int far getmaxcolor(void);
Function GetMaxColor : Word;
getmaxcolor(MaxColor)     (o)
          (integer)
```

Parameter:
MaxColor   (Turbo Prolog) contains an integer value for the maximum
               color in the current color palette.

Examples:
See **getpalette**.

Reference:
getdefaultpalette, getpalette, getpalettesize, setpalette, setallpalette

Obtains the integer code for the highest resolution mode for the current   **getmaxmode**
driver.

Syntax:
```
int far getmaxmode(void);
Function GetMaxMode : Word;
```

Examples:
The following examples use **getmaxmode** to help perform a mode switching operation.

```
void sethigh(void)        /* Turbo C */
{
    int  grmode,  maxmode;

    grmode = getgraphmode();
    maxmode = getmaxmode();
    if (grmode != maxmode)  setgraphmode(maxmode);
}


Procedure SetHigh;        {Turbo Pascal}
Var
    GrMode, MaxMode : Integer;
Begin
    GrMode  := GetGraphMode;
    MaxMode := GetMaxMode;
    If GrMode <> MaxMode Then  SetGraphMode(MaxMode);
End;
```

Reference:
getmodename, getmoderange

Remarks:
This routine is not provided with Turbo Prolog.

getmaxx

Obtains the maximum horizontal coordinate for the active graphics adapter and mode.

Syntax:
```
int far getmaxx(void);
Function GetMaxX : Integer;
getmaxx(Xmax)        (o)
        (integer)
```

Parameter:
Xmax   returns the maximum horizontal coordinate (Turbo Prolog only).

Examples:
The following routines use **getmaxx** and **getmaxy** to check a set of coordinate points to see if they are in range.

```
int checkpoints(int x1, int y1, int x2, int y2) /* Turbo C */
{
    if ((x1 > getmaxx()) || (x2 > getmaxx()))
        return -1;
    if ((y1 > getmaxy()) || (y2 > getmaxy()))
        return -1;
    return 0;
}
```

```
{Turbo Pascal}
Function CheckPoints(X1, Y1, X2, Y2 : Integer) : Integer;
Var X, Y : Integer;
Begin
    X := GetMaxX;    Y := GetMaxY;
    If (X1 > X Or X2 > X ) Then CheckPoints := -1;
    If (Y1 > Y Or Y2 > Y ) Then CheckPoints := -1;
    CheckPoints := 0;
End.
```

```
include "GRAPDECL.PRO"    /* Turbo Prolog */
predicates
    check_points(integer, integer, integer, integer, integer)
clauses
    check_points(X1, _, X2, _, ReturnVal) :-
        getmaxx(MaxX),
        X1 > MaxX; X2 > MaxX,
        ReturnVal = -1.
    check_points(_, Y1, _, Y2, ReturnVal) :-
        getmaxy(MaxY),
        Y1 > MaxY; Y2 > MaxY,
        ReturnVal = -1.
    check_points(_, _, _, _, ReturnVal) :-
        ReturnVal = 0.
```

Reference:
getmaxy, getx

Remarks:
Both Turbo C and Pascal return the maximum horizontal coordinate as a
function return value.

getmaxy   Obtains maximum vertical coordinate for the active graphics adapter
and mode.

Syntax:
```
int far getmaxy(void)
Function GetMaxY : Integer;
getmaxy(Ymax)     (o)
        (integer)
```

Parameter:
Ymax   returns the maximum vertical coordinate (Turbo Prolog only).

Examples:
See **getmaxx**.

Reference:
getmaxx, gety

Remarks:
Both Turbo C and Pascal return the maximum vertical coordinate as a
function return value.

getmodename   Obtains the name of the active graphics mode. The name is returned as a
string of characters.

Syntax:
```
char *far getmodename(int modenumber);
Function GetModeName(ModeNumber : Word) : String;
getmodename(ModeNumber, ModeName)     (i,o)
        (integer, string)
```

Parameters:
modenumber   an integer code that specifies the graphics mode.
modename   the returned name of the requested mode number
                 (Turbo Prolog only).

Examples:
See **getgraphmode**.

Reference:
getmaxmode, getmoderange

Obtains the ranges of graphics modes for a given driver.   **getmoderange**

Syntax:
```
void far getmoderange(int graphdriver, int far *lomode,
                      int far *himode);
Procedure GetModeRange(GraphDriver : Integer; Var LoMode,
                      HiMode : Integer);
getmoderange(GraphDriver, Lomode, Himode)     (i,o,o)
         (integer, integer, integer)
```

Parameters:
graphdriver   integer code which references a driver.
lomode, himode   the low and high modes.

Examples:
See **getgraphmode**.

Reference:
getgraphmode, getmaxmode, getmodename, setgraphmode

Remarks:
This routine is not available for Turbo Pascal.

Obtains information about the active color palette including its size and   **getpalette**
colors.

Syntax:
```
void far getpalette(struct palettetype far *palette);
Procedure GetPalette(Var Palette : PaletteType);
getpalette(Palette)     (o)
         (bgi_ilist)
```

Parameters:
palette   Turbo C and Turbo Pascal use a predefined data type called
        palettetype to store the palette information. These data types
        are defined as:

```
#define MAXCOLORS  15  /* Turbo C */
struct palettetype {
    unsigned char size;
```

```
                    signed char colors[MAXCOLORS + 1];
            };

            Const MaxColors = 15;      {Turbo Pascal}
            Type
                PaletteType = Record
                Size : Byte;
                Colors : Array[0..MaxColors] of Shortint;
                End;
```

In Turbo Prolog the parameter is:

Palette　　a returned list of the colors stored in the palette.

Examples:

The following examples illustrate how colors in the palette can be read and altered by using the **getdefaultpalette, getpalette, setallpalette,** and **setpalette** routines.

```c
#include <graphics.h>     /* Turbo C */
#include <conio.h>


main()
{
    int graphdriver = DETECT, graphmode;   /* autodetection */
    struct palettetype curpalette, *defpalette;
    int i, palsize, nomatch;

    initgraph(&graphdriver, &graphmode, "");
    nomatch = 0;
    palsize = getpalettesize();      /* get palette size */
    getpalette(&curpalette);
    defpalette = getdefaultpalette();
    for (i = 0; i < palsize; i++) {   /* compare palettes */
        if ((*defpalette).colors[i] != curpalette.colors[i])
            nomatch++;
    }
    if (nomatch != 0) {
        setpalette(1, MAGENTA);   /* change the first color */
        setcolor(1);                /* use the first color */
        line(100, 100, 140, 140);
        setallpalette(&curpalette);    /* restore to default */
```

```
            getch();
        }
        restorecrtmode();
        printf("\nThe current palette has %d colors that \
                are different than the default.", nomatch);
        closegraph();
}


Program Palette_Change;   {Turbo Pascal}
Uses Graph;
Var
    GraphDriver, GraphMode, NoMatch : Integer;
    PalSize, I : Integer;
    CurPalette, DefPalette : PaletteType;
Begin
    GraphDriver := Detect;
    InitGraph(GraphDriver, GraphMode, '');
    NoMatch := 0;
    PalSize := GetPaletteSize;
    GetPalette(CurPalette);
    GetDefaultPalette(DefPalette);
    For I := 0 To PalSize Do Begin   {compare palettes}
        If DefPalette.Colors[I] <> CurPalette.Colors[I] Then
            NoMatch := NoMatch + 1;
    End;
    If (NoMatch <> 0) Then Begin
        SetPalette(1, Magenta);   {change the first color}
        SetColor(1);                   {use the first color}
        Line(100, 100, 140, 140);
        SetAllPalette(CurPalette);    {restore to default}
        Readln;
    End;
    RestoreCrtMode;
    Writeln('The current palette has ',NoMatch,
    ' colors that are different than the default.');
    CloseGraph;
End.
```

Reference:
getdefaultpalette, getmaxcolor, getpalettesize, setallpalette, setpalette

Remarks:
The default colors and sizes for the standard graphics adapters (CGA, EGA, and VGA) are presented in the discussion entitled Working with Colors.

getpixel　　Gets the color of a pixel at a specified position.

Syntax:
```
int far getpixel(int x, int y);
Function GetPixel(X, Y : Integer) : Word;
getpixel(X, Y, Color)    (i,i,o)
         (integer, integer, integer)
```

Parameters:
x, y　　the horizontal and vertical position of the pixel.
color　　the integer color code of the pixel (Turbo Prolog).

Examples:
See **putpixel**.

Reference:
getcolor, putimage, putpixel

Remarks:
Because the Turbo C and Pascal versions of **getpixel** are functions, a parameter is not needed to return the color code of the pixel. The color of the pixel is returned as the function's returned value.

gettextsettings　　Obtains information about the current text settings.

Syntax:
```
void far gettextsettings(struct textsettingstype far *textinfo);
Procedure GetTextSettings(Var TextInfo : TextSettingsType);
gettextsettings(Font,Direction,CharSize,Horiz,Vert)    (o,o,o,o,o)
                (integer, integer, integer, integer, integer)
```

Parameters:
In Turbo C and Pascal the parameter **textinfo** is defined as:

```
struct textsettingstype {
    int font;
```

```
    int direction;
    int charsize;
    int horiz;
    int vert;
};


Type TextSettingsType = Record        {Pascal}
    Font : Word;
    Direction : Word;
    CharSize : CharSizeType;
    Horiz : Word;
    Vert : Word;
End;
```

In Turbo Prolog the parameters are:

Font   an integer code that indicates the current font style.
Direction   the direction (horizontal or vertical) of the text.
CharSize   the size of the active font.
Horiz, Vert   the horizontal and vertical justification styles.

Examples:

The following examples illustrate how the **gettextsettings** routine is used
to determine the settings of graphics text.

```
/* Turbo C */
#include <graphics.h>
main()
{
    int graphdriver = DETECT, graphmode;   /* autodetection */
    struct textsettingstype textinfo;

    initgraph(&graphdriver, &graphmode, "");
    gettextsettings(&textinfo);
    if (textinfo.font != SMALL_FONT)
        settextstyle(SMALL_FONT, HORIZ_DIR, 1);
    moveto(100,100);
    outtext("Text displayed at 100, 100");
    getch();
    closegraph();
}
```

```
Program CheckText;   {Turbo Pascal}
Uses Graph;
Var
    GraphDriver, GraphMode : Integer;
    TextInfo : TextSettingsType;
Begin
    GraphDriver := Detect;
    InitGraph(GraphDriver, GraphMode, '');
    GetTextSettings(TextInfo);
    If TextInfo.Font <> SmallFont Then
        SetTextStyle(SmallFont, HorizDir, 1);
    MoveTo(100,100);
    OutText('Text displayed at 100, 100');
    Readln;
    CloseGraph;
End.


include "GRAPDECL.PRO"   /* Turbo Prolog */
predicates
    check_text
clauses
    check_text :-
        initgraph(detect, 0, GraphDriver, GraphMode, ""),
        gettextsettings(Font, _,_,_,_),
        Font <> small_FONT,
        settextstyle(small_FONT, horiz_DIR, 1),
        moveto(100,100),
        outtext("Text centered at 100, 100"),
        readchar(_),
        closegraph.
```

Reference:
outtext, outtextxy, settextjustify, settextstyle, setusercharsize, textheight, textwidth

getviewsettings   Gets information about the current viewport.

Syntax:
```
void far getviewsettings(struct viewporttype far *viewport);
Procedure GetViewSettings(Var ViewPort : ViewPortType);
```

```
getviewsettings(Left,Top,Right,Bottom,ClipFlag)    (o,o,o,o,o)
              (integer, integer, integer, integer, integer)
```

Parameters:

In Turbo C and Turbo Pascal the parameter viewport is defined as:

```
struct viewporttype {      /* Turbo C */
    int left, top, right, bottom;
    int clipflag;
};


Type ViewPortType = Record       {Turbo Pascal}
    x1, y1, x2, y2 : Word;
    Clip : Boolean;
End;
```

In Turbo Prolog, the parameters are:

left, top   the upper left corner of the viewport.
right, bottom   the lower right corner of the viewport.
clipflag   determines if graphics are clipped to the active viewport.
                   If this parameter is nonzero, graphics are clipped.

Examples:

The following examples illustrate how a set of coordinate points are tested
to see if they fit inside the current viewport.

```
/*   Turbo C   */
void inrange(int x1, int y1, int x2, int y2)
{
    struct viewporttype viewprt;

    getviewsettings(&viewprt);
    if (x1 < viewprt.left) viewprt.left = x1;
    if (y1 < viewprt.top) viewprt.top = y1;
    if (x2 > viewprt.right) viewprt.right = x2;
    if (y2 > viewprt.bottom) viewprt.bottom = y2;
    setviewport(viewprt.left, viewprt.top, viewprt.right,
              viewprt.bottom, viewprt.clipflag);
}
```

```
{Turbo Pascal}
Procedure InRange(XL, YT, XR, YB : Integer);
Var
    ViewPrt : ViewPortType;
Begin
    GetViewSettings(ViewPrt);
    If (XL < ViewPrt.x1) Then ViewPrt.x1 := XL;
    If (YT < ViewPrt.y1) Then ViewPrt.y1 := YT;
    If (XR > ViewPrt.x2) Then ViewPrt.x2 := XR;
    If (YB > ViewPrt.y2) Then ViewPrt.y2 := YB;
    SetViewPort(ViewPrt.x1, ViewPrt.y1, ViewPrt.x2,
                ViewPrt.y2, ViewPrt.Clip);
End;


include "GRAPDECL.PRO"     /* Turbo Prolog */
predicates
    inrange(integer, integer, integer, integer)
    switchg(integer, integer, integer)
    switchl(integer, integer, integer)
clauses
    inrange(X1, Y1, X2, Y2) :-
        initgraph(detect, 0, GraphDriver, GraphMode, ""),
        getviewsettings(Left, Top, Right, Bottom, Clip),
        switchl(X1,Left,A),
        switchl(Y1,Top,B),
        switchg(X2,Right,C),
        switchg(Y2,Bottom,D),
        setviewport(A,B,C,D,Clip).
    switchg(Val1, Val2, Val3) :-
        Val1 > Val2,
        Val3 = Val1.
    switchg(_,Val2,Val2).
    switchl(Val1, Val2, Val3) :-
        Val1 < Val2,
        Val3 = Val1.
    switchl(_,Val2,Val2).
```

Reference:
clearviewport, getx, gety, setviewport

Remarks:
When the graphics system is initialized with the **initgraph** routine, the viewport is set to the dimensions of the full screen by default. If the clipping is turned off for the viewport, graphics are drawn faster, because the drawing routines do not have to test for clipping.

Gets the current horizontal coordinate.   **getx**

Syntax:
```
int far getx(void);
Function GetX : Integer;
getx(Xcur)      (o)
    (integer)
```

Parameter:
Xcur   the horizontal coordinate (Turbo Prolog only).

Examples:
The following examples illustrate how the horizontal and vertical coordinates are read using the **getx** and **gety** routines.

```
#include <graphics.h>    /* Turbo C */
main()
{
    int graphdriver = DETECT, graphmode;   /* autodetection */
    int x, y;

    initgraph(&graphdriver, &graphmode, "");
    line(50, 50, 100, 100);
    linerel(30, 20);
    x = getx();
    y = gety();
    line(75, 75, x, y);
    getch();
    closegraph();
}


Program ReadXY;   {Turbo Pascal}
Uses Graph;
```

```
Var
    GraphDriver, GraphMode : Integer;
    X, Y : Integer;
Begin
    GraphDriver := Detect;
    InitGraph(GraphDriver, GraphMode, '');
    Line(50, 50, 100, 100);
    LineRel(30, 20);
    X := GetX;
    Y := GetY;
    Line(75, 75, X, Y);
    Readln;
    CloseGraph;
End.


include "GRAPDECL.PRO"    /* Turbo Prolog */
predicates
    get_xy
clauses
    get_xy :-
        initgraph(detect, 0, GraphDriver, GraphMode, ""),
        line(50, 50, 100, 100),
        linerel(30, 20),
        getx(X),
        gety(Y),
        line(75, 75, X, Y),
        readchar(_),
        closegraph.
```

Reference:
gety

gety   Gets the current vertical coordinate.

Syntax:
```
int far gety(void);
Function GetY : Integer;
gety(Ycur)     (o)
    (integer)
```

Parameter:
Ycur   the vertical coordinate (Turbo Prolog only).

Examples:
See **getx**.

Reference:
getx

Resets all of the graphics attributes to their default settings.   **graphdefaults**

Syntax:
```
void far graphdefaults(void);
Procedure GraphDefaults;
graphdefaults
```

Reference:
initgraph, setgraphmode

Remarks:
The default settings for all of the languages are listed in Table 4.13.

Table 4.13. Default graphic settings

Component	Setting
Current position (CP)	Upper left corner (0,0)
View port	Full screen dimensions (0,0, width–1, height–1)
Palette	Default for the current adapter
Drawing color	The maximum color
Background color	Color 0 in the palette
Line style	Solid line
Fill color	The maximum color
Fill style	Solid fill
Font size	1
Font direction	Horizontal
Font justification	Left and top

grapherrormsg   Returns an error message string for a given error code.

Syntax:
```
char *far grapherrormsg(int errorcode);
Function GraphErrorMsg(ErrorCode : Integer) : String;
```

Parameter:
errorcode   the integer error code.

Examples:
See **graphresult**.

Reference:
graphresult

Remarks:
This routine is not provided with Turbo Prolog. The error codes are listed under the discussion What to Do if Something Goes Wrong.

_graphfreemem   Frees up a block of memory allocated by the BGI. This function is called internally by the BGI when the graphics system is closed.

Syntax:
```
void far _graphfreemem(void far *ptr, unsigned size);
```

Parameters:
*ptr   pointer to the memory area to free up.
size   the size of the memory area.

Example:
Here is an example of a user-defined BGI memory deallocation routine written with **_graphfreemem**.

```
void far _graphfreemem(void far *ptr, unsigned size)
{
    if (ptr != NULL) {
        printf("\nThe memory freed up is %d bytes", size);
        farfree(ptr);
    }
}
```

Reference:
_graphgetmem, setgraphbufsize

Remarks:
This routine is only provided with Turbo C. To use it in a program, you
must declare it with the same format as its definition.

Allocates a block of memory for the BGI. This function is called internally   **_graphgetmem**
by the BGI when the graphics system is initialized.

Syntax:
```
void far *   _graphgetmem(unsigned size);
```

Parameter:
size   the size of the memory block to allocate.

Example:
The following example illustrates how you can write your own memory
allocation routine.

```
void far * _graphgetmem(unsigned size)
{
    char *ptr;
    ptr = farmalloc(size);
    if (ptr != NULL) {
        printf("\nThe memory allocated is %d bytes", size);
        return(ptr);
    } else printf("\nMemory allocation error");
}
```

Reference:
_graphfreemem, initgraph, setgraphbufsize

Remarks:
This routine is only provided with Turbo C.

Obtains an error code for last invalid graphics call.   **graphresult**

Syntax:
```
int far graphresult(void);
Function GraphResult : Integer;
```

Examples:

The following examples illustrate how the **graphresult** and **grapherror-msg** functions are used to test for and display an error message:

```c
/* Turbo C */
#include <graphics.h>
main()
{
    int graphdriver = DETECT, graphmode;   /* autodetection */
    int msgnum;
    char *errstr;

    initgraph(&graphdriver, &graphmode, "");
    line(100, 50, 200, 85);
    msgnum = graphresult();
    if (msgnum != 0) {    /* error found */
      errstr = grapherrormsg(msgnum);
      printf("\nGraphics error encountered");
      printf("\nError code is %d, error message is %s",
             msgnum, errstr);
       exit(1);
    }
    /* continue drawing graphics  ... */
    getch();
    closegraph();
}
```

```pascal
{Turbo Pascal}
Program Draw_Lines;
Uses Graph;
Var
    GraphDriver, GraphMode : Integer;
    I, MsgNum : Integer;
    ErrStr : String;

Begin
    GraphDriver := Detect;
    InitGraph(GraphDriver, GraphMode, '');
    Line(100, 50, 200, 85);
    MsgNum := GraphResult;
```

```
If MsgNum <> 0  Then Begin    {error found}
   ErrStr := GraphErrorMsg(MsgNum);
   Writeln('Graphics error encountered');
   Writeln('Error code is ', MsgNum, ' error message is ',
           ErrStr);
   Halt(1);
End;
{continue drawing graphics  ...}
Readln;
CloseGraph;
End.
```

Reference:
grapherrormsg

Remarks:
This routine is not provided with Turbo Prolog.

Obtains number of bytes needed to store a rectangular screen image.   **Imagesize**

Syntax:
```
unsigned far imagesize(int left, int top, int right, int bottom);
Function ImageSize(Left, Top, Right, Bottom : Word) : Word;
imagesize(Left, Right, Right, Bottom, Size)   (i,i,i,i,o)
          (integer, integer, integer, integer, integer)
```

Parameters:

left, top   the upper left corner.
right, bottom   the lower left corner.
size   the size of the image (Turbo Prolog only).

Examples:
See **putimage**.

Reference:
getimage, putimage

Remarks:
Both Turbo C and Pascal return the size of the screen image. If the image
size is greater than 64K, −1 is returned.

Initgraph

Initializes the graphics system by loading a specified graphics driver and setting the graphics mode.

Syntax:
```
void far initgraph(int far *graphdriver, int far *graphmode,
                   char far *pathtodriver);
Procedure InitGraph(Var GraphDriver : Integer;
                    Var GraphMode : Integer; PathToDriver : String);
initgraph(GraphDriver,GraphMode,NewDriver,NewMode,PathToDriver)
         (i,i,o,o,i)
         (integer, integer, integer, integer, string)
```

Parameters:

graphdriver provides an integer code to specify which graphics driver should be used (see Table 4.14).

graphmode provides an integer code to specify the graphics mode.

pathtodriver the directory path name where the graphics driver files are stored.

newdriver (Turbo Prolog only) a return code that indicates the driver used.

newmode (Turbo Prolog only) a return code that indicates the mode used.

Examples:
See **detectgraph**.

Reference:
closegraph, **detectgraph**, **getdrivername**, **getmoderange**, **graphdefaults**, **graphresult**, **registerbgidriver**, **registerbgifont**, **setgraphmode**

Remarks:
initgraph must be called before any of the BGI routines are called except **detectgraph**.

Installuserdriver

Installs a new BGI device driver.

Syntax:
```
int far installuserdriver(char far *drivername,
                          int huge (*autodetectptr)(void));
```

Table 4.14. Graphics drivers supported

Value	C Driver Name	Pascal Driver Name	Prolog Driver Name
0	DETECT	Detect	detect
1	CGA	CGA	cga
2	MCGA	MCGA	mcga
3	EGA	EGA	ega
4	EGA64	EGA64	ega64
5	EGAMONO	EGAMono	egamono
6	IBM8514	IBM8514	ibm8514
7	HERCMONO	HercMono	hercmono
8	ATT400	ATT400	att400
9	VGA	VGA	vga
10	PC3270	PC3270	pc3270

```
Function InstallUserDriver(DriverName : String;
                     AutoDetectPtr : Pointer) : Integer;
```

Parameters:

*drivername   the DOS name of a graphics driver (.BGI) file. The name can contain the full directory path.

autodetectptr   a pointer to an optional autodetect function that is assigned to the new driver.

Reference:
installuserfont

Remarks:
This routine is used to install third-party device drivers to the BGI.

Loads a new font file.   **Installuserfont**

Syntax:
```
int far installuserfont(char far *fontname);
Function InstallUserFont(FontName : String) : Integer;
```

Parameter:

*fontname   the DOS name of a stroked font file. The name can contain the full directory path.

Reference:
installuserdriver

line

Draws a line between two points using absolute screen coordinates. The line is drawn in the current color and line style.

Syntax:
```
void far line(int x0, int y0, int x1, int y1);
Procedure Line(X0, Y0, X1, Y1 : Integer);
line(X0, Y0, X1, Y1)     (i,i,i,i)
     (integer, integer, integer, integer)
```

Parameters:
x0, y0   the starting end point.
x1, y1   the stopping end point.

Examples:
The following examples illustrate how a set of lines can be drawn with the three different line routines:

```
#include <graphics.h>    /* Turbo C */
main()
{
    int graphdriver = DETECT, graphmode;   /* autodetection */
    int data[ ] = {45,80, 160,160, 75,35, -60,30, 45,80};

    initgraph(&graphdriver, &graphmode, "");
    line(data[0], data[1], data[2], data[3]);
    lineto(data[4], data[5]);
    linerel(data[6], data[7]);
    lineto(data[8], data[9]);
    getch();
    closegraph();
}

Program Draw_Lines;   {Turbo Pascal}
Uses Graph;
Const   MAX_POINTS = 5;
    Data : Array [1..MAX_POINTS] Of PointType =
                ((  X : 45; Y : 80),
```

```
                    ( X : 160; Y : 160),
                    ( X : 75; Y : 35),
                    ( X : -60; Y : 30),
                    ( X : 45; Y : 80) );
Var
    GraphDriver, GraphMode, I : Integer;
Begin
    GraphDriver := Detect;
    InitGraph(GraphDriver, GraphMode, '');
    Line(Data[1].X, Data[1].Y, Data[2].X, Data[2].Y);
    LineTo(Data[3].X, Data[3].Y);
    LineRel(Data[4].X, Data[4].Y);
    LineTo(Data[5].X, Data[5].Y);
    ReadLn;
    CloseGraph;
End.


include "GRAPDECL.PRO"     /* Turbo Prolog */
predicates
    draw_lines
clauses
    draw_lines :-
        initgraph(detect, 0, GraphDriver, GraphMode, ""),
        line(45, 80, 160, 160),
        lineto(75,35),
        linerel(-60, 30),
        lineto(45, 80),
        readchar(_),
        closegraph.
```

Reference:
linerel, lineto, getlinesettings, rectangle, setlinestyle

Remarks:
To draw a line in a different style than the default, call the **setlinestyle** routine to set the line style before you draw a line.

Draws a line from the current position (CP) to a new position using relative   **linerel**
coordinates.

Syntax:
```
void far linerel(int dx, int dy);
Procedure LineRel(Dx, Dy : Integer);
linerel(Dx, Dy)     (i,i)
        (integer, integer)
```

Parameters:

dx, dy   the relative horizontal and vertical distance used to draw the line. Either of these values can be specified as a positive or a negative number.

Examples:
See **line**.

Reference:
line, lineto, getlinesettings, rectangle, setlinestyle

Remarks:
After the line is drawn, the new CP is determined by adding the offset (**dx,dy**) to the previous CP.

lineto   Draws a line from the current position (CP) to a new position that is specified in absolute coordinates.

Syntax:
```
void far lineto(int x, int y);
Procedure LineTo(X, Y : Integer);
lineto(X, Y)     (i,i)
      (integer, integer)
```

Parameters:

x, y   the end point for the line. This location becomes the new CP after the line is drawn.

Examples:
See **line**.

Reference:
line, linerel, getlinesettings, rectangle, setlinestyle

Moves the current position (CP) to a relative distance from the CP in the   **moverel**
active viewport.

Syntax:
```
void far moverel(int dx, int dy);
Procedure MoveRel(Dx, Dy : Integer);
moverel(Dx, Dy)     (i,i)
        (integer, integer)
```

Parameters:
dx, dy   the offset to move the CP.

Examples:
The following examples illustrate how graphic objects are drawn with the
moverel and the **moveto** routines.

```
#include <graphics.h>    /* Turbo C */
main()
{
    /* autodetection */
    int graphdriver = DETECT, graphmode;
    initgraph(&graphdriver, &graphmode, "");
    rectangle(100,100,200,200);
    moveto(100,200);
    lineto(200,100);
    moverel(-100,0);
    lineto(200, 200);
    getch();
    closegraph();
}


Program Draw_Graphics;    {Turbo Pascal}
Uses Graph;
Var
    GraphDriver, GraphMode : Integer;
Begin
    GraphDriver := Detect;
    InitGraph(GraphDriver, GraphMode, '');
    Rectangle(100,100,200,200);
```

```
        MoveTo(100,200);
        LineTo(200,100);
        MoveRel(-100,0);
        LineTo(200, 200);
        Readln;
        CloseGraph;
End.

include "GRAPDECL.PRO"    /* Turbo Prolog */
predicates
    draw_graphics
clauses
    draw_graphics :-
        initgraph(detect, 0, GraphDriver, GraphMode, ""),
        rectangle(100,100,200,200),
        moveto(100,200),
        lineto(200,100),
        moverel(-100,0),
        lineto(200, 200),
        readchar(_),
        closegraph.
```

Reference:
linerel, moveto

moveto

Moves the current position (CP) to a new position.

Syntax:
```
void far moveto(int x, int y);
Procedure MoveTo(X, Y : Integer);
moveto(X, Y)    (i,i)
        (integer, integer)
```

Parameters:
x, y   the new CP.

Examples:
See **moveto**.

Reference:
lineto, moverel

Displays a text string at the current position in the active viewport. The text **outtext** string is displayed with the current size, font, direction, and justification settings.

Syntax:

```
void far outtext(char far *textstring);
Procedure OutText(TextString : String);
outtext(TextString)        (i)
        (string)
```

Parameter:

textstring   the string to display in the current viewport.

Examples:

The following examples illustrate how a specific text string is displayed.

```
#include <graphics.h>    /* Turbo C */
main()
{
    int graphdriver = DETECT, graphmode;   /* autodetection */

    initgraph(&graphdriver, &graphmode, "");
    settextjustify(CENTER_TEXT, TOP_TEXT);
    settextstyle(SMALL_FONT, HORIZ_DIR, 1);
    moveto(100,100);
    outtext("Text centered at 100, 100");
    getch();
    closegraph();
}


Program DisplayText;    {Turbo Pascal}
Uses Graph;
Var
    GraphDriver, GraphMode : Integer;
Begin
    GraphDriver := Detect;
    InitGraph(GraphDriver, GraphMode, '');
    SetTextJustify(CenterText, TopText);
    SetTextStyle(SmallFont, HorizDir, 1);
    MoveTo(100,100);
```

```
        OutText('Text centered at 100, 100');
        Readln;
        CloseGraph;
End.


include "GRAPDECL.PRO"    /* Turbo Prolog */
predicates
    display_text
clauses
    display_text :-
        initgraph(detect, 0, GraphDriver, GraphMode, ""),
        settextjustify(center_TEXT, top_TEXT),
        settextstyle(small_FONT, horiz_DIR, 1),
        moveto(100,100),
        outtext("Text centered at 100, 100"),
        readchar(_),
        closegraph.
```

Reference:
gettextsettings, outtextxy, textheight, textwidth

outtextxy   Displays a text string at specified position.

Syntax:
```
void far outtextxy(int x, int y, char far *textstring);
Procedure OutTextXY(X, Y : Integer; TextString : String);
outtextxy(X, Y, TextString)    (i,i,i)
          (integer, integer, string)
```

Parameters:
x, y   the absolute coordinate position where the text is displayed.
textstring   the text string to display.

Examples:
The following examples display a text string with default settings at location 100,100.

```
#include <graphics.h>    /* Turbo C */
main()
{
```

```
    int graphdriver = DETECT, graphmode;   /* autodetection */

    initgraph(&graphdriver, &graphmode, "");
    outtextxy(100,100, "Text displayed at 100,100");
    getch();
    closegraph();
}
```

```
Program DisplayText;   {Turbo Pascal}
Uses Graph;
Var
    GraphDriver, GraphMode : Integer;
Begin
    GraphDriver := Detect;
    InitGraph(GraphDriver, GraphMode, '');
    OutTextXY(100,100, 'Text displayed at 100,100');
    ReadLn;
    CloseGraph;
End.
```

```
include "GRAPDECL.PRO"        /* Turbo Prolog */
predicates
    display_text
clauses
    display_text :-
        initgraph(detect, 0, GraphDriver, GraphMode, ""),
        outtextxy(100,100, "Text displayed at 100,100"),
        readchar(_),
        closegraph.
```

Reference:
gettextsettings, outtext, textheight, textwidth

Draws and fills a pie slice with the current drawing color and pattern fill   **pieslice**
style.

Syntax:
```
void far pieslice(int x, int y, int stangle, int endangle,
                  int radius);
Procedure PieSlice(X, Y : Integer; StAngle, EndAngle, Radius : Word);
```

```
pieslice(X, Y, Stangle, Endangle, Radius)     (i,i,i,i,i)
            (integer, integer, integer, integer, integer)
```

Parameters:
x, y   the center point for the pie slice.
stangle, endangle   the starting and ending angles.
radius   the radius in pixels.

Examples:
The following examples illustrate how pie slices are drawn with **pieslice**
and **sector**.

```
#include <graphics.h>          /* Turbo C */
main()
{
    int graphdriver = DETECT, graphmode;   /* autodetection */

    initgraph(&graphdriver, &graphmode, "");
    pieslice(100, 100, 90, 120, 50);
    sector(100,100, 90, 120, 50, 30);
    getch();
    closegraph();
}


Program Draw_Pie;   {Turbo Pascal}
Uses Graph;
Var
    GraphDriver, GraphMode : Integer;
Begin
    GraphDriver := Detect;
    InitGraph(GraphDriver, GraphMode, '');
    PieSlice(100,100, 90, 120, 50);
    Sector(100,100, 90, 120, 50, 30);
    Readln;
    CloseGraph;
End.


include "GRAPDECL.PRO"      /* Turbo Prolog */
predicates
    draw_pie
```

```
clauses
    draw_pie :-
        initgraph(detect, 0, GraphDriver, GraphMode, ""),
        pieslice(100,100, 90, 120, 50),
        sector(100,100, 90, 120, 50, 30),
        readchar(_),
        closegraph.
```

Reference:
arc, ellipse, fillellipse, sector, setfillstyle

Copies a bit image onto the screen.   **putImage**

Syntax:
```
void far putimage(int left, int top, void far *bitmap,
                  int op);
Procedure PutImage(Left, Top : Integer; Var BitMap;
                   Op : Integer);
putimage(Left, Top, Bitmap, Op)      (i,i,i,i)
        (integer, integer, string, integer)
```

Parameters:
left, top   upper left corner where the image is written.
bitmap   references the stored bit image.
op   the copy operation code (see Table 4.15).

Table 4.15. **Values for op parameter**

Value	C Name	Pascal Name	Prolog Name	Function
0	COPY_PUT	NormalPut	copy_PUT	Copy
1	XOR_PUT	XORPut	xor_PUT	Exclusive OR
2	OR_PUT	OrPut	or_PUT	Inclusive OR
3	AND_PUT	AndPut	and_PUT	AND
4	NOT_PUT	NotPut	not_PUT	Copy inverse

Examples:
The following examples illustrate how the **putimage** and **getimage** routines are used to move a region of the screen.

```c
#include <graphics.h>    /* Turbo C */
main()
{
    int graphdriver = DETECT, graphmode;   /* autodetection */
    unsigned rectsize;
    void *imagebuf;

    initgraph(&graphdriver, &graphmode, "");
    rectangle(40,40, 100,100);   /* draw graphics */
    rectsize = imagesize(40,40,100,100);
    imagebuf = malloc(rectsize);   /* allocate memory for image */
    getimage(40,40,100,100,imagebuf);
    putimage(80,80, imagebuf, COPY_PUT);
    free(imagebuf);
    getch();
    closegraph();
}
```

```pascal
Program Move_Image;   {Turbo Pascal}
Uses Graph;
Var
    GraphDriver, GraphMode : Integer;
    RectSize : Word;
    ImageBuf : Pointer;
Begin
    GraphDriver := Detect;
    InitGraph(GraphDriver, GraphMode, '');
    Rectangle(40,40, 100,100);            {draw graphics}
    RectSize := ImageSize(40,40,100,100);
    GetMem(ImageBuf, RectSize);    {allocate memory for image}
    GetImage(40,40,100,100,ImageBuf^);
    PutImage(80,80, ImageBuf^, NormalPut);   {move image}
    FreeMem(ImageBuf, RectSize);
    ReadLn;
    CloseGraph;
End.
```

```prolog
include "GRAPDECL.PRO"    /* Turbo Prolog */
predicates
    move_image
```

```
clauses
    move_image :-
        initgraph(detect, 0, GraphDriver, GraphMode, ""),
        rectangle(40,40, 100,100),  /* draw graphics */
        getimage(40,40,100,100,ImageBuf),
        putimage(80,80, ImageBuf, copy_PUT), /* move image */
        readchar(_),
        closegraph.
```

Reference:
getimage, imagesize, putpixel

Remarks:
This routine along with **getimage** is useful for performing animation. You
can use it to perform graphics techniques such as rubberbanding lines.

Displays a pixel in a specified color.   **putpixel**

Syntax:
```
void far putpixel(int x, int y, int pixelcolor);
Procedure PutPixel(X, Y : Integer; PixelColor : Word);
putpixel(X, Y, Pixelcolor)     (i,i,i)
        (integer, integer, integer)
```

Parameters:
x, y   position of the pixel.
pixelcolor   the color code specified as an integer value.

Examples:
The following examples illustrate how the **putpixel** and **getpixel** routines
test and set the color of a rectangular region of the screen.

```
#include <graphics.h>    /* Turbo C */
main()
{
    int graphdriver = DETECT, graphmode;   /* autodetection */
    int i, j, pcolor, curcolor;

    initgraph(&graphdriver, &graphmode, "");
    for (i = 50; i <100; i++)
```

```
        for (j = 50; j <100; j++)   {
            pcolor = getpixel(i, j);
            curcolor = getcolor();
            if (pcolor != curcolor) putpixel(i,j,curcolor);
        }
        getch();
        closegraph();
}


Program Check_Pixels;   {Turbo Pascal}
Uses Graph;
Var
    GraphDriver, GraphMode : Integer;
    I, J, PColor, CurColor : Integer;
Begin
    GraphDriver := Detect;
    InitGraph(GraphDriver, GraphMode, '');
    For I := 50 To 99 Do
        For J := 50 To 99 Do Begin
            PColor := GetPixel(I, J);
            CurColor := GetColor;
            If PColor <> CurColor Then PutPixel(I,J,CurColor);
        End;
    Readln;
End.
```

Reference:
getimage, putimage

rectangle   Draws a rectangle in the current line style and color.

Syntax:
```
void far rectangle(int left, int top, int right, int bottom);
Procedure Rectangle(Left, Top, Right, Bottom : Integer);
rectangle(Left, Top, Right, Bottom)       (i,i,i,i)
           (integer, integer, integer, integer)
```

Parameters:
left, top   the upper left corner.
right, bottom the lower right corner.

Examples:
See **moverel**.

Reference:
bar, bar3d, line, setcolor, setlinestyle

Registers a BGI graphics driver. A driver can be loaded from disk or can   **registerbgidriver**
be linked in as a .OBJ file.

Syntax:
```
int registerbgidriver(void (*driver)(void));
Function RegisterBGIDriver(Driver : Pointer) : Integer;
```

Parameter:
driver   the name of the registered driver.

Examples:
The following examples illustrate how the **registerbgidriver** and **regis-terbgifont** routines load and register graphics hardware and font drivers.

```
#include <graphics.h>    /* Turbo C */
main()
{
    /* DETECT is defined in graphics.h */
    int graphdriver = DETECT;
    int graphmode;

    /* must register driver first */
    if (registerbgidriver(EGAVGA_driver) < 0) exit(1);
    if (registerbgifont(small_font) < 0) exit(1);
    initgraph(&graphdriver, &graphmode, "");
    rectangle(0, 0, 639, 199);
    outtextxy(100,100, "Text displayed in small font");
    getch();
    closegraph();
}


Program Driver_Demo;       {Turbo Pascal}
Uses Graph, Drivers;
Var
    GraphDriver, GraphMode : Integer;
```

```
Begin
    If RegisterBGIDriver(@EGAVGADriver) < 0 Then Exit;
    If RegisterBGIFont(@SmallFont) < 0 Then Exit;
    GraphDriver := Detect;
    InitGraph(GraphDriver, GraphMode, "");
    Rectangle(0, 0, 639, 199);
    OuttextXY(100,100, "Text displayed in small font");
    Readln;
    CloseGraph;
End.
```

References:
initgraph, installuserdriver, registerbgifont

Remarks:
A complete discussion of the techniques involved in loading and registering drivers and fonts is presented in the discussion entitled Loading Graphics and Font Drivers.

registerbgifont   Registers a BGI font driver.

Syntax:
```
int registerbgifont(void (*font)(void));
Function RegisterBGIFont(Font : Pointer) : Integer;
```

Parameter:
font   the name of the registered font.

Examples:
See **registerbgidriver**.

References:
initgraph, installuserdriver, registerbgidriver

restorecrtmode   Restores the screen to the mode it was in before a graphics mode was selected.

Syntax:
```
void far restorecrtmode(void);
Procedure RestoreCRTMode;
restorecrtmode
```

Examples:

The following examples illustrate how the **restorecrtmode** routine along with the **setgraphmode** routine can be used to switch back and
forth between a graphics mode and a text mode.

```c
#include <graphics.h>    /* Turbo C */
#include <conio.h>
main()
{
    int graphdriver = DETECT, graphmode;   /* autodetection */

    printf("\nIn text mode");
    getch();
    initgraph(&graphdriver, &graphmode, "");
    line(50, 50, 100, 100);    /* draw a line */
    getch();
    restorecrtmode();      /* back to text mode */
    printf("\nNow in text mode again");
    setgraphmode(graphmode);   /* back to graphics */
    rectangle(30, 30, 100, 100);
    closegraph();
}
```

```pascal
Program Switch_Modes;    {Turbo Pascal}
Uses Graph, Crt;
Var
    GraphDriver, GraphMode : Integer;
Begin
    GraphDriver := Detect;
    Writeln('In text mode');
    Readln;
    InitGraph(GraphDriver, GraphMode, '');
    Line(50, 50, 100, 100);    {draw a line}
    Repeat Until KeyPressed;
    RestoreCrtMode;      {back to text mode}
    Writeln('Now in text mode again');
    SetGraphMode(GraphMode);     {back to graphics}
    Rectangle(30, 30, 100, 100);
    CloseGraph;
End.
```

```
include "GRAPDECL.PRO"    /* Turbo Prolog */
predicates
    switch_modes
clauses
    switch_modes :-
        write("\nIn text mode"),
        readchar(_),
        initgraph(detect, 0, GraphDriver, GraphMode, ""),
        line(50, 50, 100, 100),    /* draw a line */
        readchar(_),
        restorecrtmode(),        /* back to text mode */
        write("\nNow in text mode again"),
        setgraphmode(GraphMode),        /* back to graphics */
        rectangle(30, 30, 100, 100),
        closegraph.
```

Reference:
getgraphmode, getmoderange, initgraph, setgraphmode

sector

Draws and fills an elliptical pie slice with the current drawing color and pattern fill style.

Syntax:
```
void far sector(int x, int y, int stangle, int endangle,
                int xradius, int yradius);
Procedure Sector(X, Y : Integer; StAngle, EndAngle, XRadius,
                YRadius : Word);
pieslicexy(X, Y, Stangle, Endangle, Radius)    (i,i,i,i,i)
    (integer, integer, integer, integer, integer)
```

Parameters:
x, y	the center point for the pie slice.
stangle, endangle	the starting and ending angles.
xradius, yradius	the horizontal and vertical radii in pixels.

Examples:
See **pieslice.**

Reference:
arc, ellipse, fillellipse, pieslice, setfillstyle

Sets active page for graphics display. **setactivepage**

Syntax:
```
void setactivepage(int pagenum);
Procedure SetActivePage(PageNum : Word);
setactivepage(PageNum)      (i)
            (integer)
```

Parameter:
pagenum   the page number to make active.

Reference:
setvisualpage

Changes all palette colors. **setallpalette**

Syntax:
```
void far setallpalette(struct palettetype far *palette);
Procedure SetAllPalette(Var Palette);
setallpalette(Palette)      (i)
            (bgi_ilist)
```

Parameter:
palette   contains the palette color information. This data structure
            is presented with the **getpalette** routine.

Reference:
getpalette, getpalettesize, setpalette, setrgbpalette

Sets the X and Y aspect ratio for the active graphics hardware and mode.   **setaspectratio**

Syntax:
```
void far setaspectratio(int xasp, int yasp);
Procedure SetAspectRatio(Xasp, Yasp : Word);
setallpalette(Xasp, Yasp)      (i,i)
            (integer, integer)
```

Parameters:
xasp, yasp   the new horizontal and vertical aspect ratios.

Examples:
See **getaspectratio.**

Reference:
getaspectratio

setbkcolor   Sets the background color.

Syntax:
```
void far setbkcolor(int color);
Procedure SetBkColor(Color : Word);
setbkcolor(Color)     (i)
          (integer)
```

Parameter:

color   an integer color code (0–15) that specifies the new background color. The tables of the background colors and codes for each of the languages are presented at the beginning of this section.

Examples:
See **getcolor.**

Reference:
getbkcolor, getcolor, getpalette, setallpalette, setpalette, setcolor

setcolor   Sets the active drawing color.

Syntax:
```
void far setcolor(int color);
Procedure SetColor(Color : Word);
setcolor(Color)     (i)
      (integer)
```

Parameter:

color   an integer color code that specifies the new drawing color. The tables of the background colors and codes for each of the languages are presented earlier in this section.

Examples:
See **getcolor.**

Reference:
getbkcolor, **getcolor**, **getmaxcolor**, **getpalette**, **setallpalette**, **setpalette**, **setbkcolor**

Remarks:
The maximum number of colors that are available for a given graphics adapter and mode can be obtained by calling **getmaxcolor**.

Selects a user-defined fill pattern and color.   **setfillpattern**

Syntax:
```
void far setfillpattern(char far *pattern, int color);
Procedure SetFillPattern(Pattern : FillPatternType; Color : Word);
setfillpattern(Pattern, Color)      (i,i)
            (bgi_ilist, integer)
```

Parameters:
pattern   specifies the user-defined fill pattern.
color   specifies the fill color.

Examples:
See **getfillstyle**.

Reference:
getfillpattern

Remarks:
The user-defined fill pattern is created using bit settings. The technique for defining a pattern is presented with the **getfillstyle** routine.

Selects the current fill pattern and color.   **setfillstyle**

Syntax:
```
void far setfillstyle(int pattern, int color);
Procedure SetFillStyle(Pattern : Word; Color : Word);
setfillstyle(Pattern, Color)      (i,i)
            (integer, integer)
```

Parameters:
pattern   specifies one of the twelve BGI supported fill patterns.
color   specifies the fill color.

Examples:
See **getfillstyle**.

Reference:
getfillsettings, setfillpattern

Remarks:
The fill pattern set by this routine is used for drawing graphics with the following routines: **bar, bar3d, fillpoly, floodfill, pieslice, sector.**

setgraphmode   Sets the system to graphics mode and clears the screen.

Syntax:
```
void far setgraphmode(int mode);
Procedure SetGraphMode(Mode : Integer);
setgraphmode(Mode)     (i)
          (integer)
```

Parameter:
mode   the graphics mode to select.

Examples:
See **getgraphmode**.

Reference:
getgraphmode, getmoderange, initgraph, restorecrtmode

Remarks:
To use this routine, **initgraph** must have been previously called.

setlinestyle   Sets the current line width and style.

Syntax:
```
void far setlinestyle(int linestyle, unsigned upattern,
                      int thickness);
Procedure SetLineStyle(LineStyle, Pattern, Thickness : Word);
setlinestyle(LineStyle, Upattern, Thickness)     (i,i,i)
          (integer, integer, integer)
```

Parameters:

linestyle the line style specified as an integer code (see Table 4.16)
upattern the user line style pattern specified as a 16-bit pattern.
thickness the line thickness (see Table 4.17). Two styles are supported: normal = 1 pixel wide, thick = 3 pixels wide.

Table 4.16. Line style codes

Value	C Name	Pascal Name	Prolog Name
0	SOLID_LINE	SolidLn	solid_LINE
1	DOTTED_LINE	DottedLn	dotted_LINE
2	CENTER_LINE	CenterLn	center_LINE
3	DASHED_LINE	DashedLn	dashed_LINE
4	USERBIT_LINE	UserBitLn	userbit_LINE

Table 4.17. Line thickness codes

Value	C Name	Pascal Name	Prolog Name
1	NORM_WIDTH	NormWidth	norm_WIDTH
3	THICK_WIDTH	ThickWidth	thick_WIDTH

Examples:

The following examples illustrate how line styles are set.

```
#include <graphics.h>    /* Turbo C */
main()
{
    int graphdriver = DETECT, graphmode;  /* autodetection */
    struct linesettingstype oldline;

    initgraph(&graphdriver, &graphmode, "");
    getlinesettings(&oldline);
    if (oldline.linestyle == USERBIT_LINE) {
      setlinestyle(USERBIT_LINE, 0x0F0F, NORM_WIDTH); /* dashed */
      circle(100, 100, 50);
    }
```

```
    else  {   /* use a predefined pattern */
       setlinestyle(CENTER_LINE, 0, THICK_WIDTH);
       rectangle(50,50,100,100);
    }
    setlinestyle(oldline.linestyle, oldline.upattern,
                 oldline.thickness);
    getch();
    closegraph();
}
```

```pascal
Program SetStyle;   {Turbo Pascal}
Uses Graph;
Var
    GraphDriver, GraphMode : Integer;
    OldLine : LineSettingsType;
Begin
    GraphDriver := Detect;
    InitGraph(GraphDriver, GraphMode, '');
    GetLineSettings(OldLine);
    If OldLine.LineStyle = UserBitLn Then Begin
       SetLineStyle(UserBitLn, $0F0F, NormWidth); {dashed}
       Circle(100, 100, 50);
    End
    Else Begin              {use a predefined pattern}
       SetLineStyle(CenterLine, 0, ThickWidth);
       Rectangle(50,50,100,100);
    End;
    SetLineStyle(OldLine.LineStyle, OldLine.Pattern,
                 OldLine.Thickness);
    CloseGraph;
End.
```

```prolog
include "GRAPDECL.PRO"     /* Turbo Prolog */
predicates
    set_style
    set_pattern(integer)
clauses
    set_style :-
       initgraph(detect, 0, GraphDriver, GraphMode, ""),
       getlinesettings(LineStyle, Pattern, Thickness),
```

```
      set_pattern(LineStyle),
      setlinestyle(LineStyle, Pattern, Thickness),
      readchar(_),
      closegraph.
   set_pattern(userbit_LINE) :-
      setlinestyle(userbit_LINE, $0F0F, norm_WIDTH), /* dashed */
      circle(100, 100, 50).
   set_pattern(_) :-
      setlinestyle(center_LINE, 0, thick_WIDTH),
      rectangle(50,50,100,100).
```

Reference:
getlinesettings

Changes a color in the active color palette.   **setpalette**

Syntax:
```
void far setpalette(int index, int color);
Procedure SetPalette(Index : Word; Color : Byte);
setpalette(Index, Color)    (i,i)
          (integer, integer)
```

Parameters:
index   the palette index (0-15).
color   the color to replace.

Examples:
See **getpalette**.

Reference:
getpalette, getpalettesize, setallpalette, setrgbpalette

Changes a color in the active color palette.   **setrgbpalette**

Syntax:
```
void far setrgbpalette(int colornum, int red, int green, int blue);
Procedure SetRGBPalette(ColorNum, Red, Green, Blue : Word);
setrgbpalette(ColorNum, Red, Green, Blue)    (i,i,i,i)
              (integer, integer, integer, integer)
```

Parameters:
colornum   the palette entry to be loaded.
red, green, blue the color components.

Reference:
getpalette, getpalettesize, setallpalette, setrgbpalette

settextjustify Sets the text justification style.

Syntax:
```
void far settextjustify(int horiz, int vert);
Procedure SetTextJustify(Horiz, Vert : Word);
settextjustify(Horiz, Vert)   (i,i)
                (integer, integer)
```

Parameters:
horiz the horizontal justification code.
vert the vertical justification code.

The justification codes for each language are listed in Table 4.18.

Table 4.18. Horizontal and vertical justification codes

Value	C Name	Pascal Name	Prolog Name	Type
0	LEFT_TEXT	LeftText	left_TEXT	Horizontal
0	BOTTOM_TEXT	BottomText	bottom_TEXT	Vertical
1	CENTER_TEXT	CenterText	center_TEXT	Both
2	RIGHT_TEXT	RightText	right_TEXT	Horizontal
2	TOP_TEXT	TopText	top_TEXT	Vertical

Examples:
See **outtext** and **textheight**.

Reference:
gettextsettings, outtext, outtextxy, settextstyle, setusercharsize, textheight, textwidth

Sets the current text style. **settextstyle**

Syntax:
```
void far settextstyle(int font, int direction, int charsize);
Procedure  SetTextStyle(Font, Direction : Word;
                        CharSize : CharSizeType);
settextstyle(Font, Direction, CharSize)    (i,i,i)
            (integer, integer, integer)
```

Parameters:

font the font style specified as an integer code (see Table 4.19).
direction the horizontal or vertical direction code (see Table 4.20).
charsize the scaling size for the character set.

Table 4.19. Font styles

Value	C Name	Pascal Name	Prolog Name	Style
0	DEFAULT_FONT	DefaultFont	default_FONT	Bit-Mapped font
1	TRIPLEX_FONT	TriplexFont	triplex_FONT	Triplex
2	SMALL_FONT	SmallFont	small_FONT	Small
3	SANSSERIF_FONT	SansserifFont	sansserif_FONT	Sansserif
4	GOTHIC_FONT	GothicFont	gothic_FONT	Gothic

Table 4.20. Direction codes

Value	C Name	Pascal Name	Prolog Name
0	HORIZ_DIR	HorizDir	horiz_DIR
1	VERT_DIR	VertDir	vert_DIR

Examples:
See **outtext** and **textheight**.

Reference:
gettextsettings, outtext, outtextxy, settextjustify, setusercharsize, textheight, textwidth

setusercharsize   Defines the size for displayed stroke font characters. The size is specified as a multiplication factor.

Syntax:

```
void far setusercharsize(int multx, int divx, int multy, int divy);
Procedure SetUserCharSize(MultX, DivX, MultY, DivY : Word);
setusercharsize(Multx, Divx, Multy, Divy)     (i,i,i,i)
                  (integer, integer, integer, integer)
```

Parameters:

multx, multy   specify the height and width multiplication factors.

divx, divy   specify the height and width division factors. The horizontal and vertical size of a character is defined by using the following ratios:

multx/divx — horizontal scale factor.
multy/divy — vertical scale factor.

Examples:

```
#include <graphics.h>     /* Turbo C */
main()
{
    int graphdriver = DETECT, graphmode;   /* autodetection */
    int textht, textwt;

    initgraph(&graphdriver, &graphmode, "");
    settextjustify(LEFT_TEXT, TOP_TEXT);
    settextstyle(DEFAULT_FONT, HORIZ_DIR, USER_CHAR_SIZE);
    moveto(50, 50);
    textht = textheight("Test string");
    textwt = textwidth("Test string");
    setusercharsize(100, textht, 50, textwt);
    outtext("Test string");
    getch();
    closegraph();
}


Program SizeText;   {Turbo Pascal}
Uses Graph;
Var
```

```
    GraphDriver, GraphMode : Integer;
    TextHt, TextWt : Integer;
Begin
    GraphDriver := Detect;
    InitGraph(GraphDriver, GraphMode, '');
    SetTextJustify(LeftText, TopText);
    SetTextStyle(DefaultFont, HorizDir, 0);
    MoveTo(50, 50);
    TextHt := TextHeight('Test string');
    TextWt := TextWidth('Test string');
    SetUserCharSize(100, TextHt, 50, TextWt);
    OutText('Test string');
    ReadLn;
    CloseGraph;
End.


include "GRAPDECL.PRO"   /* Turbo Prolog */
predicates
    size_text
clauses
    size_text :-
        initgraph(detect, 0, GraphDriver, GraphMode, ""),
        settextjustify(left_TEXT, top_TEXT),
        settextstyle(default_FONT, horiz_DIR, 0),
        moveto(50, 50),
        textheight("Test string", TextHt),
        textwidth("Test string", TextWt),
        setusercharsize(100, TextHt, 50, TextWt),
        outtext("Test string"),
        readchar(_),
        closegraph.
```

Reference:
gettextsettings, settextstyle

Sets the current viewport.   **setviewport**

Syntax:
```
void far setviewport(int left, int top, int right, int bottom,
                     int clipflag);
```

```
Procedure SetViewPort(Left, Top, Right, Bottom : Integer;
                        ClipFlag : Boolean);
setviewport(Left, Top, Right, Bottom, ClipFlag)    (i,i,i,i,i)
                (integer, integer, integer, integer, integer)
```

Parameters:

left, top   the upper left corner of the viewport.
right, bottom   the lower right corner of the viewport.
clipflag   determines if graphics are clipped to the active viewport.
                      If this parameter is nonzero, graphics are clipped.

Examples:
See **getviewport**.

Reference:
clearviewport, getviewsettings

setvisualpage   Sets the visual graphics page number.

Syntax:
```
void far setvisualpage(int pagenum);
Procedure SetVisualPage(PageNum : Word);
setvisualpage(PageNum)    (i)
                (integer)
```

Parameter:
pagenum   an integer code that specifies the active visual page.

Reference:
setactivepage

setwritemode   Sets the writing mode for the line-drawing graphics routines.

Syntax:
```
void far setwritemode(int writemode);
Procedure SetWriteMode(WriteMode : Integer);
setwritemode(WriteMode)    (i)
                (integer)
```

Parameter:
writemode   specifies the write mode. The modes supported are:

Value	C Name	Pascal Name	Prolog Name
0	COPY_PUT	CopyPut	CopyPut
1	XOR_PUT	XorPut	XorPut

The **CopyPut** (value = 0) mode is used to overwrite whatever is currently on the screen with the new line that is drawn. The **XorPut** (value = 1) mode is used to perform an XOR (exclusive OR) operation.

Remarks:
The writing mode set by this routine affects only the following drawing routines: **drawpoly, line, linerel, lineto,** and **rectangle.**

Obtains the height of a text string in pixels. The current (active) font size and multiplication factor are used to calculate the height of the string.   **textheight**

Syntax:
```
int far textheight(char far *textstring);
Function TextHeight(TextString : String) : Word;
textheight(TextString, Height)   (i,o)
         (string, integer)
```

Parameters:
textstring   the string used for sizing.
height   (Prolog only) this variable stores the height in pixels of the text string.

Examples:
The following examples illustrate how text is displayed in different styles.

```
#include <graphics.h>    /* Turbo C */
main()
{
    int graphdriver = DETECT, graphmode;   /* autodetection */
    int textht, textwt;

    initgraph(&graphdriver, &graphmode, "");
    settextjustify(LEFT_TEXT, TOP_TEXT);
    settextstyle(DEFAULT_FONT, HORIZ_DIR, 1);
```

```
    moveto(100,100);
    textht = textheight("Test string");
    textwt = textwidth("Test string");
    if ((textht < 100) && (textwt < 100))
        outtext("Test string");
    getch();
    closegraph();
}


Program SizeText;   {Turbo Pascal}
Uses Graph;
Var
    GraphDriver, GraphMode : Integer;
    TextHt, TextWt : Integer;
Begin
    GraphDriver := Detect;
    InitGraph(GraphDriver, GraphMode, '');
    SetTextJustify(LeftText, TopText);
    SetTextStyle(DefaultFont, HorizDir, 1);
    MoveTo(100,100);
    TextHt := TextHeight('Test string');
    TextWt := TextWidth('Test string');
    If (TextHt < 100) AND (TextWt < 100) Then
        OutText('Test string');
    Readln;
    CloseGraph;
End.


include "GRAPDECL.PRO"   /* Turbo Prolog */
predicates
    size_text
clauses
    size_text :-
        initgraph(detect, 0, GraphDriver, GraphMode, ""),
        settextjustify(left_TEXT, top_TEXT),
        settextstyle(default_FONT, horiz_DIR, 1),
        moveto(100,100),
        textheight("Test string", TextHt),
        textwidth("Test string", TextWt),
        TextHt < 100,
```

```
TextWt < 100,
outtext("Test string"),
readchar(_),
closegraph.
```

Reference:
gettextsettings, outtext, outtextxy, settextstyle, textwidth

Remarks:
This routine, along with **textwidth**, is useful for determining if a string will
fit in a specified region before the string is actually displayed. If you are
creating presentation graphics with labels, such as bar or pie charts, you'll
find these routines to be very valuable.

Obtains the width of a text string in pixels. The current (active) font size   **textwidth**
and multiplication factor is used to calculate the width of the string.

Syntax:
```
int far textwidth(char far *textstring);
Function TextWidth(TextString : String) : Word;
textwidth(TextString, Width)    (i,o)
        (string, integer)
```

Parameters:
textstring the string used for sizing.
width   (Prolog only) this variable stores the width in pixels of the
                text string.

Examples:
See **textheight**.

Reference:
gettextsettings, outtext, outtextxy, settextstyle, textheight

String

Processing

Introduction

Strings are important and popular data structures found in all programming languages. Simply viewed, strings are arrays of characters. However, because these sequences of characters normally store readable text, they are treated as a special type of array. There are two types of strings: fixed and dynamic. Fixed strings have their maximum size predefined, whereas dynamic strings can change their sizes at run-time. Often, dynamic strings also have an upper limit imposed on their size, due to limitations imposed by the hardware, the underlying operating system, or both. However, these limits still offer a generous size for dynamic strings.

In this section, we'll look at the string routines and the techniques for processing strings in each of the languages.

Overview

Programming languages generally implement strings in one of two ways:

1. The string structure reserves a one byte memory location to keep track of the current length. Because a byte cannot store a value higher than 255, the string cannot exceed 255 characters. When a word is used instead, the string size can be up to 64K.
2. A string delimiter is maintained after the last character. Usually, the null character (that is, ASCII 0) is used for this purpose. This is also known as the *ASCIIZ string*. To determine the length of a string, for example, characters are counted until the null character is encountered. This scheme works equally well with fixed and dynamic strings. In fact, this scheme enables a language, such as C, to employ the same routines for both fixed and dynamic strings.

Strings in Turbo BASIC

Turbo BASIC supports strings that are up to 64K in size. The size of a string does not have to be predefined, so Turbo BASIC strings may be considered as dynamic with a 64K hardware limitation. The first character in a string is at index 1. Simple string typed variables need no special declarations, whereas arrays of strings must have their array bounds defined. A string variable is normally identified by using a $ after the name of the variable.

This is the prevalent convention. You can also use the **DEFSTR** declaration to declare variables, having names that begin with certain letters, as strings. In this case, the $ is optional.

Strings in Turbo C

Turbo C implements fixed and dynamic strings that are delimited by the null character (represented by **\0** in C). The first character in a string is at index 0. Strings are declared as arrays of characters in C, as shown below:

```
char string1[81] = "The Last Emperor";
char string2[] = "The Day of the Jackal"
char lonStr[1001];
char *ptr1 = string1;
char *ptr2 = string2;
```

The technique of accessing strings via pointers is used extensively in C. In fact, C string management functions are built using a pointer to characters to access strings. An interesting feature of such functions, in general, is their ability to work on the trailing part of a string. This is illustrated in the following short program:

```
#include <stdio.h>
#include <string.h>

main()
{
    char string[81] = "When you see him, say hi!";
    char *ptr = string;

    strupr(ptr+strlen("When")+1);
    printf("String is %s\n", ptr);
}
```

When the above program runs, it displays the string **"When YOU SEE HIM, SAY HI!"**. By employing pointer arithmetic, **ptr+strlen("When")-1** points to the substring **" you see him, say hi!"** and not the whole string. Similarly, other C functions are able to work on the trailing part of a string using a pointer accompanied by an offset value.

Strings in Turbo Pascal

Turbo Pascal implements fixed strings that are up to 255 characters long. The first character in a string is at index 1. The index for 0 is the byte used to store the current string length. Thus, **Ord(Message[0])** returns the length of the string **Message**. Conversely you can alter the length of a string by accessing index 0 in the following manner:

```
Message[0] := Chr(New_String_Length);
```

The **String** and **String[<***size***>]** data type identifiers declare standard strings in Turbo Pascal. When **String** is used, a string of 255 characters is created. Examples are shown below:

```
Type String40 = String[40];
     LString = String[255];
Var Message : String;          {255 characters}
    Warning : String[80];      {specify size with declaration}
    Name : String40;           {user-defined string identifier}
    BigStr : LString;          {user-defined string identifier}
```

Strings in Turbo Prolog

Turbo Prolog supports strings that are up to 64K long. String variables are created and removed dynamically, in a manner very similar to BASIC. This is especially true for strings that are local to predicates. However, the predicate that passes string arguments declares the string type (no string length needs to be specified). This is demonstrated below in the predicate **prompt_str** that prompts the user for a string with a specified maximum string length. The predicate's parameter **LeString** has been identified in the predicates section as a string.

```
predicates
    go
    prompt_str(string, integer)
clauses
    prompt_str(LeString, StrLen) :-
        write("Enter a string (up to ",StrLen," chars) : "),
        readln(LeString),
```

```
    str_len(LeString, LeStrLen),
    LeStrLen <= StrLen.
/* recursive call to obtain a string of length StrLen */
prompt_str(LeString, StrLen) :-
    prompt_str(LeString, StrLen).
go :-
    prompt_str(LeString, 10),
    write("String '", LeString,
        "' matches the length requirements"), nl.
```

Because Turbo Prolog does not support arrays, to access a specific character in a string you must resort to using one of the built-in Prolog string processing predicates. To the veteran procedural-language programmer this means adapting to a different way of thinking.

Turbo BASIC

The major string processing routines in Turbo BASIC are covered next.

Returns the ASCII code number of the first character in its argument.　**ASC**

Syntax:
ASC(S$)

Parameter:
S$　the string containing one or more characters. In a multicharacter string, the ASCII code of the first character is returned. If a null string is supplied, a zero is returned.

Examples:

```
ASC("")  'returns 0
ASC("A")  'returns 64
ASC("AND")  'returns 64
```

Returns the binary string equivalent of a number.　**BIN$**

Syntax:
BIN$(N)

Parameter:

N   a numeric constant, variable, or expression in the range of –32768 to 65553. The value of **N** is rounded to the nearest integer before the binary number image is created. The two's complement binary number is produced by the function for a negative argument.

Example:

The following example is a function that reports whether a certain bit of a number is 1 or 0. The function checks for bad arguments and returns –1 if they are found.

```
DEF FNGetBit%(N%, BitNumber%)
    S$ = BIN$(N%) ' get the binary number image
    DO WHILE LEN(S$) < 8
        S$ = "0" + S$ ' pad with leading zero
    LOOP
    IF (BitNumber% < LEN(S$)) AND (BitNumber% >= 0) THEN
        FNGetBit% = VAL(MID$(S$,LEN(S$)-BitNumber%,1))
    ELSE
        FNGetBit% = -1 ' error code
    END IF
END DEF
```

CHR$ Returns the character that corresponds to the ASCII code number of the argument.

Syntax:

CHR$(ASCII.CODE%)

Parameter:

ASCII.CODE%   an integer constant, variable, or expression in the range of 0 to 255.

Restrictions:

If the argument of **CHR$** is out of range, a run-time error occurs.

Examples:

```
CHR$(64) 'returns "A"
CHR$(ASC("h")) 'returns "h"
```

Converts a number into a string containing the hexadecimal image of that **HEX$**
number.

Syntax:
```
HEX$ (N)
```

Parameter:

N   a numeric constant, variable, or expression in the range of –32768 to
65553. The value of **N** is rounded to the nearest integer before the
hexadecimal number image is created. The two's complement binary
number is produced by the function for a negative argument.

Example:
The following program prints a simple decimal-hexadecimal conversion
table.

```
PRINT "DECIMAL      HEX"
PRINT "_____    ____"
FOR I% = 0 TO 255
   PRINT USING "  ###    /    /";I%,HEX$(I%)
NEXT I%
```

Returns the position of a substring in a string.   **INSTR**

Syntax:
```
INSTR([Offset,] String$, SubString$)
```

Parameters:

Offset   the number of leftmost characters of **String$** to skip before
string matching is tested.

String$ the main string.

SubString$ the smaller pattern string.

Remarks:
If the substring finds no match, **INSTR** returns a zero. By contrast, a
successful match returns the index to the first character of **String$** in which
Substring$ occurs (if an offset is used, then the location is that of the first
character after the offset).

If **Substring$** is a null string, **INSTR** returns 1 if **Offset** is omitted or
the value of **Offset** itself if it is used.

Restrictions:
INSTR is case sensitive. For example, the statement **INSTR("HELLO","hello")** will return a zero. To make **INSTR** case insensitive, use either the **UCASE$** or **LCASE$** functions to convert both string arguments to either upper- or lowercase. An example is shown below:

```
INSTR("UCASE$("Hello world"),UCASE$("hello world") 'returns 1
```

Examples:
```
INSTR("Hello World","Hello") 'returns 0
INSTR("Hello World","Hello") 'returns 1
INSTR(2,"Hello World","Hello") 'returns 0
```

LCASE$

Returns a string with all of its characters in lowercase.

Syntax:
```
LCASE$(S$)
```

Parameter:
S$ a string whose characters are to be converted into lowercase letters.

Examples:
```
LCASE$("HELLO") 'returns "hello"
LCASE$("Hello"+" "+"World") 'returns "hello world"
LCASE$("greetings!") 'returns "greetings!"
```

LEFT$

Returns the leftmost specified number of characters in a string.

Syntax:
```
LEFT$(S$,N)
```

Parameters:
S$ the source string.
N   the number of characters in S$ that are returned. The value of **N** must be in the range of 0 to 32767. If **N** is zero, a null string is returned by the function. If **N** exceeds the actual length of S$, the entire string is returned.

Examples:
```
LEFT$("Hello World",5) 'returns the string "Hello"
LEFT$("Hello World",22) 'returns "Hello World"
```

Returns the length of a string.   **LEN**

Syntax:
```
LEN(S$)
```

Parameter:

S$ the string constant, variable, or expression whose length is sought. A null string causes **LEN** to return a 0.

Examples:
```
LEN("Hello There") 'returns 11
LEN("HELLO"+" "+"WORLD") 'returns 11
```

Extracts or replaces a substring.   **MID$**

Syntax:
```
MID$(S$,First[,Count])
```

Parameters:

S$ the source string.

First   the index of the string character where extraction starts or where the character is overwritten. If you are extracting a substring and **First** is greater than the length of S$, a null string is returned. The values of this parameter must be:

$$1 <= First <= LEN(S\$) <= 32767$$

Count   the length of the extracted substring. The range of values is 0 to 32767. If **Count** is omitted or if it is greater than the available number of characters, **MID$** returns the rightmost part of S$, starting at character **First**.

Examples:
```
MID$("Smiles",2,4) returns the string "mile"
MID$("Smiles",2) returns the string "miles"
MID$("Smiles",2,40) returns the string "miles"
```

This program illustrates how a substring is replaced:

```
CLS
A$ = "The first time I saw your face"
```

```
PRINT A$
B$ = "first"
C$ = "last "
' use exact character count
MID$(A$, INSTR(A$, B$), LEN(A$)) = C$
PRINT A$
B$ = "face"
C$ = "ears"
' omit character count altogether
MID$(A$, INSTR(A$, B$)) = C$
PRINT A$
B$ = C$
C$ = "head"
' use a character count that exceeds the actual
' number of overwritten characters
MID$(A$, INSTR(A$, B$), 1000) = C$
PRINT A$
END
```

When the above program runs, the following is displayed on the screen:

```
The first time I saw your face
The last  time I saw your face
The last  time I saw your ears
The last  time I saw your head
```

OCT$ Converts a number into a string containing the octal image of that number.

Syntax:
OCT$ (N)

Parameter:
N   a numeric constant, variable, or expression in the range of −32768 to 65553. The value of **N** is rounded to the nearest integer before the octal number image is created. The two's complement binary number is produced by the function for a negative argument.

Example:
The following program prints a simple decimal-octal conversion table.

```
PRINT "DECIMAL      OCTAL"
PRINT "_____    ____"
FOR I% = 0 TO 255
   PRINT USING "  ###    /    /";I%,OCT$(I%)
EXT I%
```

Return the rightmost specified number of characters in a string.   **RIGHT$**

Syntax:
RIGHT$(S$,N)

Parameters:

S$ the source string.

N   the number of characters in S$ that are returned. The value of **N** must
be in the range of 0 to 32767. If **N** is zero, a null string is returned
by the function. If **N** exceeds the actual length of S$, the entire string
is returned.

Examples:
```
RIGHT$("Hello World",5)  'returns the string "World"
RIGHT$("Hello World",22) 'returns "Hello World"
```

Returns a string that is made up entirely of spaces.   **SPACE$**

Syntax:
SPACE$(N)

Parameter:

N   a numeric constant, variable, or expression in the range of 0 to 32767.

Example:
The following function enables you to emulate centered text in a string
before sending it to a printer or a text file.

```
DEF FNCenter$(Message$)
   L% = LEN(Message$)
   FNCenter$ = SPACE$(40 - L / 2) + Message$
END DEF
```

STR$

Converts a number into a string.

Syntax:
STR$ (N)

Parameter:
N   a numeric constant, variable, or expression.

Remarks:
If the argument of **STR$** is not negative, there is a leading space in the resulting string.

Examples:
```
STR$ (10)    'returns  " 10"
STR$ (8/10)  'returns  " 0.8"
STR$ (-8/10) 'returns  "-0.8"
```

STRING$

Returns a string made up of multiple copies of a specified character.

Syntax:
STRING$ (Count, ASCII.Code | S$)

Parameters:

Count	a number that specifies the size of the created string with values in the range of 1 to 32767.
ASCII.Code	the ASCII code of the character used to create the string. The values of this parameter must be in the range of 0 to 255.
S$	a string expression whose first character is used to create the string.

Example:
The next function takes a message string and produces a string by centering the message string and surrounding it with underscore characters.

```
DEF FNCenter2 (Message$)
    L = LEN (Message$)
    B$ = STRING$ (30 - L div 2, "_")
    FNCenter2 = B$ + " " + Message$ + " " + B$
END DEF
```

Returns a string with all of its characters in uppercase. **UCASE$**

Syntax:
UCASE$(S$)

Parameter:
S$ string whose characters are to be converted into uppercase letters.

Examples:
```
UCASE$("hello") 'returns "HELLO"
UCASE$("Hello"+" "+"World") 'returns "HELLO WORLD"
UCASE$("GREETINGS!") 'returns "GREETINGS!"
```

Converts the numeric string image into a number. **VAL**

Syntax:
VAL(S$)

Parameter:
S$ a string constant, variable, or expression that contains the image of
       a number.

Remarks:
The string argument may contain numeric characters in the set (0 to 9, +,
−, ., E, e, D, d) as well as other characters. When you convert a string to
a number, observe the following rules:

1. Leading spaces and tabs are ignored.
2. Conversion stops at the first character that is not in the above set.
3. If the converted string does not begin with a space, tab, or a character
in the above set, a zero value is returned by **VAL**.

Examples:
```
VAL("12") 'returns 12
VAL("1.23") 'returns 1.23
VAL("   3.4") 'returns 3.4
VAL("1.2e+02") 'returns 120
VAL("   3.4 feet") 'returns 3.4
VAL("Ampere = 1.2 Amps") 'returns 0
```

Turbo C

The major string processing functions for Turbo C are covered next.

stpcpy()

Copies one string into another.

Syntax:
```
char* stpcpy(char* target, const char* source);
```

Parameters:
target   the pointer to the string receiving the characters.
source   the pointer to the string containing the source characters.

Result:
Returns the pointer to the target string.

Example:
The following program copies the literal string **"Turbo Modula-2"** into a string variable.

```
#include <stdio.h>
#include <string.h>
main()
{
    char strng[81];

    stpcpy(strng,"Turbo Modula-2");
    puts(strng); /* displays "Turbo Modula-2" */
}
```

strcat()

Appends the contents of the source string to the target string.

Syntax:
```
char* strcat(char* target, const char* source);
```

Parameters:
target   a pointer to string being concatenated with the source string.
source   a pointer to string appended to the target string.

Result:
Returns a pointer to the concatenated string.

Example:
The next program concatenates the strings **"Turbo"** and **" C++"**.

```
#include <stdio.h>
#include <string.h>
main()
{
    char* strng = "Turbo";

    strcat(strng," C++");
    printf("%s\n", strng); /* displays "Turbo C++" */
}
```

Examines the target string for the first occurrence of a given character.   **strchr()**

Syntax:
```
char* strchr(const char* target, int ch);
```

Parameters:
target   a pointer to the string being scanned.
ch   the character being searched for in the target string.

Result:
Returns a pointer to the first occurrence of the character **ch** in the string
target. If the character does not occur in the string, the function returns
a **NULL**.

Example:
The following program scans for the colon character in a string.

```
#include <stdio.h>
#include <string.h>
main()
{
    char str[81] = "DataFrame:Word Folder:C Book";
    char* strng;

    strng = strchr(str, ':');
    puts(strng); /* displays ":Word Folder:C Book" */
}
```

strcmp()   Compares two strings.

Syntax:
```
int strcmp(const char* strng1, const char* strng2);
```

Parameters:
strng1, strng2   the pointers to strings being compared.

Result:
Returns the outcome of the comparison:

< 0 when strng1 is less than strng2
= 0 when strng1 is equal to strng2
> 0 when strng1 is greater than strng2

Example:
The following program compares the strings **"Turbo C++"** and **"Turbo Pascal"**:

```
#include <stdio.h>
#include <string.h>
main()
{
    char* string1 = "Turbo C++";
    char* string2 = "Turbo Pascal";
    int i;

    i = strcmp(string1, string2);
    if (i > 0)
        printf("'%s' > '%s'\n", string1, string2);
    else if (i < 0)
        printf("'%s' < '%s'\n", string1, string2);
    else
        printf("'%s' = '%s'\n", string1, string2);
}
```

The program displays:

```
'Turbo C++' < 'Turbo Pascal'
```

because **"Turbo C++"** is less than **"Turbo Pascal"** (this is decided by comparing the seventh character in each string).

Compares two strings without case sensitivity.   **strcmpI()**

Syntax:
```
int strcmpi(const char* strng1, const char* strng2);
```

Parameters:
strng1, strng2   the pointers to strings being compared.

Result:
Returns the outcome of the comparison:

< 0 when strng1 is less than strng2
= 0 when strng1 is equal to strng2
> 0 when strng1 is greater than strng2

Example:
The next program compares the strings **"Turbo C++"** and **"turbo classical"**:

```
#include <stdio.h>
#include <string.h>
main()
{
    char* string1 = "Turbo C++";
    char* string2 = "turbo classical";
    int i;

    i = strcmp(string1, string2);
    if (i > 0)
        printf("'%s' > '%s'\n", string1, string2);
    else if (i < 0)
        printf("'%s' < '%s'\n", string1, string2);
    else
        printf("'%s' = '%s'\n", string1, string2);
}
```

The program displays:

```
'Turbo C++' < 'turbo classical'
```

because **"Turbo C++"** is greater than **"turbo classical"**.

strcpy() Copies one string into another.

Syntax:
```
char* strcpy(char* target, const char* source);
```

Parameters:
target a pointer to the string receiving the characters.
source a pointer to the string containing the source characters.

Result:
Returns the pointer to the target string.

Example:
The following program copies the literal string **"Turbo Modula-2"** into a string variable.

```
#include <stdio.h>
#include <string.h>
main()
{
    char strng[81];

    strcpy(strng,"Turbo Modula-2");
    puts(strng); /* displays "Turbo Modula-2" */
}
```

strcspn() Scans **strng1** and returns the length of the leftmost substring in **strng1** that is totally void of the characters of the substring **strng2**.

Syntax:
```
int strcspn(const char* strng1, const char* strng2);
```

Parameters:
strng1 a pointer to the string being examined for the absence of the characters of string **strng2**.

strng2   a pointer to the string containing the characters not sought in
string **strng1**.

Result:
Returns the length of the leftmost substring in **strng1** that is totally void
of the characters of the substring **strng2**.

Example:

```
#include <stdio.h>
#include <string.h>
main()
{
    char strng[81], substr[81];
    int i;

    do {
        printf("Enter a string -> ");
        gets(strng);
    } while (strlen(strng) == 0);
    do {
        printf("\nEnter a character-set string -> ");
        gets(substr);
    } while (strlen(substr) == 0);
    i = strcspn(strng, substr);
    if (i >= 0)
        printf("A character in the substring is found \
                at index %d\n", i);
    else
        puts("No character in the substring matches the string");
}
```

A sample run of the above program is shown below:

```
Enter a string -> Here we go again
Enter a character-set string -> aioeu
A character in the substring is found at index 1
```

Duplicates the string-typed argument. The **malloc()** function is called to **strdup()**
allocate the required space.

Syntax:
```
char* strdup(const char* strng);
```

Parameter:
strng   a pointer to the source string.

Result:
Returns the pointer to the memory location containing the newly created string. A **NULL** is returned if the memory allocation fails.

Example:
```
#include <stdio.h>
#include <string.h>
main()
{
    char* strng1 = "The rain in Spain", strng2;

    strng2 = strdup(strng1);
    /* strng2 is now "The rain in Spain" */
    /* verify that strng1 is equal to strng2 */
    if (strcmp(strng1, strng2) == 0)
        puts("Yes, strdup works fine");
    else
        puts("Oh! Oh! Something went wrong!");
}
```

stricmp()   Compares two strings without making a distinction between upper- and lowercase characters.

Syntax:
```
int stricmp(const char* strng1, const char* strng2);
```

Parameters:
strng1, strng2   pointers to the strings being compared.

Result:
Returns the outcome of the comparison:

< 0 when strng1 is less than strng2
= 0 when strng1 is equal to strng2
> 0 when strng1 is greater than strng2

Example:
```
#include <stdio.h>
#include <string.h>
main()
{
    char strng1[81];
    char strng2[81];
    int i;

    do {
        printf("Enter first string -> ");
        gets(strng1);
    } while (strlen(strng1) == 0);
    do {
        printf("\nEnter second string -> ");
        gets(strng2);
    } while (strlen(strng2) == 0);
    i = stricmp(strng1, strng2);
    if (i == 0)
        printf("\nString '%s' is equal to '%s'\n", strng1, strng2);
    else if (i > 0)
        printf("\nString '%s' is greater than '%s'\n",
                strng1, strng2);
    else
        printf("\nString '%s' is less than '%s'\n", strng1, strng2);
}
```

A sample session with the above example is displayed below:

```
Enter first string -> turbo pascal
Enter second string -> Turbo Pascal
String 'turbo pascal' is equal to 'Turbo Pascal'
```

Obtains the length of a string.   **strlen()**

Syntax:
```
unsigned strlen(char* source);
```

Parameter:
source   a pointer to the string whose length is sought.

Result:
Returns the length of the string argument.

Example:
```
#include <stdio.h>
#include <string.h>
main()
{
    char str[11], bigstr[81];
    unsigned i;

    do {
        printf("Enter a string of up to 10 characters -> ");
        gets(bigstr);
        i = strlen(bigstr);
    } while (i > 10 && i == 0); /* data entry verification */
    /* copies contents of bigstr into str */
    strcpy(str, bigstr);
    printf("The contents of str are: %s\n",str);
}
```

strlwr()   Converts the uppercase characters of a string to lowercase.

Syntax:
```
char* strlwr(char* source);
```

Parameter:

source   a pointer to the string whose characters are being converted to lowercase.

Result:
Returns a pointer to the argument string.

Example:
The following program prompts you to enter a string and converts it into lowercase. The program prompts you for the number of leading characters to leave unaltered. A zero input results in converting the entire string into lowercase.

```
#include <stdio.h>
#include <string.h>
```

```
main()
{
    char str[81];
    int len;
    int skip;

    do {
        printf("Enter a string -> ");
        gets(str);
        len = strlen(str);
    } while (len == 0);
    do {
        printf("\nEnter number of leading characters \
                to leave unchanged : ");
        scanf("%d", &skip);
    } while (skip < 0 && skip >= len);
    strlwr(str+skip);
    printf("\nThe lowercase version is\n%s\n", str);
}
```

A sample session with the above program is shown below:

```
Enter a string -> A BRAVE NEW WORLD!
Enter number of leading character to leave unchanged : 1
The lowercase version is
A brave new world!
```

Appends up to a specified number of characters from the source string to **strncat()**
the target string.

Syntax:
```
char* strncat(char* target, const char* source, int numchars);
```

Parameters:

target	a pointer to the string receiving additional characters from the source string.
source	a pointer to the string supplying the target string with additional characters.
numchars	the number of source string characters concatenated to the target string.

Result:
Returns a pointer to the target string.

Example:
```
#include <stdio.h>
#include <string.h>
main()
{
    char* str1 = "Hello I am ";
    char* str2 = "Thomas Jones";

    strncat(str1, str2, strlen("Thomas"));
    puts(str1); /* displays "Hello I am Thomas" */
}
```

strncmp()   Compares a specified number of leading characters in two strings.

Syntax:
```
int strncmp(const char* strng1, const char* strng2, int numchars);
```

Parameters:

strng1, strng2   the pointers to the strings being compared.
numchars   the maximum number of characters to be compared.

Result:
Returns the outcome of the comparison:

< 0   when strng1 is less than strng2
= 0   when strng1 is equal to strng2
> 0   when strng1 is greater than strng2

Example:
This program employs a simple method to find out just how many leading characters match in two strings.

```
#include <stdio.h>
#include <string.h>
main()
{
    char* strng1 = "Turbo C 2.0";
```

```
    char* strng2 = "Turbo Pascal";
    int i, j = 0, len;

    len = strlen(strng1);
    if (len > strlen(strng2))
        len = strlen(strng2);
    for (i = 0; i < len && j == 0; i++)
        j = strncmp(strng1, strng2, i+1);
    printf("The first %d characters match in both strings\n",--i);
    /* displays "The first 6 characters match in both strings" */
}
```

Compares a specified number of leading characters in two strings without **strncmpi()**
case sensitivity.

Syntax:
```
int strncmpi(const char* strng1, const char* strng2, int numchars);
```

Parameters:
strng1, strng2   the pointers to the strings being compared.
numchars   the number of characters in the string comparison.

Result:
Returns the outcome of the comparison:

< 0 when strng1 is less than strng2
= 0 when strng1 is equal to strng2
> 0 when strng1 is greater than strng2

Example:
This program employs a simple method to find out just how many leading
characters match in two strings.

```
#include <stdio.h>
#include <string.h>
main()
{
    char* strng1 = "Turbo C 2.0";
    char* strng2 = "turbo Pascal";
    int i, j = 0, len;
```

```
        len = strlen(strng1);
        if (len > strlen(strng2))
        len = strlen(strng2);
        for (i = 0; i < len && j == 0; i++)
            j = strncmpi(strng1, strng2, i+1);
        printf("The first %d characters match in both strings\n",--i);
        /* displays "The first 6 characters match in both strings" */
}
```

strncpy()   Copies a number of characters from the source string to the target string. Character truncation or padding may be performed, if necessary.

Syntax:
```
char* strncpy(char* target, const char* source, int numchars);
```

Parameters:

target   a pointer to the string receiving copies of characters from the source string.

source   a pointer to the string supplying the target string with characters.

numchars   the number of source string characters copied to the target string.

Result:
Returns a pointer to the target string.

Example:
```
#include <stdio.h>
#include <string.h>
main()
{
    char* str1 = "Pascal";
    char* str2 = "Hello there";
    int space_location;

    space_location = strcspn(str1, " ");
    strncpy(str1, str2, space_location);
    printf("String str1 is now '%s'\n", str1);
    /* String str1 is now 'Hello ' */
}
```

Compares a specified number of leading characters in two strings without **strnicmp()** case sensitivity.

Syntax:

```
int strnicmp(const char* strng1, const char* strng2,
            unsigned numchars);
```

Parameters:

strng1, strng2   the pointers to the strings being compared.
numchars   the number of characters in the string comparison.

Result:

Returns the outcome of the comparison:

< 0 when strng1 is less than strng2
= 0 when strng1 is equal to strng2
> 0 when strng1 is greater than strng2

Example:

The following program enables you to compare a number of leading characters in the strings **"turbo basic"** and **"Turbo Pascal"**.

```
#include <stdio.h>
#include <string.h>
main()
{
    char* strng1 = "turbo basic";
    char* strng2 = "Turbo Pascal";
    int i, n, len;

    len = strlen(strng1);
    do {
        printf("Enter number of characters to compare [ < %d] : ",
                len);
        scanf("%d", &n);
        printf("\n\n");
    } while (n < 1 && n > len);
    i = strnicmp(strng1, strng2, n);
    if (i == 0)
        printf("\nThe first %d characters match\n", n);
```

```
        else
            printf("\nThe first %d characters do not match\n", n);
    }
```

A sample session with the above program is shown below:

```
Enter number of characters to compare [ < 12] : 5
The first 5 characters match
```

strnset()   Overwrites a number of characters in a string with duplicate copies of a single character.

Syntax:
```
char* strnset(char* target, int pattern, int numchars);
```

Parameters:

target   a pointer to the string filled with multiple copies of the character pattern.

pattern   the character used to overwrite part or all of the target string.

numchars   the length of the target string overwritten by multiple copies of the pattern character.

Result:
Returns a pointer to the target string.

Example:
The next program enables you to enter a string, a character, and the number of times the entered character should overwrite the leading part of the string. This function does not increase the length of the string.

```
#include <stdio.h>
#include <string.h>
#include <conio.h>
main()
{
    char ch, message[80];
    int i, len;

    do {
        printf("Enter a string -> ");
```

```
        gets(message);
        len = strlen(message);
    } while (len == 0);
    printf("\nEnter a character -> ");
    ch = getche();
    do {
        printf("\nEnter the number of repeated characters : ");
        scanf("%d", &i);
    } while (i > len && i <= 0);
    strnset(message, ch, i);
    printf("The input string is now '%s'\n", message);
}
```

A sample session with the above program is shown below:

```
Enter a string -> The Little Prince
Enter a character -> !
Enter the number of repeated characters : 3
The input string is now '!!! Little Prince'
```

Searches the target string for the first occurrence of any character in the   **strpbrk()**
pattern of characters.

Syntax:
```
char* strpbrk(const char* target, const char* pattern);
```

Parameters:
target   a pointer to the string being examined for the occurrence of any
         pattern character.
pattern   a pointer to the string containing the pattern characters.

Result:
Returns a pointer to the first occurrence of any pattern character in the target
string.

Example:
```
#include <stdio.h>
#include <string.h>
#include <conio.h>
main()
```

```
{
    char str[81], substr[81];
    char* ptr;

    do {
        printf("Enter a string -> ");
        gets(str);
    } while (strlen(str) == 0);
    do {
        printf("\nEnter the string of characters -> ");
        gets(substr);
    } while (strlen(substr) == 0);
    ptr = strpbrk(str, substr);
    if (ptr != NULL)
        printf("\nMatching substring is '%s'\n\n", ptr);
    else
        printf("\nNo character in '%s' matched\n\n", substr);
}
```

A sample session with the above program is shown below:

```
Enter a string -> SQRT((X + Y) * Z)
Enter the string of characters -> ()+*/-
Matching substring is '((X + Y) * Z)'
```

strrchr()   Searches a string for the last occurrence of a pattern character.

Syntax:
```
char* strrchr(const char* target, char pattern);
```

Parameters:

target   a pointer to the string examined for the last occurrence of a pattern character.

pattern   the pattern character.

Result:
Returns a pointer to the sought character, or **NULL** if character is not found.

Example:
```
#include <stdio.h>
#include <string.h>
```

```
#include <conio.h>
main()
{
    char str[81], substr;
    char* ptr;

    do {
        printf("Enter a string -> ");
        gets(str);
    } while (strlen(str) == 0);
    printf("\nEnter a character -> ");
    substr = getche();
    ptr = strrchr(str, substr);
    if (ptr != NULL)
        printf("\nThe trailing substring is '%s'\n", ptr);
    else
        printf("\nCharacter %c is not found in string '%s'\n",
                substr, str);
}
```

The following is a sample session with the above program:

```
Enter a string -> Hello how are you doing?
Enter a character -> o
The trailing substring is 'oing?'
```

Reverses the order of the string characters.   **strrev()**

Syntax:
```
char* strrev(char* string);
```

Parameter:
string   a pointer to the string whose characters are reversed by this
              function.

Result:
Returns a pointer to the reversed string.

Example:
```
#include <stdio.h>
#include <string.h>
```

```
main()
{
    char string[81];

    do {
        printf("Enter a string -> ");
        gets(string);
    } while (strlen(string) == 0);
    printf("The reverse of string '%s' is ", string);
    strrev(string);
    printf("'%s'\n\n", string);
}
```

A sample session with the above program is shown below:

```
Enter a string -> Hello
The reverse of string 'Hello' is 'olleH'
```

strset()

Replaces the contents of a string with a pattern character.

Syntax:
```
char* strset(char* target, char pattern);
```

Parameters:

target   a pointer to the string whose contents are replaced by multiple copies of the pattern character.

pattern   the pattern character filling the target string.

Result:
Returns a pointer to the target string.

Example:
```
#include <stdio.h>
#include <string.h>
#include <conio.h>
main()
{
    char str[81], char substr;

    do {
```

```
        printf("Enter a string -> ");
        gets(str);
    } while (strlen(str) == 0);
    printf("Enter a character -> ");
    substr = getche();
    strset(str, substr);
    printf("The string is now '%s'\n\n", str);
}
```

Here is a sample session with this example:

```
Enter a string -> Hello there
Enter a character -> +
The string is now '+++++++++++'
```

Returns the number of characters in the leading part of the string that **strspn()**
matches any character in the string pattern.

Syntax:
```
int strspn(const char* target, char* pattern);
```

Parameters:

target   a pointer to the string examined for containing the pattern char-
               acters.

pattern   a pointer to the string containing the pattern characters.

Result:
Returns the length of the leading substring that matches characters of the
pattern string.

Example:
```
#include <stdio.h>
#include <string.h>
main()
{
    char str[81];
    int index = 0;

    do {
        printf("Enter a string -> ");
```

```
            gets(str);
        } while (strlen(str) == 0);
        index = strspn(str, " ");
        printf("There are %d leading whitespace characters \
                    in your string.\n",index);
    }
```

A sample session with the above program is shown below:

```
Enter a string -> '     Hello there'
There are 5 leading whitespace characters in your string.
```

strstr()   Scans a string for the first occurrence of a substring.

Syntax:
```
char* strstr(const char* string, const char* substr);
```

Parameters:
string   a pointer to the main string being examined for the occurrence
           of the substring.
substr   a pointer to the substring that may be part of the main string.

Result:
Returns a pointer to the string location where the substring matches, or
NULL if no match occurs.

Example:
```
#include <stdio.h>
#include <string.h>
main()
{
    char str[81], substr[81], *ptr;
    unsigned index;

    puts("              0123456789!123456789!12345679!123456789");
    do {
        printf("Enter a string -> ");
        gets(str);
    } while (strlen(str) == 0);
    do {
```

```
        printf("\nEnter a substring -> ");
        gets(substr);
    } while (strlen(substr) == 0);
    ptr = strstr(str, substr);
    index = (unsigned) (ptr - str);
    if (ptr != NULL)
        printf("\nSubstring is located at character %u\n", index);
    else
        puts("No match was found");
}
```

A sample session with the above program is shown below:

```
                    0123456789!123456789!12345679!123456789
Enter a string -> The first time I saw your face
Enter a substring -> time
Substring is located at character 10
```

Converts a string into a double value. String conversion is stopped when   **strtod()**
an unrecognizable character is scanned.

Syntax:
```
double strtod(const char* numimage, char** endptr);
```

Parameters:
numimage   a pointer to the string containing the image of a double number.

endptr   a pointer to the character that stopped the scan.

Result:
Returns a double-typed value or **HUGE_VAL** if an overflow occurs.

Example:
```
#include <stdio.h>
#include <stdlib.h>
main()
{
    char strng[31];
    char** c;
    double x;
```

```
printf("Enter a number : ");
gets(strng);
x = strtod(strng,c);
printf("The number is %lf\n",x);
}
```

strtok()

Searches the target string for tokens. A string supplies the set of delimiter characters. The example shows how this function works in returning the tokens in a string.

Syntax:
```
char* strtok(char* target, const char* delimiters);
```

Parameters:
target   a pointer to the string containing the tokens.
delimiter   a pointer to the string containing the delimiter characters.

Result:
Returns a pointer to a token found in the target string.

Example:
```
#include <stdio.h>
#include <string.h>
#include <conio.h>
main()
{
    char* str = "(Base_Cost+Profit) * Margin";
    char* tkn = "+* ()";
    char* ptr = str;

    clrscr;
    puts(str);
    /* the first call looks normal */
    ptr = strtok(str, tkn);
    printf("\n\nis broken into: %s",ptr);
    do {  /* must make first argument a NULL character */
        ptr = strtok('\0', tkn);
        if (ptr != NULL) printf(" ,%s",ptr);
    } while (ptr != NULL );
    printf("\n\n");
}
```

This program displays the following when it is run:

```
(Base_Cost+Profit) * Margin

is broken into: Base_Cost, Profit, Margin
```

Converts a string into a long integer. String conversion is stopped when **strtol()**
an unrecognizable character is scanned. The string image may be that of
decimal, octal, and hexadecimal numbers.

Syntax:
```
long strtol(const char* numimage, char** endptr, int base);
```

Parameters:
numimage   a pointer to the string containing the image of a long integer.
endptr   a pointer to the character that stopped the scan.
base   the radix of the resulting long integer.

Result:
Returns the value of the converted string, or 0 if an error occurs in the
conversion.

Example:
```
#include <stdio.h>
#include <stdlib.h>
main()
{
    char strng[31];
    char** c;
    long i;

    printf("Enter an integer : ");
    gets(strng);
    i = strtol(strng,c,10);
    printf("The number is %ld\n",i);
}
```

Converts a string into an unsigned long integer. String conversion is stopped   **strtuol()**
when an unrecognizable character is scanned. String image may be that of
decimal, octal, or hexadecimal numbers.

Syntax:
```
unsigned long strtuol(const char*, numimage, char** endptr,
                      int base);
```

Parameters:

numimage   a pointer to the string containing the image of an unsigned long integer.

endptr   a pointer to the character that stopped the scan.

base   the radix of the resulting unsigned long integer.

Result:

Returns the value of the converted string or 0 if an error occurs in the conversion.

Example:
```
#include <stdio.h>
#include <stdlib.h>
main()
{
    char strng[31];
    char** c;
    unsigned long i;

    printf("Enter an unsigned integer : ");
    gets(strng);
    i = strtuol(strng,c,10);
    printf("%lu\n",i);
}
```

strupr()   Converts the lowercase characters of a string to uppercase.

Syntax:
```
char* strupr(char* string);
```

Parameter:

string   a pointer to the string whose characters are converted to uppercase.

Result:

Returns a pointer to the converted string.

Example:

```c
#include <stdio.h>
#include <string.h>
main()
{
    char str[81];
    int len, skip;

    do {
        printf("Enter a string -> ");
        gets(str);
    } while ((len = strlen(str)) == 0);
    do {
        printf("\nEnter number of leading characters to \
                leave unchanged : ");
        scanf("%d", &skip);
    } while (skip < 0 && skip >= len);
    strupr(str+skip);
    printf("The uppercase version is\n%s\n", str);
}
```

A sample session with the above program is shown below:

```
Enter a string -> a brave new world!
Enter number of leading characters to leave unchanged : 1
The uppercase version is
a BRAVE NEW WORLD!
```

Turbo Pascal

The major string processing routines for Turbo Pascal are covered next.

Returns the character with the indicated ASCII code number.   **Chr**

Syntax:

```pascal
Function Chr(Ascii : Byte) : Char;
```

Parameter:

Ascii   the ASCII code number for the character to be returned by the
    Chr function. The value must be in the range 0 to 255.

Example:
This procedure sends a beep through the computer's speaker.

```
Procedure Beep;
{print ASCII code 7 to beep}
Begin
    Write(Chr(7));
End; {Beep}
```

Concat

Concatenates a series of strings. This function is implemented to enable you to port programs from other Pascal implementations. Usually, the + operator performs the same task as this function.

Syntax:
```
Function Concat(s1, s2 [,s3,...,sn] : String) : String;
```

Parameters:
s1, s2, ...   the strings to be concatenated.

Example:
```
Program Test_Concat;
{$V-}
Type String80 = String[80];
Var s1, s2, s3, BigStr : String80;
Begin
    s1 := 'Turbo ';
    s2 := 'Ada ';
    s3 := 'version 1.0';
    BigStr := Concat(s1, s2, s3);
    Writeln(BigStr); {displays 'Turbo Ada version 1.0'}
End.
```

Copy

Returns a substring extracted from a bigger string.

Syntax:
```
Function Copy(Strng : String; Index : Integer; Count : Integer);
```

Parameters:
Strng   the source string.
Index   the index of the first character in the string to be copied. If it is

> greater than the actual length of the string, the function returns an empty string.

Count the number of characters to be copied. If this exceeds the number of available characters, the extra is ignored.

Example:

The following program contains the function **GetWord** that returns an English space-delimited word from a string. The word is selected by supplying a character index. The index may point to any nonspace letter of the word. If the index points to a space character, the next word is extracted.

```
Program Test_Copy;
{$V-}
Type String80 = String[80];
Var Strng : String80;
    Index : Byte;


Function GetWord(Strng : String80; Start : Byte : String80;
Var First, Count, Strlen : Byte;
    NotFound : Boolean;
Begin
    Strlen := Length(Strng);
    If (Strng = '') Or (Start > Strlen) Then Begin
        GetWord := '';
        Exit;
    End;
    {backtrack to the beginning of the word}
    While (Start > 0) And (Strng[Start] <> ' ') Do
        Dec(Start);
    If Strng[Start] = ' ' Then Inc(Start);
    First := Start;
    Count := 0;
    NotFound := True;
    While (Start <= Strlen) And NotFound Do
        If Strng[Start] = ' ' Then
                NotFound := False
        Else Begin
                Inc(Start);
                Inc(Count);
```

```
        End;
    GetWord := Copy(Strng, First, Count);
End; {GetWord}

Begin
    Repeat
        Write('Enter a string -> ');
        Readln(Strng); Writeln;
    Until Length(Strng) > 0;
    Write('Enter the index -> ');
    Readln(Index); Writeln;
    Writeln('Word is ',GetWord(Strng, Index));
End.
```

A sample session with the above program is shown below:

```
Enter a string -> Lady Ada Augusta Byron
Enter the index for a word : 7
Word is Ada
```

Delete   Deletes a portion of a string.

Syntax:
```
Procedure Delete(Var Strng : String; Start : Integer;
                     Count : Integer);
```

Parameters:

Start   the first character of **Strng** to be deleted. If the value **Start** is greater than the string length, no characters are removed.

Count   the number of characters to be deleted. If there are actually fewer characters to delete than the number specified by **Count**, the extra is ignored.

Strng   the processed string.

Example:
The following program contains a procedure to remove the first occurrence of a substring from a string using the **Delete** routine.

```
Procedure Test_Delete;
{$V-}
```

```
Type String80 = String[80];
Var Strng, SubStr : String80;

Procedure RemoveStr(Var Strng : String80; SubString : String80);
Var Start : Integer;
Begin
    If (SubString = '') Or (Strng = '') Then Exit;
    Start := POS(SubString, Strng);
    If Start > 0 Then Delete(Strng, Start, Length(SubString));
End; {RemoveStr}

Begin
    Strng := 'The rain in Spain stays mainly in the plain';
    SubStr := 'in Spain ';
    Writeln(Strng); {displays 'The rain stays mainly in the plain'}
End.
```

Inserts a substring into a string.   **Insert**

Syntax:
```
Procedure Insert(SubStr : String; Var Strng : String;
                 Index : Integer);
```

Parameters:
SubStr   the substring to be inserted in **Strng**.

Index   the character location of **Strng** where the substring is inserted. If the value of **Index** exceeds the current string length, the substring is appended, if space allows.

Strng   the expanded string. If the inserted substring causes the main string to exceed its maximum size, the extra trailing characters of the substring are truncated.

Example:
The following program contains the procedure **ReplaceStr** to replace one string with another. The procedure checks the validity of its arguments and exits if the main and/or the search strings are null.

```
Program Test_Insert;
{$V-}
Type String80 = String[80];
Var Strng, Find, Replace : String80;
```

```
Procedure ReplaceStr(Var Strng : String80;
                        FindStr, ReplaceStr : String80);
Var Start : Integer;
Begin
   If (Strng = '') Or (FindStr = '') Then Exit;
   Start := Pos(FindStr, Strng);
   If Start > 0 Then Begin
      Delete(Strng, Start, Length(FindStr));
      If ReplaceStr <> '' Then Insert(ReplaceStr, Strng, Start);
      End; {If}
End; {ReplaceStr}
Begin
   Repeat
      Write('Enter a string -> ');
      Readln(Strng);
   Until Length(Strng) > 0;
   Repeat
      Write('Enter the search substring -> ');
      Readln(Find);
   Until Length(Find) > 0;
   Write('Enter the replacement substring -> ');
   Readln(Replace);
   ReplaceStr(Strng, Find, Replace);
   Writeln('String is now "', Strng,'"');
End.
```

A sample session with the above program is shown below:

```
Enter a string -> Turbo Pascal 4.0
Enter the search substring -> Pascal
Enter the replacement substring -> Ada
String is now "Turbo Ada 4.0"
```

Length

Returns the length of a string.

Syntax:

```
Function Length(Strng : String) : Integer;
```

Parameter:

Strng   a string constant, variable, or expression whose length is sought.

Examples:

```
Length('Hello There') returns 11.
Length('HELLO'+' '+'WORLD') returns 11.
```

Returns the ordinal number of an ordinal-type.   **Ord**

Syntax:

```
Function Ord(Member) : LongInt;
```

Parameter:

Member   an ordinal-typed variable (integer, character, set member).

Remarks:

With character-type arguments, **Ord** returns the ASCII code number.

Example:

The following program contains a procedure to convert a string to lower-case. The procedure uses both the **Chr** and **Ord** functions to achieve the sought character case conversion.

```
Program Test_Ord;
{$V-}
Type String80 = String[80];
Var Message : String80;

Procedure LoCaseStr(Var Strng : String80);
Var strlen, shift : Byte;
    ch : Char;
Begin
    shift := Ord('a') - Ord('A'); {calculate ASCII value shift}
    strlen := Length(Strng);
    While strlen > 0 Do Begin
        ch := Strng[strlen];
        If ch In ['A'..'Z'] Then Begin {uppercase letter?}
                ch := Chr(Ord(ch) + shift);
                Strng[strlen] := ch
        End;
        Dec(strlen);
    End; {While}
End; {LoCaseStr}
```

```
Begin
    Write('Enter a string -> ');
    Readln(Message); Writeln;
    LoCaseStr(Message);
    Write('The lowercase version is "', Message, '"');
End.
```

Pos

Locates the first character position of a substring in a string.

Syntax:

```
Function Pos(SubStr : String; Strng : String) : Byte;
```

Parameters:

SubStr   the search substring.
Strng   the main string.

Remarks:

If **SubStr** is not found in **Strng**, a zero value is returned. The **Pos** function is case sensitive.

Example:

The following function is a modified version of the **Pos** function that also uses **Pos**. With the **IPos** function you can use an offset in bypassing a specified number of leading string characters.

```
Function IPos(SubStr, Strng : String; StartIndex : Byte) : Byte;
Var Strpos : Byte;
Begin
    If (Strng = '') Or (SubStr = '') Then Begin
        IPos := 0;
        Exit;
    End; {If}
    Strpos := 0; {initialize with default function value}
    If (StartIndex > 0) And (StartIndex <= Length(Strng)) Then Begin
        {clip leading part of the string Strng?}
        If StartIndex > 1 Then Delete(Strng, 1, StartIndex);
        Strpos := Pos(SubStr, Strng);
        If (Strpos > 0) And (StartIndex > 1) Then
                Inc(Strpos, StartIndex);
    End; {If}
```

```
    IPos := Strpos {return function value}
End; {IPos}
```

Transforms a number into a string.   **Str**

Syntax:
```
Str(X : <any numeric type> [: Width [:Decimals]],Var Strng : Char);
```

Parameters:

X	the numeric expression to be converted.
Width, Decimals	formatting specifiers that work in a manner very similar to that in **Write** and **Writeln**.
Strng	the string image of numeric expression.

Example:
```
Procedure Test_Str;
Var Str1, Str2 : String[80];
    I : Integer;
    X : Real;
Begin
    X := 355.0 / 113.0;
    I := 355 div 113;
    Str(X:21:5,Str1);
    Str(I:10,Str2);
    Writeln('The string image of ',X,' is ',Str1);
    Writeln('The string image of ',I,' is ',Str2);
End.
```

Converts a character to uppercase.   **UpCase**

Syntax:
```
Function UpCase(Ch : Char) : Char;
```

Parameter:
Ch   input character whose uppercase is sought.

Example:
The following program contains a procedure that converts a string to uppercase characters.

```
Program Test_UpCase;
{$V-}
Type String80 = String[80];
Var Message : String80;

Procedure UpCaseStr(Var Strng : String80);
Var strlen : Byte;
Begin
    strlen := Length(Strng);
    While strlen > 0 Do Begin
        Strng[strlen] := UpCase(Strng[strlen]);
        Dec(strlen);
    End; {While}
End; {UpCaseStr}

Begin
    Write('Enter a string -> ');
    Readln(Message); Writeln;
    UpCaseStr(Message);
    Write('The uppercase version is "', Message, '"');
End.
```

Val   Converts a string containing the image of a number into a number.

Syntax:
```
Procedure Val(Strng : String; Var Number; Var Error : Integer);
```

Parameters:

Strng   a string containing the image of a number. The string may contain only a correct numeric image. Leading spaces are allowed. Any other character before or after the numeric image results in a conversion error.

Number   number converted from string.

Error   the index of the first character that causes conversion error. A zero value indicates that the conversion was successful.

Example:
```
Program Test_Val;
Var X : Real;
    Error : Integer;
Begin
```

```
    Val('      1.23',X,Error);
    Writeln(Error); {displays a zero}
    Writeln(X); {displays 1.23 in scientific format}
    Val('      1.23 Hello',X,Error);
    Writeln(Error); {displays a non-zero value}
    Writeln(X); {displays zero in scientific format}
End.
```

Turbo Prolog

The major string processing predicates for Turbo Prolog are covered next.

Converts between a character and its ASCII code number.   **char_Int**

Syntax:
```
char_int(TheChar, ASCII_Code)      (i,o),  (o,i),  (i,i)
        (char, integer)
```

Parameters:

TheChar   the character converted to or from, or compared with an ASCII code.

ASCII_code   the ASCII code converted to or from, or compared with a character.

Example:
The following program tests the various flow patterns of predicate **char_int**.

```
predicates
    go
    copy_int_to_char          /* test (o,i) */
    copy_char_to_int          /* test (i,o) */
    compare_char_int          /* test (i,o) */

clauses
    copy_int_to_char :-
        write("Enter an ASCII code integer -> "),
        readint(LeInt),
        char_int(LeChar, LeInt),
        write("You typed the ASCII code for character '",
```

```
            LeChar, "'"), nl.
      copy_char_to_int :-
          write("Enter a character -> "), readchar(LeChar),
          write(LeChar), nl,
          char_int(LeChar, LeInt),
          write("You typed a character whose ASCII code is ",LeInt),
          nl.
      compare_char_int :-
          write("Enter an ASCII code integer -> "),
          readint(LeInt), nl,
          write("Enter the character with the above ASCII code -> "),
          readchar(LeChar), write(LeChar), nl,
          char_int(LeChar, LeInt),
          write("The character matches the ASCII number you typed"),
          nl.
      compare_char_int :-
          write("The character does not match the ASCII number"), nl.
      go :-
          nl, nl, nl,
          copy_int_to_char, nl, nl,
          copy_char_to_int, nl, nl,
          compare_char_int.
```

A sample session with the above program created by calling the predicate **go** is shown below:

```
Enter an ASCII code integer  -> 65
You typed the ASCII code for character 'A'

Enter a character  -> B
You typed a character whose ASCII code is 66

Enter an ASCII code integer  -> 67
Enter the character with the above ASCII code -> C
The character matches the ASCII number you typed
```

format   Creates a string containing the formatted values of multiple arguments.

Syntax:
```
format(ImageString,FormatString,Arg1,Arg2,...,Argn)   (o,i,i,...)
       (string,...,string,anytype,...,anytype)
```

Parameters:

ImageString   the string containing the formatted values of the arguments.

FormatString   the format control string.

Arg1, ..., Argn   the arguments for the format string.

Remarks:

The format control string contains regular text mixed with format specifier characters. The latter have the general form of **%-m.pf**. The optional hyphen signals that the field should be left justified. The optional **m** indicates the minimum field size. The optional **p** is used to define the precision for floating-point numbers, or the maximum number of characters to be printed for a string. The optional **f** specifies the exact format. These formats are shown in Table 5.1.

Table 5.1. Parameter settings for the format predicate

Format	Purpose
f	Fixed-decimal notation used for real numbers.
e	Scientific notation used for real numbers.
g	Shortest format used for real numbers.
d	Decimal representation for integers and characters.
u	Unsigned decimal representation for integers and characters.
x	Hexadecimal representation for integers and characters.
c	Character representation for integers and characters.
s	String representation for strings and symbols.
R	Database reference number for ref domain.
X	Long hexadecimal representation for strings and database reference numbers.

Example:

The following example tests the various formats supported by this predicate.

```
predicates
    go
clauses
```

```
go :-
    Pi = 355.0 / 113.0,
    I = 123,
    format(Image1,"pi = %f using fixed decimal format",Pi),
    write(Image1), nl,
    format(Image2,"pi = %e using scientific notation",Pi),
    write(Image2), nl,
    format(Image3,"pi = %g using the shortest format",Pi),
    write(Image3), nl,
    format(Image4,"I = %d using decimal format", I),
    write(Image4), nl,
    format(Image5,"I = %u using unsigned-number format", I),
    write(Image5), nl,
    format(Image6,"I = %x using hexadecimal format", I),
    write(Image6), nl,
    format(Image7,"The ASCII code %d is character %c" , I, I),
    write(Image7), nl,
    MyName = "Billy Jo Bob",
    format(Image8,"Howdee! My name is %s", MyName ),
    write(Image8), nl,
    format(Image9,"The ASCII code for %c is %d", 'A','A'),
    write(Image9), nl.
```

A sample session with the above program is shown below:

```
pi = 3.1415929204 using fixed decimal format
pi = 3.1415929204E+00 using scientific notation
pi = 3.1415929204 using the shortest format
I = 123 using decimal format
I = 123 using unsigned-number format
I = 7B using hexadecimal format
The ASCII code 123 is character {
Howdee! My name is Billy Jo Bob
The ASCII code for A is 65
```

frontchar

Extracts the leading character of a string.

Syntax:

```
frontchar(MainString, LeadingChar, TailString)    (i,o,o), (i,i,o),
        (string, char, string)          (i,o,i), (i,i,i), (o,i,i)
```

Parameters:

MainString   the main string broken into or made up of **LeadingChar** and **TailString**. Its size cannot exceed 64K.

LeadingChar   the first character of the main string.

TailString   the tail substring.

Remarks:

(i,o,o)   breaks main string into leading character and tail substring.

(i,i,o)   succeeds if **LeadingChar** is the first character of **MainString**. When it succeeds, this pattern returns the **TailString**.

(i,o,i)   succeeds if the **TailString** is the tail substring of **MainString**. When it succeeds, this pattern returns the **LeadingChar**.

(i,i,i)   succeeds if **MainString** = **LeadingChar** + **TailString**.

(o,i,i)   builds the main string by prepending **LeadingChar** to **TailString**.

Example:

The following program tests the various flow patterns of predicate **frontchar**.

```
predicates
    go
    get_char_str                    /* test (i,o,o) */
    get_str                         /* test (i,i,o) */
    get_char                        /* test (i,o,i) */
    check(string, char, string)
    check_char_str                  /* test (i,i,i) */
    build_str                       /* test (o,i,i) */

clauses
    get_char_str :-
        write("Enter a string -> "), readln(LeString),
        frontchar(LeString, LeadingChar, TrailingString),
        write("The leading character is ",LeadingChar), nl,
        write("The rest of the string is ", TrailingString), nl.
    get_str :-
        write("Enter a string -> "), readln(LeString),
        write("Enter a leading character -> "),
        readchar(LeChar),
        write(LeChar), nl,
        frontchar(LeString, LeChar, TrailString),
```

```
        write("The trailing string is ", TrailString), nl.
get_char :-
    write("Enter a string -> "), readln(LeString),
    write("Enter the trailing substring  -> "),
    readln(TailString),
    frontchar(LeString, LeChar, TailString),
    write("The leading character is ", LeChar), nl.
check(LeString, LeChar, TailString) :-
    frontchar(LeString, LeChar, TailString),
    write("Strings and character match"), nl.
check(_, _, _) :-
    write("Strings and character do not match"), nl.
check_char_str :-
    write("Enter a string -> "), readln(LeString),
    write("Enter the leading character -> "),
    readchar(LeChar),
    write(LeChar), nl,
    write("Enter the trailing substring  -> "),
    readln(TailString),
    check(LeString, LeChar, TailString).
build_str :-
    write("Enter the leading character -> "),
    readchar(LeChar),
    write(LeChar), nl,
    write("Enter the trailing substring  -> "),
    readln(TailString),
    frontchar(LeString, LeChar, TailString),
    write("The new string is ", LeString), nl.
go :-
    get_char_str,
    get_str,
    get_char,
    check_char_str,
    build_str.
```

A sample session with the above program is shown below:

```
Enter a string -> the man
The leading character is t
The rest of the string is he man
```

```
Enter a string -> TProlog
Enter a leading character -> T
The trailing string is Prolog

Enter a string -> TProlog
Enter the trailing substring  -> Prolog
The leading character is T

Enter a string -> what
Enter the leading character -> w
Enter the trailing substring  -> hat
Strings and character match

Enter the leading character -> S
Enter the trailing substring  -> now
The new string is Snow
```

Divides a string into two substrings.   **frontstr**

Syntax:
```
frontstr(NumberChars,MainString,LeadString,TailString)  (i,i,o,o)
        (integer, string, string, string)
```

Parameter:
NumberChars the size of the leading substrings. If the value of this parameter equals the size of the main string, then the leading substring is assigned the main string while the tail substring returns a null string. If the value of this parameter exceeds the length of the main character, the predicate fails.

Example:
The next program tests the predicate **frontstr**.

```
predicates
    go
clauses
    go :-
        write("Enter a string -> "), readln(LeString),
        write("Enter number of characters to put in first ",
            "substring -> "),
```

```
readint (Count),
frontstr(Count, LeString, Substr1, Substr2),
write("Substring # 1 is '", Substr1, "'"), nl,
write("Substring # 2 is '", Substr2, "'"), nl.
```

A sample session with the above program is shown below:

```
Enter a string -> Ada Augusta Byron
Enter number of characters to put in first substring -> 4
Substring # 1 is 'Ada '
Substring # 2 is 'Augusta Byron'
```

fronttoken   Extracts or prepend space-delimited tokens to a string.

Syntax:
```
fronttoken(MainString, Token, TailString)    (i,o,o), (i,i,o),
           (string, string, string)          (i,o,i), (i,i,i), (o,i,i)
```

Parameters:

MainString   the main string containing space-delimited tokens.

Token   the leading token in the main string. Tokens are a set of characters that constitute

1. a name in agreement with Turbo Prolog syntax.
2. a string image of an integer or a real number.
3. a single character, except for the space that acts as a token delimiter.

TailString   the tail substring containing other tokens.

Remarks:

(i,o,o)   extracts the leading token from the main string.

(i,i,o)   succeeds if **Token** is the leading token in **MainString**. When it succeeds, the pattern returns the **TailString** with the rest of the tokens found in the main string.

(i,o,i)   succeeds if **TailString** contains the tokens in **MainString**, except the first one. When it succeeds, this pattern returns the leading token found in the main string.

(i,i,i)   succeeds if prepending the **Token** parameter to the tokens of **TailString** matches the tokens in **MainString**.

(o,i,i)   builds the main string by prepending the **Token** parameter to the tokens of **TailString**.

Example:
The following program tests the various flow patterns of the string handling predicate **fronttoken**.

```
/* NOTE: the predicate frontchar is used to pad or strip the leading
space from the string containing the trailing tokens. */

predicates
    go
    check_tokens            /* test (i,i,i) */
    get_rest_tokens         /* test (i,i,o) */
    get_tokens              /* test (i,o,o) */
    build_token             /* test (o,i,i) */
    get_token               /* test (i,o,i) */
clauses
    check_tokens :-
        write("Enter a set of tokens -> "), readln(LeString),
        write("Enter the first token in the string -> "),
        readln(Token),
        write("Enter the trailing tokens -> "),
        readln(TailTokens),
        frontchar(RestTokens, ' ', TailTokens),
        fronttoken(LeString, Token, RestTokens),
        write("All right! Tokens do match").
    check_tokens :-
        write("Sorry! Tokens do NOT match").
    get_rest_tokens :-
        write("Enter a set of tokens -> "), readln(LeString),
        write("Enter the first token -> "), readln(Token),
        fronttoken(LeString, Token, TailTokens),
        frontchar(TailTokens, ' ', RestTokens),
        write("The trailing tokens are '", RestTokens, "'"), nl.
    get_tokens :-
        write("Enter a set of tokens -> "), readln(LeString),
        fronttoken(LeString, Token, TailTokens),
        write("The leading token is '", Token, "'"), nl,
        frontchar(TailTokens, ' ', RestTokens),
        write("The trailing tokens are '", RestTokens, "'"), nl.
    build_token :-
        write("Enter the leading token -> "), readln(Token),
        write("Enter the trailing tokens -> "),
```

```
        readln(TailTokens),
        frontchar(RestTokens, ' ', TailTokens),
        fronttoken(LeString, Token, RestTokens),
        write("The new set of tokens is '", LeString, "'"), nl.
    get_token :-
        write("Enter a set of tokens -> "), readln(LeString),
        write("Enter the trailing tokens -> "),
        readln(TailTokens),
        frontchar(RestTokens, ' ', TailTokens),
        fronttoken(LeString, Token, RestTokens),
        write("The leading token is '", Token, "'"), nl.
    get_token :-
        write("Sorry! Main tokens and trailing tokens do not match"),
        nl.
    go :-
        nl, nl, nl,
        check_tokens, nl, nl,
        get_rest_tokens, nl, nl,
        get_tokens, nl, nl,
        build_token, nl, nl,
        get_token.
```

A sample session with the above program is shown below:

```
Enter a set of tokens -> To be or not to be
Enter the first token in the string -> To
Enter the trailing tokens -> be or not to be
All right! Tokens do match

Enter a set of tokens -> Water is a liquid
Enter the first token -> Water
The trailing tokens are 'is a liquid'

Enter a set of tokens -> Turbo Prolog 2.0
The leading token is 'Turbo'
The trailing tokens are 'Prolog 2.0'

Enter the leading token -> Turbo
Enter the trailing tokens -> C++
The new set of tokens is 'Turbo C++'
```

```
Enter a set of tokens -> Pascal is better than BASIC
Enter the trailing tokens -> is better than BASIC
The leading token is 'Pascal'
```

Verifies whether a string represents a valid Turbo Prolog name.   **isname**

Syntax:
```
isname(TestedString)      (i)
     (string)
```

Parameter:
TestedString   string tested for being a valid Turbo Prolog name.

Example:
The following program demonstrates the use of the **isname** predicate by
recursively prompting the user for a valid name, until one is keyed in.

```
predicates
    get_name(string)
    go
clauses
    get_name(ValidName) :-
        write("Enter a valid Prolog name -> "),
        readln(ValidName),
        isname(ValidName).

    /* recursive call used to repeatedly prompt the user for a  */
    /* valid Prolog name until one is obtained */
    get_name(ValidName) :-
        get_name(ValidName).
    go :-
        get_name(Prolog_Name),
        write("'", Prolog_Name,"' is a valid Turbo Prolog name"),
        nl.
```

A sample session with the above program is shown below:

```
Enter a valid Prolog name -> !@#$
Enter a valid Prolog name -> ---
Enter a valid Prolog name -> ok_here_it_is
'ok_here_it_is' is a valid Turbo Prolog name
```

str_char   Provides a two-way conversion between a string and a character.

Syntax:
```
str_char(TheString, TheChar)     (i,o), (o,i), (i,i)
        (string, char)
```

Parameters:

TheString   a string that contains a single character.

TheChar   the character compared, converted to, or converted from **TheString**.

Remarks:

(i,o)   converts **TheString** to **TheChar**. This predicate fails if **TheString** contains more than one character.

(o,i)   converts **TheChar** into a single-character string.

(i,i)   compares a single-character string with a character.

Example:

The next program tests the various flow patterns of predicate **str_char**.

```
predicates
    go
    copy_char_to_str          /* test (o,i) */
    copy_str_to_char          /* test (i,o) */
    compare_str_char          /* test (i,o) */
clauses
    copy_char_to_str :-
        write("Enter a character  -> "), readchar(LeChar),
        str_char(LeString, LeChar),
        write(LeString), nl,
        write("You typed ",LeString), nl.
    copy_str_to_char :-
        write("Enter a character (then press Enter)  -> "),
        readln(LeString),
        str_char(LeString, LeChar),
        write("You typed ",LeChar), nl.
    copy_str_to_char :-
        write("You entered more than one character!") , nl.
    compare_str_char :-
        write("Enter a character  -> "), readchar(LeChar),
```

```
        write(LeChar), nl,
        write("Enter a character (then press Enter)  -> "),
        readln(LeString),
        str_char(LeString, LeChar),
        write("The single-character string matches the ",
            "character you typed"), nl.
    compare_str_char :-
        write("The string you entered does not match the ",
            "character"), nl.
    go :-
        nl, nl, nl,
        copy_char_to_str, nl, nl,
        copy_str_to_char, nl, nl,
        compare_str_char.
```

A sample session with the above program is shown below:

```
Enter a character  -> M
You typed M


Enter a character (then press Enter)  -> h<CR>
You typed h


Enter a character  -> i
Enter a character (then press Enter)  -> ii<CR>
The string you entered does not match the character
```

Converts strings to integers and vice versa.   **str_int**

Syntax:
```
str_int(StringImage, Number)    (i,o), (o,i), (i,i)
        (string, integer)
```

Parameters:
StringImage   a string containing the image of an integer.
Number   the integer converted to/from **StringImage**.

Remarks:
(i,o)   converts the string into an integer. If **StringImage** is not a valid
         image of an integer, the predicate fails.

(o,i)   converts the integer into its string image.

(i,i)   compares an integer and its string image.

Example:

The following program tests the various flow patterns of predicate **str_int**.

```
predicates
    go
    copy_int_to_str              /* test (o,i) */
    copy_str_to_int              /* test (i,o) */
    compare_str_int              /* test (i,o) */
clauses
    copy_int_to_str :-
        write("Enter an integer  -> "), readint(LeInt),
        str_int(LeString, LeInt),
        write("You typed string '",LeString, "'"), nl.
    copy_str_to_int :-
        write("Enter a string  -> "), readln(LeString),
        str_int(LeString, LeInt),
        write("You typed the integer ",LeInt), nl.
    compare_str_int :-
        write("Enter an integer  -> "), readint(LeInt), nl,
        write("Enter the string image of the above number  -> "),
        readln(LeString),
        str_int(LeString, LeInt),
        write("The string matches the integer you typed"), nl.
    compare_str_int :-
        write("The string you entered does not match the integer"),
        nl.
    go :-
        nl, nl, nl,
        copy_int_to_str, nl, nl,
        copy_str_to_int, nl, nl,
        compare_str_int.
```

A sample session with the above program is shown below:

```
Enter an integer  -> 55
You typed string '55'
```

```
Enter a string   -> 67
You typed the integer 67

Enter an integer  -> 41
Enter the string image of the above number  -> 41
The string matches the integer you typed
```

Returns or verifies the length of a string.   **str_len**

Syntax:
```
str_len(TheString, Length)    (i,o), (o,i), (i,i)
        (string, integer)
```

Parameters:

TheString   the role of this parameter varies greatly with the flow pattern used with the predicate.

Length   the role of this parameter varies greatly with the flow pattern used with the predicate.

Remarks:

(i,o)   returns the length of the string argument.

(o,i)   creates a space-filled string whose length is specified by **Length**.

(i,i)   compares the actual length of **TheString** with the value of **Length**.

Example:

The next program tests the various flow patterns of predicate **str_len**.

```
predicates
    go
    get_len                  /* test (i,o) */
    make_str                 /* test (o,i) */
    check_len                /* test (i,i) */
    prompt_str(string, integer)
clauses
    get_len :-
        write("Enter a string -> "), readln(LeString),
        str_len(LeString, StrLen),
        write("You typed ",StrLen," characters"), nl.
    make_str :-
        write("Enter size of blank-filled string to create -> "),
```

```
            readint(LeSize),
            str_len(LeString, LeSize),
            write("You created a string"), nl,
            write("|",LeString,"|"), nl.
    check_len :-
            write("123456789012345678901234567890"), nl,
            write("          1         2         3          4"),
            nl, nl,
            write("Enter the size of the string you want to type -> "),
            readint(LeSize),
            write("Enter the string -> "), nl, readln(LeString),
            str_len(LeString, LeSize),
            write("On the money!"), nl.
    check_len :-
            write("Sorry! The string you entered did not match ",
                 "the length"), nl.
    prompt_str(LeString, StrLen) :-
            write("Enter a string (up to ",StrLen," chars) -> "),
            readln(LeString),
            str_len(LeString, LeStrLen),
            LeStrLen <= StrLen.


    /* recursive call to obtain the string with the */
    /* length requirement */
    prompt_str(LeString, StrLen) :-
            prompt_str(LeString, StrLen).
    go :-
            nl, nl, nl,
            get_len, nl,
            make_str, nl,
            check_len, nl,
            write("                                        1234567890"),
            nl,
            prompt_str(LeString, 10),
            write("String '", LeString,
                 "' matches the length requirements"), nl.
```

A sample session with the above program is shown below:

```
Enter a string -> Dirck Bogart
You typed 12 characters
```

```
Enter size of blank-filled string to create -> 5
You created a string
|    |
12345678901234567890123456789012345678901234567890
          1         2         3         4
Enter the size of the string you want to type -> 6
Enter the string ->
Joseph
On the money!

Enter a string (up to 10 chars) -> Keith Weiskamp
Enter a string (up to 10 chars) -> Namir Shammas
Enter a string (up to 10 chars) -> Billy Bob
String 'Billy Bob' matches the length requirements
```

Converts a string to a real number and vice versa.   **str_real**

Syntax:
```
str_real(StringImage, Number)     (i,o), (o,i), (i,i)
        (string, real)
```

Parameters:
StringImage   a string containing the image of a real number.
Number   the real number converted to/from **StringImage**.

Remarks:
(i,o)   converts the string to a real. If **StringImage** is not a valid image
        of a real, the predicate fails.
(o,i)   converts the real to its string image.
(i,i)   compares a real and its string image.

Example:
The following program tests the various flow patterns of predicate **str_real**.

```
predicates
    go
    copy_real_to_str                /* test (o,i) */
    copy_str_to_real                /* test (i,o) */
    compare_str_real                /* test (i,o) */
clauses
    copy_real_to_str :-
```

```
            write("Enter a real number  -> "), readreal(LeInt),
            str_real(LeString, LeInt),
            write("You typed the string '",LeString, "'"), nl.
        copy_str_to_real :-
            write("Enter a real number  -> "), readln(LeString),
            str_real(LeString, LeInt),
            write("You typed the number ",LeInt), nl.
        compare_str_real :-
            write("Enter a real number  -> "), readreal(LeInt), nl,
            write("Enter the string image of the same ",
                  "real number -> "),
            readln(LeString),
            str_real(LeString, LeInt),
            write("The string matches the real number you typed"), nl.
        compare_str_real :-
            write("The string you entered does not match the real ",
                  "number"), nl.
        go :-
            nl, nl, nl,
            copy_real_to_str, nl, nl,
            copy_str_to_real, nl, nl,
            compare_str_real.
```

A sample session with the above program is shown below:

```
Enter a real number  -> 55.5
You typed string '55.5'


Enter a string  -> 67.7
You typed the number 67.7


Enter a real number  -> 41.4
Enter the string image of the same real number  -> 41.4
The string matches the real number you typed
```

upper_lower   Converts uppercase strings to lowercase strings and vice versa.

Syntax:
```
upper_lower(UpcaseString, LocaseString)    (i,o), (o,i), (i,i)
        (string, string)
```

Parameters:

UpcaseString   the string argument designated to contain uppercase characters.

LocaseString   the string argument designated to contain lowercase characters.

Remarks:

(i,o)   converts a string to lowercase characters.

(o,i)   converts a string to uppercase characters.

(i,i)   performs a case-insensitive comparison of the **UpcaseString** and **LocaseString**.

Example:

The next program tests the various flow patterns of predicate **upper_lower**.

```
predicates
    go
    to_upper          /* test (o,i) */
    to_lower          /* test (i,o) */
    ignore_case       /* test (i,i) */
clauses
    to_upper :-
        write("Enter a string -> "), readln(LeString),
        upper_lower(UpperStr, LeString),
        write("The uppercase version is '", UpperStr, "'"), nl.
    to_lower :-
        write("Enter a string -> "), readln(LeString),
        upper_lower(LeString, LowerStr),
        write("The lowercase version is '", LowerStr, "'"), nl.
    ignore_case :-
        write("Enter string # 1 -> "), readln(LeString1),
        write("Enter string # 2 -> "), readln(LeString2),
        upper_lower(LeString1, LeString2),
        write("Strings match (overlooking the case of their ",
              "letters)"), nl.
    ignore_case :-
        write("Strings do not match"), nl.
    go :-
        nl, nl, nl,
        to_upper, nl, nl,
```

```
        to_lower, nl, nl,
        ignore_case.
```

A sample session with the above program is shown below:

```
Enter a string -> William Tell
The uppercase version is 'WILLIAM TELL'

Enter a string -> Neil Armstrong
The lowercase version is 'neil armstrong'

Enter string # 1 -> turbo prolog
Enter string # 2 -> Turbo Prolog
Strings match (overlooking the case of their letters)
```

Math
Routines

Introduction

While all four Turbo languages support predefined mathematical functions, the list of functions varies among the languages. Throughout the years, a standard of minimal math functions has evolved. All four of the Turbo languages support this standard set. Surprisingly, Turbo C provides the largest library of math functions. A few math functions in one or more Turbo languages are available as operators in other Turbo languages. For example, the BASIC **INCR** and Pascal **Inc** functions are available as the C ++ and += operators. In this section, we'll cover all of the math routines available for each of the languages.

Summary of the Math Routines

Table 6.1 compares the math functions for the Turbo languages.

Table 6.1. Math functions provided with the Turbo languages

Function	BASIC	C	Pascal	Prolog
Absolute value	ABS(X)	abs(i)	Abs(X)	abs(X)
		fabs(x)		
		labs(l)		
		cabs(c)		
Arccosine		acos(x)		
Arcsine		asin(x)		
Arctangent	ATN(X)	atan(x)	ArcTan(X)	arctan(X)
		atan2(x)		
Ceiling of a number	CEIL(X)	ceil(x)		
Common logarithm	LOG10(X)	log10(x)	log(X)	
Cosine of an angle	COS(X)	cos(x)	Cos(X)	cos(X)
Decrement a number	DECR I,N	–= opr	Dec(I,N)	
Exponential	EXP(X)	exp(x)	Exp(X)	exp(X)
Floating modulo		dmod(x,y)		
Floor of a number	INT(X)	floor(x)	Int(X)	
			Trunc(X)	trunc(X)
			Round(X)	round(X)
Hyperbolic cosine		cosh(x)		
Hyperbolic sine		sinh(x)		

Table 6.1. Math functions provided with the Turbo languages (continued)

Function	BASIC	C	Pascal	Prolog
Hyperbolic tangent		tanh(x)		
Hypotenuse of a right angle		hypot(x,y)		
Calculate X*2^ex		ldexp(x,ex)		
Increment a number	INCR I,N	+= opr	Inc(I,N)	
Integer division	/ opr	div(i,j)	Div opr	
		ldiv(i,j)		
Logarithm base 2	LOG2(X)			
Natural logarithm	LOG(X)	log(x)	Ln(X)	ln(X)
Polynomial value		poly(x,i,c[])		
Power of X to Y	^ opr	pow(x,y)		
Random number	RND	rand()	Random(I)	random(Max, RndInt)
		random(i)		random(RealNum)
Randomize seed	RANDOMIZE	randomize()	Randomize	
Sign of a number	SGN(N)			
Sine of an angle	SIN(X)	sin(x)	Sin(X)	sin(X)
Split double into integer & fraction		modf(x,ip)		
Split number into mantissa & exponent		frexp(ma,ex)		
Square of a number			Sqr(X)	
Square root	SQR(X)	sqrt(x)	Sqrt(X)	sqrt(X)
Tangent of an angle	TAN(X)	tan(x)	Tan(X)	tan(X)
Two raised to a power	EXP2(X)			
Ten raised to a power	EXP10(X)	pow10(i)		

Translating programs that extensively use math functions between the Turbo implementations (mostly BASIC, Pascal, and C) is very easy, because generally the functions work similarly in all of the languages. For those functions found in one language and not another, a user-defined function should not be hard to write to assist in the translation.

TIP

In the remainder of this section, we cover all of the math functions and predicates for each of the Turbo languages.

Turbo BASIC

Here we cover the major math routines for Turbo BASIC.

ABS

Returns the absolute value of the numeric argument.

Syntax:
```
ABS(X)
```

Parameter:
X   the numeric argument (all integer and floating-point types).

Examples:
```
ABS(-4) 'returns 4
ABS(-1.23) 'returns 1.23
```

ATN

Returns the trigonometric arctangent in radians.

Syntax:
```
ATN(X)
```

Parameter:
X   the numeric argument whose radian angle is sought.

Example:
The following program converts rectangular coordinates to polar coordinates.

```
DEFDBL A-Z
INPUT "Enter X : ";X : PRINT
INPUT "Enter Y : ";Y : PRINT
Modulus = SQR(X*X + Y*Y)
Angle = ATN(Y/X)
PRINT "Modulus = ";Modulus
PRINT "Angle = ";Angle;" radians"
END
```

CEIL

Yields an integer greater than or equal to its argument.

Syntax:
```
CEIL(N)
```

Parameter:

N   a numeric constant, variable, or expression.

Example:

The subsequent example displays the ceiling values for real numbers to illustrate the rounding effect.

```
FOR I! = 0.0 TO 2.0 STEP 0.25
    PRINT I!,CEIL(I!)
NEXT I!
```

Calculates the cosine of an angle.   **COS**

Syntax:

```
COS(Angle)
```

Parameter:

Angle   the angle measured in radians whose cosine is desired.

Example:

The following program converts polar coordinates to rectangular coordinates.

```
DEFDBL A-Z
INPUT "Enter modulus : ";Modulus : PRINT
INPUT "Enter Angle : ";Angle : PRINT
X = Modulus * COS(Angle)
Y = Modulus * SIN(Angle)
PRINT "X = ";X
PRINT "Y = ";Y
END
```

Decrements a numeric variable.   **DECR**

Syntax:

```
DECR X [,<Decrease>]
```

Parameters:

X   a numeric variable (integer or real) to be decremented. No constants or expressions are allowed.

Decrease   the magnitude of change in **X**. If this parameter is omitted, the default value of 1 is used. Can be a constant, variable, or expression.

Example:
```
I% = 100
X# = 100
Sum# = 0
DO
    DECR I%,2 ' decrement I% by 2
    DECR X#, 0.15 ' decrement X# by 0.15
    INCR Sum#, X#
LOOP UNTIL I% <= 0
PRINT "Sum = ";Sum#
```

EXP

Computes the exponential value.

Syntax:
```
EXP(X)
```

Parameter:

X   the numeric argument (integer or floating-point types).

Example:
```
DEFDBL A-Z
INPUT "Enter initial concentration ";C0 : PRINT
DO
    INPUT "Enter reaction rate constant ";K : PRINT
LOOP UNTIL K > 0;
FOR T% = 0 TO 100 STEP 5
    C = C0 * EXP(-K * T%)
    PRINT "Concentration = ";C;" at ";T%;" minutes"
NEXT T%
END
```

INCR

Increments a numeric variable.

Syntax:
```
INCR X [,<Increase>]
```

Parameters:

X   a numeric variable (integer or real) to be incremented. No
            constants or expressions are allowed.

Increase the magnitude of change in **X**. If omitted, the default value
            of 1 is used. Can be a constant, variable, or expression.

Example:
```
I% = 1
X# = 0
Sum# = 0
DO
    INCR I%,2 ' increment I% by 2
    INCR X#, 0.15 ' increment X# by 0.15
    INCR Sum#, X#
LOOP UNTIL I% > 100
PRINT "Sum = ";Sum#
```

Returns the largest integer equal to or less than the numeric argument of   **INT**
the function.

Syntax:
```
INT(X)
```

Parameter:

X   a numeric constant, variable, or expression.

Example:
The next program applies **INT** to a range of negative and positive numbers to illustrate the rounding effect with positive and negative numbers.

```
FOR I! = -2 TO 2 STEP 0.25
    PRINT I!,INT(I!)
NEXT I!
```

Calculates the natural logarithm.   **LOG**

Syntax:
```
LOG(X)
```

Parameter:

X   integer or floating-point value whose natural logarithm is sought.

Remarks:
LOG10 and **LOG2** are also available in Turbo BASIC to calculate the logarithms for bases 10 and 2, respectively. The argument of **LOG** must be positive.

Examples:
```
DEF FNLog10(X) = LOG(X) / LOG(10)  ' mimic LOG10
DEF FNLog2(X) = LOG(X) / LOG(2)    ' mimic LOG2
```

RANDOMIZE   Randomizes the seed that generates random numbers.

Syntax:
```
RANDOMIZE
```

Remarks:
This routine prevents the generation of the same sequence of random numbers every time you run a program during the same session.

RND   Returns a random number between zero and one.

Syntax:
```
RND [X]
```

Parameter:
X   the optional numeric constant, variable, or expression that has the following effect:

> 0	generates the next random number
= 0	repeats the last number generated
< 0	reseeds the random number generator

Example:
The next program generates 20 random numbers in the range of 0 to 1000.

```
RANDOMIZE
FOR I% = 1 TO 20
    PRINT INT(RND*1000) 'show random integers in 0-1000
NEXT I%
```

SIN   Calculates the sine of an angle.

Syntax:
```
SIN(Angle)
```

Parameter:

Angle   the angle, measured in radians, whose sine is sought.

Example:
The following program converts polar coordinates to rectangular coordinates.

```
DEFDBL A-Z
INPUT "Enter modulus : ";Modulus : PRINT
INPUT "Enter Angle : ";Angle : PRINT
X = Modulus * COS(Angle)
Y = Modulus * SIN(Angle)
PRINT "X = ";X
PRINT "Y = ";Y
END
```

Calculates the square root of a number.   **SQR**

Syntax:
```
SQR(X)
```

Parameter:

X   the non-negative numeric argument (integer or real).

Example:
The following program converts rectangular coordinates to polar coordinates.

```
DEFDBL A-Z
INPUT "Enter X : ";X : PRINT
INPUT "Enter Y : ";Y : PRINT
Modulus = SQR(X*X + Y*Y)
Angle = ATN(Y/X)
PRINT "Modulus = ";Modulus
PRINT "Angle = ";Angle;" radians"
END
```

TAN
Computes the trigonometric tangent of an angle.

Syntax:
```
TAN(Angle)
```

Parameter:
Angle   the angle, measured in radians, whose tangent is sought.

Example:
The next program returns the angle associated with an arctangent and the tangent of twice that angle.

```
INPUT "Enter an arctangent : ";X : PRINT
Angle = ATN(X);
PRINT "The angle of your arctangent = ";Angle : PRINT
Y = TAN(2 * Angle)
PRINT "The tangent of twice that angle = ";Y : PRINT
```

Turbo C

The major math functions for Turbo C are covered next.

abs()
Returns the absolute value of the integer-typed argument.

Syntax:
```
#include <math.h>
int abs(int i);
```

Parameter:
i   number whose absolute value is returned.

Example:
The next program employs a loop to prompt for an integer and to return the sum of integers between 1 and that integer. The **abs()** function converts negative entries into positive values. Entering 0 exits the loop and ends the program.

```
#include <stdio.h>
#include <math.h>
```

```
main()
{
    int i;
    double sum;

    do {
        printf("Enter a positive integer [0 to exit] : ");
        scanf("%d", &i);
        i = abs(i); /* make variable i non-negative */
        if (i > 0) {
            sum = (double) (i * (i + 1) / 2);
            printf("\nThe sum of the first %d integers = %lf\n",
                    i, sum);
        }
    } while (i > 0);
}
```

Returns the arccosine value, which lies between 0 and pi. **acos()**

Syntax:
```
#include <math.h>
double acos(double x);
```

Parameter:
x   the argument that must be in the range of 1 to –1, inclusive. Bad arguments cause the **acos()** function to return zero and set the **errno** to **EDOM** (domain error).

Example:
The subsequent program evaluates a Chebyshev polynomial of a given order and a given argument value. Both the **cos()** and **acos()** functions are used in the calculation of the Chebyshev polynomial.

```
#include <stdio.h>
#include <math.h>
main()
{
    int order;
    double x, p;

    printf("Enter order of Chebyshev polynomial : ");
```

```
    scanf("%d", &order);
    printf("\nEnter argument for Chebyshev polynomial : ");
    scanf("%lf", &x);
    p = cos(order * acos(x));
    printf("\n\nT%d(%lf) = %lf", order, x, p);
}
```

asin()

Returns the arcsine value, which lies between –pi/2 and pi/2.

Syntax:
```
#include <math.h>
double asin(double x);
```

Parameter:

x   the argument that must be in the range of 1 to –1, inclusive. Bad arguments cause the **asin()** function to return zero and set the **errno** to **EDOM** (domain error).

Example:

The subsequent program evaluates the angles of a triangle (in degrees), given the length of its three sides.

```
#include <stdio.h>
#include <math.h>
main()
{
    double angle(double, double, double);
    double a, b, c, p;

    printf("Enter the length of side 1 : ");
    scanf("%lf", &a);
    printf("\nEnter the length of side 2 : ");
    scanf("%lf", &b);
    printf("\nEnter the length of side 3 : ");
    scanf("%lf", &c);
    p = (a + b + c) / 2.0;
    printf("\nAngle opposite to side 1 = %lf\n", angle(p,b,c));
    printf("\nAngle opposite to side 2 = %lf\n", angle(p,a,c));
    printf("\nAngle opposite to side 3 = %lf\n", angle(p,a,b));
}
```

```
double angle(double p, double b, double c)
{
    return 2.0 * asin( sqrt( (p-b) * (p-c) / b / c)) *
            180.0 / (355.0 / 113.0);
}
```

Returns the arctangent value that lies between –pi/2 and pi/2.   **atan()**

Syntax:
```
#include <math.h>
double atan(double x);
```

Parameter:
x   the numeric argument whose radian angle is sought.

Example:
The subsequent program converts rectangular coordinates to polar coordinates.

```
#include <stdio.h>
#include <math.h>
main()
{
    double x, y;
    double angle, modulus;

    printf("Enter x : ");  scanf("%ld", &x);
    printf("\nEnter y : ");  scanf("%lf", &y);
    modulus = sqrt(x*x + y*y);
    angle = atan(y/x);
    printf("Modulus = %lf\n", modulus);
    printf("Angle = %lf radians\n", angle);
}
```

Returns the arctangent value that lies between –pi and pi.   **atan2()**

Syntax:
```
#include <math.h>
double atan2(double y, double x);
```

Parameters:

y, x   the numeric arguments whose ratio, y/x, is taken as the tangent of the sought angle (in radians).

Example:

The subsequent program converts rectangular coordinates to polar coordinates.

```
#include <stdio.h>
#include <math.h>
main()
{
    double x, y, angle, modulus;

    printf("Enter x : "); scanf("%ld", &x);
    printf("\nEnter y : "); scanf("%lf", &y);
    modulus = sqrt(x*x + y*y);
    angle = atan2(x,y);
    printf("Modulus = %lf\n", modulus);
    printf("Angle = %lf radians\n", angle);
}
```

cabs()

cabs() is actually a macro that returns the absolute value of a complex number. A **HUGE_VAL** is returned when the result overflows and the **errno** variable is set to **ERANGE** (out-of-range result).

Syntax:

```
#include <math.h>
double cabs(struct complex z);
```

Parameter:

z   a complex number whose structure is defined as:

```
struct complex { double x, y; }
```

Example:

```
#include <stdio.h>
#include <math.h>
main()
{
    struct complex a;
```

```
    printf("Enter the real component of a complex number : ");
    scanf("%lf", &a.x);
    printf("\nEnter the imaginary component of a \
            complex number : ");
    scanf("%lf", &a.y);
    printf("\nThe absolute value = %lf\n", cabs(a));
}
```

Returns the lowest whole number that is greater than or equal to the   **ceil()**
argument **x**.

Syntax:
```
#include <math.h>
double ceil(double x);
```

Parameter:
x   a double number whose ceiling value is sought.

Example:
The next program displays the ceiling values for numbers ranging from –2
to 2, marching in 0.25 intervals.

```
#include <stdio.h>
#include <math.h>
main()
{
    double x = -2.0;

    do {
        printf("Ceiling of %lf = %lf\n", x, ceil(x));
        x += 0.25;
    } while (x <= 2.0);
}
```

Returns the trigonometric cosine of an angle.   **cos()**

Syntax:
```
#include <math.h>
double cos(double x);
```

Parameter:

x   the angle, measured in radians, whose cosine is sought.

Example:

The next program converts polar coordinates to rectangular coordinates.

```
#include <stdio.h>
#include <math.h>
main()
{
    double x, y, angle, modulus;

    printf("Enter modulus : ");
    scanf("%lf", &modulus);
    printf("\nEnter Angle : ");
    scanf("%lf", &angle);
    x = modulus * cos(angle);
    y = modulus * sin(angle);
    printf("\nX = %lf\n",x);
    printf("Y = %lf\n",y);
}
```

cosh()

Returns the hyperbolic cosine. If the result overflows, the value **HUGE_VAL** is returned with the appropriate sign.

Syntax:

```
#include <math.h>
double cosh(double x);
```

Parameter:

x   the real value whose hyperbolic cosine is returned.

Examples:

The next program calculates the modified Bessel function of the first kind of order −1/2.

```
#include <stdio.h>
#include <math.h>
main()
```

```
{
    double x, bessel_func, pi = 355.0 / 113.0;

    printf("Enter argument : ");
    scanf("%lf", &x);
    bessel_func = sqrt(2/pi/x) * cosh(x);
    printf("\nBessel function = %lf\n", bessel_func);
}
```

Performs integer division and returns the quotient and remainder. The   **div()**
results are passed using the **div_t** data type defined as:

```
typedef struct {
    int quot;
    int rem;
} div_t;
```

Syntax:
```
#include <stdlib.h>
div_t div(int numer, int denom);
```

Parameters:
numer   the numerator.
denom   the denominator.

Example:
The next program calculates the number of disks required to store a group
of files. Using the **div()** function, the program can report whether all the
disks are used to capacity and, if not, the number of Kbytes stored in the
last one.

```
#include <stdio.h>
#include <stdlib.h>
main()
{
    int disk_size, file_sizes;
    div_t n;

    printf("Enter the capacity of each disk (in Kbytes) : ");
    scanf("%d", &disk_size);
```

```
        printf("\nEnter the total size of files to store \
                (in Kbytes) : ");
        scanf("%d", &file_sizes);
        n = div(disk_size, file_sizes);
        printf("You will need %d disks\n", n.quot+1);
        if (n.rem != 0)
            printf("The last disk will contain %d Kbytes\n",n.rem);
        else
            puts("All of the disks will be full");
    }
```

exp()

Calculates the exponential value for its argument. If an overflow occurs, the function yields the **HUGE_VAL** result and the **errno** is set to **ERANGE** (out-of-range result).

Syntax:
```
#include <math.h>
double exp(double x);
```

Parameter:

x   the argument whose exponential value is returned.

Example:
The next program tabulates the values of the concentration of a chemical reactant as a function of reaction time.

```
#include <stdio.h>
#include <math.h>
main()
{
    double c0, c, k, t;

    printf("Enter initial concentration : ");
    scanf("%lf", &c0);
    do {
        printf("\nEnter reaction rate constant : ");
        scanf("%lf", &k);
    } while (k <= 0.0);
    t = 5.0;
    while (t < 100.0) {
```

```
        c = c0 * exp(-k * t);
        printf("Concentration = %lf at %lf minutes\n", c, t)
        t += 5.0;
    }
}
```

Returns the absolute value of the double-typed argument.   **fabs()**

Syntax:
```
#include <math.h>
double fabs(double x);
```

Parameter:
x   number whose absolute value is returned.

Example:
The next program employs a loop to prompt for an integer and returns the sum of integers between 1 and that integer. The **fabs()** function converts negative entries into positive values. Entering 0 enables you to exit the loop and end the program.

```
#include <stdio.h>
#include <math.h>
main()
{
    double x, sum;

    do {
        printf("Enter a positive number [0 to exit] : ");
        scanf("%lf", &x);
        x = fabs(x); /* make variable x non-negative */
        if (x > 0.0) {
            sum = (x * (x + 1.0) / 2.0);
            printf("\nThe sum of 1..%lg = %lf\n", x, sum);
        }
    } while (x > 0.0);
}
```

Returns the greatest whole number that is less than or equal to its argument.   **floor()**

Syntax:
```
#include <math.h>
double floor(double x);
```

Parameter:

x   a double number whose floored value is sought.

Example:

The next program displays the floor values for numbers ranging from –2 to 2, marching in 0.25 intervals.

```
#include <stdio.h>
#include <math.h>
main()
{
    double x = -2.0;

    do {
        printf("Floor of %lf = %lf\n", x, floor(x));
        x += 0.25;
    } while (x <= 2.0);
}
```

fmod()   Returns x modulo y.

Syntax:
```
#include <math.h>
double fmod(double x, double y);
```

Parameters:

x, y   the numbers whose modulo is calculated, such that:

```
x = (multiplier) * y + modulo_value
```

where **modulo_value** is in the range defined by:

```
0 <= modulo_value < y
```

Example:

Using random numbers, the following program demonstrates the **fmod()** function.

```
#include <stdio.h>
#include <math.h>
main()
{
    double x, y, mv;

    randomize;
    x = (double) (random(20) + 1);
    y = (double) (random(20) + 1);
    mv = fmod(x,y);
    printf("%lg fmod %lg = %lg\n", x, y, mv);
}
```

Breaks down a number into $m * 2^n$. The function returns the value of m **frexp()**
(in the range of 0.5 to 1), whereas the pointer to the argument **expon** returns
the value of n.

Syntax:
```
#include <math.h>
double frexp(double x, int *expon);
```

Parameters:
x   the number broken down into mantissa and exponent.
expon   pointer to the exponent result.

Example:
The following program implements a simple demonstration for the use of
function **frexp()**.

```
#include <stdio.h>
#include <math.h>
main()
{
    double x, m;
    int n;

    printf("Enter a number : ");
    scanf("%lf", &x);
    m = frexp(x, &n);
    printf("\n%lg = %lg * 2^%d\n", x, m, n);
}
```

hypot()   Calculates the hypotenuse of a right triangle, given the length of the sides forming the right angle. The function returns **HUGE_VAL** in case of an overflow and also sets **errno** to **ERANGE** (out-of-range error).

Syntax:
```
#include <math.h>
double hypot(double x, double y);
```

Parameters:
x, y   the length of the sides of the right triangle forming the right angle.

Example:
The next program calculates the length of the triangle side opposite to the right angle, given the two other sides.

```
#include <stdio.h>
#include <math.h>
main()
{
    int a, b, c;

    printf("Enter side a : ");
    scanf("%lf", &a);
    printf("\nEnter side b : ");
    scanf("%lf", &b);
    c = hypot(a,b);
    printf("\nSide c = %lg\n", c);
}
```

labs()   Returns the absolute value of the long integer-type argument.

Syntax:
```
#include <math.h>
#include <stdlib.h>
long labs(long i);
```

Parameter:
i   number whose absolute value is returned.

Example:
The next program employs a loop to prompt for an integer and return the

sum of integers between 1 and that integer. The **labs()** function is used to convert negative entries into positive values. Entering zero enables you to exit the loop and end the program.

```c
#include <stdio.h>
#include <math.h>
main()
{
    long i;
    double sum;

    do {
        printf("Enter a positive integer [0 to exit] : ");
        scanf("%ld", &i);
        i = labs(i); /* make variable i non-negative */
        if (i > 0) {
            sum = (double) (i * (i + 1) / 2);
            printf("\nThe sum of the first %d integers = %lf\n",
                    i, sum);
        }
    } while (i > 0);
}
```

Calculates the value of x * 2^expon. This function is the reverse of **frexp()**.   **ldexp()**

Syntax:
```c
#include <math.h>
double ldexp(double x, int expon);
```

Parameters:
x   the mantissa (0.5 to 1).
expon   the exponent to which 2 is raised.

Example:
The next program converts a double-typed number into the mantissa and exponent using function **frexp()** and then performs the reverse conversion using function **ldexp()**.

```c
#include <stdio.h>
#include <math.h>
main()
{
```

```
double x, m;
int n;

printf ("Enter a number : ");
scanf ("%lf", &x);
m = frexp (x, &n);
printf ("\n%lg = %lg * 2^%d\n", x, m, n);
x = ldexp (m,n);
printf ("%lg * 2^%d = %lf\n", m, n, x);
}
```

ldiv()　　Performs long integer division and returns the quotient and remainder. The results are passed using the **ldiv_t** data type defined as:

```
typedef struct {
    long quot;
    long rem;
} ldiv_t;
```

Syntax:
```
#include <stdlib.h>
ldiv_t ldiv (long numer, long denom);
```

Parameters:
numer　　the numerator.
denom　　the denominator.

Example:
The next program calculates the number of disks required to store a certain amount of files. Using the **ldiv()** function, the program can report whether all the disks are used to capacity and, if not, the number of bytes stored in the last one.

```
#include <stdio.h>
#include <stdlib.h>
main ()
{
    long disk_size, file_sizes;
    ldiv_t n;

    printf ("Enter the capacity of each disk (in bytes) : ");
```

```
        scanf("%ld", &disk_size);
        printf("\nEnter the total size of files to store \
                (in Bytes) : ");
        scanf("%ld", &file_sizes);
        n = div(disk_size, file_sizes);
        printf("You will need %ld disks\n", n.quot+1);
        if (n.rem != 0)
            printf("The last disk will contain %ld bytes\n",n.rem);
        else
            puts("All of the disks will be full");
}
```

Returns the natural logarithm (taken to base e).   **log()**

Syntax:
```
#include <math.h>
double log(double x);
```

Parameter:
x   is the positive argument for the logarithm function. When a nega-
     tive value or 0 is passed to **log()**, the function returns the negative of
     HUGE_VAL, and **errno** is set to **EDOM** (Error in domain).

Example:
The following function calculates the base 2 logarithm.

```
#include <math.h>
double log2(double x)
{
    return log(x) / log(2.0);
}
```

Returns the common logarithm (taken to base 10).   **log10()**

Syntax:
```
#include <math.h>
double log10(double x);
```

Parameter:
x   is the positive argument for the logarithm function. When a negative

value or 0 is passed to **log10**(), the function returns the negative of **HUGE_VAL**, and **errno** is set to **EDOM** (Error in domain).

Example:
The following function calculates the base 2 logarithm.

```
#include <math.h>
double log2 (double x)
{
    return log10 (x)  / log10 (2.0);
}
```

max()

Returns the greater value of **a** or **b**.

Syntax:
```
#include <stdlib.h>
<type> max (<type> a,  <type> b);
```

Parameters:
a, b   the compared numbers.

Example:
The next program prompts you for two integers and returns the bigger one.

```
#include <stdio.h>
#include <stdlib.h>
main ()
{
    long a, b, big;

    printf ("Enter two numbers separated by a space : ");
    scanf ("%ld %ld", &a, &b);
    big = (long) max (a,b);
    printf ("\nThe larger of the two numbers is %ld\n", big);
}
```

min()

Returns the smaller value of **a** or **b**.

Syntax:
```
#include <stdlib.h>
<type> min (<type> a,  <type> b);
```

Parameters:
a, b   the compared numbers.

Example:
The next program prompts you for two integers and returns the smaller one.

```
#include <stdio.h>
#include <stdlib.h>
main()
{
    long a, b, small;

    printf("Enter two numbers separated by a space : ");
    scanf("%ld %ld", &a, &b);
    small = (long) min(a,b);
    printf("\nThe smaller of the two numbers is %ld\n", small);
}
```

Breaks down a number into an integer and a fraction. The function returns   **modf()**
the fraction part, whereas the integer is passed via the pointer-argument.

Syntax:
```
#include <math.h>
double modf(double x, double *intpart);
```

Parameters:
x   the number split into an integer and a fraction.
intpart   the pointer to the integer part.

Example:
The subsequent program displays the integer and fraction of pi.

```
#include <stdio.h>
#include <math.h>
main()
{
    double pi = 355.0 / 113.0, whole, fraction;

    fraction = modf(pi, &whole);
    printf("%lg = %lg + %lg\n", pi, whole, fraction);
}
```

poly()   Evaluates a polynomial.

Syntax:
```
#include <math.h>
double poly(double x, int order, double coeff[]);
```

Parameters:

x   the argument of the polynomial.
order   the order of the polynomial.
coeff[]   the array of coefficients used to evaluate the polynomial:

$$Y = c[0] + c[1] X + c[2] X^2 + c[3] X^3 + ... c[order] X^{order}$$

Example:
The next program enables you to calculate the error-function using a polynomial approximation.

```
#include <stdio.h>
#include <math.h>
main()
{
    int order = 7;
    double coeff[8] = {0.0,1.0,0.0,-0.333334,
                       0.0,0.1,0.0,-0.02381};
    double x, y, pi = 355.0 / 113.0;

    printf("Enter argument for error-function : ");
    scanf("%lf", &x);
    y = 2.0 / sqrt(pi) * poly(x, order, coeff);
    printf("\nErf(%lg) = %lg\n",x,y);
}
```

pow()   Raises **y** to the power **x**. This function returns **HUGE_VAL** in case of an overflow and also sets **errno** to **ERANGE** (out-of-range error). If the value of **x** is negative or 0 and **y** is not an integer, **errno** is set to **EDOM** (Error in domain) and the result returned is the negative value of **HUGE_VAL**. If both **x** and **y** are 0, function **pow()** returns 1.

Syntax:
```
#include <math.h>
double pow(double x, double y);
```

Parameters:

y   base number.

x   exponent.

Example:

The next program enables you to calculate the error-function using a polynomial approximation.

```
#include <stdio.h>
#include <math.h>
main()
{
   int i, order = 7;
   double coeff[8] = {0.0, 1.0,  0.0, -0.333334,
                      0.0, 0.1,  0.0, -0.02381 };
   double x, y = 0.0, pi = 355.0 / 113.0;

   printf("Enter argument for error-function : ");
   scanf("%lf", &x);
   for (i = 0; i <= order; i++)
      y += coeff[i] * pow(x, (double) i);
   y *= 2.0 / sqrt(pi);
   printf("\nErf(%lg) = %lg\n",x,y);
}
```

Raises 10 to the **expon** power.   **pow10()**

Syntax:

```
#include <math.h>
double pow10(int expon);
```

Parameter:

expon   integer power of 10.

Example:

The following program prompts for the electrical voltage and resistance. The current is calculated and if found to be less than one ampere is displayed in milliamperes (by scaling the value of the electrical current by **pow10(3)**).

```
#include <stdio.h>
#include <math.h>
```

```
main()
{
    double volt, ohm, amp;

    printf("Enter voltage (volts) : ");
    scanf("%lf", &volt);
    printf("\nEnter resistance (ohms) : ");
    scanf("%lf", &ohm);
    amp = volt / ohm;
    if (amp > 1.0)
        printf("\nCurrent = %lg amps\n", amp);
    else
        printf("\nCurrent = %lg milliamps\n", amp * pow10(3));
}
```

rand()

Returns a random integer generated using the multiplicative congruential random number generator. The range of values produced is 0 to **RAND_MAX** (defined as $(2^{15} - 1)$ in **stdlib.h**).

Syntax:

```
#include <stdlib.h>
int rand(void);
```

Example:

The following program generates 100 random numbers and reports the smallest and biggest numbers generated.

```
#include <stdio.h>
#include <stdlib.h>
main()
{
    int big, small, n, count = 99;

    n = rand;
    small = n;
    big = n;
    while (count > 0) {
        n = rand;
        small = (int) min(small,n);
```

```
        big = (int) max(big, n);
        count--;
    }
    printf("The smallest number is %d\n", small);
    printf("The largest number is %d\n", big);
}
```

Returns a random integer generated between 0 and (**upper_limit** – 1).   **random()**

Syntax:
```
#include <stdlib.h>
int random(int upper_limit);
```

Parameter:
upper_limit   the ceiling value for the returned random number.

Example:
The following program generates 100 random numbers (between 0 and 999) and reports the smallest and largest numbers generated.

```
#include <stdio.h>
#include <stdlib.h>
main()
{
    int big, small, n, count = 99;

    randomize;
    n = random(1000);
    small = n;
    big = n;
    while (count > 0) {
        n = rand(1000);
        small = (int) min(small,n);
        big = (int) max(big, n);
        count--;
    }
    printf("The smallest number is %d\n", small);
    printf("The largest number is %d\n", big);
}
```

randomize()   Reseeds the random number generator.

Syntax:
```
#include <stdlib.h>   (time.h is also required)
void randomize(void);
```

Example:
See the example for the **random**() function.

sin()   Returns the trigonometric sine of an angle.

Syntax:
```
#include <math.h>
double sin(double x);
```

Parameter:

x   the angle, measured in radians, whose sine is calculated.

Example:
The next program converts polar coordinates to rectangular coordinates.

```
#include <stdio.h>
#include <math.h>
main()
{
    double x, y, angle, modulus;

    printf("Enter modulus : ");
    scanf("%lf", &modulus);
    printf("\nEnter Angle : ");
    scanf("%lf", &angle);
    x = modulus * cos(angle);
    y = modulus * sin(angle);
    printf("\nX = %lf\n",x);
    printf("\nY = %lf\n",y);
}
```

sinh()   Returns the hyperbolic sine. If an overflow occurs, the function returns
                        HUGE_VAL with an appropriate sign.

Syntax:
```
#include <math.h>
double sinh(double x);
```

Parameter:

x   the argument whose hyperbolic sine is returned.

Example:
The next program calculates the modified Bessel function of the first kind of order 1/2.

```
#include <stdio.h>
#include <math.h>
main()
{
    double x, bessel_func, pi = 355.0 / 113.0;

    printf("Enter argument : ");
    scanf("%lf", &x);
    bessel_func = sqrt(2/pi/x) * sinh(x);
    printf("\nBessel function = %lf\n", bessel_func);
}
```

Computes the square root value of a non-negative number. With negative   **sqrt()**
arguments, this function returns 0 and sets **errno** to **EDOM** (Error in
domain).

Syntax:
```
#include <math.h>
double sqrt(double x);
```

Parameter:

x   number whose square root is sought.

Example:
The following program prompts for the area of a circle and calculates the
corresponding radius.

```
#include <stdio.h>
#include <math.h>
```

```
main()
{
    double area, radius, pi = 355.0 / 113.0;

    do {
        printf("\nEnter area of circle : ");
        scanf("%lf", &area);
    } while (area <= 0.0);
    radius = sqrt(area) / pi;
    printf("\nRadius of circle = %lg\n", radius);
}
```

srand()

Reseeds the random number generator with the seed value.

Syntax:
```
#include <math.h>
void srand(unsigned seed);
```

Parameter:
seed   the new seed value for the random number generator.

Example:
The following program generates 100 random numbers (between 0 and 999) and reports the smallest and largest numbers generated.

```
#include <stdio.h>
#include <stdlib.h>
main()
{
    int big, small, n, count = 99;

    srand(3); /* reseed random number generator with 3 */
    n = random(1000);
    small = n;
    big = n;
    while (count > 0) {
        n = rand(1000);
        small = (int) min(small,n);
        big = (int) max(big, n);
        count--;
```

```
    }
    printf("The smallest number is %d\n", small);
    printf("The largest number is %d\n", big);
}
```

Calculate the trigonometric tangent. The angles pi/2 and –pi/2 result in an infinite value for the **tan()** function. Consequently, the **tan()** function returns 0 and sets **errno** to **ERANGE** (out-of-range result).   **tan()**

Syntax:
```
#include <math.h>
double tan(double x);
```

Parameter:
x   the angle, measured in radians, whose tangent is sought.

Example:
The next program returns the angle associated with an arctangent and the tangent of twice that angle.

```
#include <stdio.h>
#include <math.h>
main()
{
    double angle, x, y;

    printf("Enter an arctangent : ");
    scanf("%lf", &x);
    angle = atan(x);
    printf("\nThe angle of your tangent = %lf\n",angle);
    y = tan(2.0 * angle);
    printf("\nThe tangent of twice that angle = %lf\n",y);
}
```

Computes the hyperbolic tangent with values ranging from –1 to 1.   **tanh()**

Syntax:
```
#include <math.h>
double tanh(double x);
```

Parameter:

x   argument for the **tanh()** function.

Example:

The following program displays a table for **tanh(x)** for values of **x** ranging between –3 and 3, in steps of 0.5.

```
#include <stdio.h>
#include <math.h>
main()
{
    double x = -3.0;

    while (x <= 3.0) {
        printf("tanh(%lg) = %lg\n", x, tanh(x));
        x += 0.50;
    }
}
```

Turbo Pascal

Here we cover the major math routines for Turbo Pascal.

Abs

Returns the absolute value of the numeric argument.

Syntax:
```
Function Abs(X : <numeric type>) : <numeric type>;
```

Parameter:

X   the numeric argument (all integer and floating-point types).

Examples:
```
Abs(-4); {returns 4}
Abs(-1.23); {returns 1.23}
```

ArcTan

Returns the trigonometric arctangent in radians.

Syntax:
```
Function ArcTan(X : Real) : Real;
```

Parameter:

X   the numeric argument whose radian angle is sought.

Example:

The subsequent program converts rectangular coordinates to polar coordinates.

```
Procedure Test_ArcTan;
Var X, Y, Angle, Modulus : Real;
Begin
    Write('Enter X : '); Readln(X); Writeln;
    Write('Enter Y : '); Readln(Y); Writeln;
    Modulus := Sqrt(X*X + Y*Y);
    Angle := ArcTan(Y/X);
    Writeln('Modulus = ',Modulus);
    Writeln('Angle = ',Angle,' radians');
End.
```

Calculates the cosine of an angle.   **Cos**

Syntax:

```
Function Cos(Angle : Real) : Real;
```

Parameter:

Angle   the angle, measured in radians, whose cosine is sought.

Example:

The next program converts polar coordinates to rectangular coordinates.

```
Procedure Test_Cos;
Var X, Y, Angle, Modulus : Real;
Begin
    Write('Enter Modulus : '); Readln(Modulus); Writeln;
    Write('Enter Angle : ');   Readln(Angle); Writeln;
    X := Modulus * Cos(Angle);
    Y := Modulus * Sin(Angle);
    Writeln('X = ',X);
    Writeln('Y = ',Y);
End.
```

Dec   Decrements an ordinal-typed variable.

Syntax:
```
Procedure Dec(Var X : <ordinal-type> [;Decrease : <ordinal-type>])
```

Parameters:
X   is an ordinal-typed variable to be decremented.
Decrease   the magnitude of change in **X**. If omitted, the default value
               of 1 is used. Can be a constant, variable, or expression.

Remarks:
No floating-type arguments can be used with **Dec**.

Example:
The next program calculates the sum of the following series:

```
100, 99, 98, 97, ..., 50
```

```
Procedure Test_Dec;
Var I : Integer;
    X, Sum : Longint;
Begin
    I := 100;
    X := 100;
    Sum := 0;
    Repeat
        Dec(I,2);        { decrement I by 2 }
        Dec(X);          { decrement X by 1 }
        Inc(Sum,X);
    Until I <= 0;
    Writeln('Sum = ',Sum);
End.
```

Exp   Computes the exponential value.

Syntax:
```
Function Exp(X : Real) : Real;
```

Parameter:
X   the numeric argument (integer or floating-point types).

Example:
The next program tabulates the values of the concentration of a chemical reactant as a function of reaction time.

```
Procedure Test_Exp;
Var C0, C, K, T : Real;
Begin
   Write('Enter initial concentration : ');
   Readln(C0); Writeln;
   Repeat
      Write('Enter reaction rate constant ');
      Readln(K); Writeln;
   Until K > 0.0;
   T := 5.0;
   While T < 100.0 Do Begin
      C := C0 * Exp(-K * T);
      Writeln('Concentration = ',C,' at ',T,' minutes')
      T := T + 5.0;
   End; { While }
End.
```

Increments an ordinal-typed variable.   **Inc**

Syntax:
```
Procedure Inc(Var X : <ordinal-type> [;Decrease : <ordinal-type>]);
```

Parameters:

Increase   the magnitude of change in **X**. If omitted, the default value of 1 is used. Can be a constant, variable, or expression.

X   is an ordinal-typed variable to be incremented.

Remarks:
No floating-type arguments can be used with **Inc**.

Example:
The next program calculates the sum of the following series:

```
5, 10, 15, 20, 25, ..., 255
```

```
Procedure Test_Inc;
Var I : Integer;
```

```
          X, Sum : Longint;
     Begin
         I := 0;
         X := 0;
         Sum := 0;
         Repeat
             Inc(I,2); { increment I by 2 }
             Inc(X,5); { increment X by 5 }
             Inc(Sum,X);
         Until I > 100;
         Writeln('Sum = ',Sum);
     End.
```

Int

Returns the integer part (as a Real) of a real number.

Syntax:
```
Function Int(X : Real) : Real;
```

Parameter:
X   the truncated number or expression whose value is rounded toward zero.

Example:
The next program displays the integer values for numbers between 2 and –2, in steps of 0.25.

```
Procedure Test_Int;
Var X : Real;
Begin
    X := 2.0;
    Repeat
        Writeln('The integer part of ',X,' is ',Int(X));
        X := X - 0.25;
    Until X < -2.0;
End.
```

Ln

Calculates the natural logarithm.

Syntax:
```
Function Ln(X : Real) : Real;
```

Parameter:

X   the numeric (integer or floating-point) argument whose natural logarithm is sought.

Remarks:

The argument of **Ln** must be positive.

Examples:

The functions shown below implement the common and base 2 logarithms.

```
Function Log10(X : Real) : Real;
Begin
    Log10 := Ln(X) / Ln(10)
End;
```

```
Function Log2(X : Real) : Real;
Begin
    Log2 := Ln(X) / Ln(2)
End;
```

Randomizes the seed that generates random numbers.   **Randomize**

Syntax:

```
Procedure Randomize;
```

Remarks:

This routine prevents generation of the same sequence of random numbers
every time you run a program during the same session. The random value
is obtained from the system clock and is stored in a predefined long integer
variable, **RandSeed**.

Returns a random number.   **Random**

Syntax:

```
Function Random(X : <integer-type>) : Word;
Function Random : Real;
```

Parameter:

X   the optional numeric constant, variable, or expression that has one
of the effects listed in Table 6.2.

Table 6.2. Use of the argument for Random

Argument Present	Type of Result	Range
No	Real	0 <= result < 1
Yes	Word	
X > 0		0 <= result < X
X <= 0		result = 0

Example:
The next code segment reseeds the random number generator and displays 20 random integers in the range of 0 to 999.

```
Randomize
For I := 1 To 20 Do
    Writeln(Random(1000));  {show random integers in 0..999}
```

Round   Rounds a real number into a **Longint**.

Syntax:
```
Function Round(X : Real) : Longint;
```

Parameter:
X   the number rounded to the nearest integer.

Example:
The next program displays rounded values for numbers between 2 and –2, in steps of 0.25.

```
Procedure Test_Round;
Var
    X : Real;
Begin
    X := 2.0;
    Repeat
        Writeln('Rounding ',X,' gives ',Round(X));
        X := X - 0.25;
    Until X < -2.0;
End.
```

Calculates the sine of an angle.   **Sin**

Syntax:
```
Function Sin(Angle : Real) : Real;
```

Parameter:
Angle   the angle, measured in radians, whose sine is sought.

Example:
The next program converts polar coordinates to rectangular coordinates.

```
Procedure Test_Sin;
Var X, Y, Angle, Modulus : Real;
Begin
   Write('Enter Modulus : '); Readln(Modulus); Writeln;
   Write('Enter Angle : ');   Readln(Angle); Writeln;
   X := Modulus * Cos(Angle);
   Y := Modulus * Sin(Angle);
   Writeln('X = ',X);
   Writeln('Y = ',Y);
End.
```

Calculates the square root.   **Sqrt**

Syntax:
```
Function Sqrt(X : Real) : Real;
```

Parameter:
X   the non-negative numeric argument.

Example:
The following program converts rectangular coordinates to polar coordinates.

```
Procedure Test_Sqrt;
Var X, Y, Angle, Modulus : Real;
Begin
   Write('Enter X : '); Readln(X); Writeln;
   Write('Enter Y : '); Readln(Y); Writeln;
   Modulus := Sqrt(X*X + Y*Y);
```

```
        Angle := ArcTan(Y/X);
        Writeln('Modulus = ',Modulus);
        Writeln('Angle = ',Angle,' radians');
    End.
```

Tan

Computes the trigonometric tangent of an angle.

Syntax:
```
Function Tan(Angle : Real) : Real;
```

Parameter:

Angle   the angle, measured in radians, whose tangent is sought.

Example:

The next program returns the angle associated with an arctangent and the tangent of twice that angle.

```
Procedure Test_Tangent;
Var Angle, X, Y : Real;
Begin
    Write('Enter an arctangent : ');
    Readln(X); Writeln;
    Angle := ArcTan(X);
    Writeln('The angle of your tangent = ',Angle);
    Writeln;
    Y := Tan(2 * Angle);
    Writeln('The tangent of twice that angle = ',Y);
    Writeln;
End.
```

Trunc

Truncates a real number into a **Longint**.

Syntax:
```
Function Trunc(X : Real) : Longint;
```

Parameter:

X   the truncated number whose value is rounded toward zero.

Example:

The next program displays truncated values for numbers between 2 and –2, in steps of 0.25.

```
Procedure Test_Trunc;
Var X : Real;
Begin
    X := 2.0;
    Repeat
        Writeln('Truncating ',X,' gives ',Trunc(X));
        X := X - 0.25;
    Until X < -2.0;
End.
```

Turbo Prolog

Here we cover the major math predicates for Turbo Prolog.

Returns the absolute value of the numeric argument.   **abs**

Syntax:
```
abs(X)      (i)
    (integer) (real)
```

Parameter:
X   the numeric argument (all integer and floating-point types).

Examples:
```
abs(-4) returns 4
abs(-1.23) returns 1.23
```

Returns the trigonometric arctangent, measured in radians.   **arctan**

Syntax:
```
arctan(X)      (i)
      (integer) (real)
```

Parameter:
X   the numeric argument for an angle whose radian is sought.

Example:
The subsequent program converts rectangular coordinates to polar coordinates.

```
predicates
    go().
goal
    go.
clauses
    go :-
        write("Enter X : "), readreal(X), nl,
        write("Enter Y : "), readreal(Y), nl,
        Modulus = sqrt(X*X + Y*Y),
        Angle = arctan(Y/X),
        write("Modulus = ",Modulus), nl,
        write("Angle = ",Angle," radians"), nl.
```

cos   Calculates the cosine of an angle.

Syntax:
```
cos(Angle)      (i)
    (integer) (real)
```

Parameter:
Angle   the angle, measured in radians, whose cosine is sought.

Example:
The next program converts polar coordinates to rectangular coordinates.

```
predicates
    go()
goal
    go.
clauses
    go :-
        write("Enter Modulus : "), readreal(Modulus), nl,
        write("Enter Angle : "), readreal(Angle), nl,
        X = Modulus * cos(Angle),
        Y = Modulus * sin(Angle),
        write("X = ",X), nl,
        write("Y = ",Y), nl.
```

div   Computes the result of integer division between two integers.

Syntax:
```
<Num1> div <Num2>      (i,i)
```

Parameters:
Both numbers must be integers. The result returned is also an integer.

Examples:
```
Result = 10 div 5
Total = NumParts div 2
```

Computes the exponential value.   **exp**

Syntax:
```
exp(X)     (i)
   (integer)  (real)
```

Parameter:
X   the numeric argument (integer or floating-point types).

Example:
The next program tabulates the values of the concentration of a chemical reactant as a function of reaction time.

```
predicates
    go()
    react(real, real, real)
goal
    go.
clauses
    react(C0, K, T) :-
        T < 100.0,
        C = C0 * exp(-K *T),
        write("Concentration = ",C," at ",T," minutes"), nl,
        T1 = T + 5.0,
        react(C0, K, T1).
    react(_, _, _).
    go :-
        write("Enter initial concentration : "),
        readreal(C0), nl,
```

```
write("Enter reaction rate constant : "),
readreal(K),   nl,
T = 5.0,
react(C0, K, T).
```

ln   Calculates the natural logarithm.

Syntax:
```
ln(X)     (i)
   (integer) (real)
```

Parameter:
X   the numeric (integer or floating-point) argument whose natural log-arithm is sought.

Remarks:
The argument of **ln** must be positive.

Example:
The predicates shown below implement the common and base 2 logarithms.

```
Log10(X, Result) :- Result = ln(X) / ln(10).
Log2(X, Result) :- Result = ln(X) / ln(2).
```

log   Calculates the common logarithm (base 10).

Syntax:
```
log(X)     (i)
    (integer) (real)
```

Parameter:
X   the numeric (integer or floating-point) argument whose common log-arithm is sought.

Remarks:
The argument of **log** must be positive.

Example:
The predicates shown below implement the natural and base 2 logarithms.

```
Loge(X, Result) :- Result = log(X) / log(10).
Log2(X, Result) :- Result = log(X) / log(2).
```

Computes modulo division between two integers.   **mod**

Syntax:
```
<Num1> mod <Num2>      (i,i)
(integer)   (integer)
```

Parameters:
Both numbers must be integers. The result returned is also an integer.

Examples:
```
Result = 10 mod 5
Total = NumParts mod 2
```

Returns a random integer between zero and an assigned upper limit.   **random**

Syntax:
```
random(UpperLimit, RandInt)   (i,o)
      (integer, integer)
```

Parameters:
UpperLimit   the upper limit for the generated random value, such that:

```
0 <= random value < UpperLimit
```

RandInt   the random integer.

Example:
The next program displays 20 random integers in the range of 0 to 999.

```
predicates
    go()
    make_rand(integer, integer)
goal
    go.
clauses
    make_rand(Count, UpperLimit) :-
        Count > 0,
```

```
        random(UpperLimit, RandInt),
        write(RandInt), nl,
        Count1 = Count - 1,
        make_rand(Count1, UpperLimit).
    make_rand(_,_).
    go :-
        I = 20,
        make_rand(I, 1000).
```

random   Returns a random real between zero and one.

Syntax:
```
random(RandReal)        (o)
        (real)
```

Parameter:

RandReal   the real-typed random number (0 <= number < 1).

Example:

The next program displays 20 random numbers in the range of 0 to 999.

```
predicates
    go()
    make_rand(integer, real)
goal
    go.
clauses
    make_rand(Count, UpperLimit) :-
        Count > 0,
        random(RandReal),
        write(RandReal * UpperLimit), nl,
        Count1 = Count - 1,
        make_rand(Count1, UpperLimit).
    make_rand(_,_).
    go :-
        I = 20,
        make_rand(I, 1000.0).
```

round   Rounds a real number into an integer.

Syntax:
```
round(X)      (o)
     (real)
```

Parameter:
X   the number rounded to the nearest integer.

Example:
The next program displays rounded values for numbers between 2 and –2, in steps of 0.25.

```
predicates
    go()
    round_num(real)
goal
    go.
clauses
    round_num(X)  :-
        X >= -2.0,
        Y = round(X),
        write("Rounding ",X," gives ",Y), nl,
        X1 = X - 0.25,
        round_num(X1).
    round_num(_).
    go :-
        X = 2.0,
        round_num(X).
```

Calculates the sine of an angle.   **sin**

Syntax:
```
sin(Angle)      (o)
    (integer) (real)
```

Parameter:
Angle   the angle, measured in radians, whose sine is sought.

Example:
The next program converts polar coordinates to rectangular coordinates.

```
predicates
    go()
goal
    go.
clauses
    go :-
        write("Enter Modulus : "), readreal(Modulus), nl,
        write("Enter Angle : "),   readreal(Angle), nl,
        X = Modulus * cos(Angle),
        Y = Modulus * sin(Angle),
        write("X = ",X), nl,
        write("Y = ",Y), nl.
```

sqrt   Calculates the square root.

Syntax:
```
sqrt(X)     (i)
    (integer) (real)
```

Parameter:
X   the non-negative numeric argument.

Example:
The following program converts rectangular coordinates to polar coordinates.

```
predicates
    go()
goal
    go.
clauses
    go :-
        write("Enter X : "), readreal(X), nl,
        write("Enter Y : "), readreal(Y), nl,
        Modulus = sqrt(X*X + Y*Y),
        Angle = arctan(Y/X),
        write("Modulus = ",Modulus), nl,
        write("Angle = ",Angle," radians"), nl.
```

tan   Computes the trigonometric tangent of an angle.

Syntax:
```
tan(Angle)      (i)
   (integer) (real)
```

Parameter:
Angle   the angle in radians whose tangent is sought.

Example:
The next program returns the angle associated with an arctangent and the
tangent of twice that angle.

```
predicates
    go()
goal
    go.
clauses
    go :-
        write("Enter an arctangent : "),
        readreal(X), nl,
        Angle = arctan(X),
        write("The angle of your tangent = ",Angle), nl,
        Y = tan(2 * Angle),
        write("The tangent of twice that angle = ",Y), nl.
```

Truncates a real number into an integer.   **trunc**

Syntax:
```
trunc(X)      (i)
     (real)
```

Parameter:
'**X**   the truncated number whose value is rounded toward zero.

Example:
The next program displays truncated values for numbers between 2 and –2,
in steps of 0.25.

```
predicates
    go()
    trunc_num(real)
```

```
goal
    go.
clauses
    trunc_num(X) :-
        X >= -2.0,
        Y = trunc(X),
        write("Truncating ",X," gives ",Y), nl,
        X1 = X - 0.25,
        trunc_num(X1).
    trunc_num(_).
    go :-
        X = 2.0,
        trunc_num(X).
```

Command-Line Arguments

Introduction

The technique of using command-line arguments originates with the C language. Because C is a function-oriented language, the idea of invoking a program as a function accompanied by arguments is a natural one. Thus, command-line arguments are the set of words that follow the program name when the program is invoked at the operating system level. The general form for using command-line arguments is:

```
A> <program name> <arg1> <arg2> <arg3> ... <argn>
```

Command-line arguments provide a powerful vehicle for controlling program execution. With the four Turbo languages, the techniques for processing command-line arguments fall into two classes. Turbo BASIC and Turbo Prolog provide built-in functions that return the string containing the entire set of command-line arguments. Consequently, it is up to the programs to extract each argument, using string manipulation functions. By contrast, Turbo Pascal and Turbo C provide more elegant routines for accessing command-line arguments. These languages enable you to obtain the argument count, as well as access each argument.

TIP

Programs that use command-line arguments should check for the correct number of arguments and provide an on-line help if the number of arguments are found to be short of the requirement.

Turbo Basic

In Turbo BASIC, the **COMMAND$** function returns a string containing the command-line arguments. This function trims off the leading and trailing spaces from the command-line argument string. In addition, the name of the program is not returned. Therefore, the first word in the command-line string returned by **COMMAND$** is the name of the first argument.

The following program uses command-line arguments to implement a simple four-function calculator. Assuming the program is compiled as **CALC.EXE**, it is invoked as:

```
A> calc <first operand> <operator> <second operand>
```

The program is responsible for extracting each of the three command-line arguments (it ignores any extra arguments). In addition, the code performs its own checking for the presence of the correct number of arguments. The label **Usage:** is jumped to when fewer arguments are detected. Two **WHILE** loops are used to delete multiple spaces that may be typed between the command-line arguments.

```
DEFDBL A-Z
S$ = COMMAND$
Ptr1% = INSTR(S$," ")
IF Ptr1% = 0 THEN GOTO Usage
' remove multiple spaces
I% = Ptr1% + 1
DO WHILE MID$(S$,I%,1) = " "
  S$ = LEFT$(S$,I%-1) + MID$(S$,I%+1)
LOOP
Ptr2% = INSTR(Ptr1%+1,S$," ")
IF Ptr2% = 0 THEN GOTO Usage
' remove multiple spaces
I% = Ptr2% + 1
DO WHILE MID$(S$,I%,1) = " "
  S$ = LEFT$(S$,I%-1) + MID$(S$,I%+1)
LOOP
X = VAL(LEFT$(S$,Ptr1%-1))
OP$ = MID$(S$,Ptr1%+1,1)
Y = VAL(MID$(S$,Ptr2%+1))

SELECT CASE OP$
    CASE "+"
        Z = X + Y
    CASE "-"
        Z = X - Y
    CASE "*"
        Z = X * Y
    CASE "/"
        IF Y = 0.0 THEN
            PRINT "Cannot divide by zero!"
        END IF
        Z = X / Y
    CASE ELSE
```

```
        PRINT "Bad operator"
        END
END SELECT
PRINT "result = ";Z
END


Usage:
    PRINT "Proper usage: calc <num1> {+|-|*\/} <num2>"
END
```

Counting Arguments

Unlike Turbo C and Pascal, Turbo BASIC does not provide a built-in routine you can use to count the number of command-line arguments passed to a program. You can, however, write one of your own by using the **COMMAND$** function. As an example, the following subroutine returns the **ParamCount%**, number of command-line arguments, as well as **ParamStr$**, the string array containing the individual arguments:

```
SUB ParseComLine(ParamCount%, ParamStr$(1))

ParamCount% = 0 ' initialize count for command-line argument
S$ = COMMAND$
IF S$ = "" THEN
    EXIT SUB ' exit if no command-line arguments exist
Ptr1% = 1
Ptr2% = INSTR(S$," ")
' loop to extract arguments, except the last one
DO WHILE Ptr2% > 0
    I% = Ptr2%+1
    ' eliminate duplicate spaces between arguments
    DO WHILE MID$(S$,I%,1) = " "
        S$ = LEFT$(S$,I%-1) + MID$(S$,I%+1)
    LOOP
    INCR ParamCount%
    ParamStr$(ParamCount%) = MID$(S$,Ptr1%,Ptr2%-Ptr1%)
    Ptr1% = Ptr2% + 1
    Ptr2% = INSTR(Ptr1%,S$," ")
LOOP
IF Ptr2% = 0 THEN Ptr2% = LEN(S$) + 1
INCR ParamCount%
ParamStr$(ParamCount%) = MID$(S$,Ptr1%,Ptr2%-Ptr1%)
END SUB
```

Turbo C

To access command-line arguments in Turbo C, the main function, **main()**, should be declared using the following convention:

```
main(int argc, char* argv[])
```

The **argc** parameter provides a count for the command-line arguments. The **argv** is a pointer to the list of arguments. Keep in mind that **argv[0]** is a pointer to the program's name and the first actual command-line argument is accessed with **argv[1]**. The argument count returned by **argc** includes an entry to account for the program's name; thus, the actual argument count is **argc − 1**.

The following program employs command-line arguments to implement a simple four-function calculator. Assuming the program is compiled as **CALC.EXE**, it is invoked as:

```
A> calc <first operand> <operator> <second operand>
```

Using **argc**, the program is able to quickly detect whether enough command-line arguments have been typed. If there are not enough arguments, a one-line help message is displayed. The **argv[]** pointers access each argument; each argument is stored as a string. The **argv[]** pointer returns an empty string when you attempt to access a nonexisting argument. In the case of this program, as in many applications, conversion between strings and numeric data is performed. In this case, the **atof()** function is used for the required conversion.

```c
#include <stdio.h>
#include <stdlib.h>
#include <string.h>
main(int argc, char* argv[])
{
    char op;
    double x, y, z;

    if (argc < 3) {
        printf("Proper usage: calc <num1> {+|-|*\/} <num2>");
        exit(0);
    }
```

```
    x = atof(argv[1]);
    op = *argv[2];
    y = atof(argv[3]);
    switch (op) {
        case '+':
            z = x + y;
            break;
        case '-':
            z = x - y;
            break;
        case '*':
            z = x * y;
            break;
        case '/':
            if (y == 0.0) {
                puts("Cannot divide by zero!");
                exit(0);
            }
            z = x / y;
            break;
        otherwise:
            puts("Bad operator");
            exit(0);
    }
    printf("result = %lg\n",z);
}
```

TIP
Turbo C also provides two global variables called **_argc** and **_argv** that you can use to access command-line arguments. These variables operate just like the **argc** and **argv[]** parameters that are passed to the function **main()**. These global variables are defined in the file **dos.h** as:

```
extern int _argc;
extern char **_argv;
```

If the header file **dos.h** is included with your program, you can access each of these variables with a simple assignment statement, as shown:

```
conut = _argc;
str = *_argv;
```

In general, we suggest that you use the parameters **argc** and **argv**[] to access command-line arguments, because these parameters are supported by the proposed ANSI standard and the global variables are not.

Turbo Pascal

Turbo Pascal provides two predefined functions to manage command-line arguments. The **ParamCount** function returns the number of arguments, whereas you use the **ParamStr(<*index*>)** function to access a specified argument number. The **ParamStr** function returns an empty string when you attempt to access a nonexisting argument.

The following program employs command-line arguments to implement a simple four-function calculator. Assuming the program is compiled as **CALC.EXE**, it is invoked as:

```
A> calc <first operand> <operator> <second operand>
```

Using **ParamCount**, the program is able to quickly detect whether enough command-line arguments have been typed. If not enough arguments are present, a one-line help message is displayed. The **ParamStr** function is used to access each argument, as strings. In the case of this program, as in many applications, conversion between strings and numeric data is performed. The Turbo Pascal **Val** intrinsic can detect strings containing corrupt images of numbers. This should be performed systematically, and any errors handled according to the application. For the simple on-line calculator, a warning message is displayed and then the program halts.

```
Program Calculator;
Var opstr : String;
    op : Char;
    ErrorCode : Integer;
    x, y, z : Real;
Begin
    If ParamCount < 3 Then Begin
        Writeln('Proper usage: calc <num1> {+|-|*\/} <num2>');
        Writeln;
    End;
    Val(ParamStr(1),x, ErrorCode);
    If ErrorCode <> 0 Then Begin
```

```
        Writeln('Bad number -> ',ParamStr(1));
        Halt;
    End;
    opstr := ParamStr(2);
    op := opstr[1];
    Val(ParamStr(3), y, ErrorCode);
    If ErrorCode <> 0 Then Begin
        Writeln('Bad number -> ',ParamStr(3));
        Halt
    End;
    Case op of
        '+' :  z := x + y;
        '-' :  z := x - y;
        '*' :  z := x * y;
        '/' :  Begin
                 If y = 0.0 Then Begin
                     Writeln('Cannot divide by zero!');
                     Halt;
                 End;
                 z := x / y;
               End;
        Else Begin
            Writeln('Bad operator');
            Halt;
        End;
    End;
    Writeln('result = ',z);
End.
```

Turbo Prolog

Turbo Prolog employs the **comline** predicate to return the command-line arguments in one string. The following program employs command-line arguments to implement a simple four-function calculator. Assuming the program is compiled as **CALC.EXE**, it is invoked as:

A> calc *<first operand> <operator> <second operand>*

The program extracts the arguments (except the last one) using the **frontto-**

ken predicate. Conversion between strings and other types is performed
using predicates like **str_real**, **str_int**, and **str_char**.

```
predicates
    calc(real, real, char, real)
    get_param(real,char,real)
    go


clauses
    calc(Z, X, '+', Y) :-
        Z = X + Y.
    calc(Z, X, '-', Y) :-
        Z = X - Y.
    calc(Z, X, '*', Y) :-
        Z = X * Y.
    calc(_, _, '/', 0) :-
        write("Cannot divide by zero"), nl, fail.
    calc(Z, X, '/', Y) :-
        Y <> 0,
        Z = X / Y.
    calc(_,_,_,Y) :-
        Y <> 0,
        write("Bad operator"), nl, fail.
    get_param(X,Op,Y) :-
        comline(DOSline),
        fronttoken(DOSline,Str1,Rest1),
        str_real(Str1, X),
        fronttoken(Rest1,OpStr,Str2),
        str_char(OpStr, Op),
        str_real(Str2, Y).
    get_param(_,_,_) :-
        write("Proper usage: calc <num1> {+|-|*\/} <num2>"),
        nl, fail.
    go :-
        get_param(X,Op,Y),
        calc(Z,X,Op,Y),
        write("result = ", Z), nl.
goal
    go.
```

Index

\n, 15,99,122
_argc, 458-459
_argv, 458-459
_chmode(), 111
_close(), 103,109
_creat(), 100-102,103
_fmode, 101,105
_graphfreemem, 241,292-293
_graphgetmem, 241,293
_open(), 103,106-107
_read(), 127
_write(),119-120

abs(), 408-409
ABS, 402
Abs, 434
abs, 443
Absolute value, 400
access(), 111
acos(), 409-410
AnyFile, 206
Append, 135,136,141,143
APPEND, 80-81
arc, 241,244-246
Arccosine, 400

Archive, 206
arcoordstype, 262
Arcsine, 400
ArcTan, 434-435
arctan, 443-444
Arctangent, 400
ASC, 335
asin(), 410-411
Assign, 134-135,136,141,143,145,147,150,155,204
atan(), 411
atan2(), 411-412
ATN, 402
att.bgi, 226

bar, 241,246-248
bar3d, 241,246-248
BGI routines
    arc, 241,244-246
    bar, 241,246-248
    bar3d, 241,246-248
    circle, 241,248-250
    cleardevice, 241,250-251
    clearviewport, 227,241,251-252
    closegraph, 233,241,252
    detectgraph, 223,232-233,241,252-254

drawpoly, 241,254-256
ellipse, 241,256-257
fillellipse, 241,257-258
fillpoly, 241,258-260
floodfill, 241,260-261
getarccoords, 241,261-263
getaspectratio, 241,246,263-265
getbkcolor, 228,241,265
getcolor, 228,241,266-268
getdefaultpalette, 229,231,241,268,282
getdrivername, 223,241,268-269,274
getfillpattern, 241,269-270
getfillsettings, 241,270-273
getgraphmode, 223,241,273-275
getimage, 241,275-276,307,309
getlinesettings, 241,276-277
getmaxcolor, 228,231,241,277
getmaxmode, 223,241,277-278
getmaxx, 241,278-279
getmaxy, 241,280
getmodename, 223,241,274,280
getmoderange, 223,241,274,281
getpalette, 229,231,241,281-284
getpalettesize, 229,231,241
getpixel, 241,284,309
gettextsettings, 241,284-286
getviewsettings, 227,241,286-289
getx, 227,241,289-290
gety, 227,241,290-291
graphdefaults, 241,291
grapherrormsg, 240,241,292,294
_graphfreemem, 241,292-293
_graphgetmem, 241,293
graphresult, 240,241,293-295
imagesize, 241,295
initgraph, 231-233,235,241,254,269,289,296
installuserdriver, 241,296-297
installuserfont, 241,297-298
line, 241,298-299
linerel, 241,299-300
lineto, 241,300
moverel, 241,301-302
moveto, 241,302

outtext, 241,303-304
outtextxy, 241,304-305
pieslice, 241,305-307
putimage, 241,307-309
putpixel, 241,309-310
rectangle, 241,310-311
registerbgidriver, 236-237,241,311-312
registerbgifont, 236-237,241,312
restorecrtmode, 233,241,312-314
sector, 241,306,314
setactivepage, 241,315
setallpalette, 229,231,241,282,315
setaspectratio, 241,246,264,315-316
setbkcolor, 228,230,241,316
setcolor, 228,241,316-317
setfillpattern, 241,317
setfillstyle, 241,317-318
setgraphbufsize, 241
setgraphmode, 223,230,233,241,313,318
setlinestyle, 241,250,318-321
setpalette, 228,231,241,282,321
setrgbcolor, 229,241
setrgbpalette, 241,321-322
settextjustify, 241,322
settextstyle, 241,323
setusercharsize, 241,324-325
setviewport, 226,228,241,325-326
setvisualpage, 241,326
setwritemode, 241,326-327
textheight, 241,327-329
textwidth, 241,329
BGI setup and use
    Closing graphic mode, 233-234
    Colors, 227-232
    Default settings, 291
    Error detection, 238-239
    File requirements/placement, 223,226
    Graphic hardware/modes, 223-225
    Initializing graphics, 231-233
    Loading drivers and fonts, 235-239,297
    Overview, 222-223
    Porting, 240
    Using graphic commands, 233
    Viewports, 225-227

BGI.LIB, 238
bgi_ilist, 254,258
bgidriver, 238
bgifont, 238
bgiobj, 235
BIN$, 335-336
Binary files, Turbo Basic
    Overview, 78,79
    Reading, 95-97
    Writing to, 88-89
Binary files, Turbo Prolog: see
    Text/binary files, Turbo Prolog
BINARY, 80
BINOBJ, 236-237
BIOS, 14
Bios, 211,213-214,218
bioskey(), 14-15
BLOAD, 96-97
BlockRead, 150
BlockWrite, 143-144
Borland Graphic Interface: see
    BGI routines
    BGI setup and use
    Linking BGI drivers
BSAVE, 89
Buffer, 99
BW40, 36,48
BW80, 36,48

C40, 36,48
C80, 36,48
cabs(), 412-413
ceil(), 413
CEIL, 402-403
Ceiling of number, 400
cga.bgi, 226
cgets(),15-16
char_int, 379-380
Character input
    Turbo BASIC, 2-3
    Turbo C, 11-15
    Turbo Pascal, 39-40
    Turbo Prolog, 53-57

Character output
    Turbo Basic, 6
    Turbo C, 18-20
    Turbo Pascal, 41-42
    Turbo Prolog, 62-63
chdir(), 192
CHDIR, 186,189
ChDir, 200,201-202
CheckSnow, 48
chmode(), 103
CHR$, 336
Chr, 369-370
circle, 241,248-250
cleardevice, 241,250-251
clearerr(), 131
clearviewport, 227,241,251-252
clearwindow, 69
close(), 103,109
Close, 136,142,144,148,151
CLOSE, 80-81,85,87-88,93-96
closefile, 162-163
closegraph, 233,241,252
clreol(), 33
ClrEol, 46
clrscr(), 33,38
ClrScr, 46,50
colorsetup, 69
COM1, 138
com1, 166,178
COM1:, 83
COM2, 138
COM2:, 83
COMMAND$, 454-456
Command-line arguments, Turbo BASIC
    COMMAND$, 454-456
    Counting arguments, 456
    Overview, 454
Command-line arguments, Turbo C
    _argc, 458-459
    _argv, 458-459
    main(), 457-458
    Overview, 454, 457
Command-line arguments, Turbo Pascal
    Overview, 454,459

ParamCount, 459
ParamStr, 459
Command-line arguments, Turbo Prolog
    comline, 460
    Overview, 454, 460
CON, 138,147
Concat, 370
conio.h, 12,29,34
consult, 171,173,175-177
Consultable files: see
    Database files, Turbo Prolog
Copy, 370-372
cos(), 413-414
COS, 403
Cos, 435
cos, 444
cosh(), 414-415
Cosine, 400
cprintf(), 33
cputs(), 21,33
creat(), 100-102,103,106,110
creatnew(), 100-102,103
creattemp(), 100-102,103
CRT (TPU), 39,40,43,44,46,47,48,155
CSRLIN, 10
Cursor control
    Turbo Basic, 7-10
    Turbo C, 29-33
    Turbo Pascal, 43-44
    Turbo Pascal, 66-68
cursor, 66-68
cursorform, 68
CVD, 93-94
CVI, 93-94
CVL, 93-94
CVMD, 93-94
CVMS, 93-94
CVS, 93-94

Database files, Turbo Prolog
    Overview, 158
    Reading, 175-178
    Writing, 171-173

DateTime, 209
Dec, 436
DECR, 403-404
Decrement a number, 400
DEF SEG, 89,97
DEFSTR, 333
Delete, 372-373
deletefile, 160-161
delline(), 33
DelLine, 46
detectgraph, 223,232-233,241,252-254
Device/filenames
    Turbo BASIC, 83
    Turbo C, 98
    Turbo Pascal, 138
    Turbo Prolog, 161
dir, 216-217,218
dir.h, 190,198
Direct video output
    Turbo C, 34-35
    Turbo Pascal, 47-48
    Turbo Prolog, 72
Directory, 206
directvideo, 34-35
DirectVideo, 47-48
disk, 211
div(), 415-416
div, 444-445
Division, 400
DO-LOOP UNTIL, 4
DOS directory control, Turbo BASIC
    Change, 186-187
    Display, 189
    Make,187-188
    Move files, 189
    Overview, 186
    Remove, 188-189
    Rename files, 189
DOS directory control, Turbo C
    Change, 192
    Current dir/drive, 191-192
    File attributes, 198
    File date/time, 198

File/dir search, 197-200
Make, 193
Overview,190
Remove, 194
Rename, 195-196
DOS directory control, Turbo Pascal
Change, 201-202
Current dir, 200-201
File attributes, 208
File time/date, 208-209
File/dir search, 206-208
Make, 202
Move file, 204
Overview, 200
Remove, 203
Rename, 204
DOS directory control, Turbo Prolog
Change, 211-212
Current dir, 211
Display, 212,216-217
File attributes, 218
File/dir search, 218
Make, 213,214
Overview, 211
Remove, 214,215
Rename file, 217
dos.h, 100,102,458
DosError, 207
drawpoly, 241,254-256

edit, 169
egavga.bgi,226
ellipse, 241,256-257
eof(), 129-130
Eof, 156
eof, 161,179-180
EOF, 90,92,113,122,130
Erase, 134,135
errno, 130,133
existfile, 159-160,170,218-219
existwindow, 69
exp(), 416-417
EXP, 404

Exp, 436-437
exp, 445-446
Exponential, 400,401

FA_ARCH, 198
FA_DIREC, 198
FA_HIDDEN, 101,198
FA_LABEL, 198
FA_RDONLY, 101,198
FA_SYSTEM, 101,198
fabs(), 417
fclose(), 103,108-109
fcloseall(), 103,108-109
fcntrl.h, 105
fdopen(), 110-111
feof(), 129-130
ferror(), 131-132
ffblk, 198
fflush(), 103,108
fflushall(), 103,108
fgetc(), 122
fgetchar(), 122
fgetpos(), 111
fgets(), 122
Field delimited, 78
Field variable conversion, Turbo BASIC, 86,93-94
FIELD, 85-86,93
field_attr, 61,64-65,72-75
field_str, 60-61,64-65
File buffering, 99-100
File handle, 99
File of Char, 136,145
File of, 140,147,148
File pointers, 88,95
File, 143,150
FILE, 98
file_str, 169-171,175,217
filelength(), 111,118,129
filemode, 163-164
fileno(), 111,118
FilePos, 142-143,144-145,148-149,151-152
filepos, 161,175,180
FILES, 189

Files, Turbo Basic
    Binary, 78-79
    Closing, 80-81
    Creating, 79-80
    Deleting, 79
    Initializing, 81
    Management, 79
    Mapping fields, 85,93
    Overview, 78
    Random access, 78
    Reading, 89-97
    Sequential, 78,81-85
    Writing to, 81-89
Files, Turbo C
    Access codes, 106
    Attribute codes, 101,104
    Closing, 103,108-109
    Creating, 100-102
    Deleting, 100,102-103
    End-of-file, 129-130
    Error handling, 130-133
    Error messages, 131
    Initializing, 109-111
    Modes, 105
    Opening, 103-108
    Overview, 97-100
    Permission codes, 101,107
    Reading, 121
    Status, 111
    Writing to,112-121
Files, Turbo Pascal: see
    Text files, Turbo Pascal
    Typed files, Turbo Pascal
    Untyped files, Turbo Pascal
Files, Turbo Prolog: see
    Database files, Turbo Prolog
    Text/binary files, Turbo Prolog
FileSize, 142-143,144-145,148-149,151-152
Fill patterns, 271
fillellipse, 241,257-258
fillpoly, 241,258-260
findfirst(), 197-199
FindFirst, 206-208

findnext(), 197-199
FindNext, 206-208
floodfill, 241,260-261
Floor of a number, 400
floor(), 417-418
Flush, 135
flush, 181
fmod(), 418-419
Font files, 226
Font style codes (BGI), 323
fopen(),103-105
Format code
    Turbo BASIC, 8
    Turbo C, 18,23,25,28
    Turbo Pascal, 42
    Turbo Prolog, 66
format, 380-382
Formatted input
    Turbo BASIC, 7
    Turbo C, 23-27
    Turbo Pascal, 42
    Turbo Prolog, 64
Formatted output
    Turbo BASIC, 7
    Turbo C, 27-29
    Turbo Pascal, 42-43
    Turbo Prolog, 65-66
fprintf(), 112-117
fputc(), 112-113
fputchar(), 112-113
fputs(), 112-113
framewindow, 69
fread(), 122,126
freopen(),103,110,111
frexp(), 419
frontchar, 382-385
frontstr, 385-386
fronttoken, 386-389,460-461
fscanf(), 122,124-125
fseek(), 119,127
fstat(), 111
ftell(), 111
fwrite(), 112,117-119,120

GET$, 95
GET, 93
getarccoords, 241,261-263
getaspectratio, 241,246,263-265
getbkcolor, 228,241,265
getc(), 11
getch(), 11-12
getchar(), 11-12
getche(), 11-12,33
getcolor, 228,241,266-268
getcurdir(), 191
getcwd(), 191
getdefaultpalette, 229,231,241,268,282
GetDir, 200-201
getdrivername, 223,241,268-269,274
getenv(), 200
GetFAttr, 208
getfiletime(), 111
getfillpattern, 241,269-270
getfillsettings, 241,270-273
GetFTime, 208
getgraphmode, 223,241,273-275
getimage, 241,275-276,307,309
getlinesettings, 241,276-277
getmaxcolor, 228,231,241,277
getmaxmode, 223,241,277-278
getmaxx, 241,278-279
getmaxy, 241,280
getmodename, 223,241,274,280
getmoderange, 223,241,274,281
getpalette, 229,231,241,281-284
getpalettesize, 229,231,241
getpixel, 241,284,309
gets(), 15-16
gettext(), 33
gettextinfo(), 31,33
gettextsettings, 241,284-286
getviewsettings, 227,241,286-289
getx, 227,241,289-290
gety, 227,241,290-291
goth.chr, 226
gotowindow, 69
gotoxy(), 29-31,33,38

GotoXY, 43,46,50
grapdecl.pro,225,243
graph.tpu, 225,243
graphdefaults, 241,291
grapherrormsg, 240,241,292,294
Graphic drivers, 226
graphics.h, 225,243
graphics.lib, 225,235
graphresult, 240,241,293-295

herc.bgi, 226
HEX$, 337
Hidden, 206
highvideo(), 38-39
HighVideo, 52-53
Hyperbolic cosine, 400
Hyperbolic sine, 400
Hyperbolic tangent, 401
hypot(), 420
Hypotenuse, 401

I/O devices, 158
I/O functions: see
    Keyboard I/O, Turbo Basic
    Keyboard I/O, Turbo C
    Keyboard I/O, Turbo Pascal
    Keyboard I/O, Turbo Prolog
    Screen I/O, Turbo Basic
    Screen I/O, Turbo C
    Screen I/O, Turbo Pascal
    Screen I/O, Turbo Prolog
ibm8514.bgi, 226
imagesize, 241,295
Inc, 437-438
INCR, 404-405
Increment, 401
initgraph, 231-233,235,241,254,269,289,296
INKEY$, 3-5
inkey, 55-56
INPUT #, 90
INPUT$, 90
INPUT, 2-3,5.80-81,89
Insert, 373-374

insline(), 33
InsLine, 46
installuserdriver, 241,296-297
installuserfont, 241,297-298
INSTR, 337-338
INT, 405
Int, 438
io.h, 98,100,129
IOResult, 157
isatty(), 111
isname, 389

Keyboard I/O, Turbo BASIC
    Overview, 2
    INPUT, 2-5
    INKEY$, 3-5
    LINE INPUT, 5
Keyboard I/O, Turbo C
    Overview, 11
    bioskey(), 14-15
    cgets(),15-16
    getc(), 11
    getch(), 11-12
    getchar(), 11-12
    getche(), 11-12,33
    gets(), 15-16
    getw(), 17
    scanf(), 13-14,23-27
    ungetc(), 12-13
    ungetch(), 12-13
Keyboard I/O, Turbo Pascal
    Overview, 39
    Readln, 39-41
    ReadKey, 39-40
    KeyPressed, 40
Keyboard I/O, Turbo Prolog
    Overview, 53
    readchar, 53-54,56-57
    unreadchar, 54
    readln, 54-55,57-58
    inkey, 55-56
    keypressed, 56
    readint, 57-58

readreal, 57-58
str_int, 58-59
str_real, 58-59
str_char, 55
keyboard, 178
KEYBOARD, 91
Keyboard, 147
KeyPressed, 40
keypressed, 56
KILL, 79
KYBD:, 91

labs(), 420-421
LAST, 35
Last, 48
LCASE$, 338
ldexp(), 421-422
ldiv(), 422-423
LEFT$, 3,338
LEN, 3,339
Length, 374-375
LINE INPUT #, 90
LINE INPUT, 5
Line style/thickness codes (BGI), 319
line, 241,298-299
linerel, 241,299-300
linesettingstype, 276
lineto, 241,300
Linking BGI drivers
    Turbo C, 235-236
    Turbo Pascal, 236-237
    Turbo Prolog, 237-238
litt.char, 226
Ln, 438-439
ln, 446
LOC, 95,96
LOCATE, 9-10
LOF, 96
log(), 423
LOG, 405-406
log, 446-447
log10(), 423-424
Logarithm, 400,401

Low level I/O system, Turbo C
  Closing files,109
  Creating files, 100-102
  Deleting files, 102-103
  File error handling, 133
  Opening files, 103,106-108
  Overview 97-100
  Reading files, 127-129
  Writing to files, 119-121
Low-level I/O, 11
lowvideo, 38-39
LowVideo, 52-53
LPT1, 138
LPT1:, 83
LPT2, 138
LPT2:, 83
LPT3, 138
LPT3:, 83
lseek(), 111
LSET, 85-86

main(), 457-458
makewindow, 69-71
Math functions, Turbo C
  abs(), 408-409
  acos(), 409-410
  asin(), 410-411
  atan(), 411
  atan2(), 411-412
  cabs(), 412-413
  ceil(), 413
  cos(), 413-414
  cosh(), 414-415
  div(), 415-416
  exp(), 416-417
  fabs(), 417
  floor(), 417-418
  fmod(), 418-419
  frexp(), 419
  hypot(), 420
  labs(), 420-421
  ldexp(), 421-422
  ldiv(), 422-423

log(), 423
log10(), 423-424
max(), 424
min(), 424-425
modf(), 425
poly(), 426
pow(), 426-427
pow10(), 427-428
rand(), 428-429
random(), 429
randomize(), 430
sin(), 430
sinh(), 430-431
sqrt(), 431-432
srand(), 432-433
tan(), 433
tanh(), 433-434
Math predicates, Turbo Prolog
  abs, 443
  arctan, 443-444
  cos, 444
  div, 444-445
  exp, 445-446
  ln, 446
  log, 446-447
  mod, 447
  random, 447-448
  round, 448-449
  sin, 449-450
  sqrt, 450
  tan, 450-451
  trunc, 451-452
Math routines, Turbo Basic
  ABS, 402
  ATN, 402
  CEIL, 402-403
  COS, 403
  DECR, 403-404
  EXP, 404
  INCR, 404-405
  INT, 405
  LOG, 405-406
  RANDOMIZE, 406

RND, 406
SIN, 406-407
SQR, 407
TAN, 408
Math routines, Turbo Pascal
Abs, 434
ArcTan, 434-435
Cos, 435
Dec, 436
Exp, 436-437
Inc, 437-438
Int, 438
Ln, 438-439
Randomize, 439
Random, 439-440
Round, 440
Sin, 441
Sqrt, 441-442
Tan, 442
Trunc, 442-443
max(), 424
MID$, 339-340
min(), 424-425
MKD$, 86
mkdir(), 193
MKDIR, 187
MkDir, 200,202-203
MKI$, 86
MKL$, 86
MKMD$, 86
MKMS$, 86
MKS$,86
mod, 447
modf(), 425
Modulo, 400
MONO, 36
Mono, 48
moverel, 241,301-302
movetext(), 33
moveto, 241,302

NAME, 189-190
nondelimited, 78

normvideo(), 38-39
NormVideo, 52-53
NUL, 138
NULL, 199
Numeric input
Turbo BASIC, 5
Turbo C, 17-18
Turbo Pascal, 41
Turbo Prolog, 57-59
Numeric output
Turbo BASIC, 6
Turbo C, 28
Turbo Pascal, 41
Turbo Prolog, 64

O_APPEND, 106
O_BINARY,106
O_CREAT,106,107
O_RDONLY, 106
O_RDWR, 106
O_TEXT, 105,106
O_TRUNC,106
O_WRONLY, 106
OCT$, 340-341
open(), 103,106-108,133
OPEN, 79-80,85,88,93,95
openappend, 161,164-165
openmodify, 161,164-165,173
openread, 161,173,175
openwrite, 158-160,161,164-165
Ord, 334
Ord, 375-376
outtext, 241,303-304
outtextxy, 241,304-305

palattetype, 281
OUTPUT, 80-81
ParamCount, 459
ParamStr, 459
PATH, 199-200
pc3270.bgi, 226
perror(), 131-132
pieslice, 241,305-307

poly(), 426
Polynomial, 401
POS, 10
Pos, 376-377
pow(), 426-427
pow10(), 427-428
PRINT # USING, 81-84
PRINT #, 81-84
PRINT USING, 7-9
PRINT, 4,6
printer, 166,178
printf(), 20-23,27-29,114
prn, 182
PUT$, 88-89
PUT, 85-86
putc(), 19
putch(), 19-20,33
putenv(), 200
putimage, 241,307-309
putpixel, 241,309-310
puts(), 20-21
puttext(), 33
putw(), 22

rand(), 428-429
Random access files, Turbo Basic
    Overview, 78
    Reading, 92-95
    Writing to, 85-87
random(), 429
Random, 439-440
random, 447-448
RANDOM, 80
randomize(), 430
RANDOMIZE, 406
Randomize, 439
read(), 127-129,133
Read, 145-147,148
Read, 46
readchar, 53-54,56-57,64,159,174
readdevice, 161,162,174,178,182
readint, 160,174
readint, 57-58

ReadKey, 39-40
Readln, 39-41,46,145-147
readln, 54-55,57-58,160,174,182
ReadOnly, 206
readreal, 57-58,160,174
readterm, 160,173,174
rectangle, 241,310-311
registerbgidriver, 236-237,241,311-312
registerbgifont, 236-237,241,312
remove, 103
removewindow, 69
rename(), 195-196
Rename, 135,200,204-206
renamefile, 217-218
repeat-fail, 179
Reset, 135,145,147,150
resizewindow, 69
restorecrtmode, 233,241,312-314
rewind(), 110-111,131
Rewrite, 135,136,141,143
RIGHT$, 341
rmdir(), 194
RMDIR, 188
RmDir, 200,203-204
RND, 406
Round, 440
round, 448-449
RSET, 85-86

S_IREAD | S_IWRITE, 101,107
S_IWRITE, 101,107,111
S_READ, 101,107
sans.chr, 226
save, 171-173,175
scanf(), 13-14,16-18,23-27
scr_attr, 60,62,72-75
scr_char, 60,62,64
Screen I/O, Turbo BASIC
    Overview, 2
    CSRLIN, 10
    LOCATE, 9-10
    POS, 10
    PRINT, 4,6

SPC(), 6
TAB(), 6
WRITE, 6
Screen I/O, Turbo C
  BW40, 36
  BW80, 36
  C40, 36
  C80, 36
  clreol(), 33
  clrscr(), 33
  cprintf(), 33
  cputs(), 21,33
  delline(), 33
  directvideo, 34-35
  gettext(), 33
  gettextinfo(), 31,33
  gotoxy(), 29-30,33
  highvideo(), 38-39
  insline(), 33
  LAST, 35
  lowvideo(), 38-39
  MONO, 36
  movetext(), 33
  normvideo(), 38-39
  Overview, 10-11
  printf(), 20-23,27-29
  putc(), 19
  putch(), 19-20,33
  puts(), 20-21
  puttext(), 33
  putw(), 22
  text_info, 34
  textattr(), 38
  textbackground(), 36-38
  textcolor(), 36-38
  textmode(), 33,35-36
  wherex(), 29-31,33
  wherey(), 29-31,33
  window(), 32-33
Screen I/O, Turbo Pascal
  BW40, 48
  BW80, 48
  C40, 48

C80, 48
CheckSnow, 48
ClrEol, 46
ClrScr, 46,50
DelLine, 46
DirectVideo, 47-48
GotoXY, 43,46,50
HighVideo, 52-53
InsLine, 46
Last, 48
Low-Video, 52-53
Mono, 48
NormVideo, 52-53
Overview, 39
Text Attr, 49-52
Text Background, 49-52
TextColor, 49-52
TextMode, 45-49
WhereX, 43-44,46
WhereY, 43-44,46
WindMax, 46-47
WindMin, 46-47
Window, 44-46,48
Write, 41-42,46-47
Writeln, 41-42,46-47
Screen I/O, Turbo Prolog
  clearwindow, 69
  colorsetup, 69
  cursor, 66-68
  cursorform, 68
  existwindow, 69
  field_attr, 61,64-65,72-75
  field_str, 60-61,64-65
  framewindow, 69
  gotowindow, 69
  makewindow, 69-71
  Overview, 59-60,62
  removewindow, 69
  resizewindow, 69
  scr_attr, 60,62,72-75
  scr_char, 60,62,64
  scroll, 69
  shiftwindow, 69

snowcheck, 72
window_attr, 69,72-75
window_str, 61,63,69
windowcolors, 69
write, 62-64
writef, 62-65
screen, 166,178
SCRN:, 82
scroll, 69
searchpath(), 199-200
SearchRec, 207
sector, 241,306,314
Seek, 141-142,144,148,150-151
SEEK, 88-89,95
Sequential files, Turbo BASIC
    Overview, 78
    Reading, 89-92
    Writing to, 81-85
setactivepage, 241,315
setallpalette, 229,231,241,282,315
setaspectratio, 241,246,264,315-316
setbkcolor, 228,230,241,316
setcolor, 228,241,316-317
setfillpattern, 241,317
setfillstyle, 241,317-318
setgraphbufsize, 241
setgraphmode, 223,230,233,241,313,318
setlinestyle, 241,250,318-321
setpalette, 229,231,241,282,321
setrgbcolor, 229,241
setrgbpalette, 241,321-322
SetTextBuf, 135,152-156
settextjustify, 241,322
settextstyle, 241,323
setusercharsize, 241,324-325
setviewport, 226,228,241,325-326
setvisualpage, 241,326
setwritemode, 241,326-327
shiftwindow, 69
sin(), 430
SIN, 406-407
Sin, 441
sin, 449-450

Sine, 401
sinh(), 430-431
snowcheck, 72
sopen(), 103
SPACE$, 341
SPC(), 6
SQR, 407
sqrt(), 431-432
Sqrt, 441-442
sqrt, 450
Square root, 401
Square, 401
srand(), 432-433
standard I/O, 97
stat.h, 100
stdaux, 98
stderr,98, 132,182
stdin, 12,15,19,27,98,122,182
stdio.h, 11-12,97,129,131
stdout, 19,20,98,182
stdprn, 98
stpcpy(), 344
STR$, 342
Str, 210,377
str_char, 55,390-391,461
str_int, 58-59,391-393
str_len, 122,393-395
str_real, 58-59,395-396,461
strcat(), 344-345
strchr(), 345
strcmp(),346
strcmpi(),347
strcpy(), 348
strcspn(), 348-350
Stream I/O system, Turbo C
    Closing files,108-109
    Creating files, 100-102
    Deleting files, 102-103
    EOF detection, 129-130
    File error handling, 130-132
    Initializing files, 109-111
    Opening files, 103-105
    Overview 97-100

Reading block data, 126-127
Reading files, 121-127
Reading formatted data, 124-126
Reading unformatted data, 122-124
Writing to files, 112-119
Writing unformatted data, 112-113
Writing blocks, 117-119
Writing formatted data, 113-117
Stream I/O, 11
Stream pointers, 98
Streams
    Binary, 99
    Text, 99
stricmp(), 350-351
String input
    Turbo BASIC, 5
    Turbo C, 15-17
    Turbo Pascal, 41
    Turbo Prolog, 57
String output
    Turbo BASIC, 7
    Turbo C, 29
    Turbo Pascal, 41-42
    Turbo Prolog, 63-64
String processing functions, Turbo C
    stpcpy(), 344
    strcat(), 344-345
    strchr(), 345
    strcmp(), 346
    strcmpi(), 347
    strcpy(), 348
    strcspn(), 348-350
    stricmp(), 350-351
    strlen(), 351-352
    strlwr(), 352-353
    strncat(), 353-354
    strncmp(), 354-355
    strncmpi(), 355-356
    strncpy(), 356
    strnicmp(), 357-358
    strnset(), 358-359
    strpbrk(), 359-360
    strrchr(), 360-361

strrev(), 361-362
strset(), 362-363
strspn(), 363-364
strstr(), 364-365
strtord(), 365-366
strtok(), 366-367
strtol(), 367
strtuol(), 367-368
strupr(), 368-369
String processing predicates for Turbo Prolog
    char_int, 379-380
    format, 380-382
    frontchar, 382-385
    frontstr, 385-386
    fronttoken, 386-389
    isname, 389
    str_char, 390-391
    str_int, 391-393
    str_len, 393-395
    str_real, 395-396
    upper_lower, 396-398
String processing routines, Turbo Basic
    ASC, 335
    BIN$, 335-336
    CHR$, 336
    HEX$, 337
    INSTR, 337-338
    LCASE$, 338
    LEFT$, 338
    LEN, 339
    MID$, 339-340
    OCT$, 340-341
    RIGHT$, 341
    SPACE$, 341
    STR$, 342
    STRING$, 342
    UPCASE$, 343
    VAL, 343
String processing routines, Turbo Pascal
    Chr, 369-370
    Concat, 370
    Copy, 370-372
    Delete, 372-373

Insert, 373-374
Length, 374-375
Ord, 375-376
Pos, 376-377
Str, 377
UpCase, 377-378
Val, 378-379
STRING$, 342
String, 334
String[], 334
Strings
  Overview, 332
  Structure, Turbo BASIC, 332-333
  Structure, Turbo C, 333
  Structure, Turbo Pascal, 334
  Structure, Turbo Prolog, 334-335
strlen(), 351-352
strlwr(), 352-353
strncat(), 353-354
strncmp(), 354-355
strncmpi(), 355-356
strncpy(), 356
strnicmp(), 357-358
strnset(), 358-359
strpbrk(), 359-360
strrchr(), 360-361
strrev(), 361-362
strset(), 362-363
strspn(), 363-364
strstr(), 364-365
strtok(), 366-367
strtol(), 367
strtord(), 365-366
strtuol(), 367-368
strupr(), 368-369
sys_errlist, 130,133
sys_nerr, 130
SysFile, 206
system, 213-216

TAB(), 6
tan(), 433
TAN, 408

Tan, 442
tan, 450-451
Tangent, 401
tanh()433-434
tell(), 111
Text Attr, 49-52
Text Background, 49-52
Text files, Turbo Pascal
  Buffers, 152-155
  Closing, 136
  Creating, 134
  Deleting, 134
  Eof detection, 156
  Error detection, 157
  I/O redirection, 155-156
  Initializing, 136
  Opening, 134-135
  Overview, 133-134
  Reading, 145-147
  Writing to, 136-140
Text justification codes (BGI), 322
Text windows
  Turbo C, 31-39
  Turbo Pascal, 44-53
  Turbo Prolog, 68-70
Text, 136,145
Text/binary files, Turbo Prolog
  Closing, 162
  Creating, 158-160
  Deleting, 160-161
  Eof detection, 179-180
  Flushing buffer, 180-181
  I/O redirection, 182-183
  Initializing, 163-164
  Modes, 164
  Opening, 161-164
  Output devices, 166
  Overview, 158
  Pointers, 180
  Predefined domains, 178
  Reading strings, 175
  Reading, 173-175
  Writing strings, 169-171

Writing to, 164-171
text_info, 34
textattr(), 38
textbackground(), 36-38
textcolor(), 36-38
TextColor, 49-52
textheight, 241,327-329
textmode(), 33,35-36
TextMode, 45-49
textsettingstype, 284-285
textwidth, 241,329
Time, 208
trip.chr, 226
Trunc, 442-443
trunc, 451-452
Truncate, 141-142,144,148,10-151
Typed files, Turbo Pascal
    Closing, 136,142,148
    Creating, 134
    Deleting, 134
    Eof detection, 156
    Error detection, 157
    File size, 142-143,148-149
    File-type variables, 140-141,147
    I/O redirection, 155-156
    Initializing, 136
    Opening, 134-135
    Output mode, 141,147-148
    Overview, 133-134
    Reading, 147-149
    Writing to, 136,140-143

ungetc(), 12-13
ungetch(), 12-13
unlink(), 102-103
UnPackTime, 208-209
unreadchar, 54
Untyped files, Turbo Pascal
    Closing, 136,144,151
    Creating, 134
    Deleting, 134
    Eof detection, 156
    Error detection, 157

File size, 144-145,151-152
File-type variables, 143,150
I/O redirection, 155-156
Initializing, 136
Opening, 134-135
Output mode, 143,150
Overview, 133-134
Reading, 149-152
Writing to, 136,143-145
UPCASE$, 343
UpCase, 377-378
upper_lower, 396-398

VAL, 343
Val, 378-379,459
vfprintf(), 112-117
viewporttype, 287
VolumeID, 206
vprint, 114
vscanf(), 122,124

wherex(), 29-31,33
WhereX, 43-44,46
wherey(), 29-31,33
WhereY, 43-44,46
WHILE, 92
While-Do, 156-157
WindMax, 46-47
WindMin, 46-47
window(), 32-33
Window, 44-46,48
window_attr, 69,72-75
window_str, 61,63,69
windowcolors, 69
WRITE #, 84-85,91
write(), 119-121,128
write, 62-64,160,165,181
Write, 41-42,46-47,136-140,141
WRITE, 6
writedevice, 161,162,164,178,182
writef, 62-65,160,165
Writeln, 41-42,46-47,136-140

Disk Order Form

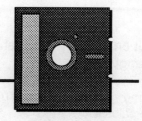

If you'd like to use the code presented in this book but you don't want to waste your time typing it in, we have a very special offer for you. We are making available a set of diskettes that contain all of the major programming examples presented in this book.

To order your disks, fill out the form below and mail it along with $24.95 in check or money order (orders outside the U.S. add $5 for shipping and handling) to:

> Keith Weiskamp
> Turbo Libraries Disk
> 3120 E. Paradise Ln., Suite 12
> Phoenix, AZ 85023

- -

Please send me _____ copies of the Turbo Libraries Disks at $24.95 each (orders outside the U.S. add $5 shipping and handling). Please make checks payable to Keith Weiskamp.

_____
Name

_____
Address

_____
City   State   Zip Code

_____
Telephone

A Special Offer From Wiley

Don't miss out on the only comprehensive reference series on all Borland's high-level Turbo languages.

• Please send me _____ copy(ies) of **Turbo Language Essentials** (1-60907-2) @ $24.95 plus applicable sales tax.

• Please send me _____ copy(ies) of **Turbo Algorithms** (1-61009-7) @ $26.95 plus applicable sales tax.

NAME _____

COMPANY _____

ADDRESS _____

CITY _____ STATE/ZIP _____

TELEPHONE _____

Method of Payment (please make payment to John Wiley & Sons)
❐ Payment Enclosed (Wiley pays postage)   ❐ Bill me   ❐ Bill Company
❐ VISA   ❐ MASTERCARD (Sales tax, postage and handling will be added.)

Expiration Date _____/_____/_____   Card No. _____

SIGN HERE: _____
Order invalid if not signed. Offer good in U.S. and Canada only.

- - - - ✂ -

To get the most out of the Turbo languages, you'll want to add these two books written by the authors of *Turbo Libraries* to your personal library:

✓ *Turbo Language Essentials* —a complete source to the language fundamentals and advanced concepts of all four Borland's high-level Turbo languages.

✓ *Turbo Algorithms* — provides an in-depth look at how practical algorithms are implemented in each high-level Turbo language.

To order, fill out the form above and mail it along with your payment to:

John Wiley & Sons, Inc.
Order Department
1 Wiley Drive
Somerset, NJ 08850-1272